Fr. Leslie Rumble

Radio Replies

The Catholic Answers Edition

Radio Replies

The Catholic Answers Edition

Published by Catholic Answers, Inc.
2020 Gillespie Way
El Cajon, California 92020
1-888-291-8000 orders
619-387-0042 fax
catholic.com
Printed in the United States of America

ISBN 978-1-938983-69-6 hardcover
ISBN 978-1-938983-74-0 paperback
ISBN 978-1-938983-70-2 Kindle
ISBN 978-1-938983-71-9 ePub

Contents

Editor's Note

The Catholic Answers edition of *Radio Replies* is an abridgement of three volumes by the same name, published beginning in 1938 through a collaboration between Australian radio apologist Fr. Leslie Rumble—the "replies" are in his voice—and his American counterpart Fr. Charles M. Carty. This editor has sought to shave the thousands of questions and replies in those volumes to a more manageable size: eliminating many instances of repetition, excising anachronisms (save a few that have been retained for their charm), and combining and consolidating where it seemed fitting.

To modern sensibilities, perhaps the most striking feature of the 836 replies given in this book is their faintly pugnacious tone. It seems inconsonant with our gentler age of ecumenism. But for much of the forty years that Fr. Rumble spent as the original and then foremost radio apologist, the English-speaking world was marked by a native and casual anti-Catholicism. That demanded a certain posture of response, and this posture is evident in the force, wit, and certitude found in each of the good priest's defenses of the Church and its teachings.

It's true that many Catholics today feel beleaguered by moral relativism and general unbelief, but fortunately the presumption of enmity, the naked distrust, with which Catholics in England and her former colonies once had to contend daily is for most of us an alien experience. But if things continue on their current path it may not always be thus. And so I'm grateful to Fr. Rumble for his mettle; may it inspire us now and in the future.

—*Todd Aglialoro*

Foreword

Discovering the multi-volume edition of *Radio Replies* years ago, as I was making my way back to the fullness of the Catholic Faith, was quite a jolt (the good kind). I had never encountered keen logic and precisely compressed argumentation before. Arcing like a laser beam through the fog of my Catholicism Lite, those books made hamburgers out my sacred cows and demolished the -isms I had imbibed, such as indifferentism, relativism, and "dissentism."

The key to appreciating most fully this new Catholic Answers edition is to keep in mind that its original audience was not readers but listeners. These "radio replies" are a series of transcribed scripts drawn from the live show—titled *Question Box Sessions*—of the original radio apologist, Fr. Leslie Rumble. The Australian priest's format was simple, and, until he began in 1928, had never been done before on radio: answering challenging questions about the Faith mailed in from the public, much of which was anti-Catholic.

Modern readers can't help but wince now and again at the bluntness of some of the questions and replies. I know I did. Didn't our mothers tell us not to argue about religion and politics? Yet Rumble violates that advice with brio. The thing to be noticed, however, is he answers every question—no matter how sarcastically framed, no matter the emotions they are designed to inflame—like an honest and sincere inquiry. Even when he's clearly irritated by a rudely posed objection, he never replies with mere snark. The good priest wants to connect with the inquirer in the midst of disagreement.

One is tempted to indulge in some schadenfreude whenever Fr. Rumble takes apart, bolt by bolt, what the questioner must have thought was a convincing argument against the Faith. But, again, he knew the right *what* must be conveyed in the right *way*. Significantly, in this edition he uses the words *love* 186 times and *truth* 163 times. Not a bad "communication ratio" formula to keep in mind when speaking to someone outside the Church.

The sheer range of Fr. Rumble's knowledge is impressive. It has been said that the same basic objections to the Faith never go out of style—they just keep getting recycled. And *Radio Replies* seems to cover them all, giving cogent answers to questions about everything from God's existence to the the historicity of the Bible; from sexuality to socialism; from the papacy to miracles to Marian dogmas to the Inquisition; and more. Regardless of the subject, the answers take at face value the biblical warning that God's people "are destroyed due to lack of knowledge" (Hos. 4:6). If souls really do hang in the balance, then answers to questions touching upon salvation that are not founded upon the truth are worse than worthless.

A Minnesota priest named Charles Mortimer Carty believed the same thing. Fr. Carty hosted his own radio show in St. Paul, Minnesota, yet he felt that the printed word was needed to preserve and amplify its efforts. The word of God focuses often on the sense of *hearing* as the primary way we receive his self-disclosure in Christ. We learn that "that faith comes by hearing" in various ways (Mark 3:8; Luke 4:21, 8:10-15; Acts 19:5; Romans 10:17; Galatians 3:2). And so radio is uniquely suited to the work of evangelization. But its nature is fleeting; tracts, booklets, and books are needed to congeal, as it were, its contents.

Soon after Fr. Carty discovered his Australian counterpart, the two priests joined forces—with astounding results. In 1934, Fr. Carty published four short collections of Fr. Rumble's on-air questions and answers, selling seven million copies; out of the union of the spoken word and the written, a classic was born. Rumble & Carty did for Catholicism what Hope & Crosby did for comedy and Rogers & Hammerstein did for musicals.

One reason for his success, something of which the casual reader may not be aware, is that Fr. Rumble knew all about the inherent tension that comes with sharing the Faith with family members. Growing up Anglican in Sydney, young Leslie was exposed to many differing beliefs, including within his own family. His father, Harry Rumble, had converted to Catholicism in 1908 but then left the Church. His famous son eventually became a Catholic and was drawn to become a priest—putting a ten-year strain on the relationship between father and son.

But God's providence was at work. Most of his family also came back to the Faith, and not long after his ordination to the priesthood, Fr. Rumble gave them all Holy Communion. His radio apostolate continued until 1968, when glaucoma and other health problems forced his retirement. Fr. Rumble died in 1975 having spent his life making Christ and his Church better known and better loved.

★ ★ ★

Fr. Rumble's radio ministry arose during a renaissance of Catholic apologetics that emerged first out of England. Sterling figures such as Bl. John Henry Cardinal Newman, Fr. Ronald Knox, Fr. C.C. Martindale, Frank Sheed, Hilaire Belloc, G.K. Chesterton, and Arnold Lunn provided well-dressed ways to "always be prepared to make a defense to any one who calls you to account for the hope that is in you" (1 Pet. 3:15). In that era, Catholicism in the English-speaking world went from second-class religion to the thinking man's faith, a magnet for intellectuals.

The Catholic Answers apostolate—certainly its flagship radio show, *Catholic Answers Live*—today stands on the shoulders of Rumble and Carty. As evangelists and apologists, we are in their debt.

I think this dynamic priestly duo also knew exactly what they were doing when they tapped a rising radio star named Fulton J. Sheen to write the bracing preface—a classic in its own right—for their first volume. As a spiritual son of Venerable Archbishop Fulton Sheen, the first radio and television evangelist, I am at once humbled and thrilled to help him reintroduce twenty-first-century readers to this exceptional resource on the art and science of Catholic apologetics.

—Patrick Coffin
Host, *Catholic Answers Live*

Introduction to the First Edition

There are not more than a hundred people in the United States who hate the Catholic Church. There are millions, however, who hate what they wrongly believe to be the Catholic Church—which is, of course, quite a different thing.

These millions can hardly be blamed for hating Catholics because Catholics "adore statues"; because they "put the Blessed Mother on the same level with God"; because they say "indulgence is a permission to commit sin"; because the pope "is a fascist"; because the "Church is the defender of capitalism." If the Church taught or believed any one of these things it should be hated; but the fact is that the Church does not believe or teach any one of them. It follows then that the hatred of the millions is directed against error and not against truth. As a matter of fact, if we Catholics believed all of the untruths and lies which were said against the Church, we probably would hate the Church a thousand times more than they do.

If I were not a Catholic, and were looking for the true Church in the world today, I would look for the one Church which did not get along well with the world; in other words, I would look for the Church which the world hates. My reason for doing this would be that if Christ is in any one of the churches of the world today, he must still be hated as he was when he was on Earth in the flesh. If you would find Christ today, then find the Church that does not get along with the world.

Look for the Church that is hated by the world, as Christ was hated by the world. Look for the Church which is accused of being behind the times, as our Lord was accused of being ignorant and never having learned. Look for the Church which men sneer at as socially inferior, as they sneered at our Lord because he came from Nazareth. Look for the Church which is accused of having a devil, as our Lord was accused of being possessed by Beelzebub, the Prince of Devils. Look for the Church which, in seasons of bigotry, men say must be destroyed in the name of God as men crucified Christ and thought they had done a service to God. Look for the Church which the world rejects because it claims it is infallible, as Pilate rejected Christ because he called himself the Truth. Look for the Church which is rejected by the world as our Lord was rejected by men.

Look for the Church which amid the confusion of conflicting opinions, its members love as they love Christ, and respect its voice as the very voice of its Founder, and the suspicion will grow that if the Church is unpopular with the spirit of the world, then it is unworldly, and if it is unworldly, it is otherworldly. Since it is otherworldly it is infinitely loved and infinitely hated as was Christ himself. But only that which is divine can be infinitely hated and infinitely loved. Therefore the Church is divine.

If then, the hatred of the Church is founded on erroneous beliefs, it follows that the basic need of the day is instruction. Love depends on knowledge, for we cannot aspire to nor desire the unknown. Our great country is filled with what might be called marginal Christians, i.e., those who live on the fringe of religion and who are descendants of Christian-living parents, but who now are Christians only in name. They retain a few of its ideals out of indolence and force of habit; they know the glorious history of Christianity only through certain emasculated forms of it, which have married the spirit of the age and are now dying with it. Of Catholicism and its sacraments, its pardon, its grace, its certitude and its peace, they know nothing except a few inherited prejudices. And yet they are good people who want to do the right thing, but who have no definite philosophy concerning it. They educate their children without religion, and yet they resent the compromising morals of their children. They would be angry if you told them they were not Christian, and yet they do not believe that Christ is God. They resent being called pagans and yet they never take a practical cognizance of the existence of God.

There is only one thing of which they are certain and that is that things are not right as they are. It is just that single certitude which makes them what might be called the great "potentials," for they are ready to be pulled in either of two directions. Within a short time they must take sides; they must either gather with

Christ or they must scatter; they must either be with him or against him; they must either be on the cross as other Christs, or under it as other executioners. Which way will these marginal Christians tend? The answer depends upon those who have the Faith. Like the multitudes who followed our Lord into the desert, they are as sheep without a shepherd. They are waiting to be shepherded either with the sheep or goats. Only this much is certain. Being human and having hearts they want more than class struggle and economics; they want Life, they want Truth, and they want Love. In a word, they want Christ.

It is to these millions who believe wrong things about the Church and to these *marginal Christians* that this book is sent. It is not to prove that they are "wrong"; it is not to prove that we are "right"; it is merely to present the truth in order that the truth may conquer through the grace of God. When men are starving, one need not go to them and tell them to avoid poison; nor to eat bread because there are vitamins in bread. One need only go to them and tell them that they are starving and here is bread, and the laws of nature will do the rest. *Radio Replies* goes out on a similar mission. Its primary task is not to humble the erroneous; not to glorify the Catholic Church as intellectual and self-righteous, but to present the truth in a calm, clear manner in order that with the grace of God souls may come to the blessed embrace of Christ.

It is not only the point of *Radio Replies* to prove that the Church is the only completely soul-satisfying Church in existence at the present day; it is also to suggest that the Catholic Church is the only Church existing today which goes back to the time of Christ. History is so very clear on this point it is curious how many minds miss its obviousness. When therefore you, the readers of *Radio Replies,* wish to know about Christ and about his early Church, and about his mysteries, we ask you to go not only to the written records but to the living Church which began with Christ himself. That Church, or that Mystical Person which has been living all these centuries, is the basis of our faith and to us Catholics it speaks this way:

"I live with Christ. I saw his Mother and I know her to be a Virgin and the loveliest and purest of all women in heaven or on Earth; I saw Christ at Caesarea-Philippi, when, after changing Simon's name to Rock, Christ told him he was the rock upon which the Church would be built and that it would endure unto the consummation of the world. I saw Christ hanging on a cross and I saw him rise from his tomb; I saw Magdalene rush to his feet; I saw the angels clad in white beside the great stone; I was in the Cenacle room when doubting Thomas put fingers into his hands; I was on Olivet when he ascended into heaven and promised to send his Spirit to the apostles to make them the foundation of his new Mystical Body on earth. I was at the stoning of Stephen, saw Saul hold the garments of those who slew him, and later I heard Saul, as Paul, preach Christ and him crucified; I witnessed the beheading of Peter and Paul in Rome, and with my very eyes saw tens of thousands of martyrs crimson the sands with their blood, rather than deny the faith Peter and Paul had preached unto them.

"I was living when Boniface was sent to Germany, when Augustine when to England, Cyril and Methodius to the Poles, and Patrick to Ireland; at the beginning of the ninth century I recall seeing Charlemagne crowned as king in matters temporal as Peter's vicar was recognized as supreme in matters spiritual; in the thirteenth century I saw the great stones cry out in tribute to me, and burst into Gothic cathedrals; in the shadows of those same walls I saw great cathedrals of thought arise in the prose of Aquinas and Bonaventure, and in the poetry of Dante.

"In the sixteenth century I saw my children softened by the spirit of the world leave the Father's house and reform the faith instead of reforming discipline which would have brought them back again into my embrace; in the last century and at the beginning of this I heard the world say it could not accept me because I was behind the times. I am not behind the times, I am only behind the scenes. I have adapted myself to every form of government the world has ever known; I have lived with caesars and kings, tyrants and dictators, parliaments and presidents, monarchies and republics. I have welcomed every advance of science, and were it not for me the great records of the pagan world would not have been preserved. It is true I have not changed my doctrine, but that is because the 'doctrine is not mine but his who sent me.' I change my garments which belong to time, but not my Spirit which belongs to eternity.

"In the course of my long life I have seen so many modern ideas become unmodern, that I know I shall live to chant a requiem over the modern ideas of this day, as I chanted it over the modern ideas of the last century. I celebrated the nineteen-hundredth anniversary of the death of my Redeemer and yet I am no older now than then, for my Spirit is eternal, and the eternal never ages. I am the abiding Personage of the centuries. I am the contemporary of all civilizations. I am never out of date, because the dateless; never out of time, because the timeless.

"I have four great marks: I am One, because I have the same Soul I had in the beginning; I am Holy, because that Soul is the Spirit of holiness; I am Catholic, because that Spirit pervades every living cell of my Body; I am Apostolic, because my origin is identical with Nazareth, Galilee, and Jerusalem. I shall grow weak when my members become rich and cease to pray, but *I shall never die.* I shall be persecuted as I am persecuted now in Mexico and Russia; I shall be crucified as I was on Calvary, but I shall rise again, and finally when time shall be no more, and I shall have grown to my full stature, then shall I be taken into heaven as the bride of my Head, Christ, where the celestial nuptials shall be celebrated, and God shall be all in all, because his Spirit is Love and Love is Heaven."

—Rt. Rev. Msgr. Fulton J. Sheen, D.D.

Chapter 1

God

1. Is it not God's will that all should be Catholic?

It is. For Christ established the Catholic Church and bade her go and teach all nations, baptizing them in the name of the Father, and of the Son, and of the Holy Spirit. But he said also, "He that believes and is baptized shall be saved; he that believes not shall be condemned." He thereby tells us that not all who hear the truth will accept it. He himself did not convert all to whom he preached, and we must not be surprised if we ourselves have the same experience. In individual cases, however, we must refuse to judge as to the degree to which even those who have heard the truth concerning the Catholic Church apprehend its significance. Their responsibility in remaining non-Catholics must be left to God. In the meantime we can but pray for them, patiently bearing the trial that those we love show no present signs of conversion to Catholicism, or the fact that they are not converted as quickly as we would wish. God's time is the best time. It is for us to plead that he may give them the grace of the Catholic Faith, and that they may correspond with that grace despite all difficulties.

2. What is the evidence for God's existence, apart from the Bible?

What do you mean by evidence? Some people think that evidence must be seen and touched, as an animal sees a patch of grass and eats it. But men are not mere animals. They have reason, and can appreciate intellectual evidence. For example, the evidence of beauty in music or in painting is perceived by man's mind, not by his senses. An animal could hear the same sounds, or see the same colors, without being impressed by their harmony and proportion. Apart from the Bible altogether, reason can detect sufficient evidence to guarantee the existence of God.

There are many indications, the chief of which I shall give you very briefly: The first is from causality. The universe, limited in all its details, could not be its own cause. It could no more come together with all its regulating laws than the Golden Gate Bridge could just happen, or a clock could assemble itself and keep perfect time without a clock maker. On the same principle, if there were no God, there would be no you to dispute his existence. What is created supposes a Creator who is uncreated, or the problem goes on forever; the whole endless chain of dependent beings as unable to explain itself as each of its links. It is rational to argue to an uncreated clock maker. It is not rational to ask, "Who created this uncreated clock maker?" God was not created. If he were, he would be a creature and would have a creator. His creator would then be God, and not he himself. God always existed. He never began, and will never cease to be. He is eternal.

A second indication is drawn from the universal reasoning, or, if you wish, intuition of men. The universal judgment of mankind can no more be wrong on this vital point than the intuition of an infant that food must be conveyed to the mouth. The stamp of God's handiwork is so clearly impressed upon creation, and, above all, upon man, that all nations instinctively believe that there is a God. The truth is in possession. Men do not have to persuade themselves that there is a God. They have to try to persuade themselves that there is no God. And no one yet who has attained to such a temporary persuasion has been able to find a valid reason for it. Men do not grow into the idea of a God; they endeavor to grow out of it.

The sense of moral obligation confirms these reasons. In every man there is a sense of right and wrong. A man knows interiorly when he is doing wrong. Something rebukes his conduct. He knows that he is going against an inward voice. It is the voice of conscience, dictating to us a law we did not make and which no man could have made, for this voice protests whether other men know our conduct or not. This voice is often quite against what we wish to do, warning us beforehand, condemning us after its violation. The law dictated by this voice of conscience supposes a lawgiver who has written his law in our hearts. And as God alone could do this, it is certain that he exists.

Finally, justice demands that there be a God. The very sense of justice among men, resulting in courts of law, supposes a just God. We did not give ourselves our sense of justice. It comes from whoever made us, and no one can give what he does not possess himself. Yet justice cannot always be done by men in this world. Here the good often suffer, and the wicked prosper. And even though human justice does not always succeed in balancing the scales, they will be balanced someday by a just God, who most certainly must exist.

3. What do you mean by the term God?

God is a spiritual, substantial, personal being, infinite in intelligence, in will, and in all perfection, absolutely simple or lacking composition, immutable, happy in himself and by himself, and infinitely superior to all that is or can be conceived apart from himself. He is incomprehensible in his infinite perfection by all lesser intelligences, although knowable as to the fact of his existence as living Creator and Lord of heaven and earth, almighty, eternal, immense, and distinct from all that he has created.

If God ever had a beginning, then before he began there was nothing. Now nothing, with nothing to work upon, and no faculties with which to work, could never turn its nonexistent self into something. But there is obviously something, and there can never have been a time when there was nothing. God at least must always have existed, and if no one is responsible for his beginning, there is no one who could possibly bring his existence to an end. He always will be. God rightly declared himself the eternally existent Being when he said to Moses, "I am Who am."

4. Is it not possible that matter itself is eternal?

I admit that it would be possible for an eternal Cause to produce eternally some basic created reality. We know from Revelation that God did not create from eternity. But it would have been possible for him to do so. However, you must note this: The appeal to the eternity of matter, which cannot be proved, does not exclude the necessity of an *outside Cause.* The mere duration of a thing does not explain its existence. You cannot explain a running train by saying innocently, "Why, it was always running." In the universe we see a succession of causal mutations, each succeeding stage being caused by a preceding stage, and in turn causing a subsequent stage. Every element is dependent, and no one element can explain itself independently of the rest. And if each link in a chain is dependent, the whole chain is dependent. An eternal series of dependent and caused things can be reasonably explained only by One who is independent and uncaused, who exists with a complete self-sufficiency not to be found in finite things.

In passing, let me call your attention to the problem of life. Even if matter is eternal, there was certainly a time when life did not exist on this Earth, and certainly a time when it began to exist. Any belief that it began spontaneously, and without the creative power of God, is unworthy of a reasonable man.

You do not believe that the universe can be explained in terms of the material only. Most certainly I do not. The mere materialist offers explanations that do not even deserve a place in the catalogue of errors. They are too puerile. Of visible things materialism gives explanations one would expect from a prattling baby or from a lunatic. Of invisible things and spiritual things it gives no explanation at all. It constructs bodies with smaller bodies, like a child playing with a set of blocks, and it gets quite out of breath by the time it gets to things of the mind. It contradicts itself by speaking of laws of matter, for a law is a decree formulated by reason, and reason is not material. Materialists prove God every time they speak in order to deny him. For at the back of every denial of God there is the idea of God. No man can believe in truth, or appreciate goodness, or seek happiness, without tending toward the Author of these things. Yet each of these ideas leads to God. Materialism is not rational, and its only real appeal lies in the fact that it makes the universe the magnificent plaything of man's pride and gives him a free field for his passions.

5. What becomes of God when you think of the misery and starvation in the world?

We have already seen that there is a God. Inability to comprehend every detail in the universe does not prove that there is no God but merely the limited capacity of the finite human mind. However, the human mind can propose certain principles that go a long way toward the removal of difficulties.

First, evil is really the negation or privation of good, and if there is evil in the world, there is also much good that can be accounted for only by the existence of God.

Second, the fluctuations of this mutable life cannot affect God's existence. Meaning, you cannot have God when things seem to be all right and annihilate him when things seem to go wrong. If God exists before things go wrong, he still exists despite the unhappiness of an individual. And note that word *individual*. Viewing the race as a whole, we find that life is a mixture of comfortable and uncomfortable things. When we are happy, others are suffering. When we are suffering, others are happy. We cannot say that God exists for the happy ones and simultaneously does not exist for the unhappy ones. We must not take local and individual views only but a universal outlook.

Third, and particularly as regards the uneven distribution of this world's goods with consequent starvation for some, God's providence has not failed. Man's administration is at fault. While individuals suffer lack, we know that the world has produced enough wheat, fruit, meat, and wool to feed and clothe everyone. God has not failed to provide enough to fill every mouth. But he has given this world over to the administration of men, and it is their bad management they must correct rather than blame God. At least their incapable administration should teach them the saving grace of humility.

God permits these things only because he knows that there is a future life where he will rectify and compensate all inequalities.

In the meantime, he draws good out of these miseries, for they teach men not to set their hopes entirely upon this world as if there were no other and help to expiate the sins of mankind. If we cannot be entirely happy here, let us at least make sure of being happy in the next life.

We might say, "If God is good, why did he allow his Son to go through excruciating torture?" Sin is the real evil, not suffering. Christ found happiness in proving his love by suffering, a greater good than mere health. And the miseries of this world have driven thousands to God, who would have been self-sufficient and independent only for the naturally insoluble problem of suffering. If only for this reason, we can discern an indication of God's goodness in it.

6. If God is loving, just, and all-powerful, why does he permit moral evil, or sin?

Because God is Love, he asks the freely given love of man and not a compelled love. Because he is just, he will not deprive man of the free will that is in accordance with his rational nature. Nor is this against the omnipotence of God, for even his power does not extend to contradictory things. Man cannot be free to love and serve God without being free to reject him and rebel against him. We cannot have it both ways. Even God, if he wants men to be free, cannot take from them the power to choose evil. If he enforces goodness, he takes away freedom. If he leaves freedom, he must permit evil, even though he forbids it. It is man's dignity that he is master of his own destiny instead of having to develop just like a tree that necessarily obeys natural law. Men, as a matter of fact, misused their freedom, and sin and brutality resulted. But it was impossible to give man the gift of freedom and the dignity of being master of his own destiny without risking the permission of such failures.

7. I get so indignant when I see suffering that I agree with the axiom, "The only excuse for God is that he does not exist."

First, if there is no God, indignation is absurd. For then suffering is a necessary result of blind material forces. You might just as well get indignant with the sun for rising later in wintertime.

Second, the absurdity of the axiom you quote should be evident from the fact that any excusing supposes someone at fault; and if God is at fault, he exists. But let me add that if he does exist, he cannot be at fault.

Meantime, the only explanation of evil is that God does exist. Evil cannot exist apart from positive beings to experience it. God did not create evil, but he did create all positive beings, permitting them to lack normal perfection at times.

Again, if you say that there is evil, therefore, there is no God, I reply, "There is good, therefore, there is a God." And my reason is stronger than yours, because the good certainly outweighs the evil in this world. And the good cannot be explained without God, while the evil can be explained with God. He permitted it only because he was good and powerful enough to draw from it a benefit greater than any harm it can effect.

8. Face the dilemma. God could either prevent evil or not. If he can but will not, he is not good; if he cannot, he is not all powerful.

That dilemma is invalid. If a dilemma is to be valid, the disjunction must be complete, exhausting all possibilities. There must be no room for the reply, "Datur tertium"—there is a third possibility. Your dilemma fails, if evil and pain and suffering are useful. What if the evils we see in this world are the necessary condition of a higher good? What if, still more, they are indispensable to the progress of man and the realization of his destiny—if someday they are to be compensated by an eternity of happiness? In any case, for a dilemma to be valid, the inference from each alternative in itself must be certain and indisputable. Neither of your alternatives is even reasonable.

Absolutely speaking, God could annihilate the whole of creation, and then, of course, there would be no problem of evil in the universe. But assuming that God wants this type of world, then pain and suffering are a necessary condition; and it was certainly better to permit them than not to create a universe in which it was possible for them to occur.

As it is, your very terms involve a contradiction. In practice, the assertion that if God cannot remove all pain he is not all powerful means, where physical pain is concerned, that if God cannot have sensitive beings without their being sensitive, he is not all powerful! For, granted the power of sensation, our sensations will be pleasant and unpleasant even with the variations of the weather! Where moral evil is concerned, your assertion means, "If God cannot have free and morally responsible beings who are not really free and morally responsible, he is not all powerful." For, granted freedom of will, moral evil is a necessary possibility.

9. Do you believe literally in God as Creator of all things, visible and invisible?

Yes. But remember that things, whether visible or invisible, are things insofar as they have positive being. Now try to follow carefully this treatment of the subject.

Evil, as such, whether physical or moral, is not a positive entity but is a privation of due perfection. God has created every positive entity, but he does not directly produce those privations of perfection that are called evils.

Take the physical evil of a decayed tooth. God is the cause of all the positive being involved. That part of the tooth which is not yet decayed, but which is still good, owes its existence to God. The existent nerves owe their being to God and are good nerves. Their perfectly good registrations letting us know that the tooth is out of order are due to God's causality. But the real evil is the absence of a healthy tooth and of right order in the nerves. Even the germs that consumed the tooth are quite good germs so far as their being goes. Even the process of consuming the tooth was excellent as a process.

But the evil element is reduced to absence of order and absence of a healthy tooth; and absences of perfection are not caused by any positive action of God. God permits them, if you wish, insofar as he does not choose to prevent corrosive processes, or to produce a good tooth as fast as it is eaten away.

In all this I do not deny that pain is a positive experience. Owing to the absence of a healthy tooth, there is quite a positive vibration of the exposed nerve giving positively painful registrations. But the positive action is a good activity; the evil is merely lack of due order. And while God is the Creator of all positive entities, he is not the Creator of a lack of what should be there.

The same principle applies to moral evil. The will and the action by which I choose are good in themselves. The evil is the lack of moral rectitude—again an absence of something that should normally be there. And God does not cause the absence of what should be present.

Why he permits the nonexistence or the privation of due order in created things is another question. We are dealing with the causality of God. God is not the cause of evil as such.

10. How can you admit that evil is positively experienced by us yet deny its very existence?

I do not admit that we positively experience evil. We positively experience good registrations telling us that perfection is wanting. The registrations are positive, but they tell us of an absence of perfection. Positive entities alone really exist—good thus far—that lack the full measure of goodness that they ought to have. The evil is the privation or limitation of entity, not an entity itself.

11. If God's providence rules all things, is it not an insult to him to put lightning conductors on churches?

No. It would be an insult and a sin of presumption to expect God to do immediately those things that we ourselves are capable of doing with such powers as he has bestowed upon us. He does not give us our natural intelligence for nothing but expects us to use it. We are expected always to do all that we are capable of doing, and then we ask God to supply for our incapacity in things beyond our ability.

12. You should not seek your God's forgiveness; he should seek yours.

Such a remark illustrates a great truth. As men cease to believe in and esteem God, they begin to believe in and esteem themselves.

They lose the sense of sin and become more and more unconscious of their moral failings. Thus, it is quite common for unbelievers to assert that they do not believe in religion and at once to catalogue their own virtues. Almost instinctively they add, "I don't pray, but I'm as good as those who do. I live a good clean life, owe no man anything, help my fellow men, etc." Conscious of their rectitude, they feel that they deserve only the best, and naturally they resent misfortune. They smart under suffering and trial with a sense of injured innocence. And they cry out that, if there be a God, he is greatly to be blamed. Conscious only of their own virtue, they do not dream that they need any forgiveness. But believing their sufferings undeserved, they talk of God begging their pardon.

On the other hand, the more one believes in and esteems God, the less he believes in and esteems himself. Any good that is in him he attributes to God; and he is keenly conscious of his own shortcomings as being his own work. Aware of his sins, he is not astonished that suffering and trial should be his lot. Instead of thinking that he deserves only the best, he knows that he deserves only the worst. He therefore asks God to forgive him his sins and is grateful to God for treating him so much more gently than justice would demand.

13. If God is present everywhere in the world, is not creation so inseparable from God as to be part of him?

God does exist everywhere. He therefore coexists with all created beings. Yet he cannot be identified with created beings. He is in a totally different order of existence. The concept is not difficult. Thought and matter are in different orders of being, yet both coexist in the same head. A man's material brains could be weighed on a pair of scales; but that would not be weighing the thoughts produced by his soul with the help of those brains. So, too, a current of electricity occupies the same space as solid copper wire; but that mutual presence does not make the copper wire part of the electricity. God's presence everywhere does not make created things part of God. As a matter of fact, God is a purely spiritual

Being who cannot have parts. Also, created things are finite or limited, and God is infinite. The finite cannot be part of the infinite. While the universe has its very being "in" God because God is everywhere, God infinitely transcends the universe, differing from it in substance, nature, power, and perfection and constituting a world of mysterious reality in himself.

The natural world is full of contradictions, and there can be no contradictions in God. The true and the false, good and evil, all manner of imperfections, ignorance, and knowledge, the conscious and the unconscious, constant movement and change—all these cannot possibly be synthesized into one Being called God. We know how different men desire different things and will different things. Men are obviously distinct from one another. They cannot, therefore, be identical with one and the same God. So if you are God, I am not. If I am God, you are not. And it is impossible to say that all is God. Yet if all is not God, all nature is not divine. The whole of creation may be the effect of divine activity, but the effect certainly is distinct from God.

14. Is everything that happens to man God's will?

From the negative point of view we can certainly say that those things that happen to men would not happen did God will that they should not happen. But, from the positive point of view, the question arises, "Though nothing can happen against God's will, does God positively will all that does happen?" The answer is—not necessarily.

In some cases a death, and all its circumstances, are God's positive will. In other cases, it may be merely God's permissive will. There is a difference between God's positive and God's permissive will. For example, if an employer orders a representative to go from London to Sri Lanka, when the latter goes, he fulfills the positive will of his employer. On the other hand, the employer might express a preference that the representative should go via Capetown rather than via Suez, yet add, "I leave it to you to go via Suez if you prefer." If the representative goes via Suez, it is not against the will of his employer. It is at least with the permissive will of that employer, though not a formal command of his positive will. This is merely to show that there is a difference between a positive will and a permissive will; and it is an example that must be kept in mind when dealing with the question of moral and physical evil.

Since God forbids murder, it cannot be God's positive will that anyone should commit murder. At the same time, while people are morally obliged by the commandment "Thou shalt not kill," they are no more physically compelled to keep that commandment than any other. For God has positively willed that man should be capable of a free choice between good and evil. And God's positive will that man should be free to choose the good must carry with it his permissive will of the evil should man abuse his liberty. If, then, a man commits murder, somebody will be murdered, and that also must be included in God's permissive will. So at least we must say that it was God's permissive will that the murdered man should die in that manner. But one could conceive a case where it would even be God's positive will. If a man were bent on murdering somebody despite God's prohibition, God could positively will that his victim should be one man rather than another. Then it would not be his positive will that the murderer should violate the law, yet it would be his positive will that the victim should meet with such a manner of death rather than another.

15. Does it not seem strange that God, knowing what would happen, should create man free to please or offend him? If he could not foresee the future it could be more easily understood.

If God could not foresee the future, instead of being more easily understood, things would be absolutely inexplicable. It is precisely because he foresaw the future, and the greater good he will draw out of these present evils, that he has permitted them.

But, apart from this, why did God, knowing what would happen, create men free to please him or offend him?

First, because his foreknowledge in no way makes anyone offend him. Knowledge does not cause things to happen. Things which happen give rise to the knowledge of them.

Second, God gave us free will so that we might have the nobler dignity of being masters of our own destiny, not having to serve him necessarily and blindly as do trees and inanimate planets and stars. God did not want a forced love from beings capable of an intelligent appreciation of the good. But once God makes man free, man is free either to love God or to reject God; to serve him or to rebel against him. That is, physically. No man is morally free to reject God. God, therefore, forbids that, warning us of its disastrous results.

At any rate, there is a God, and we are free. If we cannot see a satisfactory explanation of the difficulties that occur to us, then we trust God in such matters. Many speculative questions that human curiosity would like to have solved have been left mysteries, either because our minds could not grasp the solution even if they were explained or simply because God does not choose to justify himself to his own creatures yet.

16. Did not humanity originally begin with polytheism and gradually evolve toward monotheism?

No. Humanity began with monotheism, and multitudes degenerated into polytheism. At first sight the most primitive traditions found in the Vedic books seem polytheistic; but a deeper scrutiny shows an individual Deity, and indicates that the plurality of gods is really a plurality of effects or created manifestations. This ancient tradition was a survival of the primitive convictions of our first parents. But even as the Jews were always prone to fall into polytheism despite the special protection of God, so the Gentile nations degenerated in their religious notions, and the idea of a plurality of gods became quite common among the rank and file of peoples. The great Greek philosophers Aristotle and Plato, though in general practice conforming to popular notions, discerned, however, by reason that polytheism was absurd and theoretically maintained that there could be but one Deity. They saw that polytheism was an error and that error supposes a truth of which it is the corruption. They both allude to ancient traditions confirming their views. Philologically, also, no plural terms existed prior to singular terms precisely because multitude is subsequent to unity; and the notion of a plurality of gods presupposed a notion of the one God.

17. Despite all your arguments, I refuse to believe in a God we can't understand.

That is unreasonable. In any case, you can understand that there is a God, even though you cannot fully understand the nature of God. God must surpass the capacity of the human mind or he would not be God at all. You must not confuse mystery with absurdity. Tell me that blind matter produced the universe, and I admit the absurdity. But mystery is the very opposite of absurdity. The absurd is false, contradictory, incoherent. But mystery is a truth whose immensity surpasses us. When we speak of God, what we say is true as far as it goes. But human ideas will never go far enough to express God completely. We must express God as best we can, though we shall never fully succeed in expressing God as he is. And I, for one, would not believe in God unless he did surpass my own limited concepts.

Yet God is not thoroughly incomprehensible to us. We can attain to a certain degree of knowledge concerning him, even though we cannot form an adequate concept of him. The finite human mind can conceive the fact that there is a Being not finite as are the things that Being has made. It can affirm perfections of God, denying the imperfections associated with limited creatures and attributing the purified perfections to him in an altogether higher and nobler order of being. Any perfections affirmed of God must be with the proviso that God transcends created nature and that we intend them as they must be in an order above that of nature. In other words, we intend them as they are in the supernatural order and as known to God himself. Even as an animal can know that a human being has certain knowledge without comprehending the precise quality of that knowledge, so human beings can know that God possesses certain perfections without fully comprehending their precise quality as they are in God.

Chapter 2

Man

18. What is a man?

Man is a living being endowed with a sensitive material body and a spiritual soul that is immortal of its very nature and which rejoices in the two spiritual faculties of intelligence and free will. We may speak of a man "having a soul"; however, man is a composite being consisting of both body and soul, the soul, of course, being the nobler component element.

The Bible says that God breathed the breath of life into the body and it became a *living soul.* That breath of life was either a definite something or it was nothing. But you cannot tell me that nothing vitalized that body. It was a definite something, and that something was a created human intelligent soul.

Again, if man does not have a soul, then instead of being composed of body and soul, he is a body. And if that body is a soul, then a soul wears boots! However you quote the Bible, the authority of which we shall consider later, you will notice that Christ clearly showed the difference between the material body and a spiritual soul when he said, "See my hands and my feet, that it is I myself; handle me, and see; for a spirit has not flesh and bones as you see that I have" (Luke 24:39). A body of flesh and bone could never become a living soul. Man was but named after the superior element of his being.

19. The question is ever arising as to whether man appeared suddenly on the Earth by a special creative act of God or whether he evolved.

The evolution of man's body would not be opposed to any defined doctrine of the Church, though it is far from being a proven fact, and the probabilities are against it. But man as a reasoning, thinking, spiritual being certainly did not evolve. His possession of intelligence introduces a new fact into the universe, for intelligence differs entirely from material conditions and development. It is a spiritual power and must come from the realm of spiritual being. We maintain, therefore, that the soul, to which intelligence belongs, is a special creation by God in each case simultaneously with its infusion into the material embryo as soon as that embryo is fit to receive it; and that is at the moment of conception.

20. If descent from animals is proved, would it mean that God only added the faculty of reason to the brute soul in order to make it human?

First, I do not believe that the descent of man from brute animals will ever be proved.

Second, even if it were proved, it would not mean that God had merely to endow an animal with the faculty of reason. God would have to create a human soul endowed with reason and will and infuse that soul to supplant the existent brute soul or life-principle in the animal body selected to be the body of the first man. Personally, I do not for a moment believe that any existent animal body was chosen by God to be the recipient of the first created human soul. Such an animal body would be so unfit for the reception of an intelligent soul that the immediate formation of a human body seems far more likely than the miraculous alteration of an existent animal body.

Man's soul is certainly not the result of evolution but that it is immediately created by God. There is no dogma concerning the precise mode of formation in regard to his body. But the Church stands to the ordinary teaching that his body has not evolved from lower beings but that it also was produced by the special intervention of God. The idea that the body of man has evolved from lower animals is scientifically and philosophically highly improbable, and it cannot be held with either safety or prudence. Science has proved nothing concerning the origin of man's body and is merely in the conjectural stage. And in view of the mind of the Church, no Catholic would be justified in denying the literal, biblical account. If he may not deny it, must he therefore believe it? He must accept it as more probable than the evolutionary hypothesis. Presumption stands for the literal sense until the contrary has been demonstrated.

21. Prove that a soul does exist in man.

A living human body is not the same thing as a corpse. The soul is the difference between a corpse and a living being. A dead body cannot move, eat, think, express itself, enjoy, or be miserable. It can but fall to pieces and go back to dust. There is something that stops your body from doing that now. It is your soul. For every activity you must find a principle of operation behind it. The principle in a man that thinks and loves and is happy or miserable is a very real thing. It is not nothing, less than the very body it animates. Nor is it a chemical. No doctor, examining a corpse, can tell you what chemical is missing that it should not live. If there is nothing else but chemical substances, let doctors and scientists gather together the requisite chemicals and say, "Live!" They can effect nothing like this. There is something that chemistry cannot reach; it is the soul or spirit. Look anyone in the face, and behind those animated features, those changing expressions, in the very eyes, you will read the soul.

Sane philosophy admits a vegetative soul, a sensitive animal soul, and an immortal, spiritual, and intelligent human soul.

22. Is the soul immortal?

That the soul will, and indeed must, survive the death of the body is demonstrable from many points of view.

First, its essential structure forbids dissolution by death. Death is the disintegration of parts. Only composite things can die. Yet the soul is not composite. Its power of pure immaterial thought proves its independence of matter. It is endowed with spiritual faculties and is as spiritual as the faculties it possesses, which will enable it to live and operate when separated from the body. Not being material, it can never be destroyed or fall to pieces like matter. Nor would God endow it with a nature essentially fitted to live on just to annihilate it after all.

Second, every individual experiences a sense of moral obligation, and every obligation demands a sufficient sanction. If the State said, "This is the law," and I replied, "What if I do not observe it?" it would be ludicrous were the State to reply, "Oh, nothing will happen. I say only that it is the law. If you break it you break it, I suppose." That would be a joke, not a law. I know that I shall have to answer some day for my attitude toward the interior sense of moral obligation. I can go right through this life without encountering anyone capable of judging me concerning it. The real answer must be given at the judgment seat of God, and my soul will have to be there. Consequently, it must survive.

Third, a more universal view of human life shows us the many inequalities that offend against the sense of justice. We know that justice will be done some day, and as it is not always done in this life, it will be done in the next. This implies our presence and therefore our living on after death.

Fourth, every soul has an insatiable natural desire for happiness, and for lasting happiness. No earthly or temporal good can satisfy this hunger. Yet this innate natural tendency cannot lack its rightful object. Try to conceive the existence of the human eye, perfectly adapted to sight, yet without the possibility of light anywhere to enable it to see.

Reflection, then, upon the simple structure of the soul, upon the future administration of the sanctions attached to the moral law, upon the rectification of worldwide inequalities, and upon the teleological inclinations to a lasting and perfect good, makes it a violation of reason to deny the survival of the soul.

23. How will the soul know anything when separated from the body? When unconscious through an injury to the brain, man knows nothing.

The soul does not depend upon the body for its existence. But for the operation of thought it does need the use of that bodily organ we call the brain, so long as it exists in our present composite state. By the body the soul is linked with this material world. And at present, material impressions drawn from physical experience provide the foundation for thought. Strictly speaking, thought is independent of the brain. There is no real proportion between thought activity and brain activity. While the soul remains united to the body, an affectation of the brain can cripple the thought activities of the soul, even as a broken instrument can hinder the operations of an expert worker. But, when separated from the body, the soul will be in totally different conditions—conditions adapted entirely to its spiritual character and independent of material limitations.

24. Don't you think that the idea of immortality is due merely to the desire to live on?

I know that it is not due merely to that. Men without any desire to live on have the conviction. At the same time, normal people do desire to live on, and by such an irrepressible tendency that we must admit it to be a clear indication of immortality. I do not say that everything a person wants to be true is necessarily true. But here we have not a transitory wish, not a momentary craving, but a natural tendency implanted in our very nature and always with us. Aristotle said long ago that "nature does nothing in vain." The eye demands light, and there is light. Our very constitution demands air, and there is air. And it is part of our very nature to look forward to immortality. All men experience this urge at times. They do not have to persuade themselves that they will live on. They have to try to persuade themselves that they will not; or else they just forget it. However, in addition to this argument from purposive tendencies there are other reasons of equal and greater weight. The very nature of thought shows the soul to be immaterial and not subject to the laws of disintegration and destruction that govern all material things. We must consider, also, the facts of the moral law and the necessity of ultimate justice. All these arguments, taken together, are quite satisfactory to reason. If people say that they are not satisfied by such considerations, it is because they unreasonably expect too much. We cannot expect to prove the immortality of the soul as we can prove that lead is heavy by testing it on a pair of scales. But there are different orders of being with different orders of proof. Who would be so unreasonable as to deny the existence of humility because it can't be bought by the pound? All the reasonable proof of the immortality of the soul man can rightly demand is available.

25. Granted that human souls are immortal and endowed with intelligence and free will, do they exist in eternity before their advent to this world?

The soul is created by God at the moment of conception. Prior to its creation it is simply nonexistent. Some of the ancient Greek philosophers taught that the human soul had an existence before its union with the body and that it is imprisoned in the body as a punishment for sins committed in its previous life. Aristotle refuted these opinions, pointing out the absurdity of an intelligent soul continuing its existence but having absolutely no memory of its previous doings, discoveries, and aspirations. Again, if we turn to the idea of punishment, it is irrational to have souls punished for unknown crimes in such a way that they can neither correct their faults nor acknowledge the justice of the penalty. Finally, if the soul preexisted, it would do so as a complete entity in its own right. When united with the body, it could not form one composite personality such as we know man to be. Its presence in the body would be a kind of violent possession by an alien spirit. Such an idea is quite opposed to the naturalness of the union between soul and body—a union whose dissolution awakens so much mental apprehension and anxiety. It is certain, then, that human souls do not preexist.

26. Belief in immortality is most harmful. It diverts men's attention from the good they can do in this life.

It does just the opposite. It inspires still greater works of devotedness and charity in the cause of humanity for the love of God. And the doctrine is in the best interests of man. All mankind lifts its voice with mine. Generation after generation has agreed. In fact, it is part of man's very nature. The conviction of a future life is so deeply ingrained that it could not be based on a lie. It is as true an instinct as that of a baby who carries everything to his mouth, knowing that then it will be nourished, though he can explain nothing about the process of nutrition. Destroy man's conviction of immortality and he degenerates, even as the fish taken out of the sea will perish, or the tree torn up by the roots will die. Most of those who deny immortality are interested in denying it. Nor are they very convinced themselves of their position against immortality. They have no proof. They deny, because they don't want to prepare for it.

27. The existence of an immortal soul has no real bearing on morality.

Since there is a future life, it has a lot to do with morality. Man is endowed with reason and is bound to exercise foresight. The future as such, whether here or hereafter, is a reasonable motive for present conduct. I refrain from eating certain foods now, because reason tells me that future indigestion will result. That is reasonable conduct. I try to refrain from morally wrong conduct because it is wrong; offends God; is a personal disgrace; and will wreck my whole future existence if I persist in it and die without repentance. All these motives are good. If the nobler motives fail to impress me in a given temptation, the thought of hell at least will tend to stop me.

You will say, "So you are afraid of hell?" I reply, "Of course I am!" Knowing that hell is a reality, any sane man will live so as to avoid going there. It is not cowardice but ordinary prudence. If a man leaps for his life off a railway line as an express tears past the spot where he was standing, you would not go up to him, tap him on the shoulder, and say, "You coward, you jumped for your life through sheer fear of that train!" God gave us our reason that we might use it for our well-being, and it is quite reasonable to weigh both advantages and penalties attached to moral law.

Nor is this influence probably to the bad. The knowledge that retribution will follow violations of the moral law makes that law a real law. Could we say that all the penalties attached to the laws of the State are to the bad? Thousands of temptations to crime are resisted by citizens because of the thought of the future penalties. Nor does it matter much whether the penalty is future by a few weeks and in this life, or by some years, and in the next life. The principle is the same.

28. Right is right, and wrong is wrong, whether we are mortal or immortal.

That is true. But the difficulty is to make people do right because it is right and avoid wrong because it is wrong. We have to be trained to right conduct from childhood, and that very training demands commendation or punishment.

29. Your argument from justice weakens morality. If there were to be no rectification of things in the next life, all the more reason for men to remedy injustices in this world.

Men who give up their belief in a future life are not consumed with a passion for the rectifying of injustice in this world. On the contrary, those who lead evil lives have every reason to persuade themselves that there is no future life.

30. The injustices of this life demand another life, but I believe in reincarnation.

Justice does say that this life cannot be all. But your idea of reincarnation is a mistaken notion based upon your notion that life is impossible unless on this Earth. But there is no need for another life on this Earth, which would involve further inequalities. There is a better life than this, afterward and elsewhere. Reincarnation is a myth.

31. Is transmigration of the soul and our return in animal forms impossible?

Yes. The human soul is essentially an intellectual being, and the nature God has given to man demands a proportionately constructed bodily counterpart. An intellectual soul united with a body incapable of cooperating in thought processes, as, for example, a human soul inhabiting a dog, would be a metaphysically repugnant monstrosity, and a direct contradiction of divine wisdom. Moreover, God has revealed that it is appointed unto man to die once and after that the judgment. We do not come back as animals and die again. Also, the judgment of each soul concerns its final destiny and does not allow for another temporary and earthly existence. So our returning in animal forms is outside the realm of both possibility and fact.

32. I am perfectly happy in this world, and will be quite content if death ends all.

No man is either perfectly happy or perfectly miserable in this life. Life is a succession of days alternating between joy and suffering. There are enough miseries in this life to prevent perfect happiness yet enough happiness to compel us to look beyond this world for the complete fulfillment of lawful hopes. If death did end all, of course, you would be neither contented nor discontented. You would be nonexistent. And it is absurd to say that you are perfectly happy and to give that as a reason for being content even now with the prospect of death ending all. If you said that you were perfectly miserable and that you longed for death to end everything, you would speak more intelligently, even though that, too, would be an exaggeration.

33. So you deny that I am perfectly happy?

Yes. You will never come to a stage when all your desires are quite satisfied while you are still in this life. If you were perfectly happy, and in want of nothing more, why did you bother writing in order to secure a further knowledge you did not possess? One who has all he wants seeks nothing more.

34. What is the attitude of the Catholic Church toward the survival of animal souls?

Catholic philosophers reject belief in the immortality of animal souls, chiefly on the score of their nonspiritual operations. A study of animal psychology reveals nothing that transcends the sensitive and material order, and there can be no reasonable doubt but that death terminates the existence of animals both as regards body and soul. Revelation gives no indication that animals will have a future life; in fact, the general trend of God's revelation seems to exclude it.

35. Each animal seems to have its own distinctive personality. And noble animal traits often exceed those of men.

Personality supposes intelligence, and a moral responsibility following upon free will, that no one would attribute to mere animals. Each animal may have distinctive characteristics; but we are not justified in attributing personality to them in the strict sense of the word.

The good instincts of animals, for which they are not morally responsible, may be preferable to the vices of men as such. But the very moral degradation of a man who chooses vice rather than virtue indicates a nobler type of being than any mere animal that is incapable of truly moral conduct.

36. If we deserve to survive, don't animals, by their virtues, deserve the same?

Strictly speaking, we cannot attribute virtues to animals. They may have good habits, but virtue and merit suppose moral freedom, and the deliberate choice of things which are not a matter of physical necessity.

37. Many people abandon religion because the interests of animals are not made a special part of its teaching.

The interests of animals can never be a special part of reasonable religion. It is a religious duty to God and to man's own dignity to practice restraint and kindness in the use of animals. But that will result from the really important duty of worshipping and loving God and attending to the salvation and sanctification of our own souls by the practice of Christian virtue.

There is a great danger of excess in this matter. As Christian ideals fade, human beings forget their own dignity, reduce themselves to the animal level, and grow hard toward one another. And by a strange kind of distortion, the human sympathies that they cannot suppress entirely tend to go out to the animal world. Many women marry, refuse to have children, and lavish their starved instincts upon pet animals as a substitute. So we have beauty parlors for pet dogs, where ladies can take their little Pomeranians to have them "bathed, shampooed, groomed, and manicured" at a price that would provide a week's food for a starving child. I do not suggest that you would approve of such extremes, but you echo ideas that have led to them. In the meantime, if people will not practice religion to attend to the interests of their own souls, it will be quite useless for them to do so in order to attend to the interests of animals. You may think me hard, but I cannot win sympathy for religion by sympathizing with ideas utterly opposed to it by their extravagance. We must love God and let our love for God extend to all his creatures reasonably and proportionately. It is a distortion to love animals and then be prepared to love God provided we can let our love of animals extend to him also! It is essential that we have a correct knowledge of the order of things established by God, that we obtain a genuine notion of religion and of its duties, and that we fulfill those duties. Sentiment cannot be exalted to the dominant element in religion.

38. What is the purpose of life on this Earth?

Man is created to praise, love, and serve God in this life, and by doing so to attain eternal life with God hereafter. This is not our only life. It is but an infinitesimal part of it.

39. You constantly speak of some kind of a relationship between God and man.

I do. A personal God exists. Intelligent human beings exist. Those human beings owe all they have to the personal God who made them, and, being intelligent, are able to recognize that fact. Reason demands that they do so and render a suitable, practical acknowledgment of that fact to God.

40. Do these doctrines of moral obligation, sanctions, and a future life imply the freedom of man's will?

They do, for if man were not free, he could not be responsible for his conduct and could neither merit commendation by good actions nor condemnation by evil actions. If man is not free, he cannot be expected to keep laws and should not be punished for breaking them. There can be no obligation to observe a law when it is not possible to keep it. This is the judgment of every normal mind. The judicial and punitive application of human legislation is outrageous if men are not responsible for their conduct. The theorists who talk of determinism never dream of applying their doctrine in practice.

Again, consciousness affords sufficient proof for every normal man. We are not only conscious before acting that there are various courses open to us, but we are conscious that we may desist from a course of action already adopted, and after acting are conscious of self-approbation or self-reproach, realizing that we were not compelled to act that way.

Finally, the possession of reason or intelligence cannot be without freedom of will. Granted a reasoning faculty that can apprehend finite things under different aspects, free will follows. For example, the acquiring of another man's money may be considered as involving the moral evil of obtaining it by theft, or as yielding one's own goods in exchange for the sake of possessing cash. The object itself allows a man to concentrate upon one aspect or the other, proposing to himself motives for a good or an evil choice.

41. Since God willed both the death of Christ and its attendant circumstances, where was the freedom of Judas in betraying Christ?

In the passion and death of Christ many things were due to God's positive will, but many, on the other hand, were due to God's permissive will. That God merely permitted Judas to indulge an evil will, and did not positively inspire his action, is evident from the Gospel itself. Had Judas been compelled to act as he did against his own will, he would not have been morally responsible. Yet the very Gospels that tell us of the fact that he did betray Christ tell us also that he was morally guilty in doing so. Therefore, he was free not to do so. Thus Christ reproached him, "Judas, would you betray the Son of man with a kiss?" Our Lord did not say, "Judas, you have to do this, so I can scarcely blame you." So, too, in Acts 1:25, we are told that Judas "turned aside, to go to his own place." It is obvious, therefore, from Scripture, that Judas was responsible for his action.

A difficulty might arise in your mind from the fact that God had predicted through the prophets that Judas would betray Christ. But that does not prove compulsion. It was not predicted that Judas "must" betray Christ. The prediction was based on the fact that he "would" do so by his own free choice. Judas did not do so because it had been predicted. More expressly, we are certain that God's will was not impelling Judas, because we are clearly told by God's word that "Satan entered into Judas" and that he then went to the chief priests (Luke 22:3–4). Now, the will of Satan is radically opposed to the will of God. But this leads to a second possible difficulty. If not compelled by the will of God, was Judas compelled by the will of Satan? It is obvious that he was not, since the Gospels hold him to be personally responsible. If Judas did the will of Satan, it was because he freely consented to do so. There was no need for him to do so; and if he obeyed the suggestions of Satan, he did so voluntarily. We know, too, of our Lord's own efforts to win him to better dispositions prior to the crime.

42. If God knows all things beforehand, is not that the end of our freedom?

No. God's knowledge does not make us so act. An astronomer may be able to say, "There will be an eclipse of the sun." When the eclipse comes, no one says that it had to come because the astronomer said it would. The astronomer's knowledge was caused by the fact that it would come; the eclipse was not caused by the fact that he foresaw it.

God does know what you will do in the future. Yet when you do it, it will be by your own free choice. Your difficulty arises from the fact that you are speaking of God as if he were conditioned by time exactly as we are. He is not. We are space-time creatures, and God is outside all space-time limitations. Actions that, from our standpoint, must seem to be pre-known are not really pre-known to God, for "pre-known" supposes successive knowledge, and succession supposes time. God, in reality, simply "knows" in an ever-present eternity. We are quite unable to comprehend the relationship between an eternal intelligence and successive events conditioned by time. The only experience we have is of the time-sequence. I know that talk of God as being outside time is like talking color to a man born blind. But that can't be helped. We have to talk of these things. But we must realize our limitations and know that we cannot even state the problem except in terms that are incapable of expressing it adequately.

43. We cannot escape heredity. You cannot produce a thoroughbred racehorse from a pair of broken-down hacks.

If man be no more than a beast, your analogy might apply. But if man is no more than a beast, you must not be surprised if he behaves as a beast. However, man is not a mere animal. Nor is character merely a matter of bodily characteristics only. Some of the finest types of men have arisen from the most unimpressive parentage; and from the best stock defective types have resulted. Free will is a fact and a psychological factor in the development of character that cannot be ignored. And upon the use of man's free will his eternal destiny will depend.

Chapter 3

Religion

44. What do you mean by religion?

By religion I mean that act of justice by which we render to God, both privately as individuals and publicly as social beings, the honor, gratitude, and obedience due to him, and in the way prescribed by him.

45. What can religion do for God? He can need it very little.

He does not need it at all. But he must demand that we do what it is right for us to do. We are unjust if we do not return love for love and gratitude for gifts received. Our future well-being, not God's, is inextricably bound up with our fulfillment of religious duties.

46. Is the practice of religion necessary?

Yes. God has definite rights that no man is justified in ignoring. Moreover, God definitely commands you to adore and serve him. "You shall love the Lord your God … this is the great and first commandment" (Matt. 22:37-38). A man with no religion, who never worships God, never says a prayer to him, is far from fulfilling this commandment of love. It is not enough to admit offhand that God exists and then ignore his definite claims.

Prayer is conversation with God and an act of religion. To ignore prayer is to ignore God and deny his rights. Being an adult male does not exempt from this duty. Men are not less the creatures of God than women and children. Nor will heaven be less worth having for men, or hell more tolerable.

To God you are a child. There are no privileged classes in the presence of infinite Wisdom; no exemptions before an eternal God; no strength before Omnipotence. We are all children to God.

47. Religion seems to me to be based on superstition and fear.

Religion as such is certainly not based on superstition, despite the folly into which some people have fallen where religion is concerned. As regards fear, which is by no means the same thing as superstition, nor necessarily supposes it, all genuine religion is based on a reverential and proper fear of God. For the fear of the Lord is the beginning of wisdom. Craven fear has no place in genuine religion. If any people have adopted religion through motives of craven fear, their conduct would be wrong, and their dispositions would have to be condemned. Their duty would be to rise to higher motives and seek a proper spirit of religion.

48. Don't you think that where science advances, religion is rejected?

No. In some people, pretended science can destroy religion, either because of their limited mental powers or because of their pride and self-conceit. Others do not so much love science as hate religion owing to its conflict with their vices. And their continued talk of a love for science (of which they know little or nothing) is a kind of alibi by which they try to conceal their dislike of religion and pretend to impartiality. The really scientific find no tendency to abandon religion on the score of any conflicting evidence. Science has dethroned the sun-god, Jupiter, stone-gods, and other false deities. It has demolished sorcery, incantations, oracles, and other superstitions to some extent, but true religion remains; and the really scientific mind admits willingly that life is a bigger thing than this Earth and that science itself can never satisfy the needs of human nature.

The mysteries of religion do not stifle thought. They are a provocation to thought and have inspired the greatest minds. Unexplained themselves, they throw an immense amount of light on the problem of life's purpose and destiny when added to what we already know by reason itself. Though we cannot sound their full depths, we find in them the explanation of most of our noblest experiences. They are the key to life; and as life itself is mysterious, so the key to it is mysterious. A key is as intricate as the lock, or it does not fit. It is only by combining the clear and the mysterious that we arrive at a proper understanding.

We have an example of that in science itself. In spectroscopic analysis a ray of light is broken up into its various colors; but the spectrum reveals a series of dark lines that are most mysterious. Their explanation is found only by noting where they fall in relation to the colors that are clearly shown. Now, in his search for knowledge man finds that his own power of sight is limited to a very narrow band of wavelengths. He can see neither infrared nor ultraviolet rays. These would be absolute mysteries to him if he depended only on sight. But his intelligence has discovered them. Faith goes further, and by a knowledge secured from God's revelation, gets an inkling of the great mysterious reality of God himself, who clarifies the puzzling lines and dark shadows by which the whole of our knowledge and life are criss-crossed from end to end. So we find that the mysterious and the clear give the true sense to life.

49. It is my opinion that religion is a racket designed to provide a living for those who propagate it.

Do you know anything at all about Christ? Can you find anything in the four Gospels to hint that he designed his religion only to provide a living in this world? When he called his apostles to leave their ordinary means of livelihood, he did not offer them an easier and more lucrative profession. Religion, of course, like anything else is liable to abuse. Some people undoubtedly have made a money-spinning racket out of religion. And they cannot be too strongly condemned. But that does not justify your sweeping assertion that religion is designed for that purpose. If being provided with a living were the motive, I can assure you that it would never have inspired me to become a Catholic priest, nor could it inspire me to remain one. Life could offer me much more elsewhere.

A great many people talk religion but forget about it once there is any mention of self-sacrifice on behalf of religion. Genuine religion requires the fitting worship of God by man both in his social and individual capacity. Public worship requires churches, and men set apart to devote their lives to the cause of religion. Genuine religion also requires the proper education of children in their duties to God, to themselves, and to mankind; and this requires schools. Genuine religion also demands works of charity to the destitute and to the sick; and this requires orphanages, hospitals, and other institutions. All these things require money. And those who subscribe to these things do so from a sense of religion. Meantime, those who lack the same generosity sneer at the commercialism of religion.

50. You say that religion is necessary. I say that it is positively evil and degrading. It restrains our freedom.

Sincere religion spells freedom—freedom from vice, from all injustice and want of charity. There is no absolute freedom. You must be free from vice and subject to virtue, or free from virtue and subject to vice.

51. You cannot face life unaided, and reliance on God saps self-reliance and initiative and must develop the weakling.

The religious man knows that he cannot face life unaided, but that is not to his detriment. We do not ridicule a child at school who cannot face the problem of mathematics without the help of a master. If God needed help, he would be imperfect. But man is not God. He is very conscious of limitation, and if he wishes to behave as if he were God, quite self-sufficient and capable of all things, he denies the truth of his limitation. The man who realizes that he did not make the universe, which he cannot stop or rearrange anyway, is nearer the truth and behaves reasonably in asking the perfect Being who made him to preserve him from the mistakes and frailties of his own imperfection. An imperfect being should behave as if limited, not as if supremely perfect. Nor does religion sap man's self-reliance and initiative. These he uses to the full and then asks additional help from God. If a man employs extra help in his business, is he sapping his self-reliance? Must he do everything himself? No man can do everything. God helps those who help themselves, but he expects men to turn to him where they cannot help themselves. This secures full personal initiative and the help of God to supply for one's essential deficiencies. As for the developing of weaklings, read the history of the early Christians in the days of Nero and the Roman persecutions. For the love of God and with the help of God, children faced the reality of torture and suffering before which strong men quailed. The irreligious man is the weakling, shirking the duty of rendering to God what is due to God; shirking the humility of admitting that he is not infinitely perfect; shirking the greatest reality of life.

52. Religion involves the whole question of prayer, and for my part prayer is both unreasonable and useless.

Apart from the obtaining of benefits, by prayer we express our love of God and our gratitude to him and also our sorrow and regret for such sins as we have committed against him. But also prayer is a normal and intelligent means by which we obtain many blessings from God together with his protection and consolation in difficulties. Prayer is neither unreasonable nor useless.

Reason itself dictates the necessity of prayer. Reason tells you that you are not the author of your own existence, that you owe your origin, as does the whole human race, to an outside Cause who is more intelligent than the creatures of his own making. Every man also, who is not mentally deficient, knows that he himself is limited in a thousand ways—in size, in strength, in mind and will. Man is small, weak, ignorant, and inconstant. Enabled by reason to realize these imperfections, man is impelled by reason to appeal to and rely upon his Maker for the help and protection necessary lest his defects should lead to disaster. Prayer to his Maker is as natural to man as the instinct of a child to turn to its parents for help. All creatures, of course, are subject to such limitations. But man alone is conscious of them, and therefore rational people alone are given to prayer. Brute animals do not pray. It is irrational not to pray.

53. If there is a God, it should not be necessary to tell him of our needs.

We do not pray in order to inform God of our needs. We pray to fulfill a condition laid down by God for our own sakes. God demands of us the humility that acknowledges our dependence on him and the confidence that acknowledges him as our Father. Even earthly parents, who know their children's wants and intend to supply them, insist that they ask respectfully for what they need. It is in a child's own interest that he should be trained to behave properly.

God has, of course, given us very many things without any request from us. But it would not be more generous to do that always. It is more generous to secure our still greater good by making us ask. And even apart from our training in religious behavior, it is a great happiness and privilege to be allowed to converse with God concerning our own interests.

54. If God is unchangeable, can you hope to change him by fervent appeals?

God is unchangeable. But prayer is itself part of God's unchangeable providence. He has decreed that many benefits will depend upon our praying for them. We shall get them if we ask for them; if we do not pray we shall not receive them. The change is not in God.

55. For centuries humanity has prayed to God for deliverance from floods, famines, plagues, and distress; but God has ever been silent.

You can't gulp down the whole of humanity like that. For centuries some men have cursed God, some have simply ignored God, and some have prayed to God. Humanity as a whole has not prayed to God for deliverance from evils. And among those who have prayed, many have done so in order to praise God, or to thank God, or to repair their sins against God, or to ask spiritual graces from him. Prayer is not confined to the asking of temporal benefits only.

But even if you restrict your question to prayer for temporal favors, thousands would rise in protest and prove to you that prayers for temporal favors have been granted far more often than can be explained by mere coincidence. All that Christians claim as regards prayer for temporal favors is that such prayers are sometimes heard in the way we wish when God knows that the granting of our request will be really for our good. Prayer of petition is not the kind of penny-in-the-slot machine by which we obtain just what we specify, as we would obtain a box of matches.

56. God allows war to continue, though people of all religious denominations pray to him to stop it.

If the sufferings caused by war were entirely useless, it might be more difficult to answer that problem. But if men can benefit by such sufferings, a good God could certainly permit them; and if men deserved them, his justice cannot be blamed. Men do deserve such sufferings; and indeed mankind as a whole deserves more than it gets in the way of suffering. See the flood of iniquity in the world, and ask yourself whether men deserve that all things should flatter their desires. If people prayed that the war should stop, then the fact that the war moved some people to prayers they would not otherwise have said was already a good result. And prayer did produce remarkable results in various individuals during the war. If it did not make all combatants cease fighting at the various moments various unbelievers thought the war ought to end, that fact does not imply that prayer was useless.

57. I have no religion and am well off; the poor wretches who practice religion do not seem to gain much by it.

Religion is not supposed to be an easy road to temporal prosperity in things that death takes from those who have them. It is the road, not always comfortable, to never-ending and eternal happiness. We do not expect religion to result in earthly advancement. If it did, men would rush to it as a good business proposition and offer to God a devotion quite without value. Temporal things are subject to the natural course of events. You are not materially well off because you have no religion. There are thousands who have no religion and are not well off. So, too, the poor are not poor because they practice religion. There are well-to-do people who also practice their religion. And if the poor gave up their religion they would not suddenly become rich. In the meantime, you prosper because of natural circumstances or natural ability or because God is giving you temporal rewards for such good as you do. Everyone does some good sometimes. For the poor, God often reserves their compensation for the next life.

58. I have led a happy and contented life, the crux of all human endeavor. Why is religion necessary if this can be attained without religion?

If you are perfectly happy, you are the only one on Earth who is. Is there absolutely nothing further you would like to have but which you do not yet possess? Anyway, religion is not a kill-joy. One of the happiest men who ever lived was St. Francis of Assisi, born and bred in the Catholic spirit. The simplest priest finds more joy in saying one Mass, and the least of our Catholic people in one Communion, than you have experienced in your whole life. Then, too, I have already shown that death cannot end all. If it did, the religious man would hardly be able to feel a fool. But if it does not, as it cannot, you will scarcely enjoy meeting a God whom you have consistently ignored. The idea that death ends all is not the result of thought. It is the result of refusing to think.

The crux of all human endeavor ought not to be the securing of a happy and contented life in this world. Man's main duty is the religious service of God. If you are able to be happy, you owe it to God that you exist, and that those things exist that give you happiness. You, therefore, owe to God the acknowledgment of your debt to him by religious worship, offering him your praise and gratitude. To take all, and enjoy it without the slightest manifestation of gratitude to God, is both unjust and most ill-mannered.

Again, if you seek happiness, seek it properly whilst you are at it. This world is not all. Your soul is immortal, and eternity awaits you. If the sole source of your happiness lies in the things of this world, then you are living in a fool's paradise. No man can escape death, and every cause of happiness for you will be taken from you whether you like it or not. You brought nothing into this world with you, and you will take nothing of it with you when you die. Where then will you find happiness?

Religion is our bond with God who made us, and the earnest and fervent practice of religion keeps us in touch with the God whom we are to meet some day, and with whom we are to be forever, if we are to know happiness hereafter. Your own happiness, therefore, is bound up with your religious duties to God, and you owe him the acknowledgment that you can render him only by discharging the debt of religion. Neglect that duty and you are guilty of a great injustice, and you will make wreckage of your eternity. On your deathbed you may say that you "have had" many happinesses during life. But you won't have them then. They came—only to go; and the memory of them will be no compensation for the miseries you will encounter and which will never go. Be reasonably happy in this life, if you wish. But take up your duties of religion, make sure of your eternal happiness in the next life, and at all costs save your soul.

59. I have sound ideas of goodness and morality and can live up to them without religion.

Your very ideas of what is good and moral are drawn from the general Christian culture of the civilization in which you live. To want your moral standards without the religion that gave rise to them is like wanting rain without wanting the ocean from which it is drawn. Philosopher Ernest Renan admitted that to abolish Christianity, yet to wish to retain its ethics, is merely to inhale a perfume from an empty bottle. Men cannot live on perfumes; and even if they could, the emptiness of the bottle will soon mean the end of the perfume. Again, if the Christian religion is true, as it is, then it is necessary for goodness and morality. For its very acceptance will be part of morality, involving the discharging of our debt to God. Religion is as necessary to good morals as the right course is necessary to good navigation.

Reason, when it is right, is good enough as far as it goes. But it is very liable to error, and when right does not go far enough. We need the additional truth revealed by God and taught us by the Christian religion. Reason cannot refute the claims of Christ and in fact disposes us to accept them. Certainly reason cannot replace religion. It gives inadequate knowledge only and cannot give any vital impulse to observe its own moral precepts.

Man can do some good things without religion. He can refrain from drunkenness and pay his debts to his fellow men. But he cannot live a really good life unless he does the main thing for which he was made. And the main thing is that he knows, loves, and serves God and regulates his conduct toward his fellow men by motives of love for God.

60. I am honest without being religious. But I know many people who are religious without being honest.

Now you take your own virtue as a standard and proceed to find other people wanting when measured by it. It often happens that those who practice no religion canonize themselves as the models of perfection and regard religious people as sinners and hypocrites. But those who go to church are constantly told of their own failings and that they must not judge others. It would be better for you to take up your religious duties. As a matter of fact, it is impossible to be really honest without being religious. Religion is the highest form of honesty, a strict duty to God. Take this case: Jones owes one man $100 and to another $1. He pays the $1 but not the $100. Smith also owes $100 and to another $1 but pays the $100, neglecting to pay the $1. Whose is the greater dishonesty? Now, each man owes a tremendous debt to God and a lesser one to his neighbor. You may pay the lesser, but you neglect the greater. Your neighbor, who fulfills his religious duties, at least tries to pay the greater, though he may seem to you to neglect the lesser. But he is the better man, at least insofar as he attempts to pay the greater. The man who is just to his neighbor, but does not bother about his duty of religion is the kind of man who pays the baker for the bread he puts into his body but nothing to God for the body he puts the bread into. Religion is a strict duty of justice to God, acknowledging our indebtedness to him. If religious people sometimes fail in honesty toward their fellow men, I do not justify it. But their creditors are insignificant compared with the Creditor who supplied you with all you have and receives no acknowledgment from you. You are both in the wrong, but I would rather be in the position of those you condemn, if a choice had to be made, which of course has not to be made. Their religion may save them despite their faults. Your honesty will not save you.

61. I believe in God but practice no religion.

It is something to believe in God. But what notice do you take of God? You believed in the existence of your own parents, but I am sure you paid them more attention than you have ever paid to God, in whom you say you also believe. Quiet thoughts about the Almighty do not constitute religion. Religion requires much more than that.

62. I not only believe in God, I lead a clean life. Is not that enough?

On one condition—that you honestly believe no more to be necessary and have never had an opportunity of discovering the real truth. But if, for example, you have ever heard of the claims of the Catholic Church and have refused to inquire into them, I could not answer for you. If you did inquire, realized that you should become a Catholic, and refused, you would have less chance still, for you would obviously be insincere.

63. What is your idea of a good man?

One who is first just to all others, including God. His first duty is to render to God what is due to him. Secondly, and for the love of God, he renders all that is due to his fellow men. In addition he must manage himself in his own personal life, overcoming with fortitude the difficulties in the way of right conduct, and practicing temperance by restraining sensuality and other lower appetites.

64. But surely I can do that without adopting a particular form of religion. If I adopt a particular church, I antagonize my fellow men, so I keep neutral and bear ill will to none.

Once you find that God has revealed a particular form of religion, you must accept it. You will not assume any obligation to bear any ill will toward others. Rather, you will have an additional obligation to avoid it. But you are not justified in refusing to adopt that particular form of religion because you will thus antagonize your fellow men. If thus you secure the ill will of others, that is not your fault, and it is their loss. We may never let what men think of us matter more than what God thinks of us. And after all, it is God who will judge us, not our fellow men.

65. One who accepts revealed religion is expected to believe in miracles.

Revelation includes the fact that miracles have occurred.

66. Can you expect enlightened people to believe in miracles?

Yes. It is the unenlightened people from whom we expect unbelief; from people who have never bothered to examine any evidence but whose opinions are dictated by their prejudices.

67. What is a miracle?

A miracle is an extraordinary event beyond the powers and outside the scope of any created agency and therefore produced by God himself. No natural forces could account for it.

68. I could never believe in miracles. They are much too strange for me.

As an extraordinary event not due to natural causes, every miracle is calculated to surprise us to some extent. Of its very nature it is a surprising thing. But, from another point of view, we are not surprised that God should at times work miracles. He is not bound by the secondary laws he himself appointed as the normal causes of events in this universe.

We are naturally inclined to be astonished by the unusual, but we are not justified in denying the truth of an event merely because it is unusual. "The government of the whole universe is a much more wonderful thing than the multiplication of five loaves of bread," says St. Augustine, "but men are not astonished by the former because they are used to it, whilst they are astonished by the latter because it is rare." Granted an omnipotent God, it is absurd to say that miracles cannot happen. Belief in a miracle depends entirely upon the available evidence as to whether it did happen. As a matter of fact, miracles seem strange only to minds that make no allowance for God. He who lives in the presence of God is not surprised to see God act. It is as easy for God to restore life to a dead man as to preserve the life of a living man.

69. Why should people believe in miracles that happened 2,000 years ago?

Some people believe that miracles happen in our own day; others do not. I certainly believe that they can happen and am prepared to believe that any given event is a miracle, provided satisfactory evidence can be produced that it did occur and that it surpasses the capability of any natural law.

Yet even if miracles did not happen in our own times, that would not be proof that they did not happen 2,000 years ago. Events of 2,000 years ago must be judged on the evidence of what happened then, not on the evidence of what does not happen now. In other words, the historical evidence for past miracles must be examined on its own merits. It would not be disproved by any absence of miracles now. Otherwise you could prove that women never wore hoop skirts by the fact that the modern woman does not happen to do so.

70. I agree with those who wish to purify the Gospels by eliminating the miraculous element embodied in them side by side with so much good teaching.

It is impossible to eliminate the miraculous element from the Gospels without rejecting them completely as fraud and forgery. You might just as well suggest a life of Napoleon without any military exploits as suggest a life of Christ without miracles. The texts describing the miracles were there from the very beginning and were written by those who saw them and who wrote the rest of the matter contained in the Gospels. It is unreasonable to say that the authors were quite reliable in setting down what you happen to approve in the accounts of Christ but that they suddenly became unreliable in sections that do not happen to appeal to you.

The miracles in the Gospels are not legendary. They are a matter of history. Nor do they belittle Christ. There is no element in them of the merely curious, ostentatious, and puerile. They bear directly upon his mission as Redeemer. Christ manifested his goodness by curing bodies as well as souls and proved his divine power against objectors by such sayings as, "Which is easier, to forgive sin, or to say: Arise and walk?" And he bade the crippled to rise and walk, which they did. By his miracles Christ proved both the truth and the necessity of the religion he taught.

If any man could prove that the miracles recorded in the Bible did not happen, or that miracles could not happen, I would abandon Christianity altogether. But to disprove miracles you must prove one of three things: You must prove either that there is no God, or that God cannot operate independently of the laws of nature he himself established, or that the Bible is a lying forgery and not authentic history. No man can prove any of these things.

71. Are we expected to believe things to be true without any evidence for them?

We are expected to believe what God has revealed, because God must know the truth, and because he could not deceive us. Where revealed mysteries are concerned, we accept them, not because they appeal to reason as evidently true in themselves but because of God's authority. This supposes evidence, of course, that God has actually revealed the mysteries we thus accept. We believe what God says, but we must know that he said it. It will be necessary, therefore, to study the historical evidence for the fact of revelation.

72. You keep hinting that God not only demands religious worship but that he has actually specified the way in which men must offer such homage. Do you mean that God has actually told men of his demand, explaining its conditions?

Yes. God has told mankind very clearly why he created man, what is the destiny of man, and what man must do in order to attain that destiny. He sent the Prophets to teach men his will; after that he sent his own Divine Son, Jesus Christ; and Christ sent the Catholic Church—a Church still teaching with the infallible authority of God in our very midst.

Chapter 4

The Bible

73. Prove the reliability of the Gospels.

By all means, although I cannot go very deeply into the matter in the brief time at my disposal. However, I shall do my best to give the main elements.

First, the authors assigned wrote the books attributed to them. A knowledge of Hebrew shows that the authors were certainly Jews. Historical and political references show that they were Jews of the first century, for Palestine is shown under conditions before and not after the fall of Jerusalem in the year A.D. 70. Also, had they been written after that date, the writers would not have omitted to make the point that Christ's prophecy had been fulfilled. They do not mention it. All the descriptions, also, are so vivid that they could only have been written by eyewitnesses. And in addition to this internal evidence, we have solid external evidence. Thus Papias, who was the disciple of St. John the Apostle, and who certainly lived in the first century, has left it in writing that one named Matthew first wrote in Hebrew and that one named Mark wrote what he had heard of Peter. Papias could not have written this had not these two Evangelists already written their Gospels. The Muratorian Fragment, dating from at least the year 170, tells us that the third Gospel was written by Luke, the fourth by John. And there is no evidence at all to the contrary. We have not as much evidence for the authorship of many classical books, of which no one doubts. Also, the apostles and immediate disciples would not have allowed forgeries to be palmed off as genuine. Heretics and pagans would have found their strongest argument in showing the basic documents to be falsely attributed to immediate disciples of Christ. And all regions accepted these four Gospels. If they were not genuine, and one region began the fraud, the rest would have risen up in violent protest. No critic of any value denies the fourfold authorship today.

Secondly, the Gospels have never been tampered with or substantially altered. The Gospels had been multiplied by copyists and were quite familiar to the early Christians. Not all could be falsified simultaneously, and changes could easily be detected by comparison. And the early Christians were most vigilant, holding the Gospels in great veneration. Marcion the heretic fabricated a gospel in the year 110 to suit his heresy, and there was a universal protest at once. All existing manuscripts, back as far as the fourth century, quote the Gospels as they are now. No substantial alterations can have occurred since the fourth century, and they were far less likely to occur during the times nearer to the apostles. Sincere critics today admit the substantial integrity of the Gospels, and those opposed to Christianity concentrate upon other lines of attack.

Thirdly, the Evangelists were reliably informed. Rationalists take refuge in the thought that they were sincere but laboring under some strange delusion or hallucination. They have no evidence to support the contention but stake all on a preconceived improbability. They practically say, "We do not see how such things *could* happen, therefore it's no use telling us that they *did* happen." This is prejudice. A few years ago men said, "A man *could* not speak to Australia from England by telephone, and therefore we do not believe that he ever will." The fact has disproved them. A man with a theory can see almost anything, provided it supports his theory, and be blind to the most evident facts if they seem to upset his theory. Rationalists do not like the Gospel facts and therefore deny them. Forced to admit authorship, integrity, and sincerity, they say, "The writers *must* have been the victims of some hallucination." But if you wish to deny a man's right to the property next door, you must prove something, if only that his title-deeds are false.

But it is no use saying, "I do not like the man!" Meantime, all the evidence is against the position of these rationalists. They have to admit exactness as regards geographical, political, and religious conditions of Palestine. Why should they be less accurate when they describe the sayings and doings of Christ? They are perfectly sane in all their other statements. And are all *four* to have the *same* hallucination, and *all* their lives? There is no trace of fanaticism in their sober accounts; Christ had to accuse them of being "slow to believe"; enemies then and there could not deny the miracles and must have been suffering from the same hallucination; and the Jews never attempted to deny the facts. The Evangelists were quite reliably informed.

Fourthly, they were sincere. They not only knew the facts, but they told the truth. They gained martyrdom in this life and on their own principles stood to gain only hell in the next if they were lying in so important a matter. If they intended to lie, they could have painted themselves as heroes instead of depicting their own faults; and above all should not have described a mocked, humiliated, and crucified Master in order to win the veneration of men. On the Jewish material at their disposal they could not have invented the type represented by Christ as the Messiah, and if they did want to invent might just as well have painted the portrait of a far more glorious Leader from a worldly point of view. No thinker today brings the old charge that the Evangelists lied. Finally, that the statements were made under oath before God is abundantly clear. The writers call upon God to witness to the truth of what they write. St. John says, "This is the disciple who is bearing witness to these things, and who has written these things; and we know that his testimony is true." St. Paul, also: "For God is my witness, whom I serve with my spirit in the gospel of his Son." No modern court of law would reject evidence as clearly given as that for the events and utterances attributed to Christ.

74. Where are the original records?

The original documents have long since perished. The earliest copy is about fourth century, but over 1,600 years have had their effect even upon that copy. Even parchment perishes with time. There are thousands of original documents in existence. The particular original documents, the copies of which we now possess in the Gospels, have perished. But the copies are perfectly reliable, as has been established by comparison of hundreds of independent transcriptions reaching back to the times when the originals were certainly in existence.

75. Why should not a Catholic who believes in miracles expect that the original Gospel manuscripts should last forever?

Because, although a Catholic believes that miracles can occur, and have occurred when God has willed to grant them, he does not expect miracles where God has not willed to grant them, nor that God should will to grant them wherever men might think it wise that he should do so.

If the original Gospel manuscripts were in fact preserved by a miracle, you would not accept that as a miracle any more than you accept existent miracles already wrought by God. If you want miracles for your consideration, there are plenty available. "If they hear not Moses and the Prophets," said Christ, "neither will they believe if one rise from the dead." He said this because the refusal of the Jews to be guided by Moses and the Prophets was due to bad will. And a man who has a bad will and does not want to believe will not believe, no matter what motives are put before him. If you reject the Christian religion despite all its present credentials, neither would you believe even were the original Gospel manuscripts miraculously preserved.

76. Why does no reputable historian mention Christ and his wonderful works?

I have just shown that five reputable historians record the events, the four Evangelists and St. Paul. Their books are as historical as any others. Tacitus, the Roman historian, writing about seventy years after the death of Christ, mentions him, as does Josephus, the Jewish historian. Also, Roman historians were not much concerned with Palestine, an outpost of the empire, and moreover had a supreme contempt for the Jews, discounting all their doings. It is obvious also that the Jewish writers would not be bent on recording an event they would very much like to forget.

Finally, absence of evidence in other writers who do not deal *ex professo* with a given subject weighs nothing against positive evidence recorded by reliable historians.

77. Are not the Gospels entirely set in a theological context to serve theological purposes?

It would be a gross exaggeration to say that. A remarkable feature of the Gospels is their adherence to a bare delineation of facts. Even where we should expect them to make capital out of what they write, they don't. Miraculous events are given without any expressions of astonishment or triumph. Ill-treatment of their Master is recorded without a word of indignation. If the writers were bent on supporting a thesis, having little regard for historical truth, they would have been fools to invent "hard sayings" that could only alienate people; to record that Christ's own relatives thought him mad; that he was weak enough to pray that the cup of suffering might pass from him; to paint a picture of a humiliated, mocked, and crucified criminal whom they wanted men to worship; and to insist that his own people rejected him. If his own rejected him, why on Earth should others accept him? No. They record what happened as if their only interest were that of observers and narrators. I admit that the idea of theological purpose is not without application to the fourth Gospel. But that does not hinder the truth of the facts given.

78. What proof is there that the Bible is the word of God?

Let us subject the Gospels as books to all the laws of historical criticism—the same laws that we apply to other books. They prove to be reliable historical documents—indeed, there is no genuine historical document in existence if these are not so. Now, these historical documents tell us of a certain historical person who declared that he was God, justified that claim by works that no ordinary man could do, and said that he would establish an infallible church—a church still in this world.

Thus we prove Christ's life and works from historical documents. We prove his divinity from his life and works. We prove the infallible Church from the promise of this divine Person. But we do not yet say that Scripture is inspired, though of course we know that it is. But our rational grounds for that belief come from the fact that the infallible Church of Christ teaches with her authority that the Bible is inspired and the word of God, and also tells us what books comprise the Bible.

That the Bible is infinitely superior to the sacred books of other religions becomes at once apparent. The most rigid criticism shows the strictly historical character of the Bible. Fabulous narratives cannot stand this test. The supernatural character of the Bible stands out in vivid contrast when compared with the teaching of other religious documents. The Catholic Church, whose very existence in the world today cannot be explained by natural forces, guarantees the Bible as the word of God.

79. We Protestants know that the Bible is inspired without having to accept the authority of the Catholic Church. We feel that it is the word of God and know from the lofty doctrines it contains.

Your belief is right, though many Protestants are rapidly giving up that belief. For the grounds you allege for your belief scarcely provide a sufficiently rational foundation. You may feel that it is inspired, but nothing can be proved from feelings, and in any case there are others who do not feel that it is inspired. Again, while many passages contain lofty doctrines, many other passages are not lofty, and this argument cannot justify the Bible as a whole.

80. Your own proof is a vicious circle, the Church proving her own infallibility from Scripture and the inspiration of Scripture from her infallibility.

It is not a vicious circle but a lawful spiral argument of which the ends do not meet. Taking Scripture as a historical document only, the Church proves the historical fact that Christ endowed her with infallibility. Then using that infallibility she throws new light on the historical books by assuring me that they are inspired. I begin with merely historical books. I finish with inspired historical books. But I did not use inspiration as the basis of my first premise. So, too, I could prove that the present king is the rightful ruler from history only, and after that view him under the aspect of his authority, obeying his legitimate commands. Thus St. Augustine rightly said, even in the fourth century, "I would not accept the Gospels unless the authority of the Catholic Church impelled me."

You have only your fallible human opinion as proof that Scripture is not inspired. I uphold the infallible and consistent teaching of the Catholic Church. Disprove her authority to decide which books are inspired and which are not inspired, and you will have made some headway. But until you have done so, your idea is nothing more than an opinion with a value proportionate only to your limited knowledge and mental capacity. That the Catholic Church has the authority I attribute to her I shall show on another occasion.

81. Did not the selection of the Gospels to be regarded as canonical depend upon the various councils?

The selection of the Gospels depended upon the authoritative decisions of the Catholic Church, decisions formulated in her official councils and to be approved by the pope. And it is the authority of the pope that alone counts in the final analysis. Above all, such matters are not dependent upon the authority of "various" councils when you wish to include false gatherings of recalcitrant bishops whose proceedings have been repudiated by the Church and whose decisions have been declared null and void. The authority of councils can be cited only when those councils have been authorized by the Holy See, and when their decisions have been approved and sanctioned by the pope. Under these conditions, the decisions of councils are quite reliable.

82. If God is the author of the Bible, why did he select words with several meanings, knowing this would ultimately cause confusion and skepticism?

The progress and mutation of an essentially variable human language is unavoidable. And God did know that the changing mentalities of subsequent generations would lead to confusion. To obviate the danger he could do one of two things. He could stabilize human reason and prevent each human being from mistaking the original sense, or else he could establish certain men to teach in his name, and finally, if necessary, an infallible tribunal that men could consult in matters of religion. He chose the latter course and thus never intended Scripture to be the ultimate guide in religious belief. Men who will not accept the Catholic Church, but insist on puzzling out the sense for themselves, have only themselves to blame if they end in skepticism. If the government establishes an inquiry office as a guide to the city and a complete stranger refuses to use its services, he is to blame if he gets lost.

83. I read recently the statement of a Protestant bishop that Christians are not obliged to believe in the verbal inspiration and literal infallibility of the Bible.

The Catholic Church, of course, cannot accept a Protestant bishop as an authority as to what Christians are bound to believe. How the Catholic Church would view this particular utterance depends upon what he meant by "verbal inspiration" and "literal infallibility." If, by verbal inspiration, the bishop intended a dictation of the very words to the writers by God, as one dictates to a stenographer, Catholics are not obliged to believe in verbal inspiration. But we are obliged to believe that every single word as it left the hands of the original writers was written under the inspiration of God and infallibly expressed the truth intended by God. God's influence respected the psychological characteristics of the various human instruments he used, and this accounts for differences in method and style. But it is certain that the original authors wrote exactly the things willed by God so that God is truly the principal author of the Bible as it left the hands of the original writers, those writers being but the human instruments used by God. Not a word nor a sentence belonging to the original writings could be excluded from the divine influence of God's inspiration.

Secondly, we must ask what the bishop meant by "literal infallibility." If he meant that not all the Bible is infallible, and that we may distinguish between religious parts and nonreligious parts, then no Catholic could agree with him. We Catholics are obliged to believe as infallibly true every single sentence as it left the hands of the original writers. The whole of the Bible is for us the word of God. We cannot regard the Bible as a mixture of God's word and merely human thoughts or opinions. The Catholic Church has condemned the doctrine that personal interpolations by the original writers crept into their accounts, interpolations that did not fall under the inspiring influence of God.

84. Then you cling to the fundamentalist idea that the Bible is infallibly true?

I must warn you against any idea, if you entertain such an idea, that the term *fundamentalist* is sufficient to discredit the orthodox position. There are fundamental principles in every branch of knowledge: in art, literature, mathematics, and in all other forms of science. Yet no one sneers at those who cling to such fundamental principles as a basis of thought in their respective fields of knowledge. In the field of religion, also, there are fundamental principles, and they are not destroyed by cheap ridicule. If they can be really disproved, that is well and good. But no one yet has succeeded in disproving the infallible truth of the Bible. Of course, I do not mean that every interpretation individual readers choose to impose upon the Bible is infallibly true. The Bible is true in the sense in which God intended what is said in its pages, not in any alien sense in which mistaken people understand it.

85. Old Testament teaching is barbaric in parts, not in keeping with the New Testament. Nor would God inspire such a record of outrageous crimes.

Things were permitted in the Old Law not in keeping with the more perfect New Law. But the change is in the Law. There is nothing in the Old Testament that violates any attribute of God, save, of course, the sins of men described in the Old Testament. These latter are recorded not with approval but as evil to be reprehended and as motives of repentance. It is a fallacy to measure the simple blunt standards of more primitive times by modern standards. Also, these accounts prove the trustworthiness of the reports. They are not out to say only the best of Jewish heroes but narrate exploits far from flattering to the vanity of the Jews, though written by members of the race, not by enemies.

In your readings you have either understood the correct sense or you have not. If you have, you had better change your ideas. Is the Bible, the inspired word of God, going to be true when it suits your ideas, or are your ideas going to be true when they are adjusted to God's revealed truth? If God says a thing not quite in accordance with your notions, then you can be sure that your notions are wrong, and you had better renounce them, as you have had to renounce so many other mistakes during your life. Men can be so easily mistaken; God cannot be mistaken.

86. Is the Book of Genesis to be taken literally or allegorically?

Each and every word of Genesis need not be taken literally. But the substance of all facts that are fundamental in Christianity are to be taken as literally true.

The account of creation in Genesis is certainly true, though men have not fully perceived the true interpretation of every detail given in that account. There is nothing in favor of evolution to justify doubting the direct formation of Adam and Eve by God, as we shall see on another occasion.

87. Do you hold that the world was made in six days of twenty-four hours each?

No. Moses described as occurring in six days processes that took long periods. Neither the time nor the order was meant to correspond with the objective reality of the creative process itself.

88. So you interpret the Hebrew word for day as a period?

I do not. The Hebrew word *yom* used absolutely as in the Mosaic account, and in the singular, means a day of twenty-four hours and nothing else. However long the progressive work of the formation of all things took in itself—and it occupied a very long period—Moses divided his account of the whole process into six sections, allotting each section to a separate "chapter" of his narrative, metaphorically called a "day." Vast periods, therefore, were compressed into each chapter. It is one thing to say that a long period was required for the events allotted to each section of an account called for special reasons a "day"; it is quite another to say that the author intended the word day as a long period. The author intended the word "day" as men understood that word; i.e., as consisting of twenty-four hours. The works took a long period in themselves. But the author wished the various sections of his narrative to represent ordinary days of the week.

89. Why did Moses choose such an artificial classification and literary arrangement?

That should be evident from the religious lesson he desired to teach. The imagery he employed of six working days for creation was to exemplify the six days of the week on which the Jews should work; and the seventh day was to exemplify the Sabbath, or day of rest and of religious worship.

90. Did God really take a rib from Adam and make a woman therefrom?

We are bound to believe that Eve was formed from Adam. It is revealed doctrine that God "made from one every nation of men" (Acts 17:26). "For man was not made from woman, but woman from man" (1 Cor. 11:8). Nor has reason anything to say to the contrary. It is as easy for God to make a woman that way as to make Adam from the Earth or the Earth from nothing.

91. Why did God forbid the Tree of Knowledge? Having endowed man with reason, he should encourage man to advance in knowledge. And how I would have liked to have spoken to that serpent! What language did it speak?

God forbade that tree that could lead man to a knowledge of evil. He gave man reason that he might know what is right and good. It is not advancing in knowledge to acquire erroneous and evil notions. As for the serpent, if you knew what you were talking about, you would not like to have spoken to him. The language he spoke was the language of pride, sensuality, and rebellion.

92. Angels fell in love with the daughters of men and begat giants. What a legend!

Genesis 6:2 says that the sons of God took wives from the daughters of men. These sons of God were not Angels but the descendants of Seth, while carnal and fleshly men were the descendants of Cain. God was rightly angry with these mixed marriages between those who knew the true religion and those who had forgotten and abandoned it. As for the giants, the children of these unions were monsters rather in violence and wickedness than in size, though they were probably big men and independent in their self-sufficient strength.

93. Besides Adam and Eve, we read only of Cain and Abel. Whom did Cain marry?

Your knowledge is inadequate. Had you read on, you would have seen in the fifth chapter of Genesis that Adam begot Seth, and after that lived on for some 800 years, begetting sons and daughters. Cain very probably married a sister. He could even have married a niece! But that would involve the marriage of a brother and sister at some stage, or indeed of several brothers and sisters. With the cessation of necessity, such close interrelationship was forbidden. But special conditions naturally prevailed in such special circumstances as the starting of the human race. God exercised a special providence to safeguard the earliest human beings from the evils usually associated with close intermarriage. And after all, a sister would not be so closely related to Cain as Eve was to Adam. Cain's wife was not made out of his own rib! Whom Cain married precisely is not mentioned, as it is not very important. One book cannot give all the names that have occurred in history, and the Bible gives but a summary outline of chief events.

94. Do you believe with science that man has been on Earth tens of thousands of years, or do you believe the Bible story?

Science has nothing very definite to say on the subject, and in any case, the age of the human race cannot be calculated from the Bible. I certainly believe the Bible account in its own proper sense. As far as that account is concerned, man could have been on the earth a hundred thousand years. No one can say with certainty exactly how long.

95. That ark surely is a fable or symbol. Even on the measurements given it could never have contained all said to be in it.

It is not a fable, although it does symbolize the Catholic Church in which souls are saved from the moral flood of sin. It was over 400 feet long, 70 wide, and 40 deep. The flood was most probably local, and the animals were of various types from the region only of its occurrence. We are not obliged to believe that all living animals were represented, nor that all animals outside the ark were destroyed. Men themselves had not spread so far afield at that time, so Noah and his family were the sole human survivors. The flood happened; the ark was a fact; all men were drowned save Noah and those with him in the ark; that much must be accepted in the literal sense. But many subsidiary details need not be, whilst the wholesale imaginative exaggeration of those details is to be entirely rejected. A thing is credible when a sufficiently capable cause is assigned, incredible if the cause I allege could not do it. But if the cause alleged could do it, then it becomes a question of fact. Did it occur? God says that he caused the flood and its consequences. We cannot say that he is mistaken or deliberately deceiving us. I accept it. You must make your choice. But you have given no sufficient reason for unbelief in your letter.

96. Do you believe that rain for forty days could cover the whole Earth with water above the highest mountains?

The Bible attributes the flood not only to the rain but also to an invasion of water from the sea. Moreover, the flood did not cover the whole of the Earth but the whole of the particular region where it occurred. The interpretation of the flood as local is not opposed to the expression in the Bible referring to "the whole of the Earth." That is quite a usual expression for the whole of some given region. Thus, the famine in Egypt is described as a famine "over all the face of the Earth."

97. Is it not absurd not only that God should want to try Abraham's faith but that he should order Abraham to kill his own son?

God did not test Abraham in order to secure further knowledge concerning him but in order to give Abraham an opportunity of performing a meritorious act of obedience that Abraham would not otherwise have received. The trial was not necessary from God's point of view. It was necessary from Abraham's point of view. It was God's immutable will, based upon his infinite knowledge of all things, that Abraham should first be asked to offer his son; and then that he should be freed from the necessity of sacrificing that son in actual practice. But even had God intended Abraham to kill the boy, God, as supreme Lord and Master of life and death, would not have exceeded his rights.

98. Can the infallible Catholic Church give me the chemical equation of the reaction that took place when Lot's wife was turned into a pillar of salt?

The Church does not exist to dispense chemical equations. But your question is not based upon reason. Probably Sodom and Gomorrah were destroyed by natural agencies set in movement by God, with earthquakes and volcanic eruptions. Rock salt abounds in that region, and an upheaval of that material could easily have overwhelmed and embedded Lot's wife because of her delay, leaving a standing hillock of salt as her memorial.

99. In Exodus 20:5, we are told that God is a jealous God. Do you believe that to be true?

Yes, in the sense intended. Wherever there is love, there must be some kind of jealousy, for jealousy is but zeal on behalf of the object of one's love. But, just as there are different kinds of love, selfish or unselfish, so there are different kinds of jealousy.

The more one loves, of course, the more one tries to exclude whatever could come between himself and the object of his love. Where a man, however, is usually jealous of others who would take from him one whom he thinks necessary for his happiness, God is jealous of all that would prevent him from giving happiness to the souls he loves. To bring this home to the Jews, as his chosen people and the particular object of his love, God spoke to them through the prophets in a way they could understand. He told them that Israel was wedded to him; that he had espoused his chosen people; that idolatry, or worship of false gods, was simply "adultery" in his sight. And just as a man is jealous of his wife lest another should rob him of his exclusive right to her affection, so the Jews understood that, on the religious and spiritual plane, God insisted on his exclusive right to their devotedness and love. God's very justice demanded such a return for all the benefits his love had lavished upon them. His use of the human term *jealousy*, therefore, was meant to bring home to them on their own level his exclusive claim to their spiritual allegiance. But in God, the term would have to be understood in a way proper to God and not in a way proper to men.

100. How could God harden Pharaoh's heart and then punish him for not letting the Jews go?

The sense is that God permitted Pharaoh to harden his own heart. It is but a Jewish mode of speaking. Exodus 8:15 says, "Pharaoh...hardened his heart." God sent Moses to ask Pharaoh to let the Jews go, and that means that he meant Pharaoh to do so. God would not therefore have deliberately prevented Pharaoh from doing so. God permitted Pharaoh to harden his own heart just as he permits men to sin even in our own days, if they are determined to do so.

101. The crossing of the Red Sea by Moses and the Jews must surely be a fable.

No man on Earth can prove that this thing did not happen. The only argument is, "It seems to us unlikely." I reply, "Most unlikely, if anyone less than God were responsible for such a happening." But to say that God could not do it is to misunderstand the difference between the finite and Infinite, between impotence and Omnipotence.

102. Will present scientific knowledge let us admit that the sun stood still for Joshua?

Present scientific knowledge has nothing to say on the subject. With all our present knowledge we still say that the sun rises. We know that it is due to the Earth's rotation but speak of things as they appear to our senses. Joshua would have more right to laugh at us for speaking of the sun as rising, despite our boasted knowledge, than we have to ridicule his expression that the sun stood still. He experienced the phenomenon of light for a period longer than usual, and he described it by the phrase "the sun stood still." The phenomenon could have occurred by the cessation of the earth's rotation at God's bidding, or simply by his willing the light to be continued despite the ordinary movements of the Earth. However, the Church has not defined the literal truth of each and every event described in Scripture. She teaches that the Bible is the word of God, whatever is its correct interpretation. Miraculous events are to be accepted until the opposite is proved true. Exactly what God did in such cases is not certain, but presumption is for the literal fact in default of contrary evidence. The general lesson of God's providence is to be accepted without reserve.

103. Are we to believe that the story of Jonah and the whale is true?

When Christ told the story of the prodigal son, the characters of the story were not really historical persons. But the story was a true description of types and of God's mercy. Now, some authors say that the Book of Jonah narrates a kind of parable somewhat akin to the parables of Christ. Others, and more probably, say that it is actual history and that a real Jonah was really swallowed by a real fish, though not necessarily by a whale as we understand that word. The Church leaves us free to accept either view. The purpose of the Book is worthy indeed of God, teaching as it does that God much prefers to show mercy to a repentant people rather than vindicate his justice by the infliction of punishment. Nor is the story incredible even as actual fact. A thing is credible or incredible according to the presence or absence of a sufficient cause. I grant that the events in the Book of Jonah can be explained only by a miraculous intervention on the part of almighty God. But once I say that God was the agent at work, then the cause alleged could account for it and the question is not "Could it happen?" but "Did it happen?" The main reason why people doubt the fact is because they cannot see how it could happen, a thing that does not necessarily prove more than that they cannot comprehend everything. The life of a human embryo during the period of its gestation is as much a mystery according to God's natural laws as would be the life of Jonah for three days inside a large fish according to God's extraordinary intervention. And who will say that God is never free to act outside the ordinary laws he himself has established? In reality there is no more difficulty in accepting the miracle of Jonah than there is in accepting the undoubted miraculous fact of Christ's Resurrection.

104. Do you maintain that Job really existed?

Yes. He was chosen as a type and really did serve God in the midst of great trials. But the incident has been described in poetical form, allowing for the use of literary description and amplification. I could tell the same facts in dry, technical language, or in glowing prose, or in highly polished verse, and the literary form would not affect the objective historical value of the event described.

105. Is there not a parallelism between 1 Peter 1:21-25, describing the suffering servant of Isaianic prophecy, and Isaiah 40?

Of course there is. There must necessarily be a parallelism between the fulfillment of a prophecy and the prophecy itself. If there were no parallelism you would say that the prophecy was not fulfilled. If there is a parallelism, you deny the event, and accuse St. Peter of concocting a story borrowed from Isaiah!

106. Is not the parallelism too close that in any other form of literature it would be called plagiarism?

Yes, if St. Peter were not obviously describing what he himself had witnessed, and for which there is abundant other evidence. But granted the fact foreseen by the prophet as he set down its description in anticipation, it is not plagiarism for St. Peter to make use of the same expressions in his portrayal of the same reality. It was not only lawful for him to do so, it would be rather surprising if he did not. And above all when we consider the unity of the prophetic spirit throughout the Old and New Testaments, the same Holy Spirit inspired both Isaiah and St. Peter. One and the same principal Author is responsible for both accounts. And from this point of view there can be no charge of plagiarism at all.

107. Are there not difficulties in the New Testament as well as in the Old Testament?

Yes. But there are no real contradictions. To prove a contradiction you must show that the texts are undoubtedly authentic and that they admit of no possible conciliation. When supposed contradictions have been urged by adversaries, expert defending scholars have advanced various quite probable theories by which the difficulties would be solved. They are not obliged to prove one or other of their theories certainly true. The one who asserts contradiction declares that there is no sense in which both accounts *could* be true. The moment competent scholars offer a reasonable and probable explanation by which difficulties would be reconciled, necessary contradiction is excluded. Even if rationalist critics proved every suggested explanation to be unreasonable and certainly false, they would not necessarily have proved a contradiction in Scripture. At most they would have proved that interpreters had not yet discerned the correct method of reconciling an apparent divergence.

There are no inconsistencies in any single important matter. Each Gospel is a fragmentary account, and each writer gives complementary, not contradictory, details. Supposing that I went from London to Rome for a three months' holiday but on the way broke my journey for a week in Paris. Later on I might write to a friend, "I spent my holidays in Rome." Yet to another friend I could say, "During my holidays I stayed in Paris." There is no real inconsistency, although the friends, on comparing notes, might find an apparent inconsistency. But almost at once they would say, "He might have done both. The one does not exclude the other. He omitted to mention Paris in the one account, Rome in the other." So, too, with the Gospels. One Gospel will mention details that others pass over in their brief accounts.

108. Do you maintain that mistakes and interpolations by copyists were not possible in transcriptions of the Bible?

Mistakes and interpolations were certainly possible, but by comparison of independent copies these are discoverable. Yet remember that the Catholic Church does not say that copyists were inspired. Inspiration is claimed for the original Evangelists. Insofar as later copies or versions exactly correspond with their original writings they give the inspired word of God. Insofar as they are not exact, they do not.

109. May we not assume that St. Luke and St. Matthew had no knowledge of the divine origin of Jesus Christ?

Not unless we wish to ignore evidence and credulously believe a thing merely because we wish to believe it. St. Luke records the words of the angel to Mary, "The Holy Spirit will come upon you, and the power of the Most High will overshadow you; therefore the child to be born will be called holy, the Son of God" (Luke 1:35). Matthew 1:20 records the words of the angel to St. Joseph, "Joseph, son of David, do not fear to take Mary your wife, for that which is conceived in her is of the Holy Spirit." Both St. Luke and St. Matthew, therefore, had clear knowledge of the divine origin of Christ.

110. Both give genealogies of Christ in which the names are all different.

Your difficulty arises from the idea that we have to reconcile the two sets of names given by St. Matthew and St. Luke. But that very idea is wrong. The names are meant to be different, and the Evangelists had no intention of giving the same genealogies. One gives the juridical succession through which Davidic rights descended to Joseph and his legal son—Christ. The other abstracts from this legal or juridical succession and follows the real genealogy according to consanguinity. They therefore approach the question from different viewpoints, and it is a mistake to think that they have to be reconciled. I could deal with the lineage of the pope either juridically in the papal succession, or really in his own family line; and if a man objected that the lists of names differed, I would merely reply that they were meant to differ.

111. Antiquarians say that there never was a census of the Roman Empire.

If men say that, ask them to prove it. If they could mention a thousand books that do not mention such a census, that would not prove that a census did not take place but merely that those books do not mention it. Josephus, in his *Jewish Antiquities*, describes a census of Judea, a census to which St. Luke refers in Acts 5:37. An ounce of positive evidence is worth a thousand omissions.

112. But the census mentioned by Josephus took place in A.D. 6, not at the time of Christ's birth!

There was a previous census at the time of Christ's birth of which Josephus makes no mention. St. Luke is a perfectly reliable historian. Both in his Gospel and in Acts he proves his exact knowledge of Graeco-Roman affairs and begins his Gospel with a reference to his diligence in verifying the facts he narrates. He would not at once proceed to make serious and easily avoidable errors. The census did not necessarily take place simultaneously in all parts, and the distinct census St. Luke mentions in his Gospel 2:1-5 could easily refer to a preliminary census according to Jewish customs. His very expression "In those days" suggests a long, drawn-out process.

113. St. Luke says that after his birth Jesus was taken to Nazareth and lived there, going with his parents every year to Jerusalem. He knew nothing of the flight into Egypt and the killing of the innocents.

Omission to record certain events is no argument that an author does not know of them.

114. How could the devil carry off God and set him on a hill in Galilee from which he could see all the kingdoms of the Earth?

God cannot be carried anywhere. He is a spirit and not subject to local transportation. Nor is it honest to attribute to God, making no mention of his incarnate human nature, that which happened to that human nature. The Son of God in his assumed human nature was subjected to this temptation. There is nothing repugnant in the devil being allowed to carry a material object to a height. The devil is a spiritual being, and if God, a spiritual being, can create a material universe, a spiritual being can certainly receive the power to make displacements in the universe. As for seeing all the kingdoms of the Earth, we can see in two ways—by eyesight or by intellectual vision. In this case, mental vision was sufficient.

115. St. Matthew says that Jesus rode into Jerusalem on an ass and a colt.

St. Matthew does not say that. He says that "they brought the donkey and the colt, and put their garments on them, and he sat on them" (Matt. 21:7). St. Matthew means simply that Jesus sat on the garments which they had placed on one of the animals, namely, the colt.

116. The authors of the second and third Gospels are more wary; they mention an ass only. But the author of the fourth Gospel tries to trim the story by employing a colt only.

Rather than suspect yourself of being wrong, you would accuse St. Matthew of falling into error, and the authors of the other Gospels you would charge with a wariness that amounts to conscious fraud. But there are a few things to be noticed. The authors of the other Gospels would not have been wary if, knowing what St. Matthew had recorded, they deliberately contradicted him. After all, he was an Evangelist out for the good of the same religion as themselves. Were they thinking of being wary, they would have stood to him at all costs. Again, if the authors of the other Gospels were shrewd tricksters, warily bent on trimming their story to suit their purpose, they may as well have done it right through their accounts, eliminating every awkward, humiliating, and unattractive feature of their description of themselves and of Christ. But no. They were patently honest throughout. The charge of trickery is absurd. You will say that if they were not stepping warily they were mistaken, for they contradict one another and St. Matthew. But here it is you yourself who would be mistaken. They do not contradict one another. For whilst St. John speaks of a colt, as you say, St. Mark and St. Luke merely use an alternative Greek word for the same thing. Do they, then, contradict St. Matthew by mentioning one animal only where he mentions two? No. Omission is not denial. They give the essential fact that Jesus rode into Jerusalem on a colt. St. Matthew states the same thing, giving the additional detail that the mother of the colt was brought along with it. There is no contradiction in that.

117. Christ praises marriage saying that, "For this reason a man shall leave his father and mother and be joined to his wife." But St. Paul says, "It is well for a man not to touch a woman."

There is no contradiction in that. Our Lord says that, if a man does marry, he leaves father and mother in order to live with his wife. But he himself counsels the renunciation of marriage for the sake of the kingdom of heaven (Matt. 19:12). St. Paul therefore declares that one who chooses not to marry makes quite a good choice. The context shows, of course, that St. Paul had in mind not any merely selfish motives but a choice based upon the idea of self-sacrifice, and a complete consecration of oneself to the love of God and the service of one's fellow men.

118. Both St. Peter and St. Paul say that we must be subject to our masters; yet Christ says that one only is your master, and St. Paul himself says, "Do not become slaves of men."

There is no conflict here. Christ was not referring to ordinary relationships between masters and servants but used the term *master* in the sense of *teacher*; and he declared that he only was the source of doctrine and that all were to be taught by him and to hand on his teachings. No one was to set himself up as an independent teacher in his own right. Such words certainly do not deny the necessity of obedience on the part of servants to the authority of masters in ordinary everyday affairs. The explanation of St. Paul's words "Do not become slaves of men" is given by St. Paul himself. He is speaking of our allegiance to Christ as Christians and merely declares that that allegiance must never be abandoned in favor of men. We must regard our souls as belonging to Christ and to no one else. But this does not exempt us from duties within their own proper limits to earthly employers and masters. In fact, St. Paul adds, "Let everyone remain in the condition of life wherein he was called, but abide therein with God." Servants of men will, therefore, remain servants of men; but once they have become Christians they will regard their duties as duties to be fulfilled for the love of God, and not as before, a matter of routine and with no spiritual motives whatever.

119. St. Paul told the Ephesians that they were saved by faith, and not by works; while St. James says that by works a man is justified, and not by faith alone.

St. Paul's doctrine is that good works cannot contribute to a man's salvation before he is united with Christ by faith. Because the gift of faith is supernatural, no previous good works can deserve it. A man can ask the gift of faith from God, and if he receives it, it is the first step toward his salvation. St. James tells us that after a man has received the gift of faith he is expected to live up to it. The two passages show that both faith and a life of good works in accordance with faith are necessary if one is to be justified in God's sight. Such has ever been the Catholic doctrine, and it excludes the two extremes of rationalism and early Protestantism. For the rationalist says that natural goodness without faith is enough for any man; whilst the early Protestants attacked the Catholic doctrine that good works are necessary for salvation, and taught that salvation depends on faith alone. But I have said enough to show that there is no trace of contradiction between St. Paul and St. James in this matter.

Chapter 5

Christianity

120. Why did God delay the sending of his Son?

Man has always had a religion taught by God. But this religion falls into four great divisions:

1. The religion of Adam, who was instructed immediately by God. This was the first stage and is known as the religion of innocent man.

2. After Adam's fall, Adam handed on to his children the truth about God and the duty of worshipping him. Thus Abel offered sacrifice. The traditions were transmitted by Adam's posterity, but memories faded. Still, conscience always dictated what was naturally right, and this period could be called the period of natural law. However, God gave occasional revelations to various individuals, such as the Patriarchs, over and above the natural law, and this stage is often called the period of the patriarchal religion, or the period of pre-Mosaic unwritten law.

3. The third stage came with Moses. After the re-multiplication of the human race from Noah, men again began to forget God, and God gave to Moses a clearer exposition of religious duties to be put into writing. This is known as the stage of the written law, or that of the Mosaic religion.

4. Finally, God sent his own Son to give the more perfect law—the Christian law—that the Catholic Church teaches today in its fullness and will teach until the end of time.

The delay was adapted to mankind's natural methods of progress from the less perfect to the more perfect, so that men would be prepared by more simple doctrines for still more noble truths. It taught the human race its need of God from sad experience. It brought out the real dignity of Christ, which could thus be heralded by a long series of prophets. God is not so impatient as man. He is quite content to wait for an acorn to become an oak tree rather than create all oak trees immediately.

The religion known by the Jews before Christ was therefore but imperfect and preparatory. The religion of Christ was its perfect fulfillment.

121. Would it not have been better for God to have waited until this present time to reveal himself in the Incarnation?

You can be quite sure that, despite all human speculations, what God actually chose to do was the better thing.

122. Why, then, did God choose such an apparently unfavorable time?

The time of Christ was no more unfavorable than today. No time could be more propitious than another on the score that natural means are more readily and abundantly at hand. We are dealing with a supernatural, not a natural, religion. Faith in the teachings of Christ cannot be arrived at by any man's unaided efforts. The grace of God is required, giving a supernatural and spiritual enlightenment to the mind. So Jesus himself said, when the Jews refused to believe in him, "No one can come to me unless the Father who sent me draws him" (John 6:44). And St. Paul rightly says, "The unspiritual man does not receive the gifts of the Spirit of God, for they are folly to him, and he is not able to understand them because they are spiritually discerned" (1 Cor. 2:14). If men could see the works that Jesus did and hear the words that he said yet not believe, I do not see how other men would be any better off if they heard a description of his works by radio as they occurred, or heard his words from loudspeakers in their homes. Radio and press publicity would not necessarily have improved matters. In the meantime, the printed Gospels are within the reach of all. Of those who read them, some believe; some do not.

123. Can you show from Scripture that Christ intended this perfect development of the Mosaic religion to be distinct from the religion of the synagogue?

Yes. Referring to the future, Christ said, "I will build my Church."

The synagogue was already established. Christ prescribed new doctrines, new modes of worship, and a new form of authority. He even predicted to his apostles, "You will be beaten in the synagogues" (Mark 13:9). The intended distinction of his Church from the prefigurative synagogue is most clear.

124. The Acts of the Apostles tells us that the apostles still frequented the synagogues after the Ascension of Christ. That is not like the action of men charged to found a new Church.

Acts 3:1 would tell you that Peter and John went to the Temple at the ninth hour of prayer. But why? To tell the Jews, whom they knew to be gathered there, that they had denied the holy One, and killed the Author of life; but that he had risen from the dead and that they must accept the new religion of Christ, whereupon Peter and John were arrested and thrown into prison. That would scarcely have occurred had they gone there merely to share in the ordinary Jewish worship as of old. Again, Acts 5:42 tells us that "every day in the temple and at home they did not cease teaching and preaching Jesus as the Christ." They were certainly devoting themselves to the founding of a new Church.

125. If Christianity is the true development of the Jewish religion, why is it not the religion of the Jews today? Why did not the Jews accept Christ?

Many individuals did. As a race, the Jews did not. This was not because Christ did not sufficiently prove his mission but because the leaders of religious thought and the teachers of the people had lost the true religious spirit, had selfishly transferred their affections to a love of their own high places, and had substituted the idea of a magnificent temporal ruler for the idea of a spiritual Savior. They wanted deliverance from the tyranny of the Romans and help to trample upon them in turn. Since Christ did not fit in with their earthly notions and ambitions, the leaders rejected him. The majority of the people, dependent upon the scribes and Pharisees for religious direction, obeyed these leaders, their own fears, and their national pride. The first members of the Christian Church were individual Jews chosen by Christ to spread his doctrines among the Gentiles; and this, in accordance with Christ's own prediction in the parable of the great supper, where those first invited would not come. Indeed, an earlier warning had been given to the Jews that their birthright would pass to the Gentiles if they did not overcome their attachment to earthly ideals in the incident of Esau's selling his birthright to Jacob. Although Christianity should be the religion of the Jews, therefore, it is not, through their own fault as a race. The modern Jew takes his religion for granted without inquiring deeply into the question.

From the historical point of view there is opposition between Christianity and Judaism insofar as Judaism denies that the real Messiah has come, whilst the Christian religion affirms that he has come in the person of Christ. As a preparatory religion, Judaism was the true religion of God until such time as the Messiah should come. But it was abrogated when all that it foreshadowed was realized. The shadow gave way to the substance. And a religion that still claims to be awaiting the Redeemer of the human race after that Redeemer has come is obviously wrong and could not retain God's sanction. But apart from the question of time and fulfillment, there is an opposition between the preparatory Jewish religion and Christianity. Literal Judaism was imperfect and embodied much that was temporal and fleshly, whilst the religion of Christ is perfect and elevated to the spiritual and eternal plane. Of course, even under the old regime, the true Jew was not one who merely submitted to external rites, but he who loved God and was united in spirit with the Savior to come. But many of the Jews had fallen short of this to a very great extent and were absorbed by worldly and merely human considerations.

126. Is not Christianity a reconciliation of Greek philosophy with Judaism?

No. That explanation is the refuge of those who begin by rejecting the divine and supernatural origin of Christianity and who therefore have to find a natural explanation of its appearance in this world. Christianity originated with Christ, and nowhere is there the faintest trace of indication that Christ devoted himself to the reconciliation of Greek philosophy with Judaism. Nor could Christ possibly have drawn his doctrines from Greek philosophers, who knew absolutely nothing of the great dogmas of Christianity such as the Trinity, the Incarnation of the Son of God, redemption by the death of that Son on the cross, the Resurrection of Christ, and the whole system of supernatural grace. So new and strange to the Greeks was the Christian doctrine that to them it seemed foolishness. When St. Paul preached it to the Athenians, some mocked, whilst others said, "We will hear you again about this" (Acts 17:32). But it was certainly altogether new to them. The only possible explanation of the doctrine and teaching of Jesus is that given by himself: "My teaching is not mine, but his who sent me" (John 7:16). He declared that he had descended from heaven and was telling men of what he had seen there. And he added, "If I have told you earthly things and you do not believe, how can you believe if I tell you heavenly things?" (John 3:12). It is certain that no one has ever been less of his time than Jesus. No one was less affected by his environment and by current teachings and prejudices. And it is impossible to find a merely human source for his doctrines or to argue from them to any natural preparation or human course of study and reading.

127. You seem to think that the Christian religion is the only true religion.

I do not merely think it to be the only true religion. I know it to be so. I know that religion is as necessary to the human race as breathing. I know that there must be a true religion. I know that all other religions save that revealed by God and recorded in the Bible are false. Reason alone can provide sufficient grounds for that. Moreover, I know by the gift of divine faith that the contents of the Christian religion are true with the very truth of God.

128. Perhaps if you knew more of other religions you would not continue to be a Roman Catholic.

You have no grounds for that supposition. Of one thing I am quite certain. If there is any true religion in this world today it is the

Catholic religion. It is a choice, therefore, between Catholicism or no religion at all. But to have no religion is such a complete violation of reason that no instructed and intelligent man could entertain such an idea for a moment. You can be quite sure that I will spend the rest of my life as a Catholic and die in that faith. If such absolute certainty seems strange to you, it is only because your own religion has never been able to enkindle a similar confidence within you.

129. If you were a Muslim, you would think the same of your Islam. So, too, if you were a Buddhist.

I deny that either a Muslim or a Buddhist or a member of any other non-Christian religion can ever have the same kind of certainty concerning his religious beliefs as that which is given by that particular grace of God known as the gift of Christian faith. In the meantime, that others are convinced of the truth of their various religions merely shows that the human mind is limited; that men are affected by heredity and environment; and that they are prone to form very decided opinions without sufficient knowledge. But that does not affect the truth as it is in itself and does not make all religions equal in value.

130. Much that is in Christianity is to be found in other religions also.

It would be very surprising were that not so. Religion is natural to man; and if men try to construct religious systems in accordance with their natural instinct and needs, they will naturally hit on some truth. And the basic natural truths in their various systems tend to content those who know no other religion and to distract their attention from the accompanying human errors.

131. The Buddhist and Christian codes of conduct are apparently of similar portent.

You must not confuse external similarities in conduct with the code of that conduct. Man is essentially a social being, and it is not surprising that a leader should attract disciples and inculcate naturally good principles of morality. But the code of conduct in Buddhism differs immensely from the Christian code. Buddhism knows nothing of God nor of duties to God. It is based on a pessimistic view of life and is entirely self-centered. It teaches that man is not essentially different from animals; that he goes through a series of transmigrations, ending practically in annihilation. While Christians believe that they are created by God and owe to God obedience and worship, serving him in humility and doing all for the love of him, Buddhists regard man as a particle of a blind universe, whose whole aim is to escape distress and be at peace in this world. Even charity to others is based on love of self insofar as enmity disturbs one so much interiorly. Where Christians are saved by Christ, who is the Way, the Truth, and the Life, Buddhists need no savior. Buddha saves no one. He indicates his way, and each can attain the end by his own powers. Again there is but one Christ for all ages. But there must be a series of Buddhas, a new Buddha appearing as the work of each one fails. I cannot go through all the differences. But I have said enough to show that the codes of Buddhism and of Christianity are essentially different.

132. Has it not been claimed that Christianity copied many rules of conduct from Buddhism?

That has been claimed, but by writers who have judged too hastily from apparent resemblances. Some scholars have asserted a derivation of certain Christian practices from Buddhism; others, that later Buddhistic practices have been derived from Christianity. But deeper research has led scholars to deny both suppositions, holding that the similarities are more apparent than real; and that they are natural developments, independent of one another, from the respective aspirations of the two systems.

133. How do the personalities of Buddha and Confucius compare with that of Christ?

They cannot be ranked as on the same plane as that of Christ. Neither Buddha nor Confucius claimed to be more than ordinary human beings. They did not even claim to be able to show their fellow men the way to God, for they knew nothing of God. They claimed to show men the way to peace of soul and how to escape the worries and trials of this life. Christ claimed to be God and demanded for himself the love and absolute service of men. There is all the difference in the world between the divine personality of Christ and the merely human personalities of Buddha and of Confucius. According to Buddha's own teachings, he himself has gone through various transmigrations, having previously been a beggar, a lion, a bird, an elephant, a king, and various other types. He attained perfection, so the legend says, and had a right to enter Nirvana; but he preferred to be born again in order to teach men the road to wisdom and to freedom from the miseries of life.

Confucius was born about six years earlier than Buddha. This Chinese philosopher was a great reader and collector rather than an original thinker. He edited the ancient Chinese classics and taught a system of natural ethics. He concentrated on behavior in this world and admitted that he knew nothing beyond this world, although he did not deny a future life.

Of no other person in history could such words be written as those used by St. John in speaking of Christ: "In the beginning was the Word, and the Word was with God, and the Word was God … And the Word was made flesh, and dwelt amongst us."

134. Does not Islam worship the true God?

It does, but in the wrong way. No one with a sense of logic and a knowledge of history could accept Islam as a religion truly revealed by God. Muhammad was born about the year 570. He founded a religion of his own, blended of Arabic, Jewish, and Christian elements. But his moral standards fall infinitely below those of the Christian teachings, whilst many of his doctrines and the history of his religious movement cannot possibly claim a divine origin and protection in the light of critical analysis.

135. Most people who are Christians cannot give a valid reason for their faith. Will you give me a valid reason for your faith?

Yes.

Historically, it is certain that Christ really lived, really claimed to be God, proved that claim by his supreme command over the laws of nature established by God, taught the Christian religion, and obliged man to accept that religion.

Philosophically, Christianity alone gives an adequate solution and explanation of the origin, condition, and purpose of the human race.

Religiously, it infinitely surpasses all other forms of religion and alone completely responds to the innate religious tendencies of man.

Theologically, I am a Christian because God has given me the grace to perceive the truth of Christianity and to embrace it. Morally, I am obliged in strict justice to accept a religion specified and imposed by almighty God.

136. If acceptance of Christianity is necessary for salvation, what of those who lived before Christ?

The merits and grace of Christ were applied by God to men of goodwill in anticipation of his death on the cross. God, in his eternity, is not conditioned by time, and men could benefit by the death of Christ just as they can make use of an inheritance that is absolutely certain to be given to them in due time. The merits of Christ were applied to Jews of goodwill in virtue of their faith in a Redeemer to come. Those who through no fault of their own did not know of a Redeemer to come were saved if they obeyed the natural dictates of their conscience and repented of their failings. Every single human being has the moral standard that what is apprehended to be morally good must be done, whilst moral evil must be avoided.

137. Would you say that the world has benefited by Christianity?

Yes. It has benefited in a thousand different ways. Christianity has elevated men's thoughts to a higher level, directed men's wills to a greater good, and has indirectly affected their well-being even in this world in almost every department of life. If the world is less happy today than in years past, it is because, whilst men still profess to be Christian, they are less willing to behave as Christians and to put their principles into practice. Christianity does not force men to be good in spite of themselves.

But if men can be really miserable only by forsaking Christian principles, it shows that Christianity practiced is very likely the one true remedy. Let all men live up to Christian principles, and then if the world is not better, you can blame Christianity.

138. Christian churches are everywhere, yet misery and distress get worse all over the world!

The growth of misery and distress is not due to the multiplication of churches. Many professing Christian churches, of course, do not stand firmly for the true principles of Christ. And even the growth of the Catholic Church cannot influence much of those who will not submit to her laws. As the Church grows, so does population, and with population, evil practices. Man is endowed with intelligence, and this gives him an uncanny power of inventing new modes of iniquity that animals could not suspect. Thus we have a rotten press, the propagation of birth control, Godless education, and whatnot. The mystery is not that we have so many troubles but that the distress is not greater than it is. We can account for it only by God's mercy and by the fact that the Church does make some reparation to him in the name of mankind. If mankind got all it really deserves, you would have something to write about!

Another little matter to remember is that Christianity is not to rid the world of trouble and distress but to save souls from having to endure these things in the next life. Christianity enables people to bear gladly those sufferings that are permitted by God for their greater sanctification or as an expiation of their past sins. Also, many have been brought to God by suffering who have believed in their self-sufficient health and strength that they could manage quite well without him.

139. You speak of faith. But faith is an emotion, an involuntary action of the senses.

If that is your idea of faith, no wonder you find difficulty. But that is not faith at all, and certainly not the faith required by the Catholic Church. By faith we believe things. Now, people do not believe with their feelings and emotions. They believe with their minds. Belief is a mental conviction. If I tell a woman that her son has been killed, her faith in my knowledge and veracity will make her believe the truth that her son has actually been killed. From this knowledge emotion may follow as an effect. But an effect is not its cause. Faith, then, is not an emotion, nor is it of the senses. Faith is the intellectual admission that a certain thing is true because, although we have not seen the reality ourselves, we reasonably admit that the one who has told us must be reliably informed and not intending to deceive us. Nor is faith involuntary. If I see an accident I know that it occurred, and it is useless to tell myself that it did not occur. But if you tell me of an accident and I did not see it myself, then I have no direct evidence. All my evidence is indirect, and I can choose to believe you or not to do so. I can put my faith in what you tell me, or refuse. It should console you to know that the Catholic Church is just as opposed to the idea of faith you condemn as you yourself are opposed to it. In fact, she has solemnly defined such a type of assent to be no faith at all and forbids any priest to receive into the Church one who believes that such a caricature can do duty for the intellectual conviction known as faith.

140. I cannot understand how highly intellectual men can accept obvious legends and fairy tales as historical fact without question or doubt.

Highly intellectual men do accept the doctrines of Christianity as certain. Being highly intellectual, they have not done so without profound investigation of the reasonable grounds for their position. And knowing that such men are convinced, it is not highly intellectual conduct to reject as legends and fairy tales the doctrines they accept without making a similar investigation.

141. Do you not maintain that faith in Christianity is necessary for one's eternal salvation?

Those who do not know the facts are not required to believe doctrines of which they are unaware. Those who do know the facts cannot be saved unless they believe, for refusal is to insult the God who has deigned to reveal the truth to men.

142. If a man does not accept the Bible, can you convince him of your supernatural doctrines by reason alone?

We can prove historically that God certainly gave the Christian revelation, and right reason cannot refute the evidence. It has to admit the value of the Gospels as documentary sources. But reason alone cannot make a man accept the contents of that revelation as having binding value. Only the grace of God can do that, and the preparation best suited to the reception of the gift of faith is a good moral life and earnest prayer for the help of God.

143. Then without the grace of God one cannot have this faith?

By reason alone any ordinary man can know that God exists, that he has given a revelation to man, and any ordinary man is capable of learning the fundamental teachings of Christianity. Yet the perception of the vital force and the sheer reality of the truths God has revealed, with consequent belief in them, requires grace from God. But one who has the goodwill to submit to God's authority, and to pray earnestly for the light to know God's will, can be certain that the necessary supernatural help will be offered to him.

Mere human reasoning is not enough. Brains cannot be the condition of salvation. If so, the intellectual would have a better chance of salvation than the less intelligent. You must look round for another method of approach to the religious problem. Whilst no one asks you to go against right reason, yet you must be prepared to rise above it. St. Paul rightly says that the natural man does not perceive those things which are of the spirit of God.

144. But I cannot believe in the divinity of Christ.

Since God does not deny any man of really goodwill sufficient grace, the fault lies in your own will. You can believe, if you wish. If you have not examined the evidence for his divinity, you can do so. Until you have done so, your belief that he is not God is mere credulity. You should say, "I have no opinion on the subject. I have not studied the evidence." When you have studied the evidence carefully, you will have found at least three things:

1. The documentary evidence concerning Christ is perfectly sound.
2. Christ certainly claimed to be God.
3. He certainly did things for which God alone could be responsible.

Whether, after this, you will accept what Christ taught or reject it will be a matter for your own choice.

145. But you said that faith is necessary before one can accept Christian beliefs.

Faith is not necessary to arrive at the conviction that God has actually given a revelation to mankind, and that Christianity is that revelation. But, whilst reason can prove the fact of this revelation, faith is necessary for the full acceptance of the contents of that revelation. Quite apart from religion, this holds good in the merely natural order. There is a natural faith with which you yourself could not quarrel and which you would not dream of branding as unreasonable. Reason can justify the claims of the Christian religion to be the revelation of God. But the teachings of that religion deal with truths of the supernatural order much more above the experience of ordinary human knowledge than geneticist J.B.S. Haldane's chromosomes are above the average man's scientific experience. We, therefore, accept Christian teachings by faith; but that act of faith is reasonable in virtue of the reasonable grounds for the Christian religion as the revelation of God.

146. If such proof exists, no reasonable man in the world would remain a non-Christian!

That does not follow. There are reasonable men who have never seriously studied the evidences for Christianity. There are others who have bestowed some attention upon them but who, although reasonable in other matters, have approached this study with a prejudice that has prevented their appreciating the force of the proofs.

Others again will admit the force of the proofs but are not willing to accept by faith the teachings of the Christian religion. Instead of accepting them by faith, they seem to think that an independent proof should be offered for every single doctrine to their satisfaction; and declare that they will accept no religious truth on authority. Yet others are as convinced as I am of the truth of the Christian religion and of all its teachings, but they will not accept that religion nor those teachings because they are not prepared to fulfill the practical consequences of them. They dismiss all thought of the matter as far as possible—and remain non-Christians.

147. Surely mankind is anxious to be saved?

If we take salvation as the promise of eternal happiness and leave out all other considerations, men would certainly be anxious to get it. But if we view not the promise of future joy but the implication that men "need" to be saved, it is a different matter altogether. For the implication is that men have fallen into a rotten and depraved state from which they are incapable of escaping without the help of a savior. Human pride rebels. Men do not like to admit even to themselves that they are evil. They cry out against the doctrine of original sin, and boast that, far from having fallen, the human race has steadily risen and has a glorious future before it to be attained by its own efforts. And not only do men banish the thought of original sin. They try to banish the thought of their actual and personal sins. So a man with no religion is full of his own virtues. "I have no religion," he will say, "but I am a better man than many who profess to be religious." Pride is a great force in the world, and God himself has said that he "opposes the proud, but gives grace to the humble." But men do not like humbling themselves; and still less do they like being humbled. Despite their boasting, however, men have their vices and sins, which they do not wish to abandon. And they are not prepared to sacrifice present tangible pleasures and interests for future invisible benefits. How many people are blind to future consequences of their actions, even in this life, when in the grip of a present and urgent temptation to alluring self-satisfaction! So mankind is not always anxious to be saved if we consider not merely the future benefits of salvation but present implications and the conditions required.

148. Don't say that men do not choose to believe because the way of salvation is hard.

That is precisely what I must say. Some people are so intellectually lazy that it is too hard on them to undertake the study of God's revelation. Others are so proud that it is too hard on their self-esteem to ask them to submit to authoritative teaching of any kind. Others are so immersed in earthly ambitions that it is too hard on them to accept supernatural and spiritual ideals instead. Others again are so subject to self-indulgence in a hundred and one ways that a religion asking self-denial is altogether too hard for them to consider for a moment.

149. I believe in the little saying, "Your truth is not my truth."

On what grounds do you accept that? Truth is neither yours nor mine. It is independent of either of us. We hold things because they are true. They are not true because we happen to believe them. Again, truth is consistent. If you have the truth on a given subject, and my ideas conflict with yours, then I do not possess the truth. And if I am right, you haven't got the truth. If you wanted to go to a certain town by rail but got into the wrong train, would you ignore the stationmaster's advice and say, "Your truth is not my truth?" You would not. Why is that axiom valid only when it is a question of the way to heaven?

150. Is it a virtue to be so convinced of one's own beliefs as to exclude any possibility of being wrong?

Not if one's own beliefs happen to be the result of one's own speculations, with nothing particularly in their favor save that one desires to maintain them. It is a virtue, however, to maintain the absolute truth of what Christ has taught, once one has attained the reasonable conviction that he is God. For true virtue refuses to admit that God does not know what he is talking about, or that he is given to telling lies. It is not a question of refusing to admit a possibility of our being wrong. It is a question of refusing to admit the possibility of God being wrong. Virtue forbids blasphemous insults against God.

151. All paths lead to God.

That is rather an extreme statement. You believe in the Christian religion, and the Christian religion excludes the idea that all paths lead to God. In fact, it teaches very definitely that some paths do not lead to God. Christ himself distinguished between two roads, declaring the way leading to life to be narrow and restricted, whilst the way leading to destruction is broad and pleasant to those who are bent on self-satisfaction. St. Paul wrote to the Corinthians, "Do you not know that the unrighteous will not inherit the kingdom of God? Do not be deceived; neither the immoral, nor idolaters, nor adulterers, nor homosexuals, nor thieves, nor the greedy, nor drunkards, nor revilers, nor robbers will inherit the kingdom of God" (1 Cor. 6:9-10). We cannot therefore say that all paths lead to God.

152. Every individual must be entitled to his own religious beliefs.

That is a half-truth, and a half-truth is nearly always most dangerous. If, as Christians believe, God has revealed a religion, people are obliged to accept that religion and no other. They are no longer entitled to their own religious beliefs once God has dictated what they must believe. On the other hand, people are entitled to follow their own conscience, even though their ideas be defective or mistaken. In fact, they are obliged to live according to what they honestly deem to be true and right. Thus, for example, a Protestant, so long as he really thinks his Protestantism to be correct, is entitled and obliged to remain a Protestant. But should he discover the truth of Catholicism, he is certainly no longer entitled to remain a Protestant.

153. Since we all aim at the one destination, it cannot matter by what road we travel.

It must matter, or Christ would not have taught a new and very definite religion. After all, the Jews were aiming at the same destination as ourselves, eternal salvation and happiness with God. Yet Christ did not say that their road was good enough. Again, if God not only appoints the destination but also the road by which we must travel, we cannot say that any other road is just as good. The Catholic Church declares hers to be the only right road. Other churches dispute that and maintain that any religion will do. It is evident that the Catholic claim, if true, is most important. Study the evidence for it.

154. Provided we all strive for the one end, why worry as to who is right or wrong?

Do you really believe that Christ is the Son of God who came down from heaven to teach us the truth in the name of our Creator, and yet that it does not matter whether our ideas of that truth be right or wrong? Is it quite all right for a church to claim to be that of Christ yet to teach a whole lot of errors in his name? Do you seriously mean that there is no need to worry about that? And if it does not matter whether one is a Catholic or a Methodist because both churches are striving for the one end—to serve God—does it matter whether one is a Christian or a Muslim?

Muslims also believe in the true God and try to serve him in their own way. Now, just as you would insist that one must strive in the Christian way rather than in the Muslim way, so I insist that it must be in the Catholic way rather than in the Methodist or any other way. In other words, there is need to worry as to who is right and who is wrong.

155. God is love and therefore must be tolerant and impartial.

Because God is love, he must love the good and the true. And that excludes the bad and the false. As a Christian, too, you cannot expect God to be tolerant of insults directed against his only begotten Son. He must be partial to the doctrine taught by his own Son, and he cannot be indifferent to blasphemous denials of the veracity of Christ. Moreover, God must be partial to the exact and complete doctrine of Christ and not to incomplete or distorted doctrines proposed by men who, with no right to do so, tampered with the teachings of Christ. If you admit this, you admit that God is partial to the Catholic Church and that he is not pleased with the other churches that cannot agree amongst themselves save in their opposition to the greatest Church of all—the Catholic Church.

156. If a man is sincere, won't he attain to goodness, no matter what church he attends?

It is true that people belonging to different churches can be equally sincere in their efforts to be good. But that cannot alter the fact that the religions they profess are different. And a man who is seeking the truth will say, "Let me reflect, not on the point in which these good people do not differ but on the points in which they do differ." In other words, we must abstract from the persons professing the religions and consider the religions they profess. For it is certain that God, the supreme Truth, could not have revealed contradictory teachings. Take, for example, the infallibility of the Church. I believe that Christ meant his Church to be infallible. You do not. We cannot both be right. And as we both profess to believe in Christ, the burning problem is whether indeed Christ intended his Church to be infallible. That problem must be solved.

157. It is only natural that people should believe what they have been taught from childhood.

That is quite true, and therefore we do not blame people for mistakes for which they are not responsible. But the fact that people tend to believe what they have been taught from childhood does not make what they have been taught right. Would you say that, because a Protestant child takes it for granted that Protestantism is right, and a Catholic child takes it for granted that Catholicism is right, both Protestantism and Catholicism are equally right? They cannot be. Catholicism says that it is absolutely necessary to be subject to the pope. Protestantism says just the opposite. How can both be right?

158. I think we should die in the religion in which we are born.

That is an anti-Christian principle. Were it sound, why did not Christ tell the Jews to die in the religion in which they were born, instead of asking them to accept his religion? And, even on reason alone, must a man live and die in the religion of his parents even though he discovers it to be wrong?

159. One who leaves the religion of his parents is a traitor.

A traitor is one who leaves a cause he knows to be right, and does so from unworthy motives. But would you say that St. Paul was a traitor when he abandoned what he knew to be wrong in order to embrace the religion of Christ once he had perceived it to be right?

160. Should people change their religion when they get married?

If they discover their religion to be wrong, they should abandon it whether they marry or not. If they know it to be right, they should not abandon it for any consideration on earth. Marriage has nothing whatever to do with this question. Religion is concerned with duties to one's Creator. No desire to please a fellow creature can affect one's duties to God.

161. Should not a woman embrace the religion of her husband?

Such a principle could never be admitted. For then, were her husband a pagan, she would have to become a pagan; if a Jew, she would have to become a member of the Jewish religion; if a Methodist, or a Presbyterian, or an Anglican, or a Baptist, or anything else, she would have to become a member of one of those religions. God's rights, and the claims of conscience, would then become a mockery. The principle must stand that the relation between the soul and God cannot be affected by any relationships with human beings. This principle is of universal application.

162. Then a Protestant cannot become a Catholic in order to marry a Catholic?

That is true. However desirable it might be that both should be Catholic, if the Protestant party conscientiously believes the

Catholic religion to be wrong, he cannot possibly embrace that religion. What he can do, however, is this: He can suspect that he has not enough knowledge of the Catholic religion; or that he even has mistaken notions about it. For the sake of his wife he can therefore study the Catholic religion. Then, if he becomes convinced of its truth, he can embrace it for its own sake and for the love of God. I hope all is now clear. Marriage is not a reason in itself for the changing of one's religion. But marriage to a Catholic would certainly justify a Protestant in undertaking a close study of the Catholic religion to see whether he could conscientiously accept it.

163. It is out of place for a man to adopt his wife's religion.

As no woman should adopt a religion merely because it is that of her husband, so no man should adopt a religion merely because it is that of his wife. Every human being owes it to God to find out the true religion and, having found it, to embrace it. This obligation falls on every soul, independently of the question of sex. If the wife's religion happens to be the true religion, then the man should embrace that religion, not for his wife's sake but from a sense of duty to God. If the man's religion happens to be the true one, then the wife should join it.

164. In mixed marriages it is always the Protestant husband who is converted to the Catholic wife's religion, never the Catholic who accepts the Protestant religion. Why do Catholics cling to their position so rigidly?

Because it is certain that the Catholic party has the true religion. And therefore Catholics cling to their religion for the love of God, and of Christ, and of their own souls. Knowing that the Catholic religion is true, Catholics know that they can please God only by fidelity to their religion, and that they would offend him seriously by leaving it. Duty to God is the most important thing in life. To be what God wants her to be is a better and nobler thing for any woman than to be what her husband would like her to be. And no husband can take God's place in his wife's soul. Secondly, we must think of Christ. He established the Catholic Church only, and to that Church we owe obedience for the love of Christ. To abandon the Catholic Church is to abandon Christ and cry out with those who put him to death, "Away with him. Let him be crucified." Catholics cannot bring themselves to do that. Thirdly, we Catholics understand the duty to our own souls. Our religion is dearer to us than life itself. We know its truth and beauty and value as others do not. And we need the help our religion alone can give us. To abandon our Holy Mass, our Communions, the opportunity of sacramental absolution in confession, our devotion to our Lady, the Mother of Christ, in fact, all the privileges of our religion—one who asks us to do this does not realize what he is asking. Never can there be any peace of soul for us save in the Catholic religion.

165. I do not believe in religious discussions, which always awaken strong feelings.

Religion does not exempt us from the use of reason. The head as well as the heart has its duty. And if we are obliged to think about religious matters, there is no reason why we should be forbidden an interchange of thought with others on the subject. Why should a discussion about politics be right yet a discussion about religion be wrong? The interchange of thought by discussion has led thousands from erroneous ideas to the truth on innumerable subjects. Surely you will not say that it is good to rectify mistakes in other matters but that religious mistakes should be the accepted thing. With you, I would certainly object to quarreling over religion. But there is no need for religious discussion to develop into a quarrel. The rejection of some particular religious position is quite consistent with politeness and respect for the person who sincerely maintains that position.

166. Since quarrels do arise with much sectarian bitterness, would it not be better to avoid all discussion of religion?

If truth has any value, the search for it must go on, even though it hurts at times. After all, Christ came to teach the truth, and he was not deterred from doing so by the disturbances he caused amongst those not disposed to hear it. We know the ill-feeling he caused in many of his listeners, and what it meant to himself in the end. The fault, of course, was in the evil dispositions of his enemies. We ourselves must learn to confine our efforts to reasoned judgments on doctrines, principles, and historical facts. Great difficulty arises even here, for unconsciously there is a danger of distorting the truth itself through partisan spirit and lack of intense love for intellectual honesty. We all have the tendency to accept as true those things we would like to be true, and merely because our inclinations tend in that direction. To rise above that tendency and to put aside all likes and dislikes is almost the first requirement in all who earnestly wish to discover the truth.

167. I cannot adopt any definite profession of faith, because the heads of all the different churches disagree.

If they disagree, that shows at most that you cannot take their word on behalf of their own churches. But it does not follow that there is not a right church amongst them all. Your duty is to inquire and find the Church Christ actually established.

168. Why are not Christians united?

All who profess to be Christians, of course, ought to be united in one Church. That they are not is due to the world, the flesh, and the devil, besides the fact that human beings are very limited in intelligence and are endowed with free will.

The world has had its influence insofar as temporal and national considerations have led men to forsake original unity.

The flesh has taken its toll, men denying the faith they once professed because of its conflict with their passions.

The devil has had his share, sowing cockle amidst the wheat and choking the good grain in thousands of souls.

That men have been able to yield to these influences is due to the fact that God will not take away the gift of free will and personal responsibility from any man. As for good people who still adhere to mistaken forms of Christianity, we can account for that only by the limitations of the human mind that render it so liable to error and so little able to comprehend things in all their aspects. They concentrate on some good element retained in their mistaken form of religion and lose sight of the aspects wherein it fails.

Christ himself foresaw and predicted such divisions. "For false Christs and false prophets will arise," he said, "so as to lead astray, if possible, even the elect" (Matt. 24:24). And St. Paul warned Timothy, "For the time is coming when people will not endure sound teaching, but having itching ears they will accumulate for themselves teachers to suit their own likings, and will turn away from listening to the truth and wander into myths" (2 Tim. 4:3-4).

169. Your preceding replies are based upon a misapprehension. There is no real lack of essential unity in the Christian churches at all. All, together, form the one true Church.

However nice that looks on paper, it is impossible. We cannot hold that hundreds of conflicting churches, even those disowning each other, are all one church. The good Wesleyan who says that Rome is idolatrous would have to admit that the idolatrous Catholic belongs to the same church as himself and is equally a Christian. The notion demands not a little suppression of reason. Again, if the Catholic Church excommunicates a man, almost any Protestant Church will promptly receive him. If the Catholic Church and the Protestant Church that receives him are one and the same, you will have the same Christ accepting and rejecting the same man at one and the same time!

The Son of God, who knew that a kingdom divided against itself cannot stand, took precautions precisely to avoid such internal divisions. He declared that there would be absolute unity in both doctrine and government, and he has preserved his Church from doctrinal and disciplinary dissension. In the fourth century there was the same Catholic Church as today, and almost as many cut-off sects, Montanists, Manicheans,

Arians, Donatists, Nestorians, Pelagians, and Eutychians, were solemnly telling men that they were part of the one true Church. Sincere men like yourself were deceived and maintained many sections. But the cut-off sections died, lacking the promise of Christ. Today we have the same Catholic Church but a new host of cut-off sects—Anglicans, Wesleyans, Presbyterians, Baptists, Adventists, Christadelphians, etc.—and they have not yet lasted as long as many of the earlier heresies. They too will die, and a new lot will arise in the ages to come. But you are making the same mistake as many sincere men in the earlier centuries, thinking these man-made substitutes to be part of the one indivisible Church of Christ.

I admit that the truth can be viewed from different angles. But I deny that the truth can be different from itself. We cannot say that people who believe contradictory things are merely viewing the same truth from different angles. Of contradictories, if one is true, the other is false. For example, if a Protestant says that the Sacrifice of the Mass is blasphemy, whilst a Catholic declares it to be the highest act of worship proper to the Christian religion, would you regard those two as merely viewing the same truth from different angles? Reason itself rebels against such a supposition.

170. Did not St. Paul acknowledge the various individual churches of his time?

The churches to which St. Paul wrote were as much united as Catholics in London today are united in one Church with the Catholics in New York, Berlin, Italy, and Australia. Non-Catholics, however, are not united, have not held fast to the traditions, believe practically as they please, and have made shipwreck of the Faith as well as of disciplinary unity.

171. To my mind the whole of Christianity is like a wheel. Christ is the center, while the various churches are the spokes.

Christ forms the complete wheel, and as he identifies the Church with himself as his Mystical Body, the Catholic Church is the complete wheel, hub, spokes, and all, of Christianity in this world. And Christ prayed to his Father that the Church might be one as he and his Father are one. All non-Catholic forms of professing Christianity are broken and discarded spokes, no longer in the wheel at all as churches, whilst most of the members of these churches disown all connection with the wheel that they abandoned at the Reformation.

172. What are the essential differences between Anglicans, Methodists, Presbyterians, Lutherans, Congregationalists, Baptists, Christian Scientists, Christadelphians, Salvation Army, Pentecostals, Liberal Catholics, and the Churches of Christ?

It would take far too long to analyze the doctrines of these twelve different variations. Briefly, however, Anglicans and Liberal Catholics believe it essential to have priests and bishops. The others do not. The Liberal Catholics believe in the Sacrifice of the Mass. Anglicans do not. Leaving these two, let us turn to the others. Baptists and the Churches of Christ forbid infant baptism. Presbyterians hold to what is called the Westminster Confession and say that the ultimate authority is vested in their General Assembly. Methodism has no formal confession of faith, holding that creed is not essential. Lutherans hold that creed is essential and support the Augsburg Confession by faith, believing in the Real Presence of Christ in the Eucharist by consubstantiation as opposed to the Catholic doctrine of transubstantiation. Congregationalists say that it is not essential to have organized unity at all. Each local church is independent, the members walking by faith, each according to what he privately judges faith to imply. Christian Scientists deny the divinity of Christ and believe that Christianity is ordained to the attaining of physical health by autosuggestion blended with prayer. Christadelphians deny the immortality of the soul, believing that Christ will come again, recreate the elect, and reign over them forever on this Earth as their civil ruler. General Booth broke away from Methodism and began a social crusade with his Salvation Army. Doctrinally the Army is very vague. The Pentecostal Church thinks that all others have missed the essential thing, and its members concentrate on contact with the immediate and personal influence of the Holy Spirit, whom they gratuitously constitute their direct guide whilst they do as they please. I cannot now go more deeply into their differences; but it can be said that each sect has at least one thing it thinks essential that it believes the others to lack. Were it not so, it would never have commenced its own separate existence. If we study the origins of the different sects, we find that their founders fought almost violently for things that modern Protestants now declare to be nonessential. But how far even modern Protestants believe their differences to be nonessential is a problem. If their differences are nonessential, why do they find reunion amongst themselves so impossible a task? They talk of unity, hold conferences to discuss it, discover that their positions are essentially irreconcilable, determine not to unite after all, and tell the world that they were all good-tempered about it and that a wonderful unity was obvious in their decision to tolerate a continued lack of unity!

173. I deny that lack of unity really matters. After all, go into any Christian church, and you will hear Christ preached and the word of God spoken.

On that score, the Seventh-day Adventists, who teach that the pope is Antichrist, and the Catholic Church, which teaches that he is the very Vicar of Christ, would both be teaching doctrines equally pleasing to God! As a matter of fact, you will not hear Christ preached in *any* Christian church, for in all non-Catholic churches you will hear now one, now another distorted aspect of Christian doctrine. Even did you hear the uncorrupted word of God in some non-Catholic church, that would not make you a member of Christ's true Church.

174. When asked where his Church would be found, Jesus answered, "Where two or three are gathered in my name, there am I in the midst of them" (Matt. 18:20).

On the occasion of those words no one was asking Christ where his Church would be found. Our Lord was teaching his apostles that he would be found in his Church—a very different thing. When the Church legislates, Christ himself ratifies that legislation. Take the context. In Matthew 18:17-20, our Lord vindicates the authority of his Church when he says, "If he refuses to listen to them, tell it to the Church; and if he refuses to listen even to the Church, let him be to you as a Gentile and a tax collector." In the next verse he insists that he invests his authority in the apostles, saying, "Whatever you bind on earth shall be bound in heaven." Then he adds the reason for this by saying, "If two of you agree on earth about anything they ask, it will be done for them by my Father in heaven. For where two or three are gathered in my name, there am I in the midst of them." But even if you take the words as implying Christ's presence with all who meet in his name, you must remember that he laid down many other conditions as well. Those conditions concerning his Church demand unity in doctrine, worship, and discipline. And when he said, "If you love me, you will keep my commandments" (John 14:15), not a single one of his commandments can be excluded. Take as a test the commandment to hear and obey the Church. By what Church are you taught? What Church do you obey? The very consideration of those questions forces one to look around in order to find Christ's Church as a preliminary condition.

175. All are one who are guided by the same Holy Spirit. Jesus said, "I will ask the Father, and he will give you another Counselor, to be with you forever" (John 14:16).

Christ there promises to send the Holy Spirit as an invisible source of light and strength upon his Church. Whilst that Holy Spirit will operate within the souls of the disciples of Christ, the very promise that he will abide "forever" shows that Christ is speaking of a gift to be granted to the Church collectively, and to remain with the Church until the end of time. As a matter of fact, when Christ spoke, the Holy Spirit was already dwelling in the souls of the apostles as individuals. But he was not yet dwelling in them as a group, knitting them together in the Church they had to form. For this purpose the Holy Spirit was sent upon them collectively on Pentecost Sunday. It must be insisted upon that, whilst the Holy Spirit dwells within the souls of individual disciples of Christ, his teaching is never at variance with that of the Church. The same Holy Spirit works both in the Church and in individual souls. What the Church says to our ears the Spirit of truth says in our hearts. The same wind that fills the sails of the ship provides for the breathing of the passengers. If a man says that the Holy Spirit within him tells him something quite opposed to the teaching of the Church, then such a man is mistaking his own vain fancies for the voice of God. That is why Christ said, "[If a man] refuses to listen even to the church, let him be to you as a Gentile and a tax collector" (Matt. 18:17).

176. How can we solve the problem as to which is the true religion of Christ?

There are many ways of approaching the problem. But the simplest way is the historical way. Christ founded a Church, said that the gates of hell or forces of evil would never prevail against it, and also said that he would be with it all days until the end of the world. His Church, therefore, must still be in this world, and it must have been in the world all days since his time. That rules out all other churches except the Catholic Church; for all other churches came into existence long after Christ and have not been in the world all days since Christ. But we will see more on this subject later.

Chapter 6

Catholicism and Protestantism

177. Do you say that the Protestant faith is false?

There is no such thing as the Protestant faith. There are hundreds of varieties of Protestantism, each variety containing some true things mixed up with its own particular errors. As religious systems, I say that all Protestant sects are wrong.

Protestantism says that Scripture is a sufficient guide to salvation, although Scripture says that it is not; it denies the authority of the Church established by Christ; it has no sacrifice of the Mass; it does not believe in confession; it denies Christian teaching on marriage; it rejects purgatory, and very often its advocates refuse to believe in hell. But I could go on almost forever. In the meantime, if you give me any doctrine taught by one Protestant Church, I will produce another Protestant Church that denies it, save perhaps the one doctrine that there is a God of some sort.

178. Protestants believe the Bible to be the standard of Christian truth and the very word of God.

Many of their leading exponents dispute that today. But even amongst those who still accept the Bible there is little agreement as to what the Bible means. The Catholic Church defends the Bible as the very word of God and is alone capable of giving the authentic interpretation of the sense intended by God.

179. When did the Protestant movement begin?

In the sixteenth century, Luther, in Germany, broke away from the Catholic Church in 1517, and began to set up a new church for himself. Henry VIII, in England, abandoned the Catholic Church in 1534, when he brought in the law of his own supremacy over the Church in his own realm. It would take too long to narrate how each of the first Protestants broke away. In various ways, each rebelled against the authority of the Church and was excommunicated by the Church. Luther denied her teaching by preaching heretical doctrines. Henry VIII defended her teachings but violated the discipline of the Church.

180. Protestantism is not a protest against Christ but against the Roman Church.

Christ promised that his Church would not fail. The Protestant Reformers said that it did fail. Instead of protesting merely against the bad lives of some Catholics, and even of some priests, they went too far and protested against the Church as such, asserting that Christ had failed to keep his promise concerning it. This was a protest against Christ, who had promised to be with his Church until the end of the world. Protest as much as you like against individual abuses in the Church, but no man has the right to set up a new Church.

181. Was not the fall of the Roman Catholic Church due to the vilest practices ever recorded against any Church?

The Catholic Church did not fall. Many of her members had fallen from her standards of virtue, and this was made the excuse for their conduct by multitudes who fell from the Faith into heresy. And the children of those who then fell away from Catholicism are today falling into indifference to all religion and almost complete unbelief, whilst the Catholic Church is the one great stronghold of Christianity in the world. Even in his own day Luther admitted that the more his teachings progressed, the worse the people became. "It is clear," he wrote, "how much more greedy, cruel, immodest, shameless, and wicked the people now are than they were under the papacy."

182. Do you deny that the Church was in a state of decay prior to the Reformation?

I deny that. I do not deny that there was a widespread laxity corrupting the lives of many of the clergy and laity alike. St. Thomas More knew the society of his day very well, and he put things pithily when he said, "The world is tired of the clergy, but the clergy are not tired of the world." Yet St. Thomas More did not make the mistake of blaming the Church of Christ for the lax members in it. He blamed the lax members. And it would be a mistake to think that there was nothing but laxity in the Church in the times immediately prior to the Reformation. There were saints in those days side by side with the sinners. Read that marvelous little book, *The Imitation of Christ* by Thomas à Kempis, and try to realize that that treasure of spirituality was written by a Catholic monk during those very years of supposed universal corruption. That book represents the true ideals of the Catholic Church and is a strong condemnation of the unchristian lives of those who were a disgrace to the Christian name.

183. The Book of Revelation revealed that many of the hierarchy would fall into gross sins in the Middle Ages. History tells us that they did so.

It is a mistake to restrict the predictions of Revelation to any particular class or to any particular age. St. John sees the forces of evil ever reviving and renewing their attack against Christ and his Church. Only with the end of the world itself will the influence of Antichrist or the Beast come to an end. Through the ages surge upon surge of evil will attack the Church; now prevailing in a greater degree, now beaten back. But we need not go to the Book of Revelation for predictions of evil amongst members of the Church. Christ himself predicted them. "It is necessary," he said, "that temptations come, but woe to the man by whom the temptation comes" (Matt. 18:7). And he did not make any distinction between clergy and laity. In fact, he seems almost to have permitted the fall of Judas, one of the apostolic hierarchy, to warn us of the possibility of such things and to preserve us from undue dismay.

184. Pope Innocent III said that the Church of his day suffered from five evils and that the first of all was the evil conduct of prelates.

Be it so. But notice that Pope Innocent III, whilst aware of the abuses on the part of prelates, did not sanction them. He spoke to condemn them as not in keeping with Catholic ideals. And the obvious cure was the reform of the prelates and the stamping out of their abuses, not the dynamiting of the whole Church established by Christ and the creation of new churches by men who had no authority from God to do so. Certainly Pope Innocent himself never dreamed that such abuses could afford any excuse for leaving the Catholic Church and setting up other churches.

185. Will you set out what you consider the main causes for the loss of such multitudes to the Church at the Reformation?

There was nothing whatever wrong with the Catholic religion in itself. But there were a good many things wrong with great numbers of Catholics, or the Reformation would have been impossible. No one, simple cause can explain it. The conduct of those who left the Church must be attributed firstly to their infidelity to the grace of God in their own personal lives, and to their own pride and passions. But that so many should follow these leaders demands explanation. Mass defections from the Church were possible only in a given atmosphere. And unfortunately many factors were at hand to contribute to the disaster. Political causes had weakened the authority of the pope. Their personal ambitions made the German princes of the various small states welcome a movement that would free them from their discordant relations with the pope altogether—even religiously. The covetous and avaricious also saw the possibility of loot and plunder in the confiscation of Church property. So they supported the Protestant rebellion even by force of arms. In England the Tudor kings had immense power, and Henry VIII, when he could not get his divorce from the pope, found it comparatively easy to impose his ideas on his subjects, robbing them of the Catholic inheritance. We must remember, too, that the Renaissance had brought the revival of the pagan Greek and Latin classics, and these had corrupted the minds and the hearts of the educated classes. Moreover, many of the bishops and priests, far removed from Rome, had been too subservient to secular authority and had neglected to enforce the discipline of the Church, thus weakening their hold upon the people. Laxity amongst the clergy had given great disedification, and the delay in their reformation had paved the way for a wrong reformation by breaking away from the Church. Careless priests had left the faithful uninstructed and incredibly ignorant of their religion; and, not knowing their own faith, great numbers of simple Catholics did not discern the real evil of the separatist movement. Not knowing the truth, they were swayed by the ideas of the Reformers, who denounced Rome without demanding any higher standard of virtue than that which had prevailed. And when the temporal rulers hacked up the campaign with violence and oppression, the people simply found themselves Protestants. There were many other factors also, which a brief reply can scarcely describe. But I have said enough to show the possibility of a Reformation, with its disastrous division of Christendom amongst an ignorant, dissatisfied, and disedified laity, above all under pressure by ruling princes and grasping dukes and earls.

186. In view of all this, was not a Reformation necessary?

Undoubtedly. But there was no need for what is popularly called "The Reformation." Any abuses amongst the members of the Church will always cry out urgently for reform. But Protestantism was not a movement of real reform. It made prevalent abuses an excuse to abandon the Church altogether, instead of remaining with it and trying to effect the conversion of its lax members to better ways. Moreover, Protestantism retained many of the very abuses and merely sought to justify them by denying that they were wrong. That the Catholic Church will never do. She may have to admit sadly that her children sin; but she will never say that what is sin is not sin, as did many of the Reformers.

Eventually the Church did succeed in securing her own internal reform, so far as that is possible in a Church consisting of human beings.

187. Surely, then, you owe some thanks to Martin Luther.

Luther we cannot respect. He had no right to leave the Catholic Church and commence a church of his own under the pretense of reform. He should have remained in the true Church and labored to reform lax Catholics within it. You wash a plate that needs cleansing; you do not smash it. As a matter of fact, in 1521, the worldly minded Pope Leo X died and was succeeded by the German Pope Adrian VI. Adrian was just such a Pope as Luther pretended to demand. He was austere and holy and at once set to work to reform the members of the Church, beginning with the cardinals themselves, and battling against Italian laxity. The brave old pope would have been vastly aided by German support and the closing of the Northern Schism. But Luther made no effort to help a true reformer set in the very See whence reform ought to have come. Instead of rushing to the aid of a compatriot who was just such a head of the Church as he had declared necessary, he continued to pour forth abuse against the pope as if he were the devil. Blind passion, and not reason, was Luther's guide. Adrian VI died brokenhearted, and the real Counter-Reformation came with the Council of Trent nearly twenty years later. The widespread chaos compelled action then; but reform was due to the innate power of the living Catholic Church to renew her own vitality.

188. Was not Luther a brave man to follow his convictions despite the opposition of the Catholic Church?

He had a certain natural courage. But that was no more a virtue than the courage often found in evildoers. I do not maintain that merely human courage is the monopoly of good Christian men. However, I deny that Luther was following his sincere convictions. Rather, he followed his passions.

Luther declared that reason was of the devil and that the Christian must regard it as his greatest enemy. That Luther indulged his vices and concupiscences is clear from his writings, where he gives disgraceful descriptions of his own indulgence in everything passionate. His diaries record shocking excesses of sensuality, which could not be printed in any decent book today. A true apostle of Christ does not give vent to such expressions as "To be continent and chaste is not in me" or "Why do I sit soaked in wine." I do not say these things merely to detract from the memory of Luther.

But it is not right that people should be duped by the thought that Luther was a well-balanced and saintly reformer. He was not entirely devoid of good qualities. He was endowed with a certain kindness and generosity. But this does not compensate for his vices. He should have controlled his sentimentality and emotional nature in the light of Christian principles. He did not but gave free rein to his lower passions, calmly saying that a man has to do so and will not be responsible for such conduct.

189. Christ meant Protestantism to be, or it would not exist.

On the same reasoning you would argue that because sin exists Christ meant it to be! Christ predicted that heresies would arise but distinctly forbade men to abandon the Church and originate them.

190. Protestants have the creeds, saints' days, baptism, confirmation, and Holy Communion. These things guarantee that they are true Christians.

Some Protestants have those things, at least theoretically. Others have some of them. Others have none of them. But in any case they would not prove Protestants to be true Christians. At most they prove that some Protestants are attempting to do some Christian things. But a true Christian accepts the complete teaching of Christ and does all that he commands. And all is accepted on the authority of Christ, not on the authority of one's own human judgment. A self-made religion built upon a personally approved selection from the teaching of Christ does not give us the Christian religion.

191. There are Protestants as good as Catholics, and the Protestant Church is as good as the Catholic Church.

The idea that there are Protestants as good as Catholics has no bearing on the question. There are very good and sincere Muslims, but that does not make Islam true. And again, there is not a Protestant Church, there are dozens of different brands of Protestantism. Tell me which brand of Protestantism is as good as the Catholic Church, and I shall tell you when it started and who started it. Christ certainly did not begin it.

192. But surely the majority of the millions of Protestants would realize their mistake, if indeed they are mistaken. They would on any other important subject.

It is not certain that men would realize their mistakes on other subjects. In political and national affairs men differ hopelessly, and absurd political policies seem ever to find followers. Yet, even granted that men would realize their mistakes in other matters, they would not therefore realize the falsity of Protestantism. In the first place, religion is very different from other matters. It is not here a question of a merely intellectual admission. The acceptance of Catholicism is a complex matter demanding adherence of mind, heart, and will, under the influence of God's grace. The absence of one or other necessary condition can mean a dimming of one's powers of comprehension. And until a man sees the truth of Catholicism, he is liable to rest more or less content with the religion he has. Again, Protestant prejudice is a real, if unrealized, force in those educated under the influence of Protestantism, a force blinding people to the defects of Protestantism and to the merits of Catholicism. I remember a man who went through many forms of Protestantism, ending in Agnosticism, and who replied to my question as to whether he had ever studied Catholicism, "No. But Catholicism can't be right!" Protestantism had ceased to grip him positively, yet still left the negative poison in his system, "Rome must be wrong—I would not even consider it." Finally, and especially with Englishmen, the Protestant religion has been so blended with nationalism that it has become a matter of sentiment and patriotism. Its adherents go far more by feeling and emotion than by reason and true faith. Indeed, it has been said strongly, yet not without a degree of truth, that when an Englishman enters his church, he leaves his brains on the doormat. In other words, the average Protestant gives little real thought to his religious position at all.

193. That Protestantism commends itself more to men is evident from the fact that it is not attacked as is Catholicism.

The world is not afraid of Protestantism, which has always been ready to water down Christian obligations to suit it. But instinctively the world hates and fears the Catholic Church, which will make no compromise but insists upon the fullness of Christian doctrine, comfortable or uncomfortable. She insists upon the intellectual obedience of faith, disciplinary submission of the will, the impossibility of divorce and remarriage, the iniquity of birth control by evil means, the inadequacy of a merely secular education. Her repetition of Christ's axiom "If any man would come after me, let him deny himself and take up his cross and follow me" interferes too much with the comfort of men. If Christianity demanded merely the admission of a few religious doctrines, men would not object to it. But since it imposes moral obligations difficult for human nature, I am not surprised that men refuse it in its original and austere form when they are offered a less exacting substitute with the assurance that it is just as good.

194. Protestants claim to belong to the Apostolic Church.

The claim cannot be sustained. That Church alone can be truly apostolic that reaches back to the apostles by the historical, spiritual, and social bond of uninterrupted succession. Jesus chose and commissioned the apostles, and they formed the authoritative body in the Church. And in the same Church today there must still be an authoritative body derived from them. This derivation must be historically and socially evident in a visible Church. The whole chain depends on the first link, for that links the Church to Christ.

Protestants do not claim an apostolic character for their churches in the right sense of the word. As a rule, they seek to attach themselves to Christ directly, without any intermediary society possessing historical continuity. They rather claim to have a religion "like" that of the apostles, than one given them "by" the apostles and their lawful successors. The true Christian and Catholic doctrine is that the eternal Son of God became man in the Incarnation, thus commencing a life at once divine and human. And this life of Christ continues its activity by the Church, which is a kind of permanent social incarnation. As there is one continuous life of humanity by heredity, so the life of the Church is continuous by succession and tradition.

195. Anglicans strongly claim to be part of the Catholic Church. Your Church is the Roman Catholic Church.

It is the Catholic Church, a Church that has its headquarters at Rome, subjection to the bishop of Rome being the test of true Catholicity. Anglicans, or at least some of them, would like to pretend that we have the Roman form of Catholicity and that they have the English form. But this is mere pretense. The Catholic Church is international. The Church of England is national, its authority being vested not in a successor of the apostles but in a successor of Henry VIII.

Either ours is the Catholic Church or there is no Catholic Church. The expression "Roman Catholic," though frequently used, is really meaningless. Grammatically it involves a contradiction in terms. For the word Catholic means universal or "not limited." To use the word "Roman" as a qualifying adjective of limitation or restriction is like speaking of the "limited unlimited." Again, geographically, the Catholic Church is that Church that exists in all the different countries of the world for members of those different countries. And our Church is alone truly Catholic in that sense of the word. The Church subject to the bishop of Rome exists in every country precisely for the people of each different country. No other Church is universal in this sense of the word.

Some Anglicans claim to be part of the Catholic Church; some do not. In any case, if a stray child wandered into some home and declared that it was a member of the family, it would not avail much if the whole family declared that it was no relative at all. And despite the claims of a few Anglicans, not only Catholics but practically everyone knows that the Church of England is not a part of the Catholic Church, and that it is as Protestant as the Plymouth Brethren. Catch an Anglican off his guard, whoever he may be, and his own church never enters his head when asked to direct someone to a Catholic church. The oath taken by the King of England is as un-Catholic a formula as could well be conceived, and it definitely declares Anglicanism to be a Protestant sect cut off from, and distinct from, the Catholic Church.

196. You have said that Henry VIII started the Church of England in the sixteenth century. But history shows that the Church was in England long before Henry VIII.

History shows that the Catholic Church was in England before the time of Henry VIII. Today we have the Catholic Church and the Anglican Church, in addition, of course, to many others. The Anglican Church was unheard of until Henry VIII determined to establish it. Previously, he had been as subject to the pope as I am. The Church that history records as being in England before Henry corresponds exactly with the Catholic Church in England today under the Archbishop of Westminster. Anglicanism is the intruder.

Henry gave no Church back to England. To give back is to restore what was possessed before. But nothing like the Anglican Church had previously existed in England. You cannot term Henry's action the removing of foreign matter from an eye. Rather he removed the eye, and filled up the cavity with foreign matter. The Catholic Church was suppressed, and a new Church of England was created.

197. But the very word reformation *supposes a continuously existing body.*

Historians use the word *reformation* to designate the religious changes of the sixteenth century, but the radical change cannot be called reform. The Church of England began with a new constitution altogether, with Caesar as supreme in the things that should belong to God. Before the Reformation, the Mass was the very center and essence of religion, yet before very long it was banished and ridiculed. The new religion meant a change in both worship and discipline.

198. England would still be Catholic had not men taken to thinking.

Englishmen left the Catholic Church originally through fear for their property and their lives. Not many desired to share the fate of St. Thomas More, and dear old Henry VIII had the delightful habit of confiscating all the possessions of those who would not transfer their allegiance from the pope to himself. Four hundred years have dimmed the memory of these things, and no real thought is given to the matter by the average Englishman. But those who can and do think are rapidly giving up Protestantism and becoming either agnostics or Catholics. Unfortunately, there is no particular prejudice against becoming an agnostic, whilst there is still a strong lingering prejudice against becoming a Catholic. Also, to become a Catholic requires more thinking than to become an agnostic, and thinking is too much like hard work on such an unimportant matter as the rights of God over mankind.

199. Does the Catholic Church recognize the Greek Orthodox Church as part of itself?

No. As a matter of fact, there is no one Greek Orthodox Church. There are many independent Greek Churches. They originated by rebellion against the Catholic Church in the ninth century and have split up into many different allegiances. As long as they refuse to submit to the authority of the Catholic Church they are as much outside the Catholic Church as the Protestant variations. The Greek Churches are both schismatical and heretical. They are separated from the obedience due to the authority of Christ in his true Church. Although traditionally the Greeks are spoken of as schismatics, Rome does not regard them merely as schismatics. They are heretics also on various points of doctrine. They acknowledge no infallible head. They may retain valid orders and the Mass—things that Protestantism lost—but they have fallen into errors concerning the Holy Trinity, the Immaculate Conception, purgatory, and various other points of Christian doctrine.

200. The Baptist Church is the true Church. It really acts as did the first Christians, whilst the Catholic Church is not mentioned in Scripture as the true Church.

The Baptist Church is certainly not mentioned in Scripture. The Catholic Church is most clearly described there. In the meantime, do Baptists act as did the first Christians? Do they go to confession? Have they the sacrifice of the Mass? Baptists, like other Protestants, insist upon one thing not commanded by Christ and neglect most of the things insisted upon by him. Also, Christ said that his Church would be in the world all days from his time until the end of the world. But where was the Baptist Church before the fifteenth century? Christ certainly was not the founder of the Baptist Church. It is subject to all the defects common to other forms of Protestantism.

201. Whatever you say of other churches, you will never be able to prove that we Seventh-day Adventists are wrong whilst we remain true to the Bible.

If you were true to the Bible, no one could prove you wrong. But you are most unbiblical. Your very system leaves you without any real proof that the Bible is the inspired word of God. It cannot say what is the real sense of all that is contained in the Bible. It concentrates upon a few misinterpreted texts and ignores the whole trend of Scripture, although all Scripture is of equal value as God's word. The Catholic Church alone can guarantee Scripture as the word of God and alone can guarantee its correct meaning.

202. Why not be charitable and admit that the Salvation Army with their good works are God's people?

I charitably say that their good works are often very pleasing to God, and they themselves also, for many of them have the utmost goodwill and devotion. But charity does not oblige me to say that the true Church of Jesus Christ was founded by General Booth. However well-intentioned these good people may be, they are mistaken. Christ gave us a definite set of truths to be believed and of precepts to be fulfilled. He is a true Christian who believes all that Christ taught and does all that he commands. Members of the Salvation Army reject much of Christ's doctrine. Some say that baptism is not really necessary. All reject Christ's teaching on the Eucharist, although Christ allowed the Jews to go their own way when they refused to accept this teaching. The Army says, "Believe in the name of Christ and that you are saved by him." The Catholic Church rightly says that that is not enough and gives the advice, "Believe in Christ. Believe every single doctrine he taught, and believe that you can be saved by him provided you try to obey sincerely his moral teachings." I admit that many members of the Salvation Army try just as sincerely to live up to their inadequate knowledge of Christianity as Catholics try to live up to the full truth. In that sense they are good people. But they are not true Christians insofar as they do not accept the full truth revealed by Christ.

203. Have you any reason for the rejection of the "Witnesses of Jehovah"?

The "Witnesses of Jehovah" merely constitute a form of that sect known as the Russellites. They have no evidence whatever that Jehovah ever asked them to be his witnesses. The Russellites were named after Pastor Charles T. Russell, an American who started a new form of Protestantism. Their religion is based upon the conjecture that Christ's Second Coming is imminent. They pay little or no attention to the obvious things in Scripture but concentrate upon one point in particular that Christ purposely left obscure, saying, "It is not given to man to know these things." They regard all organized churches and their clergy as agents of Satan but entertain a special hatred of the Catholic Church, regarding the pope as the Beast predicted by Daniel and St. John. Their exegetical gymnastics in the interpretation of mystical texts is astonishing. In the meantime they claim to have originated in 1874, which is just 1,874 years too late for one who seeks the Church actually established by Christ.

204. What of Christian Science?

Christian Science was founded by Mary Baker Eddy in 1875. Mary Baker was born in 1821. She married a Mr. Asa Gilbert Eddy, after securing a divorce from Mr. Patterson, whom she had married after the death of her first husband, Colonel Glover. Despite its title, her religion is really but an unscientific heresy. It denies the existence of suffering, matter, human beings, sin, death, and a whole lot of other things that we know quite well exist.

205. Does not Christian Science rely upon prayer through belief in Christ's words, "If you ask anything of the Father, he will give it to you in my name"?

I am afraid that it requires more belief in Mrs. Eddy than in Christ. It relies also far more upon auto-suggestion and self-persuasion than upon prayer. After all, favors must be asked in the name of Christ and therefore in conformity with the will of God. But God expects us to use the natural means he has put at our disposal. His ordinary law for our health is the use of natural remedies and medical aid. It is absurd to say that he provided these things uselessly and does not intend us to use them. If we deliberately neglect God's ordinary means, we cannot expect him to help us in some extraordinary way of our own devising.

206. It is most unkind of you to speak so sarcastically of other religions. God is love.

Inquirers put their religious theories before me, and if they are illogical I say so, giving my reasons for saying so. This is not sarcasm, above all since I respect the sincerity of those whose theories are mistaken. Nor is it unkind. If you saw a sick man taking not the medicine prescribed by the doctor but some other drink by mistake, would it be kindness to keep quiet just to spare him the confusion of realizing his mistake? Whilst love may excuse the man who makes a mistake, it cannot say that the mistake is not a mistake. I deny that truth is error, or that error is truth. But I make every allowance for those who mistake error for truth.

207. Would you approve of Protestant missions in places where their work does not immediately militate against the spread of Catholicism?

Since we cannot approve of Protestantism, we cannot approve of the fact that natives are taught this or that Protestant form of Christianity. But, granted that in certain localities the choice is between their being left in their paganism or converted to

Protestantism, I have no hesitation in saying that it would be better for them to be converted to Protestantism. After all, Protestantism preaches the necessity of salvation, and Christ as the means of salvation. This element of truth may be mixed up with many errors. But the element of truth may mean the salvation of souls, whilst the errors are robbed to a great extent of their danger by the ignorance of their character on the part of those who hold them. And half a loaf is better than no bread.

208. Do you not admit that baptism administered by Protestants is valid?

If the right form is used with the normal Christian intention, Protestant baptisms are valid. But here a peculiar position arises. All the sacraments, of course, were instituted by Christ, and belong to Christ. But he founded the Catholic Church and committed his religion to her only. Therefore the sacraments without exception belong to her. Not a single valid sacrament is proper to any of the Protestant Churches. There is but one Lord, one faith, one baptism. If Protestants can administer baptism validly, it is because one need not be a priest, nor even a Christian, to administer that sacrament validly; whereas confirmation, confession, the Eucharist, extreme unction, and holy orders require a valid priesthood. Meantime, if baptism administered by Protestants is valid, the subject, though baptized in the Protestant Church, is not baptized into the Protestant Church. Christ instituted baptism into the Catholic Church, not baptism into the Protestant Church. If a child is baptized in a Protestant Church and the baptism is validly administered, the child is a Catholic and remains a Catholic until he comes to the age of reason and adopts Protestantism for itself. If I receive an adult Protestant into the Catholic Church together with his infant son, and it is certain that both have been baptized validly, I have to make the father abjure heresy and formally profess his submission to the Catholic Church; but nothing is done as regards the infant son. It is simply taught Catholic doctrine and brought up as a Catholic just as any other Catholic child. Its baptism, although administered in a Protestant Church, made it a member of the Catholic Church.

209. Is marriage between two baptized Protestants a true sacrament?

Yes. For here again, since those who make the contract are the real ministers of the sacrament, no valid priesthood is required for its administration. The Catholic Church has the right to regulate the conditions governing this sacrament, and she says that an authorized Catholic priest must be present as her official witness at the marriages of Catholics. But the priest does not administer the sacrament. The contracting parties minister it mutually by their consent. Validly baptized Protestants therefore contract sacramental marriage amongst themselves when they enter into the matrimonial contract, whether it be in their own Church or in a civil court. (I am speaking of first marriages, not of marriages subsequent to divorce, with the former spouse still living.) Here again, as a valid sacrament, such a marriage is subject to the legislative power of the Catholic Church. But because the parties are in good faith and unaware of this fact, the Catholic Church exempts Protestants from her own prescriptions for Catholics. Yet they cannot be exempted from the essential prescriptions of Christ. That is why the Catholic Church insists that a valid sacramental marriage between two Protestants can be broken only by the death of one of the parties. Even for them, divorce does not break the bond of marriage and give the right to remarry, in the sight of God.

210. Despite such concessions, Catholics are forbidden to assist with Protestants in prayer and worship.

Yes, but here I must ask you to try to view things from the Catholic standpoint. If someone asked you to join in an important enterprise, and declared that he did so in the name of the State, you would want him to prove that he had the authority of the State, and that the enterprise was within the conditions laid down by the State. If he had no authority from the State, or did not comply with its conditions, you would deny that he was acting in the name of the State. Even though he mistakenly thought he was authorized by the State, he would not really be so authorized. Now, a Catholic believes that Christ entrusted the care and administration of his religion to the Catholic Church. If we want to assemble for religious purposes in his name, it must be according to the sanction and direction of his Church, this being one of the conditions laid down by him. People assembling in the name of other religions are not really assembled in the name of Christ, however sincerely they may think it to be so. And a Catholic, granted Catholic principles, cannot sanction by his presence those religious functions organized independently of the authority of Christ and of the conditions he imposed.

211. Our Protestant ministers do not forbid us to worship with fellow Christians. They trust us.

Catholic exclusiveness is not a matter of not trusting Catholics. It vindicates the right of Jesus Christ to be worshipped only in accordance with the rules of the Church he established.

212. Will you explain just what Catholics mean by the unity of the Church?

By the unity of the Church we mean the unity of belief, worship, and government for all peoples and for all times in the one religious body. This is the first great requirement of the true Church. Unity is reality. Unity and life, in fact, go together. If the Church is the union of God with man, and man with God, how can there be several different Churches? That would mean division in the very thing that should unite us in God. If God is one, and men are one in Christ, then there can be but one Church, a divine yet human organization, of which Christ is the head, the Holy Spirit the soul, and all men members. The Church is but a continuation of Christ in this world. Therefore, St. Paul asks, "Is the body of Christ divided?" There is but one Lord, one faith, one baptism, and one Church. The Catholic Church is this one Church; and any religion that differs in character from the Catholic Church, and wishes to exist independently of it, is outside the true Church.

213. History shows that the Roman Church has had crisis after crisis. She has not always had unity but only recently has perfected her concentration.

The Catholic Church has always had unity. It is true that there has been crisis after crisis in her history. But that does not imply loss of unity. In all life, whether individual or social, civil or religious, crisis follows crisis. But where civil kingdoms have been dissolved, the Catholic Church has ever emerged with a still more concentrated unity. Today there is no possibility of a Greek schism or a Protestant reformation by any movement from within the Catholic Church. Modernism was soon settled as far as she was concerned. And all previous disloyalties and rebellions provoked a reaction of unity proving the vitality of the Catholic Church, and that will to live which is her preservation. What you call the concentration of unity in the Catholic Church is merely her interior principle of control responding to the complications incidental to growth.

214. The exclusive claims of the Catholic Church will never lead to unity. It can come only by tolerance, respect for each other, and closer cooperation.

Continued tolerance of error can never give unity in truth. By such tolerance people will remain as divided as ever in their beliefs. Respect for the persons of others should ever prevail. Closer cooperation is not enough. Perfect cooperation is necessary. But that will be possible only under a unified control. And a unified control of a perfectly united Christian Church will result only from a return of the churches that caused a division to the one fold of the Catholic Church. After all, Christ sent his Church to fight the forces of evil. If a country sent an army to resist its enemies, how would that army get on if different subordinate officers walked off with groups of soldiers, disobeying orders of the higher command, and deciding to try out what they thought to be better ideas of their own? Discipline and order are essential. Our Lord knew this and warned against such divisions, saying, "If a kingdom is divided against itself, that kingdom cannot stand." And if superior officers protested against the indiscipline of hotheaded subordinates, would you blame them? Or suggest that, since all aimed at defending the country, they should work harmoniously with these insubordinates, whilst still allowing them to do as they please?

215. To what do you attribute the seemingly incurable hostility of Protestantism to Catholic claims?

I attribute it to the growth of indifference to all religion, to lack of knowledge of the Catholic Church, to inherited prejudices against that Church, to wrong ideas of the Christian faith, and to mistaken ideas of national loyalty. There is no doubt that Protestantism in general has led to a widespread indifference to the claims of religion. People don't bother about it. At the same time, whilst Protestantism has failed to hold the multitudes who have been deprived of the Catholic Faith, it has left a lingering poison of prejudice against the Church it abandoned. So it is that Protestants, who have no particular love for their own churches, have an instinctive dread of Catholicism. It is not reasonable, and they cannot account for it. If they attempt to do so, they have to invent reasons that will not bear analysis. But the dread is there. And the more Protestant a country is, the greater its hostility toward the Catholic Church. Nonconformity, therefore, as a rule, is more hostile than Anglicanism. But besides inherited prejudices, all forms of Protestantism have a wrong idea of Christian faith. For Protestants, Christianity has become merely a subjective way of life to the exclusion of an objective acceptance of truth. They have had it drilled into them from pulpit after pulpit that "creed does not matter." That practically means that truth does not matter. They have the idea that not what a man believes, but what he does, is the sole criterion of goodness. Reason, therefore, takes a very secondary place, and religion is better measured by feelings of piety and devotion. Consequently, if Protestants have no religious feelings, they banish the whole problem. On the other hand, if they have religious feelings, they are content where they are and do not bother to inquire as to whether the form of religion they profess is right in itself or not. Finally, Protestantism and patriotism have long been associated in their minds, and they have a vague sense of disloyalty to their country in the mere thought of Catholicism. In any case, to become a Catholic is to violate the conventions. That is one of the things "not done." This is but a brief survey, and incomplete. But all these things, singly or collectively, with many others, contribute to the apathy or hostility of Protestants toward the Catholic claims.

Chapter 7

The Church and the Papacy

216. What does the word Catholic *mean?*

It is derived from the Greek language and means universal and complete. And as Christ told his apostles to go and teach all nations all his doctrines, the word *Catholic* is reserved to that Church that alone teaches all Christ's doctrines to all peoples—the Catholic Church. St. Ignatius of Antioch, about the year 110, first used the word to designate the true Church. He wrote, "Where the bishop is, there is the Catholic Church." Donatism broke away from the Church in the fourth century, just as Protestantism in the sixteenth, and St. Augustine declared that this heresy was cut off from the Catholic Church. In the same fourth century Pacian used the word Catholic as a mark of identification, saying, "Christian is my name. Catholic my surname." He did not wish to be taken for one of those who protested against the Catholic Church yet still continued to call themselves Christians.

217. In what sense do you use the word "Church"?

I intend that organized religious society of all Catholics throughout the world under the pope as their one visible head on earth.

218. Is not the sense of the word simply "congregation"?

Originally in Greek the word *ecclesia* meant an assembly of people brought together by a public crier. In biblical Greek it has many meanings, one of them being that which I usually intend. Thus, in the Old Testament, the Greek word *ekklesia* is used not to designate a mere assembly but the whole theocratic society of the Jews as the chosen nation of God. In the New Testament, the word is used also in this same sense of a united and organized body but transferred to the followers of Christ. It is in this sense that Jesus said, "I will build my Church" (Matt. 16:18).

219. I have been told that no Church came into existence until the fourth century!

That was not a correct statement. Christ personally established the Christian Church. He said clearly, "I will build my Church." He did not say, "I will see that my Church is established in the fourth century." In the first century St. Paul wrote to the Philippians blaming himself for having persecuted "the Church." How could he have done so, if the Church did not come into existence until three centuries later?

220. What is the Catholic idea of the Church?

The Church is that visible society of men upon Earth that was founded by Jesus Christ, guaranteed by him to exist all days until the end of the world, and sent by him to teach all nations with his own authority. It is one definite society for man's spiritual good, and its members are bound together by the profession of the same and complete Christian faith, by the same sacraments and worship, and by submission to the same spiritual authority vested in the successors of St. Peter—the present successor being the bishop of Rome.

221. When did the Church begin?

When Jesus called the apostles to follow him. They were taught by him, given various necessary powers to act in his name, and finally sent to all the world on Pentecost Sunday, after having received a special communication of the Holy Spirit.

222. What powers did Christ confer upon his Church?

All can really be reduced to three. First, magisterial power, or the authority to teach the truth in his name. Thus he said, "Go therefore and make disciples of all nations … teaching them to observe all that I have commanded you." Secondly, sanctifying powers for the forgiving of sin and the conferring of graces necessary for salvation and virtue. Thus he said, "If you forgive the sins of any, they are forgiven." Thirdly, legislative power, or the right to make laws for the disciplinary needs of the Church. Thus he said, "Whatever you bind on earth shall be bound in heaven, and whatever you loose on earth shall be loosed in heaven."

223. What positive proof have you that the Catholic Church is the only true Church?

The proof lies in the fact that the Catholic Church alone corresponds exactly to the exact religion established by Christ. Now, the Christian religion is that religion that:

a. was founded by Christ personally;
b. has existed continuously since the time of Christ;
c. is Catholic, or universal, in accordance with Christ's command to go to all the world and teach all nations;
d. demands that all her members admit the same doctrine;
e. exercises divine authority over her subjects, since Christ said that if a man would not hear the Church he would be as the heathen.

Now, the Catholic Church alone can claim:

a. to have been founded by Christ personally. All other churches disappear as you go back through history. Christ said, "You are Peter, and on this rock I will build my Church." There are many claimants to the honor of being Christ's Church. But among all non-Catholic churches, we find one built on a John Wesley, another on a Martin Luther, another on a Mrs. Eddy, etc. But the Catholic Church alone can possibly claim to have been built on Peter, the chief of the apostles, and one-time bishop of Rome,
b. to have existed in all the centuries since Christ;
c. that every one of her members admits exactly the same essential doctrines;
d. to be Catholic, or universal;
e. to speak with a voice of true authority in the name of God.

224. What of the test given by Mark 16:17-18, "These signs will accompany those who believe ... they will pick up serpents, and if they drink any deadly thing, it will not hurt them."

The passage you quote was never meant to indicate a permanent test of the true Church. Christ predicted that certain signs would occur to justify the preaching of his followers. He did not say that they would occur continuously, nor that every individual follower would be endowed with such miraculous powers. The signs did occur in the case of some followers of Christ in the early Church, and thus Christ's prophecy was fulfilled. Thus St. Paul himself was bitten by a deadly viper and suffered no harm, to the astonishment of the people around him (Acts 28:3). But the miracle was for the sake of the unbelievers who had no other external sign. But now that the Church has been solidly established and propagated, such extraordinary signs are not necessary. You have plenty of external evidence, now that the Church exists throughout the world and stares you in the face.

225. Modernists say that it cannot be proved that Christ ever referred to his Church as such, though he did have an idea of calling into being a community of faith.

Modernists dare not admit that Christ actually founded a visible and definite Church. If they did they would have no excuse for not submitting to the Catholic Church. Therefore, so long as they are bent on remaining non-Catholics, they must find some other solution. The concession that Jesus did intend to call into being a community of faith is a suggestion that Christ merely taught some nice moral principles and that, independently of Christ's will, later Christians were led by practical needs to adopt a discipline and establish a visible organization. So the origin of the Catholic Church can be explained by historical and natural evolution—and of course no one is obliged to accept that in the name of Christ!

226. Where in Scripture does it mention that Christ founded any such system?

In general, Christ terms his Church a kingdom, which supposes some organized authority. However, the explicit steps in the establishing of an authoritative hierarchy are clear. Christ chose certain special men, "You did not choose me, but I chose you" (John 15:16). He gave them his own mission, "As the

Father has sent me, even so I send you" (John 20:21). This commission included his teaching authority: "Make disciples of all nations ... teaching them to observe all that I have commanded you" (Matt 28:19-20); his power to sanctify—"Baptizing them" (Matt 28:19); forgiving sin—"If you forgive the sins of any, they are forgiven" (John 20:23); offering sacrifice—"Do this in remembrance of me" (1 Cor. 11:24); his legislative or disciplinary power—"He who hears you hears me, and he who rejects you rejects me" (Luke 10:16); "Whatever you bind on earth shall be bound in heaven" (Matt. 18:18); "If [a man] refuses to listen even to the Church, let him be to you as a Gentile and a tax collector" (Matt 18:17). The apostles certainly exercised these powers from the beginning. Thus we read in the Acts of the Apostles, "They held steadfastly to the apostles' teaching" (Acts 2:42). St. Paul himself did not hesitate to excommunicate the incestuous Corinthian (1 Cor. 5:5). And he wrote to the Hebrews, "Obey your leaders and submit to them" (Heb. 13:17, Douay-Rheims).

227. I am loyal to Christ, not to any supposed representatives on Earth.

No one wants you to be loyal to any supposed representatives on Earth. But loyalty to Christ demands loyalty to those commissioned by him to teach and guide in his name. Test the claims before you reject them on prejudice only.

228. Whilst I walk in the spirit, I do not think it necessary to be subject to any visible organization.

You may say that you believe it unnecessary. But pay attention to the words of Christ I have just quoted. He thought it necessary, and he has the right to map out the kind of religion we are to accept. If Christians had to accept such disciplinary authority in the time of the apostles, they must accept it now. Christianity is Christianity. It does not change with the ages. If it did, it would lose its character and not remain the religion of Christ to which religion alone he attached his promises. And remember his prediction that his flock would be one fold with one shepherd (John 10:16). You would have sheep, not gathered into one fold but straying anywhere and everywhere, having no shepherd with any real authority over them.

229. Christ converted the apostles by showing them miracles. Let the Catholic Church show us some miracles if she wants us to accept her claims.

The apostles were called to follow Christ, and they left all to follow him prior to any sight of his miracles. And later on, not all who witnessed miracles were converted to Christ by any means. The Pharisees witnessed miracles, and when Christ asked them for which of his good works they desired to stone him, they replied, "For no good work but for blasphemy; because you, being a man, make yourself God" (John 10:33). And even when the Jews who had hitherto followed him abandoned him, Jesus said, "No one can come to me unless it is granted him by the Father" (John 6:65). Miracles do not convert people. Conversion supposes interior consent to an interior grace. Christ said to St. Peter, "Blessed are you, Simon Bar-Jona! For flesh and blood has not revealed this to you, but my Father who is in heaven" (Matt. 16:17). In any case, the Church herself is a simple fact confronting mankind and demanding explanation from every thinking human being. The Catholic Church, though composed of poor humanity so liable to human frailty, is so striking in her establishment, her expansion, her unity, and fruitfulness in good works that she cannot but be of God. No merely human organization could last for two thousand years under the same conditions and spread through the whole world with the same results. Her preservation has been despite long and terrible persecutions, heresies, schisms, political enemies; frailties and crimes even of Catholics themselves, whether laity, priests, or bishops; barbarian invasions, the Reformation, various revolutions, attacks by rationalistic philosophers and the forces of materialism. The forces of growth and progress in this living Catholic Church can only be from God. She is a divine fact in this world, and if a man does not find this enough, all conceivable miracles will be unable to convert him. Christ said once, "If they do not hear Moses and the prophets, neither will they be convinced if some one should rise from the dead" (Luke 16:31).

And I say that one who is not impressed by the simple fact of the Catholic Church, staring him in the face wherever he goes in this world, would not be moved to take a practical interest in religion even did he see special and occasional miracles.

230. The Church is formed, not of those who belong to a visible organization, but of those who are born again from above and endowed with the Holy Spirit.

That could not be judged by men. No one could tell who belonged to the true Church, and who did not, according to that theory. Christ established a visible Church and appointed visible apostles. And those belonged to the Church who accepted the teaching of the apostles and persevered in the discipline imposed by them. In Acts 20:28 we read, "Take heed to yourselves and to all the flock, in which the Holy Spirit has made you guardians, to feed the Church of the Lord." How could they rule the Church if they did not know who belonged to it?

231. I have a great respect for Christ but very little for the Church.

That cannot be right. If you believe in Christ, you must consider as necessary what Christ considered necessary. To wish to believe in Christ without believing in his Church is folly itself. As a matter of fact, Jesus did not preach to the first converts; the Church preached Jesus to the people, and on the testimony of the Church they believed in Christ. And the first fact for the early Christians was belief in the mission of the Church. Through their acceptance of the Church and her authority they were led to faith in Christ.

232. You say that the pope is the lawful successor of St. Peter.

That is true.

233. Do you maintain that St. Peter was the first Pope of Rome?

Yes. The word *pope* simply means "father," and it is certain that Christ appointed Peter to be the head, or spiritual father, of the whole Christian family. Also, it is certain that he died in Rome.

234. Where in the Bible does it say that Peter was the Vicar of God?

The three classical passages in which St. Peter's supremacy over the Church is clearly shown are as follows: In the Gospel of St. Matthew 16:18-19, we find Christ saying to Peter, "I tell you, you are Peter, and on this rock I will build my Church, and the gates of Hades shall not prevail against it. I will give you the keys of the kingdom of heaven, and whatever you bind on earth shall be bound in heaven, and whatever you loose on earth shall be loosed in heaven." Christ there constituted Peter head of the Church in promise, declaring that the office would carry with it the power to act vicariously in the name of God. In St. Luke, 22:31-32, we have the words of Christ, "Simon, Simon, behold, Satan demanded to have you, that he might sift you like wheat, but I have prayed for you that your faith may not fail; and when you have turned again, strengthen your brethren." St. John, 21:15-17, tells us how Christ, after his Resurrection, commissioned St. Peter to feed his lambs, and to feed his sheep, i.e., to be shepherd over the whole flock.

235. On the strength of the text, "You are Peter, and on this rock I will build my Church," you accord Peter absolute sovereignty over the Church!

Christ alone has absolute sovereignty over the Church. St. Peter had merely a delegated authority from Christ, and it was subject to conditions imposed by Christ.

St. Peter could not change the faith taught by Christ, as he could do had he absolute authority. Had he that, he could have altered things as he pleased. But no. He had to teach what Christ taught. Therefore we do not accord St. Peter absolute authority. But we do say that the fullness of Christ's authority within the limits imposed by Christ was so given to him that all others in the Church were still more secondary in relation to Peter.

236. Why do we need a pope? Is not Jesus Christ enough?

Because we need the Church Christ thought fit to establish, with just the very constitution he gave it. And since he arranged that we should have a pope, we need a pope. One does not accept Jesus Christ who refuses to accept the provision made by Jesus Christ for the guidance of his followers through the ages.

The Church was never without a pope. From its very foundation St. Peter had been appointed pope by Christ himself when he uttered the words: "You are Peter, and on this rock I will build my Church. . . . I will give you the keys of the kingdom of heaven" (Matt. 16:18-19).

237. St. Paul wrote to Timothy that there is one mediator between God and man—Christ Jesus.

That is Catholic doctrine, but it does not obviate the necessity of a pope. Because Christ is the one Mediator, we have to accept whatever method he appoints for the exercise of his mediation. He chose to dispense the benefits of his mediation through the Church he organized, and he decided that the pope should be in supreme control of the Church in this world.

238. Paul could go straight to God through Christ Jesus.

Of course he could. So can any Catholic. But we do this by accepting the teachings of the Catholic Church and fulfilling her precepts. That is why our Lord said of his Church, "He who hears you hears me" (Luke 10:16). If you think that no agents were ever appointed by Christ to dispense grace to men in his name, the very St. Paul you quote is against you. "This is how one should regard us," he wrote to the Corinthians, "as servants of Christ and stewards of the mysteries of God" (1 Cor. 4:1). Would you reply to him, "I acknowledge no dispenser of any mysteries of God save Christ alone? I go straight to him, not to you. You can dispense nothing to me—there is one Mediator—Christ Jesus." St. Paul would say to you, "My dear child, I wrote those words, and I ought to know what they mean. They do not exclude his use of us as dispensers of his mediation to mankind. Our power and authority are his power and authority committed to us; and if you want to obey him, you will account of us as dispensers in his name, and submit to his provision for you."

As a matter of fact, St. Paul demanded absolute obedience to his commands. He forgave the sin of the incestuous Corinthian after his repentance, saying, "What I have forgiven, if I have forgiven anything, has been for your sake in the presence of Christ" (2 Cor. 2:10). Your notion that the supreme mediation of Christ excludes secondary mediators acting in the name of Christ is quite opposed to St. Paul's own teachings.

239. Who gives the pope his jurisdiction, if he is elected by men and not by God?

God ratifies the choice of those who elect him. When Matthias was elected as an apostle by the other apostles, he was elected by men and not directly by God. But God ratified their choice and granted to him also apostolic power.

240. Where was Peter given power to transmit his office to others?

Christ himself gave St. Peter the power of transmitting his privileges and authority as head of the Church by declaring that Church to be perpetual. As a building is supported by its foundation, so the whole Church will ever rest upon the constitutional office and authority to be transmitted by Peter. If the Church is to remain all days until the end of the world protected by Christ, it must remain just as he established it. No one could alter the essential constitution he gave it, or it would no longer be the same society. As the Church is perpetual, so the primacy is perpetual and, therefore, to be transmitted by Peter to his successors. Those who deny this must face the formidable consequence that the Church for nearly two thousand years has been heretical, leading the overwhelming majority of Christians through all the ages into error, so that the gates of hell have indeed prevailed against the Church Christ established and guaranteed. They must concede that the Church has no single visible head on earth, that unity in faith and worship is not necessary, and that division amongst the churches with all their variations of discipline and indiscipline is quite in accordance with the mind of Christ. And that is indeed a reduction to the absurd.

241. The servant of the servants of God! Is not the pope rather the Beast predicted by Daniel 7?

Certainly not. He would be a very peculiar representative of the Beast, so given to the love of God and man, and to prayer. I have met the present Pope (Pius XI) several times, and he is one of the gentlest men I have ever met. He scarcely opens his lips save to bless and praise God in the name of Jesus Christ.

242. I have heard that he is Antichrist and that he was described by St. John as 666, the numerical equivalent of the Latin words of the pope's title, Vicarius Filii Dei.

That interpretation is absurd and rejected by all reputable scholars, Catholic and non-Catholic alike. In any case, St. John wrote in Greek, and there is no warrant whatever for the transition to the Latin language. Moreover, whatever is the true interpretation of this mystical number, it certainly refers to some one individual being. If it referred to one particular pope, it could refer to none of the others. To which pope will people refer it? To a past pope? Then he is dead and gone, and we need not worry about him. To the present pope? He is the very antithesis of all the conditions of the Beast as described by St. John. However, the number does not refer to any of the popes at all.

243. Who is 666, if not the pope?

Many fantastic interpretations have been given, but none have been proved. The vast majority of interpreters regard the number as a mystical symbol, designating some man who will be the chief agent of Satan toward the end of the world. Some people thought it was Muhammed, saying that he died in 666, but he died in 630. Calvin wished to attribute it to Pope Boniface III or to the popes in general. His only foundation was prejudice, and his theory is utterly rejected today. Martin Luther's name, and dozens of others', have been made to signify the number in various languages, but in all these cases the wish was father to the thought and was made to supply for the lack of reason. The true solution of this question cannot be given.

244. Anyway, Scripture does not mention a pope.

Do not be misled by mere words. Later designations of an office do not alter the office, and the office of the one whom we now call the pope is clearly taught by Scripture. After all, the word *pope* simply means "father," or one with paternal authority over a household. And certainly, Scripture often likens the Church to the "Household of the Faith" and indicates one as being in supreme charge of that household.

245. St. Peter was not head of the apostles. All the apostles acted as having the same authority.

The apostles, as having been sent by Christ to all nations, had universal jurisdiction. But this universality of jurisdiction was extraordinary and did not pass to those successors whom they consecrated for particular localities. Also, whilst the apostles each rejoiced in jurisdiction over all regions, St. Peter had all authority centered in him. Hence St. Paul went to consult him at Jerusalem.

246. Why did the apostles ask Christ who was the greater among them, if they knew that Peter was the greater?

They were disputing as to who should be the greater in heaven, not concerning their office on earth. The fact that Christ replied by teaching a lesson of interior humility shows that he knew them to be referring to their personal standing in God's esteem.

247. Does Scripture show that Peter was even aware of, or openly claimed, supreme power?

Since none of the apostles disputed it, St. Peter had no need to insist upon it. All knew that Christ had said to him, "You are Peter, and on this rock I will build my Church" (Matt. 16:18). And again, "I have prayed for you that your faith may not fail; and when you have turned again, strengthen your brethren" (Luke 22:32). They knew, too, that Christ's commission to St. Peter to feed both the lambs and the sheep of the flock included themselves (John 21:15-17). Implicitly, St. Peter claimed his right by being the first to announce the Gospel after Pentecost, by conducting the election of Matthias as an apostle in place of Judas, by presiding at the Council of Jerusalem, etc. St. Paul wrote to the Galatians, 1:18, that he went to Jerusalem to see Peter and stayed there fifteen days with him. Why to Peter rather than to any other of the apostles? And why does he add that, having gone to Jerusalem, he also saw James? He does not say that he went to see such apostles as were at Jerusalem, or that he went to see James, and also happened to see Peter whilst there.

248. Yet did not James preside at the Council of Jerusalem, although Peter was present?

He did not. St. Peter presided. Acts 15:7 says, "After there had been much debate, Peter rose and said"; he then solved the question. Verse 12 tells us that after Peter had spoken all held their peace. James then spoke in support of Peter's decision, as much as to say, "Peter is right. I too think that the Gentiles should not be disquieted." St. Jerome remarks, concerning this incident, "The whole multitude held their peace, and James the Apostle together with all the priests passed over to the judgment of Peter.... Peter was the prime mover in issuing the decree." St. John Chrysostom wrote, "See the care of the teacher toward his subjects! He has the first authority in the discussion because to him all were committed."

249. But if all this is so, why did Paul boast that he resisted Peter to the face?

St. Peter was supreme head of the Church and infallible in his doctrinal teaching, but it does not follow that he would not be indiscreet in some act of administration. Now, no doctrinal error was involved in this particular case. St. Peter indiscreetly ceased to eat with the Gentiles because of the presence of some Jews. But to cease from doing a lawful thing for fear lest others be scandalized is not a matter of doctrine. It is a question of prudence or imprudence. St. Paul did not act as if he were St. Peter's superior. Nor did he boast to show the urgency of the matter; he practically said,

"I had to resist even Peter—to whom chief authority belongs." And his words derive their full significance only from the fact that St. Peter was head of the apostles. St. Cyprian, who lived in the third century, knew of this passage and certainly understood Christianity. Yet he did not perceive any objection against St. Peter's supremacy in this case. He writes, "Peter, whom the Lord chose to be first and upon whom he built his Church, did not proudly assert the primacy he possessed, nor despise Paul who had once been a persecutor of the Church; but he accepted meekly, giving us an example of patience." St. Hilary, in the fifth century, says, "Both Paul and Peter are to be admired; Paul because he did not fear to point out the right practice to his superior; Peter because, knowing that all acknowledged his primacy, he had too much humility to resent any reproach offered to himself."

250. Did not St. Paul say, "I laid a foundation. … Let each man take care how he builds upon it" (1 Cor. 3:10)?

St. Paul declares that he personally laid the foundations of a particular branch of the Church at Corinth. But Christ had founded the whole Church upon Peter. Each must take care how he builds, and St. Paul took care that the Church at Corinth would be in full accordance with the universal Church founded upon St. Peter. Anyone who departs from the authority of St. Peter is not taking care but going outside the constitution of the Church as established by Christ and severing himself from that Church.

251. I cannot believe that the Church was founded upon Peter. It was built upon Christ, who is the true foundation stone.

No one claims that St. Peter was the principal foundation stone. But that Church which is in communion with St. Peter and his successors is the genuine Church built upon the foundation of Christ. Christ himself said to Peter, "You are Peter, and on this rock I will build my Church." Christ is the solid rock upon which the Church is built. But the first rock laid upon this foundation is Peter, Christ being the principal foundation stone, Peter being the secondary foundation chosen by Christ.

252. Paul says, "No other foundation can any one lay than that which is laid, which is Jesus Christ."

If St. Paul believed that Christ was the one and only foundation, why did he write to the Ephesians, "You are ... built upon the foundation of the apostles and prophets, Christ Jesus himself being the cornerstone"? If the place of Christ did not exclude the apostles as secondary foundations, nor can it exclude the fact that St. Peter was chief of those secondary foundations.

253. Christ said, "On this rock," meaning himself, not Peter.

That is erroneous. In John 1:42, we find Christ saying to Peter, "'You are Simon ... you shall be called 'Cephas' (which means Peter)." Christ had a special purpose in thus changing his name to Cephas, or rock, a purpose manifested later on as recorded by Matthew 16:18, "You are Peter, and on this rock I will build my Church." Let us put it this way. Supposing that your name were Brown, and I said to you, "They call you Brown, but I am going to call you Stone. And upon this stone I shall build up a special society I have in mind to establish," would you believe that I was alluding to you or to myself? Now, Peter's name was Simon, and Christ changed it to Peter, or, in the original Aramaic language, Kepha, which was the word for rock or stone and which was never used as a proper name in that language. Thus he said, "You are Kepha, and on this Kepha I will build my Church." In modern English it would sound thus, "You are Mr. Stone, and on this stone I will build my Church." The word could not possibly refer to Christ in this text.

254. But in the Greek text the word for Peter is Petros, *and for stone,* petra. *They are not the same.*

All reputable scholars today, both Catholic and Protestant, admit that no valid argument against the Catholic doctrine can be built up from the different genders of *petros* and *petra*. For our Lord spoke in Aramaic, and St. Matthew wrote originally in Aramaic, a Hebrew dialect in current use when Christ lived and spoke to men. From the Aramaic a Greek translation was made.

Then from the Greek a Latin translation was made. The Latin has *Petrus* for Peter, not *Petros*. *Petros* is not Latin but Greek. Now, in Latin the word for rock, *petra*, is a feminine noun. Naturally the word was given a masculine form, *Petrus*, when applied to the man, Peter. But the external difference in the Latin or Greek forms of the word, due to considerations of gender, do not affect the question. For in the Aramaic language used by Christ there was no such difference. He said, "Thou art *Kepha*, and upon this *Kepha* I will build my Church." The word was exactly the same on each occasion. And it was because Christ used the word *Kepha* that we sometimes find Peter called *Cephas*, a Greek transliteration of the Aramaic word itself. No argument from the forms employed in the Latin or Greek translations, therefore, can avail in this matter.

255. Have not many authorities held that Christ intended to build his Church not upon Peter but upon Peter's confession of faith in his divinity?

That is an antiquated interpretation abandoned by all the best scholars, Protestants included. Christ did demand a profession of faith from Peter as a pre-required condition, after that conferring the fundamental primacy upon him personally. But to say that the profession itself was the rock has not a single valid reason in its favor. Those who adopted such an interpretation did so from their desire to avoid the Catholic doctrine. Grammatically, the Catholic interpretation is alone possible. Contextually, the whole passage obviously refers to Peter's person. "Blessed are *you* ... I say to *you* ... *you* are Peter ... I will give to you the keys, etc.," nor could the Church be built upon one article of faith. All the articles of faith are essential Christianity. The Protestant Scripture scholar Hastings says that the confession theory must undoubtedly be excluded. The German Protestant Kuinoel writes, "Those who wrongly interpret this passage as referring to the confession and not to Peter himself would never have taken refuge in this distorted interpretation if the popes had not wrongly tried to claim for themselves the privilege that was given to Peter." You see, he does not believe that the pope inherits

Peter's privileges, but he does know that Peter was personally the foundation stone. Loisy, the French rationalist, rejected the historical sense of the Gospels, but he says that it is absurd to accept that sense as do Protestants, and then violate that sense in order to avoid what they do not wish to admit.

256. Even were the office of head of the Church conferred in Matt. 16:18, surely it was withdrawn in Matt. 16:23, where Christ said to Peter, "Get behind me, Satan!"

The fact that the office was not withdrawn is clear from the later words of Christ to Peter, "And when you have turned again, strengthen your brethren" (Luke 22:32); and again, from the commission to feed the whole flock given to Peter after our Lord's Resurrection, as recorded in John 21:15-18. Prompted by love and reverence for Christ, Peter had protested that Christ ought not to suffer. And Christ would have been the first to appreciate such motives. However harsh the English may seem to be, Christ really replied gently, as if to say, "Peter, you do not yet understand the plan of God. You are letting your human affection sway your judgment. But such thoughts are opposed to my vocation. Get behind me, Satan." The word *Satan* is not used personally here, as of the devil, but in the sense of adversary, Christ intending merely, "I cannot accept the natural promptings of your affection for me." No withdrawal of office is involved.

257. I don't see how all this affects your claims for the pope. Where is the connecting link between Christ's promise to Peter and the city of Rome?

The connecting link is the fact that Peter journeyed to Rome and died there as bishop with universal jurisdiction over the whole Church.

258. I have heard it said that St. Peter never was in Rome.

You may have heard that stated, but you have never heard any proof advanced in its favor. It is simple history that St. Peter went to Rome about the year A.D. 43, went back to Jerusalem after a few years for a short time, and then returned to Rome until his death, save for very short absences. He died about the year 67, during the reign of Nero. Papias wrote, about A.D. 140, "Peter came and first by his salutary preaching of the Gospel and by his keys opened in the city of Rome the gates of the heavenly kingdom." Lanciani, the eminent archaeologist, wrote, "The presence of St. Peter in Rome is a fact demonstrated beyond a shadow of doubt by purely monumental evidence."

259. I want proof outside your Catholic tradition. Does Scripture say that St. Peter was ever in Rome?

Catholic tradition is not a matter of mere rumor and report. It is down in black and white in documents as historical as any other documents, beginning from the year 97 with the declaration of the fact by Clement. It would not matter if Scripture did not give any evidence on this point. However, it does. St. Peter ends his first epistle with the words, "She who is at Babylon, who is likewise chosen, sends you greetings; and so does my son Mark." All reputable scholars admit that the first Christians called pagan Rome Babylon on account of its vices. St. Peter, therefore, was writing from Rome. St. Paul wrote to the Colossians from Rome, sending the kind wishes of Mark, thus also indicating Mark's presence in Rome.

260. Does Scripture say that Peter was ever bishop of Rome?

Scripture tells us that he was head of the Church, which implicitly demands that he was universal bishop, and it also tells us, as I have said, that he was in Rome.

261. How can you prove that he was the first pope?

The word *pope* means Father or Head of the Church, as an ordinary father is head of a family. St. Peter was certainly in Rome, and died there as bishop. By legitimate succession the one who succeeded as bishop of Rome after Peter's death inherited the office of Head of the Church, or if you wish, as Father of the whole Christian family he was pope. All the bishops of Rome right through the centuries have belonged to the Catholic Church. No one disputes that they are known as the popes, and as St. Peter was first of that long line, Catholics rightly regard him as the first pope.

262. Can you quote any testimonies to papal claims to supremacy before the year 300?

Yes. In A.D. 96, Pope Clement of Rome wrote to the Corinthians. His letter was official, written in his capacity as successor of St. Peter, and it gave not only advice but definite commands. After his instructions he wrote, "If you obey what we have written by the Holy Spirit, you will be our joy and consolation. But if some do not obey what God has said by us, let them know that they will be involved in no small sin and danger." Harnack, the German Protestant scholar, admitted that this letter of Clement proves that the primacy of the bishop of Rome was an accepted fact even in the first century. Again, we have the testimony of St. Ignatius, bishop of Antioch from 69-107. He writes that the Church at Rome "presides over the whole assembly united in charity." And he asks for prayers for the Church in Syria confided to him subject to Christ and the supreme authority of Rome. This testimony of St. Ignatius has particular value, for St. Peter had been bishop of Antioch. If St. Peter had remained and died at Antioch, the bishop of Antioch would have obtained the supremacy. But St. Ignatius expressly rejects the idea that he has authority over the Christians at Rome and admits that the bishop of Rome is the principal and presiding bishop. Thirdly, St. Irenaeus, 130- 202, bishop of Lyons in Gaul, wrote as follows of the Roman See: "On account of its supremacy it is necessary that every Church in which is the tradition of the apostles should be in harmony or unity with this Church." Fourthly, St. Cyprian, 210-258, an African bishop, writing of certain heretics, says, "They even dare to invade the See of Peter and the principal Church whence the unity of the priesthood has its source." Again he writes, "We exhort all to acknowledge and hold that Rome is the mother and root-source of the Catholic Church."

263. All that you have said seems reasonable in itself, but this monarchical hierarchy seems so dreadfully opposed to the spirit of the Gospel, which proposes Christ as the only Mediator.

Christ is the one principal Mediator. But he himself chooses to dispense his mediation through secondary agents. There is but one king of England, but that does not deny the existence of officials to whom the royal power is delegated. If fifty officials act in the name of the king, that does not make fifty kings. Now, Christ delegated his power to priests and, as the one Mediator, acts through many channels. St. Paul wrote to the Corinthians, "This is how one should regard us, as servants of Christ and stewards of the mysteries of God" (1 Cor. 4:1). In the Epistle to the Hebrews we read that the priest "is bound to offer sacrifice for his own sins as well as for those of the people" (Heb. 5:3). This cannot refer to Christ, who certainly had not to offer for his own sins.

264. Christ said, "Come to me, all who labor and are heavy laden." But Catholics cannot go directly to him. They must approach through a complex hierarchy.

The priesthood is a form of secondary mediation appointed by Christ. To ignore his provision for the Church is to ignore Christ. We do not say that Catholics cannot directly approach Christ. They may unite themselves to him by private prayers whenever they wish. But in many matters they need also the other means appointed by Christ and committed officially to the administration of priests. Remember, too, that Christ identifies himself with his Church and meant what he said when he declared of her, "He who hears you hears me." That implies the doctrine, "He who comes to you, comes to me." In fact, when Saul was persecuting the Church, Christ appeared to him and said not, "Saul, Saul, why do you persecute the Church?" but "Saul, Saul, why do you persecute me?"

265. Priests are only men after all; and how Catholics keep their faith in them is a mystery to me.

Priests as such are not "only men" after all. They are men who have been ordained and have had confided to their keeping the very priesthood of Christ. And any reverence shown by Catholics toward their priests is reverence for this priesthood of Christ. It is not reverence for anything merely human in the priest. And Catholics so esteem the priesthood of Christ that the sight of an unworthy priest merely impresses them with the lofty character of his state. It is precisely because the priesthood is not proper to man but belongs to Christ that the necessity of valid ordination becomes evident. If it be not rightly communicated to a man, that man lacks priesthood entirely in the Christian sense of the word, no matter how firmly convinced he may be that he is a priest, and no matter how many people accept him as such. Finally, it is indeed a mystery how Catholics keep their faith in their priests. It is a mystery to priests themselves as well as to the Catholics who have that faith. For it is the mystery of grace itself—of God's working within their souls. In fact, so great is the mystery that no natural factors can account for it and we are certain of one thing only—that God must be responsible for it. And this is another indication that God is indeed with the Catholic Church as with no other.

266. Catholics call their priest "Father," yet Christ said, "Call no man your father on earth" (Matt. 23:9).

Your rigid interpretation would forbid your calling an earthly parent "father." Yet God himself, in the commandments, terms one of your parents father and tells you to honor him as such. Your text means simply, "Call no one your father as if you had no other father with rights over you." That is, you must realize that all paternity is of God, and that you owe your being, and all that you have, including your earthly father, to him. Nor can any claims of an earthly father avail against our duties to God, our heavenly Father. Meantime, Catholics do not call a priest "Father" in the same sense as that in which they call God their Father. A priest, by God's providence and by the authority of Christ, is a father in the spiritual sense, just as a natural parent is a father in an earthly sense. By administering baptism he gives spiritual life to a soul; he nourishes that life by conferring the sacraments; he warns, teaches, helps with his advice, corrects, and does all in the spiritual life that an earthly father does in the temporal order. So much so that St. Paul attributes a true paternity to himself, saying, "[I] admonish you as my beloved children. ... For I became your father in Christ Jesus through the gospel" (1 Cor. 4:14–15).

267. How is the priest a father of one's spiritual life?

In a purely spiritual sense a priest does all for the life of grace in a soul that ordinary parents do for the natural life of the children God gives them. It is the priest who gives spiritual life to souls at the baptismal font. He educates those brought forth to life in Christ by their baptismal rebirth; he teaches, warns, corrects, and advises his spiritual children and nourishes them with the bread of life in the sacraments. When souls go out of this world to meet God, it is the priest who is at their deathbeds, soothing their last hours, allaying their fears, and consoling them as no others could do. Having no family, the priest belongs to every family: and all in his parish, men, women, and children, love him and venerate him and look up to him as their spiritual guide and friend, summing up everything in that term of supreme respect and reverence—"Father." Catholics rightly, therefore, call the priest "father," not to the exclusion of their Father in heaven but as a manifestation on Earth of the supreme Fatherhood of God in the spiritual order, even as an earthly parent is a similar manifestation of that same Fatherhood in the natural order.

268. The history of the Middle Ages in Europe will prevent men from putting themselves under the domination of priests any more.

First, by becoming a Catholic, one does not put oneself under the domination of priests in any sense such as that you have in mind. Secondly, you are evidently laboring under the superstition that the Middle Ages were dark, dismal, and dominated by priestcraft. But educated people have long since grown out of that antiquated notion. Mr. Douglas Jerrold has recently written a book called *England*. He may not be a Catholic, but he is not blind to the facts of history. "It is hard," he writes, "in this age of unsatisfied desires to recapture the atmosphere of a century of fulfillment. The faith of the thirteenth century was not our faith; the belief in God had not given place to the belief in man as the mainspring of human hopes. Its economy was not ours. The means of production were, as compared with today, ludicrously poor; but on the other hand, they were in the hands of the many, not of the few. Even its politics were different, for the taxpayer was still a free agent with an effective right to decide the limits of his contribution. In the thirteenth century were laid the intellectual foundations of most of what human wisdom has to tell us of the rights of man and the order of nature, and all that modern wisdom has forgotten of man's duty to God." Such is the estimate of Douglas Jerrold, a writer who does know his subject. And he has indicated the real reasons why people do not wish to become Catholics. It is not really, as you suggest, fear of putting themselves under the "domination of priests." They are at least too sensible to believe in the fears that dread word enkindles in some timid souls. The real reasons are that belief in God has given way to belief in man as the mainspring of human hopes, and that man's duty to God has been forgotten by multitudes who, despite their profession of Christianity, are really indifferent to religion altogether.

269. I find the Catholic assumption of infallibility simply appalling!

I should be appalled if a Church claiming to be established by Christ and to speak with his authority did not claim to be infallible. A fine sort of a guide to eternal destiny God would have given us, if that guide calmly admitted that she was not sure of the road herself.

270. Upon what grounds does your Church claim infallibility?

Christ established his Church upon a foundation as solid as a rock, and declared that the gates of hell, or forces of evil, would not prevail against it. This implies the perpetual retention of the truth taught by Christ forbidding its corruption. He commanded her to teach all nations, "to observe all that I have commanded you; and behold, I am with you always, to the close of the age" (Matt. 28:20). His presence guarantees that she will ever teach a doctrine identical with his own principles. He promised that the Holy Spirit would abide with the Church forever, undoubtedly a pledge of perpetual infallibility (John 14:16). St. Paul clearly manifests this doctrine by his words, "Behave in the household of God, which is the Church of the living God, the pillar and bulwark of the truth" (1 Tim. 3:15). The early Fathers insist upon the infallibility of the Church, and reason also tells us that the unity of the Church could not be maintained if she could fail in her teaching of the truth; her very holiness forbids heresy; her catholicity demands expansion without loss of the self-same teaching; whilst her apostolicity requires perpetual duration of an unchanged apostolic doctrine. Finally, if the Catholic Church is not infallible, then there is no Church on Earth that is such as Christ predicted.

271. In my opinion your viewpoint is utterly wrong, and the foundations of your Church worm-eaten.

Worm-eaten as the foundations of the Catholic Church may seem to you, the fact remains that she keeps adding story after story to her skyscraper heights. The Arians told her that her foundations were worm-eaten in the fourth century; the Greeks in the ninth; the Protestant Reformers in the sixteenth; the rationalists in the eighteenth, and a few still continue to do so, although mere rationalism is rapidly going out of date. At present the modernists are the chief people who worry about the worm-eaten foundations of the Catholic Church. The only one who is not worrying about them is the Church herself. She just keeps on her way, never dying, but ever increasing, despite the fact that in every age outsiders have been busy composing her epitaph.

272. Protestants believe that Christian doctrine was kept pure as long as the apostles lived, but after their deaths, errors crept in.

You err both in fact and in doctrine. In fact for the apostles complained of errors, not of the Church, but of individual professing Christians even in their own days. In doctrine because you practically assert that Christ failed to preserve his Church; that the Holy Spirit did not remain with her; and that the gates of hell did prevail against her. In other words, your doctrine is that Christ could not do what he said he would do. No. Individuals in all ages have fallen into error insofar as they departed from the teachings of the Church. And in falling into error, they have fallen out of the Church, even as the Protestant Reformers themselves.

If you think that, by departing from the truth, the Catholic Church forfeited the claim to be the true Church, then you believe that the infallible retention of the teachings of Christ must be a mark of the true Church. Is your own Church, therefore, infallible? Does it even claim to be so? I admit that if the Catholic Church has failed in witnessing to the truth she is not true, and I would at once leave her. But as this would mean that Christ was unable to keep his promise, I would also abandon belief in Christ. Certainly, wherever else I might go, I would not return to a Protestant church based upon the doctrine that Christ has failed to keep his promise.

273. But you cannot tell me that the Catholic religion is carried out today in accordance with the quite simple teachings of Jesus!

Catholicity does not differ from what you call the simple teachings of Jesus, although they were not so simple as you suppose. However, the Catholic Church teaches all that Christ taught, whether his teaching was explicit or implicit. Essentially, she exists just as he would have her exist. There may have been many secondary developments during the ages, but they were all foreseen and approved by Christ. After all, Christ established a living Church, and a living Church grows. He likened it to a seed. Even as a boy grows into a man with exactly the same personality, yet with many secondary changes in size, knowledge, and manners, so too has the Church rightly developed.

274. The doctrines of the Immaculate Conception and the infallibility of the pope were not believed before 1854 and 1870, respectively, yet had to be believed after those dates.

Both doctrines were believed insofar as Catholics believed in the revelation given by Christ that contained these doctrines implicitly. When the Church defined them she merely made explicit and of faith what had been hitherto implicit. She gave not a new truth but simply made these matters clear by defining these doctrines to be part of the revelation brought us by Christ. The Church is here for that. Indeed, of what use is a teaching Church if she does not teach? All doubts concerning the correct interpretation of the original Christian doctrine on these two subjects were cleared away by these definitions, and today the 400 million Catholics in the world know the truth and accept it without hesitation.

275. It is intelligible that the whole Church would be preserved from error; but you go further, and claim that the pope is personally infallible.

It is the Catholic doctrine that he is infallible when he speaks for the whole Church in defining a question of faith or morals.

276. Was not this doctrine invented in 1870?

No. Papal infallibility was promulgated as a dogma in 1370, but the doctrine was not invented then. The Vatican Council under Pope Pius IX merely said definitely, "This is the Christian doctrine contained at least implicitly in the revelation originally given to mankind by Christ." This prerogative of infallibility was conferred upon St. Peter, and upon his successors, in virtue of Christ's choice of St. Peter as the rock-foundation of the Church; his prayer for St. Peter that his faith might not fail; and his commission to him to confirm his brethren and to feed the whole flock, lambs and sheep. The Church does not say in her definitions, "I now reveal this doctrine" but "I definitely declare this to be the doctrine revealed by Christ." If she never taught with such authority, men would say, "What is the good of the Church?" If she does teach with authority they say, "She is inventing new doctrines." After all, the Catholic Church defined the "Filioque" in 1439, and you accept that without complaining that she invented a new doctrine. Why complain when she exercises the same functions in 1870? She will define other doctrines more explicitly in future times as need arises, doctrines we already believe in believing all that has been revealed by Christ, though we do not advert to the fact that these particular doctrines are certainly included. For although the definitions will be new, they will not involve new truths of religion. Now that the personal infallibility of the pope has been defined, we know that it belongs essentially to the original teaching given by Christ.

277. If God makes the pope infallible, why does he need theologians to go into questions first and arrange what he is to define?

Infallibility is not inspiration. If God inspired the pope in his official teachings there would be no need of human research. But infallibility means that the pope acts according to all the laws of ordinary prudence, studying and comparing the doctrines of the Church before coming to a decision. When research has concluded, the pope may decide simply that the matter does not warrant definition. But if he does decide to define a given doctrine, the Holy Spirit will certainly preserve him from any error in doing so. And the defined dogma will owe its infallibility not to previous human research or ability but precisely to the assisting influence of the Holy Spirit.

278. The issue narrows down to this, that the pope is enabled by his infallibility to interpret exactly the word of God.

The doctrine is better stated negatively. Infallibility means that God will not permit the pope to define *ex cathedra*, or officially, a doctrine not in accordance with the genuine teaching of Christ. Therefore, if the pope does define a doctrine, that doctrine cannot be against the true intention of Holy Scripture.

279. What does ex cathedra *mean?*

It means that the pope must speak, where it is a question of exercising his infallibility, not as a private theologian but in virtue of his office as supreme head of the whole Church on Earth, giving a decision for all the members of the Church on a matter of faith or morals.

280. The early Church did not admit that the pope was infallible, nor did any pope before Pius IX claim such a privilege.

The doctrine is contained in Christ's words to St. Peter, and the early Church was well aware of the fact. Tertullian, about the year 200, wrote concerning St. Paul's rebuke to St. Peter, "If Peter was rebuked by Paul, it was certainly for a fault in conduct not in teaching." St. Cyprian, about 256, wrote of the See of Rome, "Would heretics dare to come to the very seat of Peter whence apostolic faith is derived and whither no errors can come." St. Augustine in the fourth century gives us the famous expression, "Rome has spoken; the cause is finished." The early popes had little need to insist often upon a doctrine that was denied by none of the faithful. The Council of Ephesus in 431 thus expressed its firm convictions, "No one doubts, nay it is known to all ages, that Peter, the chief and head of the apostles, the pillar of the faith and foundation of the Catholic Church, received the keys of the kingdom from Our Lord Jesus Christ. ... Peter, who even to these our own days, and always in his successors, lives and exercises his authority." In 451 Pope Leo wrote his decision to the bishops of the Church assembled at Chalcedon, and when the letter was read all cried out, "Peter has spoken through Leo."

281. Have you to believe the pope whether what he says is true or not?

If a thing be not true, it is not to be accepted as true, no matter who says it. But when the pope defines infallibly, he cannot say what is not true, and Catholics accept his official teaching precisely because it is infallibly true. If, prior to a definition, a Catholic was of a diverse opinion, then once the pope has given the definition, such a Catholic becomes aware that his conjecture was erroneous and abandons it in order to have the truth.

282. If you are not obliged to believe all that the pope says, why say that he is infallible?

Because he is not infallible in everything. He is infallible only when he speaks in virtue of his supreme office as head of the Church on matters of faith and morals. He notifies us when he intends to define in accordance with all the conditions required for infallibility. This restriction to set occasions is as reasonable as the restriction of the jurisdiction of a civil judge to his official decisions in court.

283. Why does not the pope define the facts about evolution?

That is a question of science, not of faith or morals. The pope is not infallible on every possible question, nor has the Church ever maintained him to be so. If you have difficulties because the pope is not infallible when he is not supposed to be infallible, you have only yourself to blame.

284. Should not every individual have the right at a reasonable age to reject what does not appeal to him?

Certainly not. On that same principle one would have the right to reject what even Christ taught, if it did not happen to suit one's own ideas. How could any Christian consider himself free to challenge the knowledge or the veracity of Christ, or his right to exact obedience to his magisterial authority? The infallibility of Christ is just as much an obstacle to our principle as the infallibility of the Catholic Church. If, however, one never has the right to reject the teaching of Christ and of his Church, a Catholic may and should verify for himself the credentials of the Catholic Church to teach mankind in the name of, and with the authority of, God. I would that every Catholic did so.

The Catholic Church is conscious of an infallibility guaranteed by God—an infallibility of which no schoolmaster can be conscious. Christ taught as one having authority, saying, "My teaching is not mine, but his who sent me" (John 7:16). And the Catholic Church speaks in the same way.

285. Has not the Church of Rome sometimes digressed from spiritual matters to matters which did not concern her, as in the Galileo case?

You have not chosen a good example. The Galileo affair, though directly a matter of science, did indirectly concern the Church and spiritual interests, owing both to the circumstances of the time, and

Galileo's own indulgence in theological speculations. The political arena would have provided better examples. But even there the Church as a Church did not digress from spiritual matters. No accepted temporal powers of the popes in past ages have ever affected the official teachings of the Church in matters of faith and morals.

286. Did not an infallible pope pronounce Galileo's theory of the revolution of the Earth around the sun to be a damnable heresy?

No. Your question implies more than can rightly be said. The Committee of Cardinals and theologians appointed by the pope to inquire into the theories of Galileo gave the verdict that they were false and contrary to Holy Scripture, and that Galileo himself was "gravely suspect of heresy." After the decision was given the pope sanctioned it. And the decision, of course, was wrong. But the conditions required for infallibility were not present in this case.

287. Besides being condemned, was not Galileo brutally tortured by the Inquisition?

No. Refusal to obey the authorities who forbade him to propagate his doctrines brought on Galileo a sentence of imprisonment, a sentence that was commuted into detention on parole in the Palace of the Grand Duke of Tuscany near Rome. From there he was allowed before long to retire to Siena, where he became the honored guest of the archbishop. We Catholics do not deny any of the facts in the Galileo case merely because we would prefer that they were not true. But, admitting all the facts of history, we are quite able to show that none of them really militates against the truth of the Catholic Church. If a man says that Galileo was condemned and imprisoned without making any exaggerated statements about his punishment or any allusion to infallibility, we are quite prepared to admit his accuracy.

288. Does not the prerogative of infallibility suggest that impurity of morals should never have existed amongst the popes?

The prerogative of infallibility, rightly understood, has no bearing on this matter at all. The exalted office of supreme head of the Church, quite apart from infallibility, certainly suggests that impurity of morals ought not to have existed amongst the popes. Hence, the distress of good Catholics when they learn that a few of the popes led unworthy lives. But not for a moment does infallibility suggest that a pope could not sin did he choose to do so. Catholics do not maintain that the pope is necessarily impeccable, or simply unable to sin. We must not confuse impeccability and infallibility. They are two totally different things.

289. Surely a leader who failed in morals would forfeit his right to be the teacher of others!

That depends entirely upon the will of the one who appoints him to be the teacher. A bad man can give quite good advice to others. But your judgment is ruled out by our Lord himself. Christ blamed the Pharisees for not living up to the moral principles appointed by God. He accused them of pride, vanity, injustice, and intolerance—worse sins than the less malicious frailties of the flesh. Yet he denied that they had forfeited the right to be teachers of others in the name of God. In Matthew 23:2-3, he said to the people, "The scribes and the Pharisees sit on Moses' seat; so practice and observe whatever they tell you, but not what they do; for they preach, but do not practice." The few bad popes said, and did not. And the Catholic Church absolutely forbids all Catholics to imitate in any way the wrong personal conduct of any bad pope. But no bad pope has ever defined a wrong doctrine, or pretended that his own wrong conduct was in accordance with Catholic moral principles.

290. I agree that the Roman Catholic Church is remarkable for its unity. But should not the true Church of Christ also be holy?

It should be, and is. Catholics, therefore, are justified in their great act of faith, "I believe in the holy Catholic Church."

291. In what particular way is your Church remarkable for holiness?

She is holy in her founder, Jesus Christ; in her teachings; in her sacramental system of grace; and in her members. There is no need to dwell on the first point. The Catholic Church alone was founded by Jesus Christ, and there can be no doubt about his holiness. On the other points I must ask you to be patient with a rather lengthy explanation. Take first the question of teaching. The Catholic Church has fought everywhere and at all times to spread and defend the full truth revealed by Christ. Where other professing Christian bodies have made outrageous concessions to rationalistic unbelief, she has remained adamant. And there is not a single dogmatic teaching of the Catholic Church that does not tend to confirm in us the will to sanctify our souls; whether it be the dogma of our origin from God by creation; or of our redemption by Christ, his Son and our Lord; or of our going back to God and to our judgment with one of three possibilities awaiting us—heaven, hell, or purgatory. Certainly, the dogma of hell has never yet induced a man to sin. The dogma of purgatory has inculcated the necessity of purifying our lives by Christian mortification and self-denial. The dogma of grace and of the supernatural rules out mere standards of outward respectability and demands that one's daily life, personal, domestic, and civic, must be inspired by a deep love of God.

If we turn from the dogmatic teachings of the Catholic Church to her moral laws, we can challenge any man to keep them and not be the better for it. So, too, we can challenge him to violate them, yet not degenerate. There is no Church on Earth which so fights to lift man above the natural and the sensual, fighting for purity of morals, the holiness of marriage, and the rights of God in every department of life. So much so that no one joins the Catholic Church sincerely without desiring a loftier standard of living than was previously proposed to him; and no one leaves the Catholic Church save for a lower standard of conduct. If Catholics go, it is not because they have discovered their Church to be untrue but because they themselves have not been true to their own conscientious obligations.

But the Catholic Church is not only holy in her teachings; she is also holy in her members. The Church certainly has the power to sanctify men in practice. But, naturally, this power will attain its object insofar as men allow themselves to be influenced by it. In general, ordinary holiness prevails amongst the vast majority of Catholics insofar as they usually keep in a state of grace and out of a state of mortal sin. They do try to keep God's laws conscientiously, often making great sacrifices to do so. They are remarkable for their fidelity to their religious duties to God; to their Sunday Mass; to the sacraments; to prayer; to fasting and other forms of self-denial; to the obligations of almsgiving and charity. Often they are ridiculed as fools and as scrupulous for this fidelity to their religion by those who regard themselves as advocates of liberty. If they sin from time to time, they are never happy in that state but are most uneasy until they recover God's grace. And always they will admit that sin is sin, acknowledging themselves to be sinners, rather than hypocritically trying to save their faces by pretending that sin is virtue and that what is unlawful is really lawful.

Turning from "ordinary" holiness, which does allow for lapses through frailty, though the greater part of life is spent in God's grace, there are hosts of Catholics who go further. They not only consistently avoid mortal sin but they labor earnestly to emancipate themselves from even venial sins. And yet others push on to the practice of heroic Christian virtue. Take the almost interminable list of canonized saints produced by the Catholic Church. They are her living miracles through the ages and her true pride and joy, as well as the delight and inspiration of Catholics the world over.

That there are bad Catholics does not affect all that I have said. Christ predicted that there would be bad Catholics. The cockle will grow side by side with the wheat. But we can account for the bad Catholics. It is for the critics of the Church to account for the good ones, and above all, for the saints who have flourished in every age of the Church.

292. The Catholic religion, if holy and true, should produce almost invariably a peculiarly excellent type of individual.

You commence with an idea which is only a half-truth. The Catholic religion is able to produce excellent types. If a man seriously wants to be good, the Catholic Church will enable him to be good as no other power on Earth. But there cannot be any guarantee that she will invariably produce excellent individuals, because that makes no allowance for the variation in the dispositions of men. Men are not inanimate objects to be sanctified against their will. So Christ compared his religion to seed that falls, some upon good ground, some upon shallow soil, and some upon stone. The seed is always equally good; but its fruit is dependent upon the quality of soil that receives it.

293. Has your disappointment with the Catholics you have met ever made you regret becoming a Catholic?

I have not met only with disappointments. Some individual Catholics have proved a disappointment insofar as they have failed to live up to their religion. They make a very poor thing of their lives considering the graces at their disposal. On the other hand, I have been greatly edified by good Catholics who do live up to their religion and who have manifested a holiness and a degree of spirituality in circumstances and places where one would scarcely expect to find a saint. But whatever my disappointment with some Catholics, never have I been disappointed with the Catholic Church. She is the true Church of Jesus Christ and is rightly described by St. Paul as "not having spot or wrinkle or any such thing" (Eph. 5:27). Her only tendency is to produce saints. Insofar as her children allow her to do so, her one effort is to destroy in them all that could prevent their becoming saints. The Catholic Church is absolutely holy in herself, and she is relatively holy in those whom she influences to the degree in which they submit to her influence. As Catholics withdraw from the practical influence of their Church, less and less, of course, is to be expected of them. But amidst all faults of human frailty, the ideals of Catholics remain as long as they retain the Faith. If they know that one who gives bad example is a Catholic, they are more horrified than they would be were he anything else. If a priest gives scandal, their misery and sorrow will scarcely bear description. And the more they love their religion the more brokenhearted they are, for the more they realize how utterly repugnant to Catholic principles and ideals is any deliberate evil in one who shares in the very priesthood of Christ.

294. Why is the city of Rome itself crowded with churches in which are stored up most of the finest and valuable art treasures on Earth?

The number of churches is due to the fact that, during the last 1,900 years, many parish churches, special shrines, and chapels to various colleges, universities, and central houses of religious orders have been built in that great center of Christendom. Not most of the art treasures on Earth are stored in them. One who could suggest that must have sedulously avoided the museums and art galleries throughout the world. If those that do exist in Rome are amongst the finest in the world, that is due to the high level of culture and genius of artists drawn from the Italian people. Their preservation in the churches is due to the fact that the artists had faith and piety enough to devote their genius to the fitting adornment of this church or that; and that the death of the artists did not make the authorities feel free to sell these offerings in honor of God's house to wealthy tourists. As a result, travelers from all over the world are still able to see them and appreciate them.

295. The wealth of the Church is a scandal, when one thinks of the poverty of Christ.

It may be that your notions of Christ's attitude toward wealth need rectifying, before we can proceed with this question.

296. Both in practice and in teaching Christ condemned wealth.

He did not.

297. In practice did he not live poorly, aiming at having no means of support?

He lived poorly himself, but he never commanded others to follow his own example in this matter. Meantime he did not aim at having no means of support. St. Luke, 8:3, speaks of many who ministered to his needs and to those of his apostles out of their possessions. He accepted their offerings, and we know that

Judas carried the common purse, which held enough to allow for almsgiving to the poor (John 13:29).

298. He visited only the poorest homes.

That is not so. He was dining in the house of a wealthy man when the woman who was a sinner came in and washed his feet with her tears.

299. He had no magnificent edifice to preach in but always spoke in the open air.

He did at times teach in the open air. But Scripture tells us that he often spoke in the Temple at Jerusalem, calling it his Father's house. And he had an immense respect for that edifice as dedicated to his Father.

300. He drove the money changers from the Temple.

That proves my assertion of his respect for that religious edifice. But it does not prove that Christ condemned money. Christ condemned the abuses of these traffickers in the Temple. They were desecrating that holy place by usury, and also as we know from various sources by selling dried peas, raisins, grapes, and apples, which should have been sold in the marketplace.

301. Was not Christ poor, and did he not forbid the hoarding up of treasure on Earth?

Christ himself set the supreme example of poverty, although, as I have said, Judas carried the purse containing money for his use and for the needs of his apostles. But Christ never commanded that his followers should adopt actual and absolute poverty. God had sanctioned the right of private property when he gave the commandment, "You shall not steal." The right to private property is therefore just and not sinful. Christ did forbid men to make earthly goods their only treasure to the exclusion of their spiritual welfare. In fact he warned those who have mammon or wealth, not necessarily to give it up but to make it their friend by giving alms to the poor.

302. He commanded the rich young man to sell all, and give it to the poor.

This was not a command, obliging in conscience. It was a special invitation that the young man was free to accept or reject. If the possession of goods as such were evil, Christ would have been recommending the young man to cause evil in the very ones who bought or accepted possession of his goods. But you have misunderstood the passage. The rich young man said to Christ, "What good deed must I do, to have eternal life?" Christ replied, "Keep the commandments." Thus he specified what was necessary for salvation. But hearing that the young man had kept them, he went further: "If you would be perfect, go, sell what you possess and give to the poor, and you will have treasure in heaven; and come, follow me." The young man turned away sad, for he had not the generosity of character required. But the Gospel does not suggest that he was lost. No man is lost who loves God enough to keep all the commandments. Meantime, in the Catholic Church, thousands of priests, brothers, and nuns have renounced all worldly possessions and have vowed poverty for the love of Christ, giving up the right to possess or administer anything in their own name. Thus the invitation of Christ is fulfilled in the religious orders of the Catholic Church.

303. Christ said that a rich man could not enter heaven.

He did not. He said that the rich would encounter special difficulties in the matter of salvation. But this is not because they are rich. It is because rich people are in danger of being so attached to their earthly goods as to forget God. The same Christ said, "Blessed are the poor in spirit." A rich man can be poor in spirit by being at least sufficiently detached from his worldly goods that he would not for all of them offend God.

304. Whatever may be said of rich individuals, the extreme wealth of your Church is a scandal, with millions crying out for bodily and spiritual help.

A family is not wealthy if it has scarcely enough to meet all its essential needs, and the Catholic Church certainly has not enough for its necessary work. Meantime she spends millions on her many works for men's temporal welfare, and is very hard put to it to provide her thousands of missionaries, who are laboring for the spiritual welfare of pagans, with the bare necessities of life. If ever a Church has tried to feed her sheep spiritually, it is the Catholic Church.

305. I don't agree with foreign missions at all. It is better to leave natives as they are. The missions do more harm than good, causing physical sufferings and mental distress.

Your opinion cannot avail against Christ's command to the Church that she must go to teach all nations. Christianity, in its true form of Catholicity, gives many helps to the attaining of eternal salvation, and it is certainly better to have those helps than not to have them. Any harm that seems to follow missionary enterprise is due to the vices of so-called Christian traders and adventurers, to the introduction of false forms of Christianity, or to the mistakes of well-meaning men. But it is never due to the spreading of Catholic doctrine as such. Pagan and even cannibal tribes, noting the beneficial effects of the coming of the Catholic missionaries, again and again send requests that they too may receive a priest to teach them.

306. Do you maintain that one is obliged to join your infallible, one, holy, catholic, apostolic, and indefectible Church, if he wishes to be saved?

If a man realizes that the Catholic Church is the true Church, he must join it if he wishes to save his soul. That is the normal law. But if he does not realize this obligation, is true to his conscience, even though it be erroneous, and dies repenting of any violations of his conscience, he will get to heaven. In such a case, it would not have been his fault that he was a non-Catholic, and God makes every allowance for good faith.

307. So I deserve hell because I am a non-Catholic?

If you say, "I know quite well that the Catholic Church is the true Church, which God obliges me to join, but what of that!" then you deserve hell. That would be a serious sin. But apparently you do not realize this obligation. Your position is based upon insufficient or false information, and this leads you to a wrong if sincere conclusion.

308. There is no need to join the Catholic Church in order to be saved. John 3:15 says, "Whoever believes in him may have eternal life."

That particular text does not say that non-Catholics will be saved. It might avail if Christ had never said anything else. But he said much else. And whosoever really believes in Christ must accept every single thing he taught and try to fulfill all that he commanded. For example, he said, "Unless your righteousness exceeds that of the scribes and Pharisees, you will never enter the kingdom of heaven" (Matt. 5:20). One could believe in Christ, yet make no effort to acquire the prescribed justice. That is why Christ said, "Not every one who says to me, 'Lord, Lord,' shall enter the kingdom of heaven" (Matt. 7:21). It is evident that you cannot attach an unconditional and universal sense to the text you have quoted. They will be saved who so believe in Christ that they are prepared to accept and to fulfill all the conditions prescribed by him.

309. I can be religious without the Church.

But you cannot thus be religious in the way God wants you to be religious. And since religion is concerned with duties to God, it is for God to dictate the terms and conditions, not for us. Your attitude is due to lack of knowledge and thought. You are contenting yourself with no more than a vague religious sentiment. But religion demands a devotedness of the whole man to God. A devotedness of mind and heart and will. That means that we must believe what God has taught, love him above all else, and serve him both by worship and obedience to his law. For all this a man must study and know just what God has revealed and not be content with a merely vague religious outlook. And as he is not only individual but also social by his very nature, man must render both private and public worship to God. Christ established a Church to teach all nations and to gather to itself all whom it leads to a belief in Christ. One who says he is religious, yet who refuses to have anything to do with the Church Christ established, simply does not know the Christian religion.

310. Religion is an individual matter. No organization can come between the soul and God.

Religion is not an individual matter. Man is a social being, and in religion more than in anything else. If, humanly, we need completing by others, much more so do we need it in divine things. The most fundamental thing of all is that which unites us most and best prevents our division from one another. And Christ employed this greatest social force by establishing a Church that he commanded to remain undivided forever and to gather all men to itself. Religion should not be an individual drop of water to be evaporated. It must express itself in a Church as a vast ocean that resists opposing forces by its very mass. Socially we live in groups, finding both utility and safety in numbers. Spiritually also we Catholics form a group in unbreakable unity. Our religion is not a mere theory or vague sentiment. It is a life—a family life—with Jesus at the head. And as the one true family, so it forms the one true Church or assembly of the faithful. In fact, the Church is but the association of souls united to God. It is impossible for the organization to come between the soul and God. For the very social grace brings the soul to God. The Church is commissioned to communicate the divine life to men. That is her ministry in the name of Christ. She is but the luminous atmosphere bringing us the light and warmth from the Sun of truth, Jesus Christ himself.

311. If one has to be a Catholic to get to heaven, I shall be glad to stay outside.

That is an absurd statement, for there is no eternal happiness outside heaven. But I understand what you mean. You believe the Catholic Church to be wrong, and you will not do what you believe to be evil that good may come. But God does not want you to do that. Nor do I. As long as you believe the Catholic Church to be wrong, you are obliged not to join it. Yet if ever God gives you the grace to perceive its truth, you will be obliged to join it no matter what the cost in renouncing your previous attachments.

312. Christ died for all. He did not say that we must all be Catholics.

Since Christ died for all, it follows that he wants all to belong to the one Church he established and endowed with his authority.

313. What are the conditions for the salvation of a good Protestant?

He must have baptism at least of desire; he must be ignorant of the fact that the Catholic Church is the only true Church; he must not be responsible for that ignorance by deliberately neglecting to inquire when doubts have perhaps come to him about his position; and he must die with perfect contrition for his sins, and with sincere love of God. But such good dispositions are an implicit will to be a Catholic. For the will to do God's will is the will to fulfill all that he commands. Such a man would join the Catholic Church did he realize that that was part of God's will. In this sense the Catholic Church is the only road to heaven, all who are saved belonging to her either actually or implicitly.

314. Tell us plainly. Do you put Church first and country second?

If there be a conflict between the two interests, I put Church first. God comes before Caesar. The Church, as the kingdom of God, is more important than any earthly kingdom. No country has rights against God. And in our own case, if there be a question of soul and body, the soul is the more important and the body must give way to its interests. It is better to die keeping God's laws than to live breaking them. If a man is faithful to God and to his conscience, there is some hope of his being faithful to lesser duties. But if a man will not be faithful to God, how can a thing so much less than God as one's country expect him to be faithful to it? Think it over.

315. But in almost every country where she exists, the Catholic Church meddles with politics and causes trouble.

Catholics are human beings with souls devoted to the service of God according to their Catholic Faith, yet with bodies which link them with this world and render them subject to social relations and duties. These duties are regulated to a great extent by civil law, and Catholics do their share as citizens in the making of those laws. But do not think that all their activities as citizens are necessarily to be attributed to them as Catholics and to be regarded as due to the influence of the Catholic Church.

316. The Catholic Church controls Italy, Spain, Ireland, and Mexico, etc. I hope it never gains political control here in America!

The majority of the people in the countries you mention happen to be Catholics. But that does not mean that the Catholic Church as a church has political control. Meantime the Church does not want political control here and would absolutely refuse on principle to accept it were it offered.

317. But you cannot deny that the Church exerts political influence, in the face of all the political diplomats at the Vatican.

The Church devotes her energies to the assisting of men in their spiritual needs. But since they are human beings in this world, these spiritual needs are often bound up with earthly cares. For men's bodily needs the Church has inspired the construction of institutions, homes, orphanages, and hospitals throughout the world. In national and civic matters also she tries to sway the conduct of men by some degree of political influence, since the politicians of this world so often trespass against God's laws. But the Church does not interfere in lawful political matters that are of civic moment only and that involve no violation of moral principles.

318. Are Catholics told in the confessional how to vote on political questions?

Not necessarily. If an anti-Christian law is proposed, the priest would probably warn his people publicly from the pulpit. In such a case he should do his best to persuade them to be true to God and vote against any law that God would forbid, repeating the words of Christ, "Render therefore to Caesar the things that are Caesar's, and to God the things that are God's." If some individual wished for personal advice in the confessional, he could ask it there. But in ordinary matters Catholics are told neither in the confessional nor from the pulpit how to vote. They are told that they are free.

Chapter 8

The Church and Scripture

319. Are not all the Christian churches based on the Bible?

The Protestant churches originally insisted that the Bible was the word of God; but they were based on the various senses their founders read into the Bible and declared to be the meaning intended by God. But the Catholic Church, although she insists that the Bible is indeed the word of God, does not base her position upon the Bible. She is not so foolish as to say, "Believe the Bible to be inspired because I tell you it is; and believe in me because the Bible, which speaks of me, is inspired." That would be a vicious circle. Of course, if a man already believes the Bible to be the inspired word of God, the Catholic Church can begin from that in her discussions with him and show that the very word of God that he accepts justifies her claims. But if a man does not accept the inspiration of the Bible, then the Catholic Church does not appeal to it as inspired. She will justify herself on the grounds of history and reason alone. Only after the man has acknowledged the reasonable character of her claims, and with the help of God's grace has attained to faith in her as the Church of God, will he be prepared to accept her teaching that the Bible is the inspired word of God. With such a man the Catholic approach differs radically from that of the Protestant churches.

320. Why is the Catholic Church antagonistic to the Bible?

She is not. She protects and defends it. But she does teach that the private reading of the Bible with reliance solely upon one's own powers of comprehension is no sure way to arrive at the truth taught by Christ. And experience bears out her teaching.

It used to be the Protestant tradition that the Catholic religion is opposed to the Bible. Now, when a man has that fixed idea firmly embedded in his mind, he gets a shock when he hears the Bible quoted in favor of Catholicism. The stronger the texts are, the greater his shock. But some people never dream that they may have been laboring under a delusion.

321. Was not the Bible unknown to the people before the Reformation?

No. Beautifully illuminated copies of Scripture, wrought by the monks, were in the charge of the clergy and the Church, and from these the word of God was carefully preached to the people. Before the invention of the printing press, a wider diffusion was impossible. When the printing press was invented by the German Catholic Gutenberg in 1445, the first book printed was a Bible, before Protestantism had come into existence.

322. Then why did Pope Clement XI in 1713 condemn the doctrine that the Bible is for all to read?

He did not condemn the doctrine that it is good to read Scripture. He condemned the theory that it is necessary to do so in order to attain Christian knowledge. Christ's method was to establish a teaching Church, it being necessary to be taught by that Church. He did not order the apostles to multiply and scatter copies of Scripture. If the reading of Scripture were necessary to salvation, what of the immense number of Christians through all the centuries prior to the invention of printing, when it was impossible to transcribe by hand sufficient copies for the multitudes? Could Christ make the possibility of his religion dependent upon the invention of the printing machine? And did he intend his religion to remain forever impossible as far as the illiterate are concerned? It is absurd to say that his religion essentially depends upon a printed book. The pope wisely condemned the proposition that the reading of Scripture is necessary to all. Every reasonable man would condemn so unreasonable a proposition.

323. Pope Pius VII in 1816 denounced Bible societies as crafty devices by which the very foundations of religion are undermined.

He condemned the circulation of inaccurate translations by Protestant societies and the Protestant principle that all should read Scripture for themselves, interpreting it according to their own private judgment, however little qualified they might be to arrive at a sound judgment. He gave as his reason that different readers would arrive at different conclusions and that the ideal given by St. Paul would be destroyed. For St. Paul wrote, "I appeal to you ... that you be united in the same mind and the same judgment" (1 Cor. 1:10). And the pope was right. The chaos in doctrinal beliefs amongst Protestants is experimental proof of it. And Pope Pius VII justly quoted St. Augustine's words, "Heresies would not have arisen unless men had read good Scripture badly, and rashly asserted their own mistakes to be the truth." But this does not prove that Rome is hostile to the Bible. The Catholic Church most carefully preserved the Bible through the ages—a most foolish procedure did she regard the Bible as evil. In fact, her solicitude for the correct understanding of the Bible, and for its integrity, is obviously dictated by a deep reverence for the word of God.

324. You seem afraid that Catholics will be harmed by the reading of Scripture.

Thousands of people have been harmed by the reading of Scripture, thinking themselves capable of interpreting it aright. The Pharisees read Scripture yet managed to use, or misuse, quotations from the Bible as an argument against Christ, just as men today quote Scripture as an argument against the true Church of Christ, the Catholic Church.

325. Does the Catholic Church accept the Bible absolutely as the very word of God?

Yes, as the various books left the hands of the original writers. Various texts in the Bible itself say that they are spoken or written with the authority and under the influence of God himself. Moreover, the supernatural character of the Bible stands out in vivid contrast when compared with the teachings of other religious documents. The fact also that the Jews always accepted the Old Testament as the word of God, and that Christians have also accepted both Old and New Testaments for so many centuries, argues to the truth of their divine inspiration. For such a conviction cannot be due to any merely human influence. Nor must we appeal only to the fact of belief in the Bible by so many diverse peoples, including men of the greatest intelligence. The Bible has had the most extraordinary effect upon the lives of men, giving rise to spiritual experiences such as no other books have occasioned. It is not that the Bible has produced a fleeting condition of religious exaltation only. It has produced permanent transformations of character that are facts to be accounted for just as the facts of chemistry or geology or of any other science. That the Bible should have such an extraordinary effect as compared with other books is intelligible if it is the word of God, not otherwise. Finally, the Catholic Church, with her infallible teaching authority, teaches that the Bible is inspired and that it is indeed the word of God. And she also tells us what books comprise the Bible.

326. Is there any difference between a Roman Catholic Bible and a Protestant Bible?

Yes. The Protestant Bible omits several books of the Old Testament that are contained in the Catholic Bible. It omits the Books of Tobias, Judith, Wisdom, Ecclesiasticus, the two books of Maccabees, and various sections of other books. Moreover, in those sections of the Bible that the Protestant version has retained there are many mistranslations.

327. You say that Protestants have omitted several Old Testament books. From what Old Testament is the Catholic canon taken?

The books of the Old Testament contained in the Catholic canon are those contained in the Greek Septuagint translation of the Hebrew Bible—a translation made at Alexandria, in Egypt, by the Jews residing there. This translation was made during the three centuries before the birth of Christ. The Jews, even of Palestine, accepted the Septuagint canon, or list of books, and our Lord himself used it in conversing with them. The Jews began to deny its authenticity only about a century after Christ, because they could not resist the arguments drawn from it and used against them by the Christians. They therefore said that it was a bad translation; that it did not agree with the Hebrew text; and they rejected it. But the use the Jews themselves had made of it for nearly four hundred years rendered their rejection of it too late. And their motives, of course, are evident. Their interest was not critical but polemical.

328. From what Old Testament is the Protestant canon taken?

When the Protestant reformers abandoned the Catholic Church, they adopted the same policy as the Jews had adopted against the early Christians and tried to cast doubt upon the Catholic versions of Scripture. They too, therefore, rejected the Septuagint canon and accepted the current Hebrew copies of the Old Testament books. The Hebrew manuscripts omitted several of the books contained in the Septuagint, and the Protestants therefore followed suit.

329. Which Bible did Christ and the apostles treat as the standard version?

Christ and the apostles used both the Hebrew Palestinian canon and the Greek Septuagint canon. Both were familiar to, and were accepted at that time by, the Jews.

330. From which Old Testament did the New Testament writers most quote when writing their books?

They quoted most often from the Greek Septuagint. In fact, of some 350 quotations, nearly 300 are taken from the Septuagint. In his *Introduction to the Sacred Scriptures*, Thomas Hartwell Horne, a Protestant writer, says that the New Testament writers had to quote from the Greek Septuagint because many for whom they wrote were ignorant of Hebrew, whereas the Greek version was generally known and read. If the Septuagint was erroneous, and its canon false, then far from quoting from it the apostles should have denounced it, and warned Christians not to use it but to use exclusively the Palestinian canon. The apostles did not do so. They sanctioned the use of the canon accepted by the Catholic Church and rejected by the Protestant reformers.

331. I have known Catholics to admit that they have never read the Bible. Why does not the Catholic Church teach it to them?

The doctrines of the Bible are taught to her people by the Catholic Church more faithfully than by any other Church. The Gospel is read to them and explained every Sunday morning at Mass, and far more people are there to hear it than you will find in the Protestant churches. Some Catholics do not read the Bible privately very much, but they know the doctrines taught by the Bible more clearly than any other people on Earth. Non-Catholic Bible readers may know many texts of Scripture, but they know very little doctrine. A Catholic may be at a loss when you quote some particular text, but he knows clearly what must be done to save one's soul—the true conditions required for this being simply unknown to hosts of non-Catholic Bible readers.

332. Can the Bible be interpreted safely only by Catholic priests?

Not always by them. Priests have made mistakes again and again in the interpretation of Scripture. In many cases the only really safe guide is the authentic ruling of the Catholic Church, to which priests and laity alike must submit. The ordinary priests do not constitute the teaching authority of the Church. The bishops collectively and in union with the pope constitute the authoritative Catholic teaching body. And their guidance is often needed, even in what would seem to be most obvious. For example, the few words "This is my body" seem clear enough. Yet men have proposed a dozen conflicting interpretations of those words!

333. The plan of salvation can be understood by the simplest person. We Protestants even tell our children to read their Bibles in order to discern it.

According to the findings of your simple readers there must be hundreds of conflicting plans of salvation, all revealed by the one Christ! As for the capacity of your children, you might as well give them the article in the Encyclopedia Britannica on Spectroscopic Analysis as the subject matter of their studies. But the Bible itself is against your theory. Thus St. Peter says that in Scripture there are certain things "hard to understand, which the ignorant and unstable twist to their own destruction, as they do the other Scriptures" (2 Pet. 3:16). To his mind the private interpretation of Scripture can be most dangerous.

I have studied Aristotelian philosophy for years and have taught that subject. Whose fault would it be if I could not write a treatise on the metaphysics of Aristotle totally devoid of obscurity for a class of children whose ages ranged from eight to ten years old? The fault would lie in the lack of capacity in the children. And the distance between the supernatural mysteries of revelation and the highest natural wisdom is infinitely greater than between the metaphysics of Aristotle and the mind of an untrained child.

334. Did God designedly make the Bible so obscure that people would be forced to seek the guidance of the Church to understand it?

No. The establishing of a teaching Church was not a consequence of the obscurity of Scripture, as if God had really intended the Bible to be the guide of men, but found that it would not work, and then decided to establish the Church. Scripture was never intended to be the final guide of men. God primarily intended to have a body of men appointed to teach in his name. Thus, in the Old Law, he says, "The lips of a priest should guard knowledge, and men should seek instruction from his mouth." As long as the Old Law obliged, Christ referred the people to that authority. In Matthew 23:2, he says, "The scribes and Pharisees sit on Moses' seat; so practice and observe whatever they tell you." In the New Law he substituted the apostolic body and their successors as teachers in his name. Some years after the Catholic Church had commenced her work of teaching mankind, a secondary record of some of the events of Christ's life, and of some of his teachings and of those of the apostles, was made. That secondary record is contained in the New

Testament, and its collected books are the "family papers" of the Catholic Church. She owns them and alone has the right to give the authentic interpretation of their meaning.

335. God has given us brains to think for ourselves. We do not need help to understand Scripture.

God had given men brains before he came to teach them himself, and he came to teach them precisely because their brains could not succeed in finding out the things that were to their peace. If you say that his revealed teachings in Scripture together with our brains are enough, those very revealed teachings tell you that they are not. Even in the Old Law God said, "The lips of a priest should guard knowledge, and men should seek instruction from his mouth" (Mal. 2:7). In the New Law Christ sent his Church to teach men, transferring to his Church that authority of God once possessed by the priests of the Old Law. In the New Testament itself we find Philip the deacon saying to the Ethiopian, who was reading Scripture, "Do you understand what you are reading?" and the Ethiopian replying, "How can I, unless some one guides me?" (Acts 8:30-31). St. Peter, too, explicitly refutes your ideas. "No prophecy of Scripture," he writes, "is a matter of one's own interpretation" (2 Pet. 1:20).

336. Peter says that "no prophecy of Scripture is a matter of one's own interpretation," but he adds, "men moved by the Holy Spirit spoke from God" (2 Pet. 1:20-21). You leave out those last words, which show that he refers to the prophets, not to ordinary readers.

The last words you quote do not qualify the preceding verse as you think. There is no doubt whatever that St. Peter warns against private interpretation in verse 20, giving the reason in verse 21. The sense is as follows: "Do not presume to think you may privately interpret Scripture for yourself. If Scripture were merely the result of natural human thought, it would be different. But it is not the result of merely human thought. The holy writers were inspired by God—and it is the Spirit of God, not your own reasoning, that can dictate the true sense." That Spirit of God operates through the Catholic Church, the appointed and authentic religious guide of men. In the same epistle, 3:16, St. Peter obviously shows that he was opposed to private interpretation when he says that there are many things in Scripture hard to be understood and which the unlearned and unstable wrest to their own destruction.

337. Did not Christ promise that he would send the Holy Spirit to teach us all truth?

He did not promise that the Holy Spirit would teach each individual separately. If every individual were under the guidance of the Holy Spirit, all who read Scripture sincerely should come to the same conclusion. But they do not. The frightful chaos as to the meaning of Scripture is proof positive that the Holy Spirit has not chosen this way of leading men to the truth. It is blasphemy to say that the Holy Spirit does not know his own mind and that he deliberately leads men into contradictory notions. Christ promised to preserve his Church as a Church by the guidance of the Holy Spirit, and the only Church that shows signs of having been preserved is the consistent Catholic Church. The individual is guided by the Holy Spirit to a certain extent in the ways of holiness, but in the knowledge of revealed truth he is to be guided by the Catholic Church, which Christ sent to teach all nations.

338. Admitting the necessity of guidance, are not our Protestant ministers as capable as Catholic priests in telling us what Scripture means?

They might be, if priests had not an infallible Catholic Church to guide them. The Catholic Church rejoices in the special assistance of the Holy Spirit, and the priest has the help of her defined doctrines and the constant Catholic tradition as a safeguard. But your Protestant ministers do not claim to be spokesmen of an infallible Church. On their own principles they have to admit that they are possibly wrong. And as a matter of fact, where all priests are agreed in the essential teachings of Scripture, your ministers come to all kinds of contradictory conclusions. The unity of teaching among Catholic priests is a greater indication of capability than the chaos that prevails outside the Catholic Church. But the capability of Catholic priests has little to do with relative personal attainments. It is derived from the authority of the infallible Catholic Church.

339. Has the ordinary reader no chance whatever of arriving at the correct sense of Scripture?

In very many isolated passages of Scripture he could certainly do so. In a great many passages he would scarcely be able to do so. In many others he would have no chance at all. There is no doubt whatever that the Bible is one of the most difficult books to understand. One needs a vast knowledge of ancient languages, history, and customs; and must be quite at home with Hebrew and Greek allegorical, metaphorical, and typical expressions, quite apart from the spiritual insight required to penetrate the loftiest mysteries. How many individuals are thus qualified? The untrained lack the historical and philological formation necessary to appreciate the true sense of what is written, and therefore make isolated texts mean what they wish, without adverting to either context or parallel passages. In *The Merchant of Venice* Shakespeare puts upon the lips of Bassanio the famous words, "In religion, what damned error, but some sober brow will bless it, and approve it with a text."

340. Protestantism and Catholicism are founded on the same basic principles, their differences being due to different interpretations of the Bible.

They are not founded on the same basic principles. In basic principles they are diametrically opposed. What is the basic principle of Protestantism? It is belief in what one thinks the Bible to mean. If a man thinks the Bible to support this or that doctrine, then it surely does so; for he cannot imagine that he might be wrong. He makes an act of faith in his own judgment. But the Catholic basic principle is very different. Instead of deciding for himself what is or is not the teaching of Christ, the Catholic is taught that teaching by the Catholic Church. He knows that his own judgment is quite likely to be wrong but that the Catholic Church cannot be wrong. How different are the basic principles of the two religions can be judged from results. For the Protestant principle leads to endless diversity, whilst the Catholic principle leads to a worldwide and international unity.

341. Are all Roman Catholic doctrines founded upon Scripture?

Not all Catholic doctrines are to be found in the Bible. But none of them is opposed to any teaching of Scripture. Some Catholic doctrines are found directly recorded in Scripture; others are logically derived from teachings recorded there; others are founded upon divine Tradition. Scripture itself guarantees divine Tradition to be a sound source of doctrine. Thus St. Paul wrote to the Thessalonians, "Brethren, stand firm and hold to the traditions which you were taught by us, either by word of mouth or by letter" (2 Thess. 2:15). The traditions that the early Christians learned by word, and that were not included in the New Testament writings, have been preserved in the Catholic Church.

342. But the Catholic believes in the Catholic Church because he thinks the Bible supports it.

That is not so. The Bible does support it, of course. But even if he never saw a Bible, the Catholic would have sufficient ground for his judgment. He knows that the Catholic priest does not preach merely his own opinions, as does the Protestant minister. He knows that his Church is not a particular sect but a vast, united, universal, apostolic Church, whose history shows the allegiance of innumerable saints and martyrs. And such a Church is impossible to account for by merely human forces. It is God's work on the very face of it. Merely human institutions have always tended to fluctuation, change, and disintegration. Empires have crumbled. No human being can get even one nation to agree, say, on political matters. How could a mere man persuade over 400 million drawn from all nations to agree on religious matters—millions who differ on almost every other conceivable subject? The

Catholic has reasonable grounds for his acceptance of the Church as the teacher of mankind in religious matters; and he submits to her authoritative teaching in matters of faith and morals rather than decide for himself what the Bible must mean.

343. You speak of the authority of the Church and the weight of Tradition. But I have been taught that Scripture is the only rule of faith.

You have been taught wrongly. Scripture itself denies that it is the only rule of faith. The last verse of St. John's Gospel tells us that not all concerning our Lord's work is contained in Scripture. St. Paul tells us over and over again that much of Christian teaching is to be found in tradition. One who clings to the reading of the Bible only might be able to cite hundreds of texts yet not know Christian doctrine by any means. In fact, the adoption of the Bible only has led to as many opinions as there are men amongst non-Catholics. Finally, Scripture tells us most clearly that the Catholic Church is the rule of faith, that Church that Christ sent to teach all nations and that he commanded men to hear and obey. He who believes in Scripture as his only guide ends by believing in his own mistaken interpretations of the Bible, and that means that he ends by believing in himself.

344. Is not the Church built on the knowledge it gets from the Bible?

No. The Catholic Church was built by Christ and upon Christ before a line of the New Testament was written. She received her doctrine immediately from the lips of Christ and is safeguarded from error in her teaching by the Holy Spirit. Between forty and eighty years after her foundation, some of her members wrote the books of the New Testament. If the Gospels were the only rule of faith, then before they were written there could have been no Christian rule of faith at all!

345. Christ gave us the command to search Scripture (John 5:39).

That was a retort, not a command, and you cannot turn a particular rebuke into a universal law. Were it a universal law, it would have been impossible of fulfillment by the vast majority during the fourteen centuries prior to the invention of the printing press! But take the context. The Jews, who boasted of their fidelity to the Mosaic Law, would not believe in Christ. He challenged them: "You search the Scriptures, because you think that in them you have eternal life; and it is they that bear witness to me." The Catholic Church could say in the same way to Protestants: "You are ever speaking of searching the Scriptures as opposed to my methods, and think in them to have everlasting life independently of me; yet the same are they that give testimony of me."

346. Do we not read that the early Christians searched Scripture daily (Acts 17:11)?

They first received the true doctrine from the teaching Church and then merely checked it in Scripture. That is the right procedure, and Catholics today do the same. But your way is not first to be taught by the Church, and then verify, but to try to make out your own religion from the Bible with an untrained mind and by that private interpretation that Scripture itself forbids.

347. Well, I am afraid of nothing as long as I have the pure word of God to fall back upon.

Without the Catholic Church you cannot prove it to be the pure word of God. Nor need anyone be afraid of the pure word of God. What we must fear is the word of God adulterated by people who read into it whatever they like.

348. Does the Catholic Church recognize any instruments not found within its Bible with the degree of solemnity as if they were?

Besides the Bible, the Catholic Church recognizes the divinely safeguarded Tradition that has been preserved and transmitted in the Church. You must remember that Christ himself established Tradition as the main vehicle by which his teachings would be preserved in the Church and communicated to men. He did not expressly order any Gospels to be written. He demanded faith in his doctrines as they were preached by word of mouth. Before the New Testament was written, the only rule of faith was the oral teaching of the apostles. Later on, part of the knowledge possessed by the apostles was committed to writing, but part only. Not all revealed truth was written down. The divine teaching has been preserved and handed down completely in the Catholic Church, both by that section written in the New Testament, and by that section of revealed truth that was not committed to writing but that is declared by the living voice of the Church. For example, which books of Scripture are canonical, the very inspiration of those books, the teachings on infant baptism, or on the matter and form of the sacraments, and many other things, are known to us by the traditional and living voice of the Church only. But as I have pointed out, Christ intended that, for he did not order anything to be written but established his Church and sent it to teach all nations what he had revealed, and its applications in practice.

349. Do you place more reliance on Catholic dogma and Tradition than on the Bible?

As remote sources of Christian doctrine, Catholics accept equally the Bible and authentic Christian Tradition. These constitute the written and unwritten word of God. The immediate guide of Catholics is the official teaching of the Catholic Church. That Church expresses from time to time in a dogma the exact sense of some doctrine contained either in Scripture or Tradition. As divine Tradition can never be opposed to Scripture, and Catholic dogma can never be opposed to either Scripture or Tradition, there can never be any question of placing more reliance on one than on the others. Of course, where a person's private interpretation of Scripture conflicts with a dogma of the Church, I would certainly place more reliance on the dogma of the Church than upon that person's private interpretation of Scripture.

350. I object to the way you put human traditions on the same level as Scripture.

As a source of doctrine, the Catholic Church relies upon divinely guaranteed Tradition, not upon merely human tradition.

This divine tradition is the teaching of Christ, given orally to the apostles and handed down in the Church, although not written in the pages of the New Testament.

351. Then you appeal to Tradition in addition to Scripture?

Yes, and I am quite biblical in doing so. Christ sent the apostles to teach all things that he had taught them. In the last verse of his Gospel, St. John tells us that not all is written in Scripture. If all is to be taught and all is not set down in Scripture, part of Christian doctrine must be elsewhere. Where? St. Paul tells us clearly. "Brethren, stand firm and hold to the traditions which you were taught by us, either by word of mouth or by letter" (2 Thess. 2:15). "Follow the pattern of the sound words which you have heard from me" (2 Tim. 1:13). "What you have heard from me before many witnesses entrust to faithful men who will be able to teach others also" (2 Tim. 2:2). All Christians from the very beginning believed that Christian revelation was contained not only in Scripture but also in tradition. Acts 2:42 tells us that "they held steadfastly to the apostles' teaching," that is, to the oral teaching of the apostles that they taught to one another and handed on to their children. Those who repudiate Tradition have lost the complete doctrine of Christ.

352. I do not question traditions contained in Scripture. I object to the Roman Traditions that are not in Scripture and that are against Scripture.

The Catholic Church rejects all traditions that are against Scripture. She accepts divine Traditions, which are complementary to Scripture and which are in perfect harmony with the principles taught in Scripture. The traditions themselves cannot be in Scripture, for the traditional word of God cannot be the written word of God. But Scripture itself says that Tradition exists and that it is of equal authority with that written word of God.

353. Did not Christ blame the Pharisees, saying, "Why do you transgress the commandment of God for the sake of your tradition?" (Matt. 15:3)?

He did, but he called it *their* tradition, condemning their erroneous and merely human tradition, not the right traditions to which, according to St. Paul, we must hold fast. You quote this text merely because it happens to contain the word *tradition*, and without any appreciation of its true sense.

354. St. Paul himself warns us, "See to it that no one makes a prey of you by philosophy and empty deceit, according to human tradition, according to the elemental spirits of the universe, and not according to Christ" (Col. 2:8).

The text warns us against wrong traditions but in no way condemns traditions that are not merely of human invention but that are according to Christ. St. Paul does not contradict his own teaching.

355. St. Peter condemns tradition, saying, "You know that you were ransomed from the futile ways inherited from your fathers" (1 Pet. 1:18).

This is not a condemnation of Christian traditions but of doctrines held by those to whom St. Peter wrote, and handed on to them by human tradition from their fathers. These were the traditions our Lord condemned in Matthew 15:3.

356. I admit the force of apostolic traditions for the early Christians. But they could be sure of them as we cannot today.

That is a dreadful statement. Were the apostolic traditions part of the Christian faith then? Is it therefore impossible to know the full Christian truth now? Did Christ mean it when he said that he would be with his Church all days till the very end of the world? Or would you suggest that he meant it but could not accomplish it? He sent the Church to teach all things, yet you say that it is impossible today. Be sure that the Catholic Church has all necessary traditions embodied in her teachings. Within her fold each succeeding generation of bishops has taught faithful men who have been fit to teach others also. But you refuse to be taught by that Church. You rely upon your own fallible judgment. And as long as you adopt that method, you will never be sure, not only of the Christian traditions, but even of the true Christian doctrine to be derived from Scripture itself.

357. What special qualifications has the Catholic Church in the interpretation of Scripture?

Very many.

The New Testament was written by members of the Catholic Church. She existed before a line of the New Testament was written. Protestantism came on the scene centuries afterward. The Gospels are really the family papers of the Catholic Church, and she alone, possessing the family traditions, can interpret what those family papers really mean.

The Catholic Church carefully and jealously preserved the Bible through the ages so that Protestants would have no Gospel were it not for her.

She has been much more faithful to Scripture than any of the Protestant churches. Whilst many Protestant leaders are prepared to sacrifice the Bible in order to appear scientific and modern, the Catholic Church consistently demands that every jot and tittle of God's word must be accepted in the original sense intended by God.

The Protestant churches owe their separate existences to the fact that each denies that the others really know what Scripture means.

The Catholic Church was established by Christ as the rule of faith, and he declared that a man is to be regarded as a heathen if he will not hear the Church. The Catholic Church is the only qualified interpreter of Scripture.

358. The Bible tells us to test everything (1 Thess. 5:21). The Catholic Church demands that her adherents test nothing, accepting all on her authority, and without question.

Have you proved all things? Your own fantastic interpretations show that you have not. The text you quote has a meaning very different from that you attribute to it. It refers to conduct. The full text is, "test everything; hold fast what is good, abstain from every form of evil." In other words, "Reflect, examine your conscience before you act, and do the right thing." In the same way, St. Paul said that one who desires to receive the Holy

Eucharist must "examine himself, and so eat of the bread and drink of the cup. For any one who eats and drinks without discerning the body eats and drinks judgment upon himself" (1 Cor. 11:28-29). Your interpretation of Catholic requirements is just as fantastic. The Catholic Church does not demand that her adherents prove nothing. She wants them to examine the reasons for their Catholic Faith and prove the claims of their Church. We prove that she is the only possible Church historically, scripturally, and logically, and that she must be infallible. Then when she speaks in the name of Christ we reasonably accept her teachings. If I consult a doctor whom I know to be competent, I accept his decisions. I do not fight every inch of the way, disputing, arguing, and challenging his statements. So, once I know that the Catholic Church is divinely qualified to speak the truth in religious matters, I accept her decisions and definitions. Nothing could be more wise than that. In fact, it would be sheer folly to do otherwise.

359. You can no more interpret Scripture for me than you can eat my dinner for me.

It is true that I can no more make you assimilate mentally and spiritually the true doctrine contained in Scripture than I can make food nourish you when you yourself do not eat that food. But, as a qualified cook could prepare food for you better than you could prepare it for yourself, so I am able to put the truth of Scripture before you as you could never discover it for yourself. I at least have given years to the study of Scripture, both privately and under qualified professors, after a long training in cognate subjects. And I have the authentic decisions of the Catholic Church always at hand for constant reference. Would you say to a trained attorney, "You can no more interpret the law for me than eat my dinner for me"? Yet the interpretation of the revealed Law of God is more difficult than the interpretation of civil law. You must remember, too, that even though it is my duty to know the authoritative teachings of the Catholic Church, I am as subject to the authority of that Church as anyone else. I do not speak in my own name but in that of the Catholic Church; nor do I ask others to do that that I am not obliged to do myself. It is not really a question of your being taught by me. We must both be taught by the Catholic Church.

Chapter 9

Catholic Dogma

360. Christianity is a way of life, not a dogmatic statement of faith.

It is difficult to follow your line of thought. Do you imagine that the moment a man makes a statement of his Christian faith he must abandon a Christian way of life? Or that, if one attempts a Christian way of life, he is at once forbidden to make any statement of his Christian faith? Christianity is a religion revealed by God to teach us the full truth about our eternal and supernatural destiny, and to give us the means of attaining that destiny through Christ, who is the heart and soul of that religion. The effect of that religion, if we accept it, try to put its precepts into practice, and use its means of grace, is a spiritual and Christian way of life in the midst of our present circumstances and duties. And part of that way of life is our obligation to believe all that God has revealed because he has revealed it.

361. Why not preach charity instead of speaking always with self-satisfaction of your "only right dogmas"?

With so many conflicting churches in existence, it is a vital matter to find the truth. If the Catholic Church were self-satisfied, she would be content to have the truth herself and not bother about those without it. As for charity, it is better to exercise charity than talk about it, and there can be no greater charity than to point out the right road to those who have missed the track.

362. Truth is too big a thing for one religion to corner!

Reason should tell you that the God who made both the universe and man must know the truth about both. It should tell you that if God definitely tells man anything, the information must be sound. It would justify the fact that God has spoken, if you would but examine the credentials of the Catholic Church. And finally, it would show you that the Catholic Church is big enough to contain all the truth revealed by God on the subject of religion.

363. Dogma will not save a single soul.

Alone it will not. But since the Catholic Church is the true Church that Christ commands us to hear, the conscious and deliberate rejection of her dogma can forfeit salvation.

364. What is the value of a creed if it does not win the souls of men to Christ?

It would still have value, even if it did not do that, provided it correctly recorded the teaching of Christ. The truth would still have its value as the truth, even if men did not live up to it. Also, even if men are not living for Christ, it is better for them to have a correct creed than a wrong one. They at least would admit the truth of his teachings even though they did not fulfill his precepts. Surely that is better than rejecting both his teachings and his precepts. Again, the sinner who has a correct creed is in a better position when he does want to yield his soul to Christ than the sinner who has mistaken ideas concerning the nature and duties of Christ's religion.

365. By what process of reasoning do you hope to win men of clean lives and unshackled intelligence to your dogmas?

The process is this. Catholic dogmas, being the truth, set the mind of man free from human errors on the subject of religion. And I argue that most normally intelligent men wish to be free from error. Again I reason that men of clean lives are well fitted to appreciate the lofty moral standards of Catholicism. The only type of which I despair is the man whose intelligence is shackled by prejudice, or by inability to rise above the crude notions usually taught in the name of a so-called rationalism.

366. So Catholics must strangle their reason and swallow anything the Church teaches, however unlikely?

The strangling of reason is left to people who are ready to believe anything they hear about the Catholic Church. But the Church herself asks no man to strangle his reason, and says that it is a heresy to say that it ought to be strangled. Nor must

Catholics accept anything, however unlikely. If a thing seems unlikely, they should suspend their judgment until they secure evidence of its truth or falsity and then decide accordingly.

367. If you had to choose between faith and reason, which would you choose?

Such a choice will never confront a Catholic. Should there seem to be a conflict, he knows that he has either wrongly conceived a doctrine to be part of the Catholic Faith, or else he has wrongly thought the adverse proposition to be reasonable. He therefore reexamines the position, knowing that he will find a mistake in his interpretation of the faith or a fallacy in his reasoning. If I knew for certain that the Church had defined a given doctrine to be a dogma of faith, and my own ideas seemed at variance with the defined dogma, I would certainly choose to believe my own ideas mistaken rather than charge the Catholic Church with error. After all, Christ guaranteed the infallibility of the teaching Church, not of every individual man. And the history of human thought is as much a history of mistakes as it is a history of truth. Absolute confidence in one's own inability to reason wrongly is itself unreasonable, and against the facts of experience.

368. Through the ages your Church has stood in the way of freedom of thought, even apart from theological matters.

That cannot be accepted. Both in theological and in secular matters she has not only left men free to think but has urged them to do so. She does take precautions to prevent people from thinking wrongly, in religious matters particularly; but that is a true service to mankind. If at times she has been over-cautious, that was a fault on the right side. Scientists who complain of the restrictions of the Church have had to unsay far more things than those subject to the said restrictions.

369. Copernicus was attacked by the Church as a heretic because he said the Earth went round the sun.

Your history is at fault. Copernicus had often spoken of his theories on that subject and, far from being condemned as a heretic, was induced by clerical friends to put them into print. Only seventy-three years after his death was his book censured, and then merely because of the use Galileo made of it. But these individual cases, even were your interpretation of them correct, would not justify a general indictment of the Church.

370. Did not Tertullian say, "I believe because it is impossible"?

Yes. But the context shows that he used those words in the sense in which St. Paul spoke of Christ crucified as being unto the Gentiles foolishness (1 Cor. 1:23). He did not mean that he was prepared to believe things repugnant to principles of right reason. There are mysteries in the natural order, and still more there are and must be mysteries in the supernatural order. If God could do only those things that are possible to men, he would be no God at all. But things that are above reason are not necessarily against reason.

371. Yet has not the Church changed quite a lot of her dogmatic teaching in deference to modern thought?

She has never changed a dogma, nor has she changed in any essential Christian truth. She does change in many secondary ways according to the needs of the time, but this occurs chiefly in matters of discipline. She has never modified her methods and teachings in deference to modern thought, very little of which really exists in average society today concerning religion—certainly not as much as in the Middle Ages.

372. Has not the Catholic Church added dogma after dogma, of which the early Christians knew nothing?

The Church has never added a single teaching of dogmatic value that was not contained in the original teachings of the apostles. Where doubts have arisen, she has officially defined the right doctrine, not giving a new doctrine but clearly expressing the exact significance of the old doctrine. And that is exactly what a teaching Church is for. Meantime, the early Christians, by believing in the doctrines of Christ, believed these truths also at least implicitly, though they could quite well have been ignorant of the later terms used to describe them.

373. But there are many individual dogmas of the Church that my reason could never accept. Take, for example, your dogma of God.

Catholic dogma concerning the existence and nature of God is in perfect harmony with the conclusions of sane philosophy, which have already been discussed.

374. I am referring to the doctrine of the Trinity. You have no sufficient reason for believing in that contradictory doctrine.

No contradiction is involved in the doctrine of the Trinity. The reason why we believe it is because God says that it is true, using terms that express it as nearly as possible in human language. As God ought to know his own intimate nature, his describing it is the best of possible reasons for believing in it.

375. Explain fully to us the Trinity in the Christian sense of the word.

No man on Earth can explain fully the Trinity. The finite mind cannot fully comprehend an infinite being. Even did God condescend to explain the doctrine fully to you, you would lack the capacity necessary in order to comprehend it.

It is a revealed mystery to be accepted as true merely because God teaches it. However, we can explain the doctrine that Christians must believe. There are three divine personalities in one divine nature—the Father, the Son, and the Holy Spirit. These three Persons are equal in all things: equally God, equally eternal, powerful, etc. God is an infinitely perfect and purely spiritual Being, active in his knowledge and love. The knowledge God has of himself is a living personality called the Son. The idea of intellectual generation is not foreign to us, for we ourselves speak of our own thoughts as concepts and as the offspring of our intelligence. The mutual and reciprocal love between Father and Son is also a living personality—the Holy Spirit. There is no contradiction in this doctrine. We do not speak of one divine nature, yet three divine natures; nor of three divine persons, yet one divine person. We speak of one divine nature, yet of three divine Persons, nature, and personality being quite different aspects of our consideration. It is as if, when dealing with the Persons, we viewed numerical distinction, as in the addition of 1+1+1 into 3; yet when dealing with the nature in which all three Persons share, that fusion that results in unity by multiplication of the same three figures—1x1x1 equals 1. Yet whilst the absence of contradiction is clear, the full significance of the triune nature of God is beyond the limited capacity of the human mind. We know the fact by revelation and believe it implicitly because God has revealed it.

376. If Christ is the Son of God, there must have been a time when he did not exist, for no one can be as old as his father.

Christ is the name given to the Second Person of the Holy Trinity in his assumed human nature. As the Christ, therefore, he was not eternal but began in time. But before the Second Person appeared on Earth in this human form, he existed as the eternal Son of God, equal with the Father in all things. But in his divine nature, if he be a son, how can he be as old as his Father? I'm afraid it is impossible to express an eternal fact in terms of time. Time is successive duration. We speak of growing old as time goes by. But in eternity there is no succession of time, and there can be no such thing as age when we speak of God. Father, Son, and Holy Spirit always exist, not existed; and they exist not for a long time, but without time. What we call "now" is only the indivisible instant that is the last moment of the past and the first moment of the future simultaneously. Our time is based upon the coming and going of movement. But there is no such thing in God. Yet the Second Person of the Holy Trinity is truly a son. A son is a being or person who derives from his father the same human nature possessed by the father. In the one God, the Second Person shares through the First Person exactly the same divine nature. And from that point of view he is the Son. But he differs from earthly sons in that he does not receive a numerically distinct nature, nor does he exist subsequently to the Father. He eternally participates in the divine nature through the Father. The word *son* in human language is the nearest inadequate approximation we can find to express the truth by analogy. To say that it completely expressed the reality would be to fall into that anthropomorphism that you would be the first to ridicule. You cannot object to the treating of God as if he were merely a kind of glorified created human being, and then refuse to believe on the score that Catholic theology does not explain him in terms that would reduce him to the same level as ourselves.

377. What does the term Holy Ghost *mean?*

It means Holy Spirit. *Ghost* is Anglo-Saxon for *spirit*, "spiritus" in Latin meaning a breath. Thus the word *spirit* is associated with human breathing as a kind of intangible impulse. Christ used the term to bring home to us that the Third Person of the Holy Trinity is the impulse of love invisible and intangible between Father and Son. Since love tends to union, and union with and in God is holiness, the Third Person is termed the Holy Spirit.

378. You teach that the Holy Spirit proceeds from the Son yet is responsible for the birth of that Son.

The eternal Son of God, in becoming man, took a human nature from the Virgin Mary. Thus was born a being who was both God and man. As God, this Second Person of the Holy Trinity always existed, and from him in eternity the Holy Spirit always proceeds, as from the Father also. In this sense the Holy Spirit does not give being to the Son. But the human nature, which began in time, was due to the operation of the Holy Spirit and was assumed by the Son. There is no inconsistency in this doctrine.

379. Are the names Father, Son, *and* Holy Spirit *merely different titles of the one Being?*

They are not merely three different titles of the one Being as if they were names only and in no sense realities. They are three relative personal aspects of one absolute and substantial Being. One and the same absolute Being can have relative aspects distinct from one another. In God, of course, we meet with what should not be an unexpected mystery. The three relative aspects of the one divine nature are personal. Our experience of finite and created man is of one nature and one person. But our knowledge of finite and created man cannot give us an adequate knowledge of the infinite Creator unless we are prepared to work on a very crude and anthropomorphic basis. The fact that in the one absolute God there are three relative Personalities, distinct in virtue of their relationship to each other yet identically possessing the divine nature, is known to us by revelation alone. And we know the fact without being able to comprehend it fully, not because of any defect in God, but because of the defect in our finite selves.

380. I certainly do not understand the mystery of the Trinity.

Centuries ago St. Augustine replied to a similar complaint with the words, "If you do understand, then that is what God is not." He meant, of course, that no human being can fully comprehend God. We cannot exclude mystery when speaking of God, for if he came within the limits of our finite intelligence he would be finite and not God at all. At the same time, we can understand on our own level what the doctrine of the Trinity means. The idea of personality is not foreign to us, nor is the idea of a given nature. If the Trinity is a mystery, it is because both the nature and the Persons in God transcend all our notions of these things, our ideas giving but a faint and most inadequate reflection of the truth. It is also a mystery because our experience is limited to a single nature with a single personality. A single divine nature with a threefold Personality is not on the same plane as any of our ordinary experiences and is known by revelation alone; and even then only insofar as human words can express the transcendent truth. But the terms are not meaningless, and we do find a profound significance in the doctrine.

381. Do you not teach that God's creative activities extended also to the production of angelic beings?

Yes. Scripture often speaks of the angels. Christ himself taught their existence. Human experience of their influence leaves no doubt on the subject. And it is reasonable that God should have completed the hierarchy of created beings by introducing purely spiritual creatures in addition to merely material and semi-material beings. Not all evidence depends upon sense experience. I have never seen an angel. I am not now in a normal condition to see one and do not expect to do so until I reach heaven. I still belong to the material world. But I believe the word of God, which should know whether or not angels exist.

382. I do not believe that any being without body, form, or shape can exist.

In that case, of course, you are purely a materialist. Not only that. You are an atheist, for such an assertion denies the very existence of God. God is a pure spirit and can certainly create beings of a purely spiritual nature.

383. Our Protestant clergyman admits that angels are not personal beings but says that they are impersonal messages or good influences from God.

That is but a concession to an unbelieving rationalism. And it is quite against the word of God. Scripture insists that they are personal beings. Christ said, "Their angels always behold the face of my Father who is in heaven" (Matt 18:10). Messages and influences are not permanent and don't see. St. Peter says, "God did not spare the angels when they sinned" (2 Pet. 2:4). Impersonal influences do not sin.

384. What form have these angels?

We cannot speak of the form or shape of purely spiritual beings. God has no form or shape. Shape supposes dimensional arrangement, and dimensions suppose quantity of matter. Angels can exert spiritual force, and even will the action of natural physical forces with God's permission. If at times they have appeared to men in bodily forms, they have but assumed appearances not proper to them, and most probably formed from the material atmospheric elements in order to manifest their presence in a way in keeping with man's lower level.

385. Then they are nothing like your winged statues?

No. God told the Jews to carve angels, with wings spread, to represent to men those swift spiritual beings to whom distance is as nothing (Exod. 25:18). But God did not say that they were exact representations of angels.

386. Will you explain a little more clearly what angels are?

Angels are purely spiritual beings. A brick is a purely material being. Man, with body and soul, is partly material and partly spiritual. God has no material body and is purely spiritual. To complete the external manifestations of his perfections, he created beings of a purely spiritual nature—angels. The angels, then, are definite beings who have the qualities belonging to our souls but not those of our bodies. Now, our souls have two chief faculties—intelligence and will, and these are possessed by angels. But since they are purely spiritual they cannot be seen by our eyes any more than can God himself.

387. Is the devil a supernatural being?

No. He is a natural angelic being, in a state deprived of supernatural grace.

388. Satan is a mythical being.

He is quite content to seem a mythical being. He has no desire to be detected in his operations and is not likely to inform you that evil suggestions are from him.

389. Who is Satan?

The word *Satan* in Hebrew means one who is adverse, and it can refer to any adversary. In that sense Christ said on one occasion to Peter, "Get behind me, Satan! You are a hindrance to me" (Matt. 16:23). Satan therefore does not always refer to the devil. But since the devil, once Lucifer or the angel of light, is the greatest of all enemies to God and mankind, the word *Satan* has been applied in a special way to him. Of all adversaries, he is *the* adversary.

390. Do you make him also a person rather than an influence?

God endowed him with an imperishable personality. He is a person who influences. A person is an intellectual being who is master of his own freely chosen activities. It does not matter whether he is of a spiritual nature, as God or the angels, or of a semi-spiritual nature, as man. The devil has intelligence and free will. He can exert a spiritual influence suggestive of evil. Many people say that they do not believe in the devil. That is quite in keeping with his wishes. But Christ definitely warns us against the evil influence of Satan.

391. Is the devil responsible for all sin?

Indirectly, yes, for he caused the fall of our first parents. Directly, no. Scripture tells us that the three great enemies of man's soul are the world, the flesh, and the devil. Men sin for mere worldly prosperity, or induced by sensual passion. At times, however, Satan directly tempts them. But Satan can do no more than suggest evil to our will; he cannot compel our assent. Man can always refuse consent to evil by the help of God's grace. "God is faithful, and he will not let you be tempted beyond your strength" (1 Cor. 10:13).

392. Since the devil has some success in persuading men to choose evil, why doesn't God do away with him to prevent further harm?

First, God will not do away with the devil, because the devil is an essentially spiritual being whose nature is immortal of its very nature. And God does not create a being endowed with immortality only to destroy it. Secondly, God knows that human souls, with the help of his grace, can themselves prevent the devil from doing them any moral harm by refusing consent to his evil suggestions. Thirdly, since there is no particular merit in being good if never tempted to do evil, God knows that the temptations of the devil are the occasion at least in which men have the chance to practice and to grow in virtue. Fourthly, since all previous generations of men have had to endure the sedulous attentions of the devil, there is no particular reason why the present and future generations should be exempt. We must battle through the same trials as others, conscious that with God's help we can come through victoriously, as so many others whose example is offered for our encouragement.

393. Are there many devils?

Yes. St. John tells us that Satan was cast out of heaven and that his angels were thrown down with him (Rev. 12:9). The devils besought Christ "If you cast us out" (Matt. 8:31), and said that they were legion (Mark 5:9).

394. Are we to suppose an eternal devil as well as an eternal God? Or did God create the devil?

We cannot suppose an eternal uncreated devil. Yet God did not create the devil as a devil. In other words, God did not create any evil spiritual being as evil. He created all things other than himself, including angels. The angels as created by God were beings of a spiritual nature, endowed with intelligence and free will; and as the terminus of God's creative action they were entirely good. But some angels misused their freedom of will, and rendered themselves evil by their opposition to the God who is goodness itself. Evil is opposed to good. He who is opposed to God is opposed to the good and renders himself therefore evil. But God is not the cause of such evil. His purpose in giving freedom of will was in order that the angels might have the great dignity of offering him not a compulsory love but a love of free choice. And he forbade that misuse of the gift of freedom that rejects the infinite goodness of its source. God could not forbid sin yet be the cause of it. St. Peter's words that God spared not the angels who sinned show that some angels fell from the good state in which they previously existed into a sinful state; that they were responsible for their own evil choice; that God had that dominion over them that could belong only to their Creator; and that God does punish deliberately chosen and unrepented wickedness.

395. Isn't Christianity rather narrow-minded, to make our Earth the center of existence and forget the millions of spheres like our own upon which life most probably exists?

Whatever may be said of possibility, there is no probability that life exists upon millions of other spheres. Probability demands at least some shred of evidence, and there is no such evidence in existence. It is possible that life exists on other spheres; but Christianity has never denied that. It is illogical to attribute to Christianity a teaching you think narrow-minded and then to transfer your epithet to Christianity, whether it contains that teaching or not.

396. If life existed on another planet, would that affect the Christian religion?

Not in the least.

397. Would Christ have redeemed such people on other worlds by his death on Calvary?

To that I can but give a conditional reply. If there are living beings on other planets, and if they are endowed with free will, and if they have sinned against the moral law of God, and if God did attach their salvation to the death of Christ on the cross, then Christ died for their salvation also. But who could verify all those "ifs"? Meantime, God has revealed to us on this Earth all that we need to know for our own needs; and such speculations concerning other possibilities are of little practical importance. The lack of such knowledge is no hindrance to our own salvation and will not excuse us if we fail to attain it.

398. What do you mean by original sin?

Actual sin is a deliberate, personal transgression of God's law. But original sin, which is inherited, does not mean that I have personally and maliciously transgressed. We must notice the difference between nature and grace. Nature is our being and all that our condition demands as rational animals. Grace means a gift or quality over and above all that our nature legitimately demands. Now, nature is fitted to know God only by deduction from created things. Yet over and above this, God's sheer goodness chose to give us what is in no way due to us, the supernatural destiny to see him face to face in heaven, and the grace to attain this vision. He promised this to Adam and, provided

Adam were faithful, to all his children. And in this supernatural matter he regarded Adam as father of the human family. Adam failed. He and his children were deprived of this supernatural destiny and of the gift of sanctifying grace. This deprivation of grace is called original sin.

399. Does God create every soul now in a state of sin?

No. God's creative activity terminates in good only. But the soul cannot normally be infused into a child of Adam without its contracting the privation of the original gratuitous gifts it was destined to receive had Adam not fallen. I say normally because God did anticipate the merits of Christ in one case, preventing the soul of the Virgin Mary from contracting original sin. Do not imagine, however, that God creates a separated soul and then infuses it. By simultaneous action the soul is created and blended with the body, thus completing a nature in a state of sin. The stain of original sin, also, differs from the stain of personal sin, which is *committed*, not *contracted*. Original sin supposes a lack of grace that would have been present, but it does not suppose a personal and malicious disposition.

400. What proof have you that original sin is inherited?

The very best—the word of the God who created us. In Psalms 51:5, we read David's testimony, "In sin did my mother conceive me." He is speaking, not of his own personal sins, nor of any actual sin of his father or mother. He is speaking of original sin derived from Adam and the first fall, tracing back to the very first beginning of human life a sin handed on with human nature from parent to child. In John 3:6, Christ demands that a man be born again of water and the Holy Spirit in baptism. A birth means a life. Rebirth means the acquiring of some new principle of life not secured by our natural birth. And baptism gives the principle of supernatural life without which we were born into this world, and the lack of which constitutes the very essence of original sin. St. Paul tells us clearly, "Sin came into the world through one man and death through sin, and so death spread to all men because all men sinned" (Rom. 5:12). Experience confirms this revealed doctrine. Our very proneness to evil argues to a privation of original rectitude. As Chesterton has well remarked, men may deny original sin, but almost the only thing they know about original innocence is that they haven't got it.

401. To brand me with sin is as unjust as hanging me for a murder I did not commit.

Original sin does not brand you with the positive guilt of actual and personal malice. It is a privation of a grace and of a destiny to which no human being has a natural right. God offered that destiny to Adam and to all his children, regarding Adam as head of the human family. Were you a married man with a family, I could certainly agree to grant to you and to each of your children a substantial recompense, provided you fulfilled certain conditions specified by me. If you failed to comply with my conditions, I could certainly cancel that recompense. Nor could your children justly complain later that I had robbed them of anything due to them. Original sin is the deprivation of a right to a happiness that was never due to us. The privation of grace is essentially the privation of something gratuitous.

402. I can understand inheriting the effects of the first sin, but why the sin itself? If my father is a thief, I share in his disgrace, but my soul is not stained by his sins.

Your father was not constituted the head of the whole human race and is but the intermediate transmitter of an individual human nature. If we inherited original sin as something of positive personal malice, it would be unjust. But we do not. Death in a state of positive and serious personal malice merits hell. But if a child dies with no personal sin, but only original sin, whilst it can never attain to the very vision of God, and thus suffers the privation of a gratuitous destiny, it will never endure the positive suffering of the lost in hell. It will be rendered happy according to its natural capacity.

403. In the Apostle's Creed Christians profess belief "in the forgiveness of sins."

Sin is undoubtedly a fact in this world; and if the true religion be for men, it cannot overlook that fact. Religion cannot abandon the sinner to himself. It is there to do something for him, and chiefly to destroy sin. The word *sin* is from the Latin word *sons* meaning "guilty"; and he who is guilty of moral evil is a sinner. Such moral evil is an offense against God.

404. Why did God give men their freedom when he knew beforehand that so many would misuse it and be lost for eternity?

Because he knew that men need not sin and that his knowledge of what would eventuate did not cause them to sin. Also, included in his knowledge of the fall of man was his knowledge of the Incarnation of his own Son by whose redemptive merits every single sinner from the time of Adam would have a true opportunity of salvation from eternal loss. Finally, God knew that, however many people do lose their souls, viewing creation as a whole and relatively to human beings, the sum total of good will far outweigh the sum total of evil. It is a mistake to concentrate on the thought of individuals who are lost. God had not to choose between creating only those who are lost, and not creating at all. He had to choose between not creating, and creating a whole human race, not one of whom need go to hell, and of which, if some do lose their souls, multitudes do not. Why should those who save their souls be deprived of eternal happiness because others, who need not do so, choose to sin and to die without repenting?

405. No man can hurt God, and I am sure that people who do wrong have no thought of offending God.

Inability to do actual harm to God personally does not mean innocence and irresponsibility. As a matter of fact, one whom we cannot hurt because of his greatness and majesty deserves the greater reverence. And one does offend God in his designs by opposing his will of perfection and order. Moral evil introduces discord and abominations into the harmony of God's work. You say that evildoers do not intend this and have no thought of offending God. It may be that sinners rarely think of this aspect. Some do. But the majority rather seek to have whatever they desire and merely ignore God's will. They would prefer to be able to sin without offending God. But that is not the wish to avoid evil. It is merely to wish that evil were good. That, however, cannot be; and they deliberately choose evil, despite God's prohibition.

406. Would you take literally Christ's words, "If your right eye causes you to sin, pluck it out and throw it away; it is better that you lose one of your members than that your whole body be thrown into hell"?

Those words are certainly not meant to be taken literally, for such mutilation of self would be sinful, and one can avoid sin without having to do that. Christ was driving home the lesson that sin as such, and above all grave sin, is the greatest of all evils. Speaking to the Jews he used a mode of speech with which they were quite familiar. He meant: "The salvation of your soul is your chief work." He chose a metaphor from surgery which, to save the body, has at times to amputate a limb or remove an organ—in those days a most painful business. And he meant, "Be ready to endure any suffering or trial rather than sin. Even had you to pluck out your eye or cut off your limbs—a thing which will never be necessary—deliberate sin would still be the worse alternative."

407. I heard a Catholic speak of two kinds of sin—mortal and venial. I couldn't believe my ears.

There certainly are two kinds of sin: some of a very grave character called mortal sin, others of a less grave character called venial. Mortal sins rob the soul of grace and forfeit one's union and friendship with God. The man who deliberately disobeys the known law of God in grave and serious matters sets himself up against God, turns away from him, and renounces his friendship. By doing so he turns his back on his eternal destiny in favor of a futile and transitory pleasure or advantage. Venial sins do not have such a far-reaching effect, but they do render one less pleasing in God's sight. The man who respects God's will in serious matters, but who offends in smaller matters, does not forfeit God's friendship altogether; and, therefore, by retaining his friendship, he maintains the true direction of his life toward God. But he does stray from the direct path of the good; and for that he will need forgiveness and have to undergo proportionate purification of soul.

408. Evil cannot be a sin more or less; it is either a sin or it is not.

Venial sin is a sin—not "more or less" a sin. But there can be sins of more or less gravity. Sin is a crime insofar as it is a violation of God's laws. Now God is not less just than men. And crimes against human laws are of more or less gravity. Thus, we have capital crimes and penal crimes. Some offenses against civil law are so venial that the highest penalty for them is a small fine. The judge may not inflict more. Murder, however, is in a different category altogether. It is a capital or mortal sin against the law, and can merit deprivation of life itself. Your own sense of justice will tell you that these distinctions between crimes against state laws are justified. And the same principle must apply to crimes against God's laws. Mortal sin puts one beyond the pale of God's friendship; venial sin does not do so, but it carries with it its just penalties.

409. The Bible certainly gives no grounds for saying that there are two kinds of sins.

That is not so. Keep in mind that mortal sin cuts one off from God's grace and friendship, whilst venial sin does not, even though it renders the soul less pleasing in God's sight. Now, the book of Sirach, in warning us against sin, says, "He who despises small things will fail little by little" (Sir. 19:1). That is, succeeding sins tend to become greater as the conscience is deadened. Proverbs 24:16 tells us that even the just man falls often. In other words, whilst remaining just or justified by grace, he still has his small sins. Christ said that it would be more tolerable for Tyre and Sidon in the day of judgment than for Bethsaida, clearly indicating degrees in guilt (Matt. 11:21). So, too, in John 19:11, Christ said to Pilate, "He who delivered me to you has the greater sin." We cannot say that "sin is sin" and that there are no different kinds of gravity.

410. The principle is at fault. All theft is sin, and hideous in God's sight. One sin is as much a sin as another.

No one suggests that lesser sins are not sins; nor that any sin is pleasing to God. All sin is hateful to him. But some sins are more hateful than others. You say that the principle behind this distinction is at fault. But take the principle that we owe obedience to the laws of the state. One who violates a traffic law violates the principle of obedience to law. So does the gangster who murders a fellow citizen. Will you say that one is just as much a violation of the law as the other, and hang them both? Or if we take simply theft, can you see no difference between the child who steals a cake from the cupboard and the cold-blooded miser who robs a widow of her life savings?

411. If there are two kinds of sins, how do you distinguish one kind from another?

By the very nature of the thing forbidden; by the necessity of particular virtues to which particular vices are opposed; and also by the extent of damage done to others where justice is concerned. For example, according to the nature of the thing forbidden, some sins are always mortal, as direct hatred of God, deliberate blasphemy, murder, adultery, etc. When measured by the necessity of virtue, a deliberate denial of one's faith is a mortal sin because it implicitly denies God. Sins against justice are measured by the seriousness of the injury done to others. The more grave the injury the graver the sin. In addition to these factors, circumstances must be taken into account, as the degree of knowledge possessed by the person offending; the degree of advertence to the law before breaking it; the extent of really malicious will entering into the evil conduct.

412. Who was Christ?

Christ was the Second Person of the Holy Trinity, existing in the human nature that was born of the Virgin Mary, yet retaining ever his divine nature. He is, therefore, God and man at one and the same time. As man he could die for his fellow human beings; as God he was able to expiate the insult offered to the divine Majesty and thus restore to men the possibility of eternal happiness.

413. Have not older religions spoken of gods with sons on Earth?

Some of them have made uncertain and vague claims, but none has made any precise claim in the full sense in which Christianity declares Christ to have been the Son of God. Nor is there a shred of evidence to show the reality of their claims, vague as they are.

414. I have discovered twenty-seven virgin-born saviors in my studies of mythology.

You would find it very difficult to name them. However, granting that you have read of some such claims, a little further study would show you that a critical and comparative examination such as Christian doctrine has had to undergo leaves these mythological claims devoid of reality, whilst the Christian fact emerges unscathed.

415. You will not admit that Christians thought it fashionable to have a virgin-born Savior, so invented or borrowed one in desperation?

Such an admission would do violence to both reason and history. The invention theory supposes that the writers of the Gospels were liars, a theory abandoned by all the critics of Christianity worthwhile. The borrowing theory involves the old *post hoc ergo propter hoc* fallacy. That one thing is prior to another does not prove that it is the cause of that other. And nowhere in heathenism can you find any real parallel with the Christian doctrine. Pagan mythologies are characterized chiefly by the complete absence of an historical element. The great German critic Harnack pointed out that the one thing fatal to all mythological references or theories is the intense repugnance felt by the early Christians for everything connected with heathen idolatry. A profound critic, he writes, "Early Christians strictly refrained from everything polytheistic and heathen, and the unreasonable method of collecting from mythologies of all peoples parallels for original Christian traditions is valueless."

416. Whence came the ancient ideas of mothers and savior-sons reconciling us with God?

A belief in a God, a sense of sin, and imagination building upon ordinary human ideas would be enough to give rise to a mythology on the subject. Yet we can even admit lingering vestiges of the knowledge of our creation by God, and of God's primitive promise to put enmities between the woman and Satan. But no mythology has produced anything like the Christian doctrine, and it is certain that adversaries have dishonestly accredited virgin births to ancient mythologies in their efforts to discredit Christianity.

417. Was not the Babylonian Astarte selected as the goddess prototype of Mary?

No. Astarte was a mythical nonhistorical person; Mary was historical. The legends concerning Astarte make her a goddess associated with all that is licentious and immoral. The historical Mary has never been regarded as a goddess and was the purest woman who ever set foot on this Earth.

418. I believe that the early Christians imported their notions of Mary and her miraculous son, Jesus, from the Egyptian Isis, virgin mother of Horus.

Even according to the primitive Egyptian legends, Isis was not a virgin mother in any sense of the word. Your theory has been exploded by scholar after scholar. As a parallel it is altogether deficient, and your theory of connection is pure guess work, against all the facts. You might just as well point to the story of any woman who ever had a child in the whole of ancient literature and cry in triumph that the Christian doctrine must have been drawn from that source. Many people are prepared to put implicit faith in any guesses that militate against Christianity, yet they ignore the most obvious facts in its favor. They keep demanding evidence, yet do not really want it and will not accept it when it is offered to them.

419. Are there not great similarities between the life of Buddha and the story of Christ?

No. Buddhism knows nothing of God in the Christian sense of the word. It is definitely pantheistic. It knows nothing of the Holy Spirit. The very story of Buddha is not the story of a birth from a virgin. And in any case, it is certain that Buddhism was not known by the early Christians, and the Gospel writers never heard of its traditions. Nor, had they heard of them, could we conceive of their appropriating or using them.

420. Is there any fundamental difference between Jesus and Socrates, Plato, Aristotle, and other great thinkers?

There are many and vast differences. Socrates and others taught the uncertain philosophical conclusions of their own limited and finite minds; Jesus taught infallible and divine truth. The fruit of the teaching of the philosophers is a merely temporal proficiency in an imperfect human knowledge and conjecture; the fruit of the doctrines of Christ is eternal happiness. In themselves the philosophers were men; but Jesus was God.

421. What proof is there that Christ was God?

His perfect fulfillment of the Messianic prophecies of the Old Testament; his personal character; his teaching; his miracles, and chiefly his Resurrection; his work in establishing a Church that has outlived empires and human institutions against tremendous opposition; the perpetual vitality of his sway over human hearts.

422. Did Christ ever say that he was God?

Yes. He declared his divinity when he said, "I and the Father are one" (John 10:30). The Jews knew it and said, "We stone you for no good work but for blasphemy; because you, being a man, make yourself God." Again, Christ accepted the supreme homage implied by the words of Thomas, "My Lord and my God!" (John 20:28). He could not have let such an expression go without correction had he not been God. We know that if any ordinary man claimed to be God, he would either be insane or untruthful. But Christ was not insane. He was ever a model of self-control, and the wisest teacher and legislator the world has seen. Nor was he a liar. His moral character forbids the possibility of a lie in so grave a matter. Christ really lived. He was not insane. He was not a liar. He claimed to be God. He accepted the adoration due to God. He is God.

423. Christ claimed not to be God but to be the Son of God.

In the case of Christ, the one does not exclude the other. St. John admits personal distinction when he says, "The Word was with God," yet asserts identity in the divine nature when he adds, "And the Word was God" (John 1:1). Christ showed the coequality of the three divine Persons in the one single divine nature when he ordered the apostles to baptize in the one name of the Father, Son, and Holy Spirit (Matt. 28:19). And he proclaimed his own identity in the divine nature with the Father by his words to Philip, who had requested, "Lord, show us the Father." Christ replied, "Have I been with you so long, and yet you do not know me, Philip? He who has seen me has seen the Father" (John 14:9).

424. Why did Christ so often call himself the Son of Man, and so rarely the Son of God? You and I are both sons of men, and also God's sons.

We are not God's sons as Christ was God's Son, for he declared himself to be the only-begotten Son, which excludes other "begotten" sons. He was the only eternal Son of God by generation. We are children of God by creation in time. But now, why did the eternal Son of God, having become man by assuming to himself the human nature born of the Virgin Mary, so frequently refer to himself as the "Son of Man" rather than as the "Son of God"? He did so because the title "Son of Man" had a special Messianic significance for the Jews. Daniel had predicted that a son of man would come with the clouds of heaven; that he would have power and glory; that all peoples and tribes and tongues would serve him; that his power would be everlasting, and his kingdom never be destroyed (Dan. 7:13-14). The Jews had first to accept Christ as the Messiah, and then his Messianic teaching of the new revelation of God. He, therefore, constantly refers to himself in the terms of Daniel's Messianic appellation. The Jews knew that it signified much more than a merely human nature. So, in his trial, when the high priest said to him, "Are you the Christ, the Son of the Blessed?" Jesus said, "I am. And you will see the Son of Man sitting at the right hand of Power, and coming with the clouds of heaven." Then the high priest cried, "Why do we still need witnesses? You have heard his blasphemy" (Mark 14:61-64). Those words are intelligible only provided Christ meant by the expression "Son of Man" that he was much more than "merely a man." Christ, together with his humanity, possessed the same divine nature as his Father, and was God in the strictest sense of the word.

425. Might not Christ have been mistaken?

No sane man could so delude himself. Such an hallucination, being not temporary but permanent, would suppose in him a pathological state of insane enthusiasm. But Christ's wisdom and balance of mind absolutely excludes this. His wisdom at the age of twelve astonished the doctors of the Law. The people were lost in admiration of his doctrine, saying, "No man ever spoke like this man!" His replies to his enemies showed the utmost prudence and genius. His tranquility under provocation and suffering does not argue to madness. Add to all this the authority of the life he lived. Very few philosophers fulfill all their own advice as did Christ. No, there is no possibility that Christ was deluded.

426. In Matthew 23:9-10, he says, "Call no man your father on earth, for you have one Father, who is in heaven. Neither be called masters, for you have one master, the Christ."

That does not prove that Christ is not God. In the first part of this text he is teaching his listeners that no earthly parental authority can supplant the authority of God. In reference to himself, however, he did not hesitate to say, "I and the Father are one." And even whilst saying that God alone is the supreme

Father and Master, he puts himself on the same level as God by saying, "You have one master, Christ." If Christ were not God, he should have said, "One is your Master—God."

427. In Matthew 24:36, he says, "But of that day and hour no one knows, not even the angels of heaven, nor the Son, but the Father only."

Christ was there speaking in virtue of his assumed human nature. The knowledge was proper to him as God, but not proper to him as man. He did not know God's moment in virtue of the human nature in which he had come to teach mankind, and he merely brought out the fact that this particular piece of information was not part of the message he had to reveal to men. Briefly, it was but a way of saying, "That is God's secret." The text in no way disproves the identity of our Lord's divine nature with that of the Father.

428. Christ did say, "Why do you call me good? No one is good but God alone."

Christ said much else also. Nor do these words imply that Christ is not God. He would not contradict himself. He knew, however, that those around him saw only his human nature or created humanity, and that they had not yet attained the faith to see beyond merely human appearances to his divinity. And he once more tried to lift their thoughts to God as the Source of all created goodness. It was a warning that we must not stop at any created goodness that is but a reflection of the infinite goodness of God and meant to lead us to him. On another occasion, when Philip said to him, "Lord, show us the Father," Christ rebuked him also for not rising above thoughts of his merely human characteristics, and said, "He who has seen me has seen the Father. ... Do you not believe that I am in the Father and the Father is in me?" (John 14:8-10).

429. You cannot deny his words, "The Father is greater than I."

I do not wish to do so. Christ was at once God and man. In his created human nature he had deliberately subjected himself to

God's will. But since in him there was but the one personality, he had to use the personal pronoun "I," whether referring to his divinity or to his humanity. If he referred to his divinity he was equal to the Father. As regards his humanity, he was less than the Father. All such difficulties are solved by a correct notion of Christ as God made man, yet made man in such a way that he never ceased to be God. Had he ceased to be God, all the real value of his life and death for us would have been lost

430. If a man really did the good works you ascribe to Christ, he would be popular. Yet the Jews crucified him.

Christ was not unpopular with all. Many believed in him and followed him. But no man would be popular even today with all if, after such evidence of power, he turned round and lashed the vices of men, divorce, birth control, impurity, drunkenness, dishonesty, irreligion, and blasphemy. Men will take all the benefits they can get, and the one who will offer benefits only will be popular. But if the same man starts to probe the conscience of the moderns, and to interfere with their private vices and self-indulgences, his popularity will soon go. Christ not only conferred physical benefits; he demanded morality and self-denial. Egotism rebelled and crucified him at the instigation of the Jewish leaders.

431. When Christ said, "I and the Father are one," he meant no more than in purpose and desire.

The unity prevailing between himself and his Father, of which Christ spoke, was more than a merely moral union of purpose and desire. It was a unity in one and the same divine nature. It was on the occasion of these words that the Jews declared themselves determined to stone him because, as they said, "You, being a man, make yourself God." They knew quite well that Jesus was claiming much more than a merely moral union with God by purpose and desire. Had Christ merely intended that, they would not have accused him of blasphemy; nor would they have wanted to stone him to death.

432. Later on Christ prayed that his disciples would be one with himself as he and his Father were one. Were his disciples one with him in any other sense than by accord?

Yes. They were one with him by the reality called grace, which incorporated them all in one and the same Christ by a physical even though spiritual union: he the vine, they the branches. At the same time, in the words you quote, Christ was stressing the necessity of complete unity, not the nature of that unity, which necessarily differs in God from that possible to man. Christ prayed that his disciples would be one in the way possible to them, as he and his Father were one in the way proper to God.

433. Does it matter whether Christ was God, or merely the divine Son of God?

What do you mean by the distinction you make? If I were to say, "So-and-so is not a man, but merely the human son of a man," I am sure you would ask me to explain myself more clearly. A son is one who is generated in the same nature as his father. A human father has a son possessing human nature also. And if Christ is the divine Son of God, he possesses the divine nature also, and is God. The only alternative is that he is not the divine Son of God but merely a human creature made by God on the same level with other human beings.

It is necessary to accept the deity of the person of Christ without any half measures. Jesus is God in virtue of his divine nature possessed in union with and equally with the Father and the Holy Spirit. The expression "divine Sonship" can be ambiguous because both words have been employed by men with various grades of meaning. People speak of a "divine poet," or of a "divinely beautiful character." A Protestant friend once told me that he believed in the divinity of Christ but not that he is God. Now, when we Catholics use the word *divine* of Christ, we mean absolutely that he is God. Again, the word "Sonship" can be ambiguous. We sometimes speak of our being the children of God by creation. At other times we may speak of sonship by adoption as opposed to actual generation. Or one may simply mean sonship by a mutual paternal and filial affection. But none of these senses means what we intend by the "divine Sonship" of Jesus. We mean by that expression that the person of Jesus is the Second Person of the Holy Trinity, eternally generated by the Father in one and the same divine nature, equal with the Father and the Holy Spirit in all things, infinitely perfect, and as truly God as the Father himself. Jesus is not only the Son of God. He is God the Son.

434. Did Christ make a mistake when he said that "this generation" shall not pass till the end of the world?

No. In that chapter of Matthew (24) he blends prophecies concerning both the destruction of Jerusalem and the end of the world. Many who were then living witnessed the destruction of Jerusalem. And even as regards the end of the world, the Christian generation will not pass away until it comes. Many superficial readers confuse the two prophecies, forgetting that Christ had no intention of giving exact information concerning the final end of all things. "But of that day and hour no one knows, not even the angels of heaven, nor the Son, but the Father only" (Matt. 24:36). In reference to this matter, there are three great generations to be considered: that of the unwritten law from Adam to Moses; that of the written law and the prophets, from Moses to Christ; and that of the Christian dispensation. God is not going to give any further revelation to man. All previous prophecies have been fulfilled in Christ, and Christ has declared that his revelation shall last till the end of time. This Christian generation shall not pass away till Christ comes, and when he does come it will be the end of the Christian era. We cannot complain that a thing has not happened before the time for it to happen has arrived.

435. Where was Christ's knowledge of future glory when he prayed to be freed from the necessity of dying?

You must remember that there were in Christ two natures, one human, the other divine. Christ suffered in his human nature, and experienced a natural human shrinking from all that awaited him. To that natural apprehension he gave expression conditionally, saying,

"If it be possible, let this chalice pass from me." But with his divine knowledge he knew God's absolute will of both his passion and subsequent glorification, for he added, not conditionally but absolutely, "Not as I will, but as you will." Long before this he had predicted that he would be put to death and that he would rise again from the dead. But despite his knowledge of the glorious sequel, his present sufferings were sufferings all the same. Knowledge of subsequent relief does not necessarily destroy the dread of a painful operation.

436. Christ found out his mistake on the cross and knew that it was all in vain when he cried, "My God, my God, why have you forsaken me?"

Christ knew that his death was not all in vain. He died to give those who want it the means to save their souls. As those who want to save their souls have the means provided by the merit of Christ's death, his sacrifice was a perfect success, accomplishing all that it was intended to accomplish. It was certainly never meant to save men even against their wills. The cry of Christ on the cross, therefore, in no way expressed a conviction that all was in vain, but indicated a desolation of soul and a mental suffering in the Passion that no other external expression could manifest more suitably. The words were uttered for our sake, and bespoke a suffering that was part of the price demanded of one enduring the penalty due to our sins.

437. Why should the innocent be condemned to death for the guilty?

It was not so much the condemnation of the innocent as the free offering of the Son of God in his human nature for the salvation of his sinful yet brother human beings. Man, bought by so great a price, is taught his true dignity in the eyes of God, learns how evil sin really is, and is moved to love one who has proved his love in so convincing a way.

438. Can one suffer vicariously for another in the sense Catholic dogma teaches?

That question is answered by the fact that Christ did suffer for us and make vicarious atonement for our sins. Christ declared that he was the Good Shepherd who would give his life for his sheep. Again, of himself he said, the Son of Man came "to give his life as a ransom for many" (Mark 10:45). At the Last Supper he said, "This is my blood of the covenant, which is poured out for many for the forgiveness of sins" (Matt. 26:28). And such was the doctrine preached by the apostles. St. Peter wrote, "You know that you were ransomed ... not with perishable things such as silver or gold, but with the precious blood of Christ" (1 Pet. 1:18–19). St. Paul wrote to the Romans, "We were reconciled to God by the death of his Son" (Rom. 5:10); to the Galatians, "I live by faith in the Son of God, who loved me and gave himself for me" (Gal. 2:20).

439. Would Christianity be anything shorn of the Crucifixion?

Absolutely speaking, there could have been a Christianity without a Crucifixion. God could have condoned the sin of mankind, and, without demanding just expiation, he could have sent his Son in human form to teach another type of Christian doctrine. But that is all in the realm of possibilities. We are concerned with facts, and as facts stand, Christianity could not be shorn of the Crucifixion. Nor could the Jewish religion. All sacrifices from Adam to Christ were figures of the Crucifixion. Abraham's willingness to offer Isaac predicted God's willingness to offer his Son, even as the paschal lamb foreshadowed Christ as the true Lamb of God who would die on the cross. Any value in the Old Testament sacrifices was derived by anticipation from the cross. God willed that the scales of justice should be balanced, and for that a man had to die for the sin of man. Yet since the infinite majesty of God had been offended, the human being chosen to expiate this infinite offense must be of infinite dignity. God the Son, therefore, became man, remaining true God, and in his human form was offered on Calvary.

440. If Christ were not God but merely a man dying for his convictions, then there was something great and grand in his sacrifice.

If Christ were not God, then he was a blasphemous liar, and not even an ordinary martyr for lofty convictions. He asserted himself to be God. The alternative to deliberate deception is that he was insane, if indeed not God, and that would render his death a pity, but not heroic. It is precisely because he was God that there is something greater and grander than anything else that has ever happened in history where the death of Christ is concerned. It is a great and grand thing for a man to choose to die for the sake of justice rather than escape death by forsaking principle. It is greater and grander to die for a friend, without any obligation of justice, and solely for the sake of charity. And our admiration is increased if one in high position, with wealth and comfort, gives his life for a nobody, some poor fellow creature who is facing disaster. And if that poor person had exhibited nothing but hatred toward his benefactor, being his declared enemy, still further is our admiration increased. But that God, infinitely superior to us, should offer himself for sinners who have used his very gifts to offend and insult him goes far beyond our ordinary ideas of heroism, nobility, and generosity; and no greater or grander sacrifice comes within the range of our wildest dreams and most extravagant imaginations.

441. You have said that the greatest of Christ's miracles was the Resurrection. But no one has ever returned from the dead!

That is a complete denial of the historical value of the Gospels. You have no proof whatever that no one has ever risen from the dead. You may not have personally witnessed such an event, but not all beyond your personal experience is necessarily false or nonexistent.

442. St. Matthew speaks of the dead appearing to many at the death of Christ but fails to give the name of even one of them or of those who received such visitations.

St. Matthew wrote a summary of events concerned with a principal character. If he had to describe in detail all connected with accessory incidents he would never be done. The proof that the Gospels as a whole are reliable history covers all these minor incidents. If a reliable historian relates that a man was killed during a street accident he is describing, and with the death of whom he is chiefly concerned, no one reasonably says, "I shall believe that man to have been killed only when you give me the names and addresses of every person in the street at the time." The absence of the names makes no difference to the fact that many came forth from their tombs as St. Matthew records.

443. Why were not such marvelous events at Christ's death, amidst preternatural darkness and earthquakes, and his Resurrection recorded by the Roman historians of the day?

Christ lived and died in a remote corner of the Roman world and had caused no political disturbance. Again, the Romans had supreme contempt for the Jews, and reports connected with Jewish religious happenings held very little interest for them. Suetonius mentions Christ briefly in his biography of Claudius; Tacitus speaks of his execution under Pontius Pilate; Phlegon, the freedman of Hadrian, records the eclipse of the sun at the death of Jesus; Celsus, the pagan philosopher, boasted of much knowledge concerning the life of Christ; Pliny the Younger mentions the Christians quite clearly together with their doctrines but again is interested only in the manner in which their existence affected Rome and Roman dominion. Josephus, the Jewish historian who was born at Jerusalem about A.D. 37, records Christ's death on the cross under Pontius Pilate and his appearance on the third day after his death to his disciples.

444. Christ was buried on Friday and rose on Sunday. Where are the three days and three nights?

We must take into account the Jewish methods of calculation prevalent at the time. The Jews used the expression three days and three nights for three periods of daylight and darkness as opposed to three periods of daylight only. Friday, Saturday, and Sunday were three periods of daylight to be taken as including periods of darkness. Whether the periods of darkness were complete or not, the Jews would speak of the whole section of time as three days and three nights. Thus in the book of Esther 4:16, the Jews were told to fast for three days and three nights. Yet after two nights according to our way of calculating, but in the third period of daylight, the fast ended.

445. Christ rose with a material body and ascended into heaven. What happens to his body in heaven?

Christ rose with a material body, but not in a material body limited by all the conditions of matter as we know them. He rose with the same, yet changed body, the change in no way altering its identity. St. Paul predicts a somewhat similar and mysterious change in our own bodies after our own resurrection. "So it is with the resurrection of the dead. What is sown is perishable, what is raised is imperishable. It is sown in dishonor, it is raised in glory. ... It is sown a physical body, it is raised a spiritual body" (1 Cor. 15:42-44). The body therefore shall rise with powers of which we have no experience yet and strangely participating in the qualities proper to spiritual beings. It is a mystery, for our present ideas are drawn from our present conditions, and we should not be surprised that we lack the capacity to understand the conditions of a state of which we have as yet had no experience at all.

446. If the Second Divine Person suffered only in his human nature, how was the atonement made by God? Catholic doctrine makes it a purely human sacrifice.

The sacrifice of Calvary was not a purely human sacrifice. The atonement was made by God because the Person whose human nature was nailed to the cross was God. The Person, and not the nature under the control of that Person, is the terminus of attribution. If I commit murder, I do it. It's no use saying, "My hand did it." The human nature that was nailed to the cross was his who was and is the Second Person of the Holy Trinity. And the sacrifice, though directly involving the death of the human nature, derived its dignity from the Person to whom it belonged. It was, therefore, an atonement of infinite value derived from the infinite dignity of the Second Person of the Holy Trinity. One may or may not agree with our explanation; but in no sense can one say that on this explanation a purely human sacrifice took place on Calvary. That could follow only if we admitted that Jesus was a purely and merely human person. That we have never admitted.

447. Let us turn from your dogma of Christ to those dogmas concerning your goddess Mary.

It would be mortal sin for any Catholic to regard Mary as a goddess. If a Catholic expressed such a belief to a priest in confession, he would be refused absolution unless he promised to renounce such an absurd idea. If you wish to attack Catholic doctrine, at least find out what Catholics do believe before you begin.

448. If you call her Queen of Heaven, do you not do her an injustice in refusing to her the title of goddess?

It would be the greatest possible injustice to regard her as a goddess. It is just to honor her even as God has honored her, which we Catholics do. Jesus is King of kings and Lord of lords, and his mother certainly possesses queenly dignity, holding the highest place in heaven next to her divine Son. But that does not and cannot change her finite and created human nature. To regard her as a goddess would be absurd.

449. Yet you insist that she is the Mother of God.

Jesus Christ is true God and true man, and as he was born of Mary she is truly the Mother of God. The Second Person of the Blessed Trinity was born of her according to the humanity he derived from her. She is not a goddess, for God did not derive his divine being from her. But she is the Mother of God, since the Second Person of the Blessed Trinity was truly born of her in his human nature.

450. How could Mary be the mother of the one who created her?

Mary owed her being, of course, to God, but this under the aspect of his eternal Nature. Subsequent to her creation that human nature was born of her that the Son of God had assumed to himself. She was, therefore, the mother of Christ. But Christ was one divine Person existing in two natures, one eternal and divine, the other temporal and human. Mary necessarily gave birth to a being with one Personality and that divine, and she is rightly called the Mother of God.

451. Does not the Catholic Church insist also upon the biologically impossible dogma of the Immaculate Conception of Mary herself?

The dogma of the Immaculate Conception of Mary has nothing to do with biology. It does not mean that she was conceived miraculously in the physical sense. She was normally conceived and born of her parents, Joachim and Ann. But in her very conception her soul was preserved immaculate in the sense that she inherited no stain of original sin, derived from our first parents.

452. Is there any evidence in Scripture that Mary was indeed never actually subject to original sin?

Yes. In Genesis 3:15, God said to Satan, "I will put enmity between you and the woman ... you shall bruise his heel." The radical enmity between Satan and that second Eve, the Mother of Christ, forbids her having been under the dominion of Satan, as she would have been had she ever contracted original sin in actual fact. In Luke 1:28, we read how the angel was sent by God to salute Mary with the words, "Hail, full of grace." Grace excludes sin, and had there been any sin at all in Mary she could not have been declared to be filled with grace. The Protestant version translates the phrase as "thou that hast been highly favored." But the Greek certainly implies "completely filled with holiness." However, complaints that our doctrine exempts Mary from the contracting of original sin are becoming more and more rare in a world that is tending to deny original sin altogether and that wishes to exempt everybody from it.

453. St. Paul says that One died for all, and therefore all were dead (2 Cor. 5:14).

Such texts must be interpreted in the light of other passages where God reveals that Mary was never under the dominion of Satan. Mary is included in these words of St. Paul juridically insofar as she was born of Adam, but she was not allowed to be born in sin to be afterward redeemed. She was redeemed by prevention.

454. St. John knew the Mother of Christ better than the others, yet he does not mention her Immaculate Conception!

In Revelation 12, he shows clearly his knowledge of the deadly opposition between Mary and Satan. His Gospel he wrote to supplement the Synoptic accounts, and sufficient details had been given concerning Mary herself by St. Luke. Omission to mention a fact in a given book is not proof that the writer did not know of it, and above all if it does not fall within the scope of his work.

455. Did the early Church know anything of this doctrine?

St. Augustine, in the fourth century, wrote, "When it is a matter of sin we must except the holy Virgin Mary, concerning whom I will have no question raised, owing to the honor due to Our Lord." St. Ephrem, also in the fourth century, taught very clearly the Immaculate Conception of Mary, likening her to Eve before the fall. The Oriental churches celebrated the feast of the Immaculate Conception as early as the seventh century. When Pope Pius IX defined the Catholic doctrine in 1854, he gave not a new truth to be added to Christian teaching but merely defined that this doctrine was part of Christian teaching from the very beginning, and that it is to be believed by all as part of Christian revelation.

456. Your infallible Church allowed St. Bernard to remain in ignorance of this doctrine.

Since the Church had not then given any infallible definition on the subject, St. Bernard naturally could not be guided by it. St. Bernard believed that Mary was born free from sin, but he was puzzled as to the moment of her sanctification. He thought the probable explanation to be that she was conceived in sin but purified, as was St. John the Baptist, prior to actual birth. But he did not regard this opinion as part of his Faith. Meantime his error was immaterial prior to the final authentic decision of the infallible Church. St. Bernard believed all that God had taught and all that the Catholic Church had clearly set forth in her definitions prior to his time.

457. Did not St. Thomas Aquinas deny the doctrine of the Immaculate Conception?

His opinion was probably much the same as that of St. Bernard. Before the definite decision of the Church was given, theologians were free to discuss the matter. But the Church has since defined that the soul of Mary was never subject for a single moment to the stain of original sin. Both St. Bernard and St. Thomas would have been very glad to have had the assistance of such a definition.

458. Why did the Church withhold that honor from Mary for so long a time?

Since Mary always possessed that honor, the Church did not withhold it from her. The definition that Mary did possess such an honor was given by the Church when necessity demanded it. There was no real dispute about this matter in the early Church. In the Middle Ages theologians attempted a deeper analysis of the privileges of Mary and, with no infallible decision of the Church to help them, some theologians arrived at defective conclusions, chiefly because of the defective psychology of the times. Some theologians held that Mary was preserved from original sin from the very moment of her conception; others said from the moment of her animation; yet others held that she was purified at a moment subsequent both to her conception and to her animation. All admitted that she was sanctified prior to her actual birth. Now that the Church has spoken there is no doubt on the subject.

459. Why call Mary a virgin, seeing that she was a mother. The linking of the two terms is an insult to reason.

The assertion that an omnipotent God is limited by the natural laws, which he himself established, is an insult to reason.

Jesus, the child of Mary, was conceived miraculously without the intervention of any human father and was born miraculously, Mary's virginity being preserved throughout. I do not claim that any natural laws were responsible for this event. I claim that God was responsible, and the only way you can show that the doctrine is not reasonable is by proving that there is no God, or that he could not do what Catholic doctrine asserts.

460. Where does it say in Scripture that Mary was ever a virgin?

Isaiah the prophet (7:14) certainly predicted a supernatural and extraordinary birth of the Messiah when he wrote, "The Lord himself will give you a sign. Behold, a virgin shall conceive and bear a son, and shall call his name Immanuel." St. Luke says, "The angel Gabriel was sent from God ... to a virgin ... and the virgin's name was Mary." When Mary was offered the dignity of becoming the mother of the Messiah, a privilege to which any Jewish maiden would ordinarily look forward with eager desire, she urged against the prospect the fact that she had no intention of motherhood. "How can this be, since I have no husband?" She does not refer to the past but by using the present tense indicates her present and persevering intention. The angel assured her that her child would be due to the miraculous operation of the Holy Spirit and that she would not be asked to forfeit the virginity she prized so highly, and then only did she consent (Luke 1:26-38). When Jesus was born, Mary had none of the suffering usually associated with childbirth. The child was born miraculously, Mary herself in no way incapacitated. She herself attended to her own needs and those of the child. "She gave birth to her first-born son, and wrapped him in swaddling cloths, and laid him in a manger" (Luke 2:7).

461. If Jesus was born of a virgin, why does he say nothing about it?

We do not know that he said nothing about it. The evangelists do not record any special utterances of Christ on this subject, but they do not pretend to record all that he ever said. St. Luke tells us that when Christ met the two disciples on the way to Emmaus, "beginning with Moses and all the prophets, he interpreted to them in all the Scriptures the things concerning himself" (Luke 24:27). There is every probability that he explained his advent into this world according to the prophecy of Isaiah. Meantime the Gospels do record the fact that Mary was a virgin, and their words are as reliable in this as when they record the utterances of Christ.

462. St. Matthew says that Joseph knew her not until she had borne a son (Matt: 1:25).

Nor did he. And the expression "till" in Hebrew usage has no necessary reference to the future. Thus in Genesis 8:7, we read that "Noah ... sent forth a raven; and it went to and fro until the waters were dried up from the earth." That expression does not suggest that it returned then. It did not return at all, having found resting places. Nor does the expression "first-born" child imply that there were other children afterward. Thus Exodus says, "The Lord said to Moses, 'Consecrate to me all the first-born.'" Parents had not to wait to see if other children were born before they could call the first their first-born!

463. Matthew 13:55-56 says, "Are not his brethren James and Joseph and Simon and Judas? And are not all his sisters with us?"

The Jewish expression "brothers and sisters of the Lord" in Scripture merely refers to relationship in the same tribe or stock. Cousins often came under that title. In all nations the word *brother* has a wide significance, as when one Mason will call another a brother-Mason without suggesting that he was born of the same mother. The same St. Matthew speaks explicitly of "Mary, the mother of James and Joseph" in 27:56, obviously alluding to a Mary who was not the mother of Jesus but who was married to Cleophas, the brother of Joseph.

464. Luke 1:36 confutes the story that there was no word in the Greek to describe James, Joseph, Jude, and Simon as cousins.

I have never heard it said that there was no word in Greek for *cousin*. It is certain that there was no word in Hebrew for cousin. The

Hebrew word for brother, *ah*, and in the Aramaic, *aha*, was used to describe brothers, half-brothers, nephews and nieces, cousins, and relatives in general. It is certain that any cousins of Jesus would have to be described in Aramaic as brethren. And, in translating the Hebrew expression literally by the Greek word for brethren, the evangelists merely followed the example already given in the Septuagint Greek version of the Old Testament.

465. There would not be two girls in the one family called Mary.

There certainly could be. And St. John, 19:25, writes that there stood by the cross of Jesus "His mother, and his mother's sister, Mary the wife of Clopas." But even here, Mary the wife of Clopas need not have been a sister in the first degree of blood relationship, but rather of the same lineage in more remote degrees of either consanguinity or affinity.

466. Why are Protestants, who believe in Scripture, so convinced that Mary had other children?

They are not inspired by love for Christ, or for the mother of Christ, or for Scripture in their doctrine. Their main desire is to maintain a doctrine differing from that of the Catholic Church. But it is a position that is rapidly going out of fashion. Learned Protestant scholars today deny as emphatically as any Catholic that Mary had other children. When our Lord, dying on the cross, commended his mother to the care of St. John, he did so precisely because he was her only child, and he knew that Mary had no other children to care for her. The idea that Mary had other children is disrespectful to the Holy Spirit who claimed and sanctified her as his sanctuary. It insults Christ, who was the only-begotten of his mother even as he was the only-begotten of his heavenly Father. It insults Mary, who would have been guilty of great ingratitude to God if she threw away the gift of virginity that God had so carefully preserved for her in the conception of Christ. It insults St. Joseph. God had told him by an angel to take Mary as his wife, and that the child to be born of her had no earthly father but was the very Son of God. God merely gave St.

Joseph the privilege of protecting her good name amongst the undiscerning Jews, and he chose a God-fearing man who would respect her. Knowing that her child was God himself in human form, Joseph would at once regard her as on a plane far superior to that of any ordinary human being, and to him, as to us, the mere thought of her becoming a mother to merely earthly children would have seemed a sacrilege.

467. You urge these privileges granted to Mary at the foundation of your devotion to her, yet Christ said, "Blessed rather are those who hear the word of God and keep it!"

Would you presume to say that Mary, whom the angel addressed as full of grace, did not hear the word of God and keep it? You have missed the sense of the passage to which you allude. In Luke 11:27, a woman praised the one who had the honor to be the mother of Christ. Christ did not for a moment deny it, as you would like to believe. The sense of his words is simply, "Yes, she is blessed. But better to hear God's word and keep it and thus attain holiness, than to be my mother. You cannot all imitate Mary by being my mother; but you can do so by hearing God's word and keeping it." The thought that those who hear God's word and keep it are rather blessed than Mary because she did not is simply absurd. "Henceforth," declared Mary prophetically, "all generations will call me blessed" (Luke 1:48). And Elizabeth saluted her with the words, "Blessed are you among women" (Luke 1:42).

468. How do you prove Mary's bodily assumption into heaven?

No Christian could dispute the fact that Mary's soul is in heaven. Christ certainly did not suffer the soul of his own mother to be lost. The doctrine of her bodily assumption after her death is not contained in Scripture, but is guaranteed by tradition and by the teaching of the Catholic Church. That Scripture omits to record the fact is no argument against it. Omission is not denial. Meantime, early traditions positively record the fact and negatively we note that, whilst the mortal remains of a St. Peter and of a St. Paul are jealously possessed and honored in Rome, no city or

Christian center has ever claimed to possess the mortal remains of our Lady. Certainly relics of our Lady would be regarded as having greater value than those of any saint or apostle, so nearly was she related to Christ. And it was most fitting that the body of Mary, who had been preserved even from the taint of original sin, should not have been allowed to corrupt. After all, it was just as easy for God to take her glorified body to heaven at once as it will be to take the glorified bodies of all the saved at the last day. However, the definite sanction of this doctrine by the Catholic Church is sufficient assurance of the fact.

469. Why do Catholics believe that Mary prays for them and helps them?

Because they believe that she is their spiritual Mother, and that she has not lost her interest in those for whom her Son died merely because she is in heaven. It is the Christian law, according to St. James, that we should pray for one another. The saints in heaven pray for us who are on Earth and still endeavoring to work out our salvation. And Mary is the greatest of the saints. It is but an application in practice of our belief in the communion of saints, a doctrine we profess every time we say the Apostle's Creed.

470. Why do they pray to her instead of to God, as Protestants do?

We do not pray to Mary instead of to God, but we pray to her as well as to God. And those who retain devotion to Mary are in the habit of offering more prayers directly to God than those who have repudiated devotion to Mary. Moreover, prayers to Mary are prayers to God through her intercession. And you cannot deny that at times it is good to have our Lady praying with us rather than to pray alone to God. Two prayers are better than one, above all when the other whom I have asked to join in my petition is the very Mother of Christ.

471. To my Protestant mind your worship of Mary is little short of idolatry.

That can be only because you have not understood Catholic doctrine on the subject. The Creator alone is God. Mary is as much a creature as any other human being. But whilst she is as much a creature as we are, we have not been honored by God nearly as much as she.

472. What is her place in the Christian religion?

Mary's place in the Christian religion should be obvious. She is the morning star preceding the Light of the World, Christ. The only difference is that all her light is derived from the Son she heralds. By God's eternal decree Mary has been associated with the highest mysteries of the Christian religion, being the very instrument of the Incarnation of the eternal Son of God, and, therefore, of our redemption. We have devotion to her both because of our admiration of her and because of her interest in our eternal welfare. When we honor Mary, of course, we are but honoring Christ in her. Without him, she would be nothing, and she would be the first to admit it. And the honor we show her cannot displease Christ. He was the best Son who ever lived, and would rather be displeased were his Mother ignored or slighted. Remember the bootblack's answer to the parson. Whilst having his boots polished, the parson saw a medal of the Virgin Mary hanging from the boy's neck on a string. "Sonny," he said, "why do you wear that?" "She is the Mother of Christ," said the boy. "But," objected the parson, "she's no different from your own mother." "No," replied the boy, "but there's a hell of a difference between the sons." We owe love and devotion to the Mother of Christ.

473. In what way did Mary take her part in the redemptive work of mankind, which was accomplished by Christ alone?

Christ was the principal author of our redemption, but there were many secondary cooperators in the work. We even find St. Paul saying that we are to fill up what is wanting to the sufferings of Christ. The explanation of this, however, would demand a treatise on the Mystical Body of Christ as comprising all the members of the Church, and I can scarcely do justice to it now. All I can say is that Mary cooperated in the redemptive work in a way quite special to herself.

As Jesus is the second Adam, so Mary is the second Eve. As our first mother Eve brought us forth to misery and suffering, so our second mother, Mary, in bringing forth our Savior brought us forth to happiness and salvation. Mary's consent was asked by God when the time for the Incarnation was at hand; she consented to the full work of Christ from the cave of Bethlehem to the cross of Calvary. She provided the very blood that was shed for us. In union with Christ she had her own passion, and Simeon rightly predicted to her, under the inspiration of the Holy Spirit, "A sword will pierce through your own soul also." With, in, and through the work of Christ her sufferings also contributed secondarily toward our redemption. And she was given to us from the cross as a mother for a mother's work. To all of us Christ said, in the person of St. John, "Behold your Mother!" We Catholics, therefore, regard Mary as our spiritual Mother, entertaining toward her the love and devotion of children. Every Christian woman, above all, should regard Mary, the Mother of Christ, as the glory of her sex.

474. Christ is said to have saved us. What does being saved mean?

A man is saved who is free forever from the prospect of going to the eternal misery of hell. The soul that is saved has necessarily been separated from this earthly life of probation and has gone either to purgatory for a time or immediately to the eternal happiness of heaven.

475. Are we assured of salvation by our belief in Christ?

No one can be sure of salvation until he is safely dead, finishing this life in a state of grace. During this life a man, no matter how just he may be, is able to forsake the path of justice and lose all the merit of previous goodness. You may think this hard, but a murder on Tuesday could not be excused on the score of almsgiving to a beggar on the previous day. Previous good actions do not justify subsequent bad ones. Thus God says, "When a righteous man turns away from his righteousness and commits iniquity … none of the righteous deeds which he has done shall be remembered" (Ezek. 18:24).

All the faith in the world could not save a sinner who intends to go on sinning. A man must repent of his sins and try to live a good life.

476. But "He who believes has eternal life" (John 6:47).

Faith in Christ is one condition of eternal life. If a man sees the facts and will not believe, he cannot be saved. If he does believe he can be saved, but it does not follow that he must be saved. By mere belief in Christ no man has certainty of salvation. St. Paul believed in Christ yet had to write, "I pommel my body and subdue it, lest after preaching to others I myself should be disqualified" (1 Cor. 9:27). In the following chapter, verse 12, he warns all of us, "Any one who thinks that he stands take heed lest he fall."

477. A man cannot save himself by his own good works.

Good works prompted by purely natural motives cannot save a man. Thus St. Paul says, "If I give away all I have, and if I deliver my body to be burned, but have not love, I gain nothing" (1 Cor. 13:3). Yet good works inspired by faith in Christ and love for Christ are necessary. "You see that a man is justified by works and not by faith alone" (James 2:24). Indeed the "Son of man is to come with his angels in the glory of his Father, and then he will repay every man for what he has done" (Matt. 16:27). In fact, such good works are necessary for salvation, for St. James says in 2:26, "For as the body apart from the spirit is dead, so faith apart from works is dead."

478. St. Paul says, "Not because of works, lest any man should boast" (Eph. 2:9).

St. Paul excludes works performed by one's own efforts independently of God's grace. No man will be able to boast that he saved himself by his own efforts and that he did not need the grace of Christ. But St. Paul did not contradict St. James who declared that "a man is justified by works and not by faith alone." And this is the teaching of Christ who said, "He who has my commandments and keeps them, he it is who loves me." And the keeping of Christ's commands means good works. We do need, besides good works, both faith and charity, and in the text you quote St. Paul is insisting upon faith as one necessary condition, a faith that is a gratuitous gift from God. But not for a moment does St. Paul mean that a man is saved by faith only, to the exclusion of good works.

479. As Christ died he said, "It is finished." He completed our salvation, and we believe in his finished work.

Christ's words, "It is finished," do not show that our salvation is completed in one glorious act. They indicate that he had fulfilled his part in the essential work of our redemption. But our part still remains. He has paid the price, but we shall be saved only if we fulfill the conditions necessary to profit by his death for us. And it is not enough to believe in the finished work of Christ by simple faith in order to secure eternal salvation in heaven with him. Christ said to the apostles, "Make disciples of all nations ... teaching them to observe all that I have commanded you" (Matt. 28:20).

480. Did not St. Peter champion salvation by works of the Jewish Law, whilst St. Paul demanded salvation by faith?

Both St. Peter and St. Paul insisted upon salvation both by faith and good works. Did St. Peter insist on salvation by works only, when he wrote, "We have been born anew ... to an inheritance ... kept in heaven for you, who by God's power are guarded through faith for a salvation ready to be revealed in the last time" (1 Pet. 1:3-5)? And how can people say that St. Paul championed salvation by faith to the exclusion of good works, when he wrote to the Galatians, "Do not be deceived; God is not mocked, for whatever a man sows, that he will also reap. For he who sows to his own flesh will from the flesh reap corruption; but he who sows to the Spirit will from the Spirit reap eternal life. And let us not grow weary in well-doing, for in due season we shall reap, if we do not lose heart. So then, as we have opportunity, let us do good to all men" (Gal.

6:7-10). He is a very shallow reader of Scripture who would confine St. Peter's teaching of salvation to works and St. Paul's to faith. But, above all, it is a mystery how anyone can say that St. Peter based salvation on works of the Jewish Law, when we find him writing in his first epistle, 1:18-19, "You were ransomed from the futile ways inherited from your fathers ... with the precious blood of Christ."

481. God must know beforehand whether a soul is born to be damned or otherwise.

No soul is born to be damned. God sincerely wills the salvation of all men and gives all men sufficient grace to be saved. In fact, he warns us all by conscience and by his commandments against the very things that could destroy our eternal happiness. He would not warn us against the things that take us to hell if he wanted us to go there. He would keep silent about them and let us go over the precipice.

482. How does Catholicism differ from Calvinism as regards predestination?

Calvinism taught that some men were predestined to heaven no matter what they might do; others were predestined to hell no matter how they might try to serve God. But the Catholic Church teaches that God sincerely wills all men to be saved and that none should be lost. Anyone who does his best with all goodwill and dies sincerely repentant of his sins can certainly attain salvation through the merits of Christ. Every such man will have the necessary grace offered to him.

483. Does not the Catholic Church teach that grace is usually given through the sacraments?

Grace is given directly in answer to prayer, but many very necessary graces are normally to be obtained only through the sacraments instituted by Christ.

484. What is a sacrament?

A sacrament is a visible rite or ceremony that signifies and confers grace. Thus baptism is a visible rite. The pouring of the water on the forehead signifies the cleansing of the soul by the grace that the action bestows.

485. Catholics seem to rely so much upon external rites such as their sacraments. A spiritual life does not require external rites.

A spiritual life to be lived by human beings requires them. We are not angels. We have both a soul and a body, and religion must cater for our complete needs. We live by our senses and acquire our certainty from sense data. Significant symbols and rites and ceremonies play a big part in the individual and social lives even of those who object to our religious rites. God himself respects our twofold spiritual and material nature and leads us to himself by means on our own level. The soul uses the bodily powers in God's service, and God uses the bodily rites called the sacraments in communicating grace to men. He wishes to sanctify man, just as man was made by him.

486. God would not employ material things in his religion.

God employed material forces in our creation, and he employs them to recreate us in grace. It is quite normal that a material element should intervene in both cases. In our natural lives we use the forces of God immanent in nature. The sacraments are the forces proper to God in our supernatural and spiritual lives.

487. Is not God himself a spirit?

He is. But we are flesh. And we have to rise above the flesh to a spiritual plane, from the natural level to the God level. To enable us to do so, the eternal Son of God came down to Earth and took flesh, obviously setting before us and using a material nature for our spiritual regeneration. It is quite in harmony with this that material and visible sacraments should be used to continue the work of our spiritual regeneration.

488. I trust in Christ and have no need of sacramental rites.

It is presumption to trust in Christ yet to despise means established by him and declared by him to be necessary. The Christ in whom you trust certainly believed in such ceremonies. He anointed the blind man's eyes with saliva and earth, and he instituted the various sacraments of the Church. If you study Scripture closely you will notice that the visible is again and again employed in the work of invisible sanctification. Your denial of sacramental and visible rites is opposed to the whole tenor of Scripture almost from beginning to end.

489. Do you insist that baptism is necessary to salvation?

Yes. Christ came to save men, and he has the right to dictate the conditions of salvation. If you offered me a fortune provided I would go to London via Suez, particularly insisting that I should go via Suez, it would be little use my saying, "Oh, I'll go via Panama—it's a much more sensible route." You would reply, "But I want you to go via Suez, or there will be no fortune." Now, Christ distinctly commanded baptism as a condition of salvation, and no arguments of men, who cannot save us, are of any avail against the authority of Christ. It is necessary to be baptized, or we shall never see God and rejoice in the happiness of heaven.

490. Then are all the unbaptized lost, whether it be their own fault or not?

No one will ever be lost save through his own fault. Christ is God, and, as God, can work with secondary causes or without them. The ordinary means of salvation is by baptism, and one who is convinced of the necessity of baptism yet deliberately refuses to receive it cannot be saved. But God can supply the grace usually given by baptism, and does so without the actual sacramental rite in two cases: if an unbaptized person dies a martyr for Christ he is credited with baptism of blood. Baptism of desire counts for the man who repents of his sins and dies with the sincere will to do God's will, yet who, through no fault of his own, does not realize the necessity of actual baptism by water, or is unable to receive it.

491. Would you explain more fully this baptism of desire?

Every human being has a conscience that dictates a natural law of moral obligation, at least when he comes to the age of reason. If a pagan knows nothing of Christianity and is ignorant of it through no fault of his own, he can at least repent of his personal sins against his conscience and desire to do the right thing. God gives every man the grace to do this much. Now, we know that a man should receive baptism. If the pagan knew this he would receive baptism. This sincere desire to do all that God would require implicitly includes the desire of baptism, and God takes the will for the deed, granting sanctifying grace. Thus such a pagan would be saved. As is clear, anyone who has attained to the use of reason would be capable of this baptism of desire.

492. Then an unbaptized infant cannot attain heaven?

An unbaptized infant cannot attain heaven.[1] Christ has said very definitely, "Unless one is born anew ... he cannot see the kingdom of God" (John 3:3). I am not more severe than Christ in my denial. He declares that the ordinary principle of life received by human generation is insufficient. We must receive an additional life of grace by baptismal rebirth. An unbaptized infant has received natural life only and had one birth only. If he dies without baptism he has no claim to the supernatural happiness of heaven.

493. Is it not unjust that such a child should be lost through no fault of its own?

Injustice is not involved in this question. When treating of original sin I explained how such a child lacks that supernatural grace that is not due to human nature and without which no one can enter heaven. Christ offers that supernatural grace to such of Adam's children as receive baptism. It is his sheer goodness that he does so, and those who have been baptized have but to congratulate themselves. Unbaptized infants, who have never

1 On this subject, the *Catechism* adds, "As regards children who have died without baptism, the Church can only entrust them to the mercy of God, as she does in her funeral rites for them. Indeed, the great mercy of God who desires that all men should be saved, and Jesus' tenderness toward children which caused him to say: 'Let the children come to me, do not hinder them,' allow us to hope that there is a way of salvation for children who have died without baptism. All the more urgent is the Church's call not to prevent little children coming to Christ through the gift of holy baptism."

committed any personal sins, will never endure any actual and positive suffering. But they will be content with natural happiness only, and will not be able to complain that they do not possess the supernatural happiness of seeing God face to face, and being happy with his own supreme happiness. If I bestow a gift upon a beggar in the presence of another, that other cannot tell me that I am obliged in justice to give him a gift also. Since the fall of the human race, we are all beggars before God as regards supernatural happiness. I admit that it would be unjust if a child innocent of any personal sin had to suffer the miseries of hell. But such is not Catholic doctrine, as I have explained.

494. Do you suggest a special state for unbaptized infants?

Yes. We call it the limbo[2] of unbaptized children. The word *limbo* is derived from the Latin word *limbus*, which means a bordering place. Limbo is an intermediate state of purely natural happiness. In that state unbaptized children will receive all the happiness proportionate to their natural capacity.

495. For this sin the just God prevents them from ever seeing him, and from ever attaining perfect happiness!

That is not true. God no more prevents them from seeing him than he can be said to prevent kittens from flying because he did not give them wings. Is God unjust to kittens because he does not make them flying foxes? Would they be justified in bitter complaints against his justice because he has not endowed them with a power with which he could have endowed them? If kittens cannot fly, it is their own natural incapability that prevents them from flying. And if unbaptized infants cannot see God after their death as God sees himself, it is their own natural incapability that prevents them from doing so. They are simply without the superadded gift of being capable of operations proper to God and retain merely

2 Certainly, in the twenty-first century the Church does not speak of limbo nearly as commonly as it did in Fr. Rumble's time. We include this reply, nonetheless, as food for reflection as well as an accurate representation of a theological concept with deep roots in the Catholic tradition.

the capability of operations proper to human nature. Again, you are wrong in saying that they are prevented from attaining perfect happiness. They do not attain the perfect happiness made possible to those who participate by baptism in the supernatural and gratuitous destiny purchased for us by Christ. But they attain a perfect happiness proportionate to their nature and all its legitimate aspirations. A kitten can be perfectly happy as a kitten, even though it does not enjoy the additional happiness of flying that is the prerogative of animals endowed with wings.

496. We Protestants are taught that when Christ said, "You must be born anew," he meant a change of heart.

That would be a most inadequate explanation. For a change of heart means conversion from unbelief to belief in Christ, and from morally evil ways to morally good conduct. It therefore means repentance. Now, our Lord did insist on repentance or a change of heart in all who sought baptism, but he did not identify it with baptism. He said, "He who believes and is baptized will be saved" (Mark 16:16). When speaking of the rite of baptism itself, he said, "Unless one is born of water and the Spirit, he cannot enter the kingdom of God" (John 3:5). You will notice here that, whilst conversion or change of heart is an interior change in our own dispositions, the new principle of life comes from forces outside us. It is something put into us and signified by an external rite. The good preparatory dispositions are from us, but the new life is not from us but from God. The washing with baptismal water signifies the cleansing of the soul from the disease of sin belonging to children of a guilty race; and the Spirit of the living God is mentioned as infusing into our souls a principle of new life altogether, which is rightly said to regenerate us and give us a new birth to a spiritual life of grace far beyond and above the merely natural life secured by natural birth.

497. What did Christ mean by "being born anew"?

The life he gives us is quite distinct from the life we secured at birth and is derived from another source. Our very nature is changed and lifted to a higher plane, a plane therefore called supernatural. The starting point for Christians is the fact that the eternal Son of God became man. But he descended to our level and shared our human nature by his human birth that he might lift us to his level and enable us to share his nature by a supernatural birth. In him, God is given to us that we may become one with God. And as surely as his human life enabled the Son of God to live and experience our life in this world, so by our rebirth into the Christ-life we are to live and experience the life of God through grace in this world and through glory in heaven. It is obvious that such an experience is proper to God and not to man, just as an intellectual life in this world is proper to man and not to a tree. A tree would have to be elevated far above its natural life to be able to converse with man and share in man's activities. The human level would be supernatural in comparison with the level of mere vegetation. Far more is the God-level supernatural in comparison with man's level. For us to live the life of God, to know as he knows, love as he loves, and be happy with his happiness, we certainly will need a new principle of life and new powers that are beyond those received by natural birth. And Christ communicates that new life to us by a baptismal rebirth that enables us to share in the divine nature and gives a thought, love, action, and destiny in common with God. And we receive the principle of that life by the sacrament of baptism in which we are born again of water and the Holy Spirit. That life is in us by grace as the life of the oak tree is in the acorn; and it is that life of grace that will attain its full development and perfection in the glorious life of eternal association with God in heaven itself under conditions infinitely above the natural conditions of life in this world. That is what Christ meant when he said, "You must be born anew."

498. Why does not the Catholic Church baptize by immersion?

Such a method of baptism, though valid, is not necessary. From the very beginning baptism was administered both by immersion and by infusion, or pouring water upon the forehead.

Immersion was never thought necessary in the Christian Church. After St. Peter's first sermon three thousand people were baptized, and it is most unlikely that it could have been by immersion, above all in the light of recent research into the water supply available in Jerusalem itself at that time. The *Didache*, or *Teaching of the Twelve*, written about the year 90, says, "Thus baptize. ... If you have not fresh water, baptize in other water. If you cannot do it in cold, use warm. If you have neither, pour out on the head water three times in the name of the Father and of the Son and of the Holy Spirit." Either form then is valid. If immersion were necessary, what would you do with bedridden invalids and the dying? Nor is the significance lost by pouring. The true significance is that grace washes the soul as water washes the body. The true sign of washing is retained by any true ablutions. Washing does not always imply the taking of a plunge bath. Burial with Christ is signified by washing away the death of sin and the resurrection to the new life of grace. In any case, Christ left the practical application of such matters to his Church, saying, "Whatever you bind on earth shall be bound in heaven" (Matt. 18:18). And he promised to be with his Church, preserving her from any misuse of this power.

499. Scripture nowhere says that infants were baptized.

It nowhere says that they were not and implicitly demands that they should be.

500. Do we not read only of adult baptisms in the New Testament?

No. We read of some adult baptisms, but they were not administered precisely because the subjects were adults but because they happened to be converted as adults. Acts 16 commemorates the reception of two complete households into the Church by St. Paul, and we are not told that the adults only in those households were received. Christ told the apostles to teach and baptize all nations, and the term "all nations" certainly includes men, women, and children. Again St. Paul tells us that baptism is the circumcision of Christians, and we know that circumcision was administered to children (Col. 2:11). Or is the New Law to be less perfect than the Old, containing no purifying rite for infants? Your ideas are opposed to the whole tenor of Christianity. Christ is the second Adam. If the children of Adam are born subject to original sin and its penalties, so they can be born again of Christ into the life of grace. Or is Adam to be able to ruin all, yet Christ be unable to save any except adults? "What is of the flesh is flesh; what is of the spirit is spirit." Children by virtue of their natural birth are of the flesh, and our Lord insists that unless one be born again he cannot enter the kingdom of God. Do not be misled by the English translation, "Unless a man be born again." The original Greek does not use the word *man* in this text; it says, "Unless anyone be born again," and a child is someone.

501. John told his converts to repent and be baptized.

He was speaking to adults, and undoubtedly adults must repent of their personal sins before they can come to God. Yet children who are incapable of personal sin and repentance are born in original sin, to destroy which is the primary purpose of baptism.

502. The Bible says, "Believe and be baptized." How can children make an act of faith?

The command to believe and be baptized was addressed to adult listeners only who, without faith, would not even see the necessity of baptism. But children belong to their parents, and the parents may certainly give their children to God, professing faith on their behalf and promising to bring them up as Christians.

503. What is confession?

Confession is a sacrament instituted by Jesus Christ by which those who fall into sin after baptism may be restored to God's grace. Confession is called the sacrament of penance because it supposes that the recipient is truly repentant of his sins. It involves the admission of one's sins made to a duly approved priest in order to obtain absolution.

504. On what scriptural authority does the Catholic Church base its practice of confession?

On the promise of Christ, as recorded in Matthew 16, that he would give the keys of the kingdom of heaven, and the power of binding and loosing, to his apostles and the Church. And again, on the fulfillment of that promise, with specific reference to absolution from sin, as recorded in John 20:23. There we are told that, having breathed upon the apostles, Christ said to them: "Receive the Holy Spirit. If you forgive the sins of any, they are forgiven; if you retain the sins of any, they are retained." By those words he gave the power to the official representatives of the Church of forgiving or not forgiving sin as they judged fit, and promised to sanction and ratify their decision.

505. All men are equal. How can a priest set himself above others and presume to be their judge?

All men equally share a common humanity, but not all are equal in office and responsibility. Also, no man could have the right to set himself above others in this matter. If Christ had not endowed his priests with power to forgive sin, they could not possess it. But he endowed them with this power, and they forgive sin not in their own name but in the name of Christ. A criminal has to answer to the state for his crimes against civil law. How then can a fellow citizen act as judge and pass sentence upon him? In his official capacity he is delegated by the state and acts in the name of the state. Now, Christ died to pay the price of our sins, and he surely has the right to say how forgiveness shall be applied. We cannot deny the right of Christ to administer forgiveness through agents of his own choosing, nor can we insist that he must forgive us on our conditions whilst we ignore his conditions.

506. We Protestants believe that God alone can forgive sin.

And that is the Catholic teaching also. But the question concerns the way in which God has chosen to administer that forgiveness. We Catholics add that God can delegate his power if he wishes, just as the supreme authority in the state can delegate a judge to administer justice. Would you deny to God that power?

507. But can you prove that God did delegate that power to men?

Yes. Christ was God, and in John 20:21-23 we read these remarkable words, "As the Father has sent me, even so I send you. And when he had said this, he breathed on them, and said to them, 'Receive the Holy Spirit. If you forgive the sins of any, they are forgiven; if you retain the sins of any, they are retained.'" Now, Christ's mission was to destroy sin, and he gave that same mission to his apostles. Knowing that their merely human power as men was quite insufficient, he gave them a special communication of the Holy Spirit for this special work. To say that Christ did not confer a true power to forgive sin is to rob the whole ceremony and the words of Christ of any real meaning. And it was obviously a power to be exercised, Christians applying to the apostles for forgiveness.

508. I believe that the apostles received the power, but it was for them only and has not been handed on in the Church.

Christ commissioned his Church to teach all nations till the end of the world. The apostles had to hand on all essential powers to their successors. And the conditions of salvation must be the same for us as for the first Christians. If those subject to the apostles had to obtain forgiveness from their fellow men, there is no reason why we should be exempt. We share the same privileges as the early Christians and must have the same obligations. Until the Reformation all Christians went to confession. In the fourth century we find St. Ambrose defending confession by saying that if a man can forgive sin by baptizing, he claims nothing greater when he claims the power to forgive sin through the sacrament of penance. That priests possessed such power was Christian doctrine in his time and is still the doctrine of the Catholic Church. The Greek Church, which broke away from the Catholic Church in the ninth century, has retained this apostolic practice. Protestantism gave up the practice in the sixteenth century because it was uncomfortable and mortifying. But once admit such a principle and one could abolish every uncomfortable commandment of God.

509. What justification is there for imposing penances in confession?

Protestants, of course, deny not only the necessity of confessing one's sins but also the obligation to make personal satisfaction for them by penitential works. For a Catholic, sufficient justification for the imposition of penances is found in the fact that the Catholic Church requires it as part of the sacrament of confession. For to that Church our Lord has said, "Whatever you bind on earth is bound also in heaven." We accept the laws of our religion because they have the authority of Christ latent within them, not because we ourselves happen to approve of their wisdom or of the reasons for them. However, there are reasons for the law that penances must be imposed upon those who seek forgiveness of sin in confession; and those reasons are based upon the known will of God in relation to the forgiveness of sins in general, and also upon the very nature of the sacrament of confession as instituted by Christ.

510. Is it possible to secure forgiveness without confessing to a priest?

Catholics who are unable to find a priest are forgiven if they make an act of perfect contrition or sorrow, but such an act supposes at least the intention of going to confession when the opportunity presents itself. For perfect sorrow supposes the will to do God's will. Protestants and other non-Catholics can also secure forgiveness by perfect sorrow, if they are not responsible for their ignorance of the law of Christ. For lack of knowledge would be a condition of true sorrow in those who do not comply with the actual law. Such people would go to confession if they realized the obligation. But who can know that he has such perfect contrition? Perfect contrition implies a hatred of the sin to be forgiven, not from any motive, but because it has offended God. It implies intense sorrow for having committed it, the will to make full reparation of the harm done, and the firm purpose to avoid committing it again. What certainty has one that he possesses such dispositions? Is his sorrow supernatural? Is his conviction of forgiveness merely self-persuasion; a case of the wish being father to the thought? He has no definite and personal revelation that he is forgiven. Catholics who receive sacramental absolution are at least not left in such doubts and anxieties, for even though their sorrow be not as perfect as it should be, the sacrament itself will supply for certain defects.

511. Can a priest forgive blasphemy against the Holy Spirit, which Christ says shall not be forgiven in this world or the next?

There is no sin too great to be forgiven provided one sincerely repents of it. Christ really referred to evil dispositions of soul that are so hardened that one will lack the will to repent. Blasphemy against the Holy Spirit is not blasphemy as commonly understood but a determined resistance to the very grace of the Holy Spirit that is meant to save us. Thus the Pharisees who saw the miracles of Christ could not deny them to be miracles; yet rather than yield to the grace being offered them, they said that Christ wrought them with the help of the devil and not by God. A man who rejects the very means God adopts to convert him is little likely to make good use of other graces offered by God, and our Lord warns us very strongly to beware of sinning against the light, since it seldom ends in repentance. Yet even such a man with the help of special grace could repent of his bad dispositions and thus be converted and forgiven. Any unforgivableness, therefore, is on account of a man's bad dispositions, not on account of the nature of the sin. There is no absolutely unforgivable sin such as cannot be forgiven even though a man repents.

512. Why should a good-living Catholic go to hell because he dies without repentance after committing mortal sin, whilst a bad Catholic, sinful all his life, repents at the last moment, and goes to heaven?

Take the good Catholic first. To live his good life he kept the commandments of God. But no observance of God's commandments gives any subsequent right to break them. If he breaks God's commandments by later mortal sin and refuses to repent, he dies in a state of mortal sin and at enmity with God. He necessarily goes to hell, though he need not necessarily have fallen into a state of sin, and further, need not necessarily have remained in such a state. A previous good life in no way justifies later sins. If a man commits murder on Wednesday, is it any defense that he did not commit adultery on the preceding Tuesday? Now, take your poor sinner who, after living a bad life, repents and saves his soul. By repentance, he recovers God's grace. And he is saved because he availed himself of God's mercy, asked for forgiveness, and died in God's friendship. The one-time good man is not lost because of his previous good life, and this man is not saved because of his previous bad life. There would be injustice if that were the case. But it is not. The one-time good man is lost because he nullified his good life by subsequent sin; the bad man is saved because he nullified his bad life by subsequent repentance and a request to share in the merits of Christ.

513. What is the Holy Eucharist?

It is a sacrament instituted by Christ in which Christ himself is truly, really, and substantially present that he may be offered in the Holy Mass as the Sacrifice of the New Law, and also that he may be received by us in Holy Communion for the spiritual refreshment of our souls.

The word *host* comes from the Latin word *hostia*, meaning *victim*. Now, the victim in the sacrifice of Calvary was Jesus Christ, and he is forever the propitiation offering himself to his Father for our sins. And because he, our victim and offering to God, is in the Holy Eucharist, the consecrated wafer is often called simply the host. The host, then, is the holy sacrament of the Eucharist in which Jesus Christ is really and substantially present under the appearances of bread. The host, or in other words, the Blessed Sacrament, was originated by Jesus Christ in the supper room at Jerusalem the night before he died, when he took bread into his hands and said, "This is my body" (Matt. 26:26).

514. Are there any signs in the host proving that he is bodily present?

No. It is a mystery of faith. All external appearances remain as before consecration, but the substance of bread and the substance of wine are changed into the substance of our Lord's body and blood. The reason why we believe is not in the host as such but in God. He has revealed this truth, and we believe because he must know and could not tell an untruth.

515. Did not the Jews think that they were asked to eat the very body of Christ? Yet he refuted them by saying that his body would ascend to heaven and that the flesh profits nothing (John 6:62-64).

When Christ promised that he would give his very flesh to eat, the Jews protested because they imagined a natural and cannibalistic eating of Christ's body. Christ refuted this notion of the manner in which his flesh was to be received by saying that he would ascend into heaven, not leaving his body in its human form upon Earth. But he did not say that they were not to eat his actual body. He would thus contradict himself, for a little earlier he had said, "For my flesh is food indeed, and my blood is drink indeed" (John 6:55). He meant, therefore, "You will not be asked to eat my flesh in the horrible and natural way you think, for my body as you see it with your eyes will be gone from this Earth. Yet I shall leave my flesh and blood in another and supernatural way that your natural and carnal minds cannot understand. The carnal or fleshly judgment profits nothing. I ask you therefore to have faith in me and to trust me. It is the spirit of faith that will enable you to believe, not your natural judgment." Then the Gospel goes on to say that many would not believe and walked no more with him; just as many today will not believe and walk no more with the Catholic Church. According to the doctrine of the Catholic Church, Christ's body is ascended into heaven. But by its substance, independently of all the laws of space that affect substance through accidental qualities, this body is present in every consecrated host.

516. If Jesus said, "This is my body," he also said, "I am the true vine," and "I am the door." In those cases it was metaphorical, for our Lord is not a vine or a door in reality. Logically, therefore, we should say, "This represents my body."

That is not a logical conclusion. In fact, it is a dreadfully shallow fallacy and quite opposed to our Lord's clear statements that I have just given you. There is no logical parallel between the words, "This is my body," and "I am the vine," or "I am the door." For the images of the vine and the door can have, of their very nature, a symbolical sense. Christ is like a vine because all the sap of my spiritual life comes from him. He is like a door, since I go to heaven through him. But a piece of bread is in no way like his flesh. Of its very nature it cannot symbolize the actual body of Christ. And he excludes that himself by saying, "The bread which I shall give for the life of the world is my flesh." That is, it is to be actually eaten, not merely commemorated in some symbolical way.

517. The use of the word "is" is explained by the fact that in the Aramaic language spoken by Jesus, there was no word for "represents."

That was a favorite argument of the early Protestants. But it has been abandoned now. First, research has shown that there were nearly forty different ways in which Christ could have said, "This represents my body," in the Aramaic language. Secondly, even prior to this research, the fact was pointed out that the Greek language abounded in symbolical expressions, and St. Mark, St. Luke, and St. Paul, who wrote in Greek under the inspiration of the Holy Spirit, should have expressed the figurative sense in that language, had the figurative sense been intended by Christ. Instead, even whilst using Greek, they select words that exclude the symbolical sense.

518. The apostles must have taken the symbolic sense, for they did not remark on the repugnant literal sense.

You overlook two points: At the Last Supper it is far more likely that the apostles would have remarked upon our Lord's words if he had meant them symbolically rather than in a literal sense. There were many other alternative expressions by which our Lord could have made it clear that he did not intend to give his actual body but merely a symbolic memento. If Christ intended to give merely a symbol of his body, and not his body at all in reality, he chose the very worst words to convey his meaning when he said without any qualification, "This is my body." It was so unnecessary to choose that expression, and so absurd, that the apostles would certainly have demanded an explanation of what he meant. But they did not. They knew that he meant what he said. You must remember that, long before the actual giving of his body to be eaten at the Last Supper, our Lord had given the apostles the opportunity to express any notions of repugnance his doctrine might awaken within them. In John 6, we read of our Lord's promise to do what he did at the Last Supper. "The bread which I shall give ... is my flesh." "Unless you eat the flesh of the Son of man," etc. Many of his listeners, rightly understanding that he meant his actual flesh, expressed their repugnance. "This is a hard saying; who can listen to it?" And they left him. Then Jesus turned to his apostles, and gave them the opportunity to express their repugnance also, and to leave him if they wished. "Will you also go away?" St. Peter replied, in magnificent faith, "Lord, to whom shall we go? You have the words of eternal life." St. Peter did not pretend to comprehend the mystery. But he knew that our Lord meant to give his very flesh in the one way that those who went had understood, and he simply accepted our Lord's assurance because of his firm faith in Christ. But the point to note is this: Having overcome any ideas of repugnance then when our Lord promised to give his very flesh as food, there is no reason to expect expressions of repugnance from the apostles when the promise was fulfilled at the Last Supper.

519. We Protestants believe that Christ's body is really present in the Eucharist, but not by transubstantiation.

The majority of Protestants believe that his body is really absent. Those who do say that they believe in his Real Presence yet deny transubstantiation illogically admit an effect yet deny the only process by which it can truly occur. If there be no transubstantiation or conversion of the substance of bread into the substance of Christ's body, then the substance of bread remains after consecration, and it is bread and not the body of Christ. People make a kind of bogey of transubstantiation as foolishly as a man would do somewhat similarly if he admitted a railway from New York to San Francisco yet refused to admit that it could be called the transcontinental railway.

520. Is Christ's body anatomically and physiologically present?

Christ's real body is present. Anatomical structure and physiological modifications belong to qualities possessed by substance. After the consecration we have the substance of Christ's body present without any external manifestation of his anatomical or physiological appearances, and the qualities of bread remaining as the object of sense perception without any substance of bread. That substance of bread has been converted into the substance of Christ's body. And as substance is the basic reality, we rightly say that the Blessed Sacrament is the very body of Christ.

521. Is Christ's body subject to processes of digestion?

The substance of Christ's body is not subject to processes of digestion or to any chemical reactions. The qualities of bread of course behave in their normal way, undergoing a change as they are affected by digestion. Our Lord's substantial presence ceases as these qualities cease to retain those characteristics proper to bread.

522. Christ is in heaven. How can you put him in the tabernacle?

No Catholic denies that Christ is continually present in heaven. He is not so present in the Eucharist that he ceases to be present in heaven. He is in heaven according to his natural though glorified form. The same Christ is in the Eucharist substantially, but not in the same way as he is present in heaven. Substance as such abstracts from limitations of place and space. Locality directly belongs to the qualities of bread that remain after consecration and indirectly only to the substantial presence of Christ's body underlying those apparent qualities.

523. What is the Mass?

The Mass is the sacrifice of the Christian dispensation in which the very body and blood of Jesus Christ under the appearances of bread and wine are offered to God by a lawfully ordained priest. This sacrifice of the Mass is offered to render honor and glory to God, to thank him for his benefits, to make reparation for the sins of mankind, and to beg of God the graces and blessings we need. It represents and continues in our midst the one great sacrifice of Jesus on the cross, and is offered for all the purposes for which he died.

524. Christ meant his disciples, each time they broke bread, to remember his death and to renew their love for him each time.

He meant that but far more also. Not only were we to remember his death for us, but he left his very body under the appearances of bread so that we might reoffer to the Father him who was our victim on the cross. Not only were we to remember his death; we were to show his death as often as the celebration occurred, thus fulfilling the prophecy of Malachi. "For from the rising of the sun to its setting my name is great among the nations, and in every place incense is offered to my name, and a pure offering; for my name is great among the nations, says the Lord of hosts" (Mal. 1:11). Nor were we merely to renew our love for him. He was to renew his life in us. So he said, "As the living Father sent me, and I live because of the Father, so he who eats me will live because of me" (John 6:57). It is difficult to understand why you should wish to belittle the greatness of his gift.

525. Hebrews 10:12, says that Christ's was a finished or perfected work or sacrifice.

The Catholic Church teaches that the sacrifice of the cross was a complete and perfect sacrifice. The Mass is not a new sacrificing of Christ in the same sense but is a new offering and application of the Christ sacrificed on Calvary. The absolute sacrifice occurred on Calvary; the Mass is a relative sacrifice, deriving its value from the cross. Just as prior to his death on Calvary, Christ offered his body and blood at the Last Supper saying, "This is my body which is for you. ... This chalice is the new covenant in my blood," so in the Mass, not now by anticipation but in retrospect, Christ the victim is offered to his Father.

526. There is only one sacrifice for Christians—that of Calvary.

The sacrifice of Calvary was a sacrifice not only for Christians but for the whole human race from the moment of the first sin. But whilst the death of Christ upon the cross was the one great absolute sacrifice, the Mass is a true and relative sacrifice applying to the souls of men the fruits of Calvary. Anyway, the doctrine that denies that the Mass is the true sacrifice in the Christian dispensation is simply anti-scriptural.

527. How do you prove that the sacrifice of the Mass is scriptural?

By religion we honor God, and the chief and highest form of worship has ever been by the offering of sacrifice. Now, God demanded continual sacrifices of various kinds from the very beginning of the human race until the coming of Christ, and it is not likely that the Christian and more perfect religion would lack a continual and regular offering of the highest act of religion. All the various sacrifices of the Jewish dispensation represented and prefigured the sacrifice of Christ on Calvary and derived all their value by anticipation from his death upon the cross. And if the Jews had to honor God by regular sacrifices, so too must Christians in the higher and more perfect New Law. But there is this difference. Whilst the Jewish sacrifices were anticipations of the sacrifice of Christ on Calvary, the Mass is a recollection and constant application of that one great sacrifice to the souls of men.

528. It is little use your telling us what ought to be, unless you can prove it as a fact from Scripture.

I can do so. The Old Testament predicts that Christ will offer a true sacrifice to God in bread and wine—that he will use those elements. And this prediction is every bit as clear as the prediction that he will also offer himself upon the cross. Thus Genesis 14:18 tells us that Melchizedek, king of Salem, was a priest and that he offered sacrifice under the form of bread and wine. Now, Psalms 110 predicts most clearly that Christ will be a priest according to the order of Melchizedek, i.e., offering a sacrifice under the forms of bread and wine. We must, then, look for some form of sacrifice differing from that of Calvary, for the Crucifixion was not a sacrifice under the forms of bread and wine. You may say that Christ fulfilled the prediction at the Last Supper, but that the rite was not to be continued. However, that admits that the rite was truly sacrificial—and the fact is that it has been continued in exactly the same sense. It was predicted that it would continue. After foretelling the rejection of the Jewish priesthood, the prophet Malachi predicts a new sacrifice to be offered in every place. "From the rising of the sun to its setting my name is great among the nations, and in every place incense is offered to my name, and a pure offering" (Mal. 1:11). The sacrifice of Calvary took place in one place only. We must look for a sacrifice apart from Calvary, one offered in every place under the forms of bread and wine. The Mass is that sacrifice.

529. Jesus gave himself under the forms of bread and wine. You are not justified in withholding the cup from the laity.

The fact that the Catholic Church does so is sufficient proof that she is justified in doing so. However, let us view the theology of the matter. Jesus gave himself under both kinds, yet he was completely present in either kind. He who receives either kind receives the whole Christ. In any case, Christ being risen dies no more. It is not possible now to separate Christ's body and blood in actual fact. Wherever Christ is, there he is whole and entire. He is wholly under the appearances of bread and wholly under the appearances of wine. In receiving the Blessed Sacrament under the form of bread the communicant receives the Blood of Christ also. In receiving under the form of wine alone he would receive the body also. There is no possibility of receiving the body of Christ without the blood of Christ.

530. I have read that primitive Christians used bread and water for the Eucharist, copying Mithraism, the rival religion that so severely challenged Christianity.

Mithraism was widespread during the first centuries of Christianity, chiefly amongst pagan Roman soldiers. This pagan and mythological religion did include in its rites a symbolical banquet of bread and water. But the rite was in no way sacramental in the Christian sense of the word and had no similarity with the Christian sacrament of the Eucharist any more than any other partaking of bread and water under any other conceivable circumstances. Above all, the statement is entirely untrue when it suggests that the use of bread and water in a Christian communion service is a reversion to primitive Christian practice. Never did the early Christians substitute water for wine in this sacramental rite. They knew quite well that water would be an invalid substance for the purposes of the Eucharist, and that the very substances used and prescribed by Christ had to be employed. As for the remark that Mithraism was a rival religion that severely challenged Christianity, I can but say that it was a prevalent form of paganism in the early centuries, rivaling the official pagan religion of Rome. But it was no more a challenge to Christianity than that same Roman paganism. Christianity rather challenged all forms of paganism rife in the Roman Empire and fought them out of existence.

531. How can marriage be a sacrament?

A sacrament is a visible rite instituted by Christ for the signifying and giving of grace. Marriage is a visible rite, witnessed by men. It has been elevated by Christ to sacramental dignity. It signifies something very sacred, the union of Christ with his Church, as St. Paul tells us in Ephesians 5:22-33. There is but one Christ and one true Church. So there must be but one husband and one wife in each case. As there is no divorce between Christ and his Church, so there can be no divorce between husband and wife. And as the union between Christ and the Church results in the production of grace, so this sacred union in marriage conveys grace to the contracting parties that they may rightly fulfill their duties to each other, and to their children, for the love of God.

532. Marriage is a legal status not subject to any spiritual law.

If no spiritual law governs marriage, why did Christ say, "Every one who divorces his wife, except on the ground of unchastity, makes her an adulteress; and whoever marries a divorced woman commits adultery"? Christ was not the civil ruler, and he had said explicitly, "Render therefore to Caesar the things that are Caesar's." If marriage belongs solely to civil authority, Christ would have left it to civil authority. And why did St. Paul say, "A man shall leave his father and mother and be joined to his wife. ... This is a great mystery, and I mean in reference to Christ and the Church." He did not say, "But I speak from the viewpoint of civil authority." Again, elsewhere he writes, "She is free to be married to whom she wishes, only in the Lord" (1 Cor. 7:39).

533. According to your doctrine, polygamy would be wrong. But the Bible permitted it.

Christ clearly tells us that whatever concessions were made in the Old Law, it was God's intention from the very beginning that a man should cleave to his wife, not to his wives, and that they should be two in one flesh. God had made concessions because of the hardness of men's hearts in the less perfect Law, but those concessions were withdrawn in the more perfect Law. Christ restored the primitive law, and said, "What therefore God has joined together, let not man put asunder" (Mark 10:2-9).

534. Does the Catholic Church forbid divorce under any circumstances?

A civil divorce on the understanding that it gives a legal right to separation, but that it in no way dissolves the latent bond of marriage and gives no right to remarriage whilst both parties still live, is permitted at times for very grave reasons. But under no circumstances does the Catholic Church permit divorce in the sense of abolishing the bond of marriage and as giving a right to remarry, where baptized people are concerned.

535. What Scripture support is there for the absolute indissolubility of Catholic marriages?

Marriage is dissolved by death. But apart from that, a perfected marriage in the Christian law cannot be dissolved. Thus, in Mark 10:11-12, our Lord says, "Whoever divorces his wife and marries another, commits adultery against her; and if she divorces her husband and marries another, she commits adultery." In 1 Cor. 7:39, St. Paul says, "A wife is bound to her husband as long as he lives. If the husband dies, she is free to be married."

536. Christ allowed divorce for one reason. He said, "Every one who divorces his wife, except on the ground of unchastity, makes her an adulteress" (Matt. 5:32).

Christ allowed permanent separation if adultery be committed, but he does not allow divorce and remarriage in the sense you intend. When he said, "Every one who divorces his wife, except on the ground of unchastity, makes her an adulteress" etc., the sense he intended was this, "Whosoever shall put away his wife (I am not speaking of mere separation without remarriage, for that is lawful in the case of fornication), but whosoever shall put away his wife ... he that marries her commits adultery." This is the only possible interpretation in the light of parallel passages. Thus St. Mark records Christ's words absolutely, "Whoever divorces his wife and marries another, commits adultery against her" (Mark 10:11). In St. Luke, also, we have the words without any parenthesis: "Every one who divorces his wife and marries another commits adultery, and he who marries a woman divorced from her husband commits adultery" (Luke 16:18). St. Paul tells us clearly, "A wife is bound to her husband as long as he lives. If the husband dies, she is free to be married" (1 Cor. 7:39). For a Christian, then, there is no such thing as divorce and remarriage whilst the first partner is still living. Attempted remarriage results in a sinful union only. You can have divorce and give up Christianity, or you can have Christianity and give up divorce. You cannot have both.

537. The civil law admits divorce and remarriage.

Civil law and divine law are not always in harmony. Politicians at times exceed their powers and make laws that are contrary to those of God. Thus they have legislated concerning matrimony with no reference to the will of Christ who raised the marriage contract to the dignity of a sacrament.

538. Your law imposes a great hardship upon the innocent party.

It is the law of Christ, not a law made by the Catholic Church. And it is at times hard upon the innocent party. But since when were we dispensed from the observance of God's laws on the score that obedience to them is inconvenient?

539. What can one do if the husband is absolutely impossible to live with, or is guilty of adultery?

Brutal cruelty and ill-treatment afford lawful grounds for separation, as also does adultery if it has not been condoned. But this separation does not break the bond of marriage. Death alone can do that, and neither is free to marry again whilst the other is still living. For grave reasons a Catholic can obtain ecclesiastical permission to have the separation rendered legal by a civil decree of divorce in order to avoid legal difficulties, but this must be on the understanding that such a decree leaves neither party free to contract another marriage whilst the other party is still living.

540. Will you kindly say whether the Catholic Church has ever granted a special dispensation for the annulment of a marriage?

The Catholic Church has often declared marriages thought to be valid to be in reality null and void. These declarations of nullity merely say that no real matrimonial bond ever existed, owing to some invalidating impediment at the time of the matrimonial contract. But you evidently have in mind the case where a marriage was not null and void from the very beginning, yet where the Catholic Church has granted a decree nullifying an existent marriage bond. The Church has the power to dissolve such a marriage, and has done so, but never in the case of two baptized Christians who have both contracted and consummated their marriage. The death of one of the parties can alone dissolve such a marriage, and the Catholic Church declares that neither she nor any other power on Earth can do so. Where other types of marriage are concerned, those who desire a decision can but submit their particular cases to the proper ecclesiastical tribunals that are appointed to consider whether the Church has the power to annul them, and whether there are sufficient reasons to justify her use of that power.

541. Where does man go after death?

His body will go temporarily back to the dust. His soul goes to the judgment of God, and thence to one of three possible states. If the soul is quite fit for heaven, it enters heaven. If it is not quite fit for heaven, it goes to purgatory. If quite unfit for heaven, it goes to hell. Thus Scripture says, "It is appointed for men to die once, and after that comes judgment" (Heb. 9:27). It tells us also that one who has been fully faithful to God will receive the invitation, "Enter into the joy of your master." One who dies in God's grace and friendship but who has not been fully faithful will be saved, according to holy Scripture, but so as by fire. One who dies rejecting God will be rejected by God and will be buried in hell.

542. No one on earth knows anything about the life beyond.

You are very dogmatic. However, I prefer to accept the authority of the God who made me and who must certainly know what is awaiting me. It is your word against the word of God. I prefer the latter.

543. Will the future differ from this life?

Yes. This life is adapted more to our material nature, the soul conforming its activities to the body it animates. In the next life the body will be adapted rather to our spiritual nature, the soul dominating. Whether the new conditions will be pleasant or unpleasant depends upon our conduct here on Earth.

544. Your pleasant or unpleasant conditions suppose the dogmas of heaven and hell, dogmas that reason cannot accept.

The dogmas of heaven and hell guarantee the conditions. Nor is there anything in those dogmas that conflicts with sane reason.

545. What do you mean by hell?

Hell is the eternal lot of misery awaiting those who die in a state of grave sin and at enmity with God. Before the general resurrection, the soul alone experiences this misery; after the resurrection, the body will be reunited with that soul and will share in the misery, being tormented by created elements even as the person forsook God during life for the enjoyment of created things. The chief misery will be the sense of having lost the happiness of the vision of God; the other will be the torment of fire.

546. What evidence have you that such a hell exists?

The very best. The God who made us tells us that he also has made a hell. There is a hell in which both the bodies and the souls of the lost will be afflicted. Thus the gentle Christ himself warns us, "It is better that you lose one of your members than that your whole body go into hell" (Matt. 5:30). Remember that all shall rise someday, the good and bad alike, the body sharing in the fate of the soul. "All who are in the tombs will hear his voice and come forth, those who have done good, to the resurrection of life, and those who have done evil, to the resurrection of judgment" (John 5:28-29). Those who are lost will go to everlasting fire. Christ calls it "unquenchable fire" (Mark 9:44). He tells us of the grim sentence, "Depart from me, you cursed, into the eternal fire prepared for the devil and his angels" (Matt. 25:41). Such a solemn utterance of the judicial sentence demands the literal sense. Judges do not speak in metaphors at such moments, "Let him be hanged—but of course only metaphorically." And it will be conscious suffering. Our Lord says, "Their worm does not die, and the fire is not quenched" (Mark 9:48). And again, "There will be weeping and gnashing of teeth" (Matt. 13:50). Continued conscious suffering is the fate of the lost. And reason demands such a fate. When a man sins gravely, he chooses between God and a thing forbidden by God. He cannot have both, and he prefers to renounce God rather than the created good. If he dies without repentance his will is still alienated from God. He would do the same thing again if he got the chance. And as long as these dispositions last he must *do* without God, and happiness. These dispositions lasting forever once this probationary life is over, so will the penalty.

547. Do you maintain that there is a real fire in hell?

Yes. The fire of hell is a real and created fire that will affect even the bodies of men who die at enmity with God. I grant that it will differ in various characteristics from natural fire as we know it. Christ chose the word fire as being that element best known to us that produces results most similar to the effects of the fire of hell. Yet fire as we know it depends upon combustion. The fire of hell will not depend upon being constantly fed with fuel but upon God's will, the principle of all existing things. If God can will that fire should exist with the aid of fuel to which he gave its properties, he certainly can produce and conserve fire by simply willing it, and without the aid of created fuel. Thus he manifested to Moses a bush in flames yet unconsumed.

548. Will men's bodies go to hell as well as their souls?

If men die in such a state as to deserve hell, both their bodies and souls will endure the misery. Thus, in St. John's Gospel, 5:28–29, Christ is recorded as saying, "The hour is coming when all who are in the tombs will hear his voice and come forth, those who have done good, to the resurrection of life, and those who have done evil, to the resurrection of judgment." At that last judgment men will be present in their complete personality, body and soul. And they will reap one of two destinies, heaven or hell. The complete human being will be either saved or lost. Such is the teaching of Christ, and one must accept it or cease to claim to be a Christian.

549. How can fire affect a spiritual being such as the devil?

By the restriction of its activities according to the limitations of the created agent of torture, and by the intellectual apprehension of the suffering fire normally causes. But difficulties concerning its method of action make no difference to the fact that it exists.

550. Boundless mercy seems to contradict eternal misery, don't you think?

I don't. Boundless mercy *supposes* the possibility of eternal misery. There is no room for mercy unless there be misery, and no room for boundless mercy unless we suppose boundless misery.

Boundless mercy is a mercy that forgives that which does deserve boundless misery. But mercy is not forced upon people. It must be asked for and accepted. It cannot be rejected and at the same time be enjoyed. And if a person is in a state of sin deserving boundless or eternal misery, yet rejects the offer of boundless mercy, what is there left but hell? If you assert that because God is boundless in his mercy, as he is, no one could go to eternal misery, will you say that there is no hell? Or that God has made a hell knowing that it was quite unnecessary as it is to be eternally untenanted? And what will you do with Satan? Is he not in that everlasting suffering prepared for him and his angels? He who proves too much proves nothing. There is something wrong with an argument that ends in the denial of known facts. God is a God of boundless mercy. He has revealed that there is a hell of eternal misery. There is no contradiction. People can escape the boundless misery by a sincere appeal to God's boundless mercy.

551. Such a doctrine is against the weight of enlightened reason.

It is not. It is reason enlightened by God that accepts the doctrine. If you are speaking of natural enlightenment, then the first thing that such enlightenment admits is its own deficiency and limitation. It is the very unenlightened man who will admit eternal happiness because he likes it and deny eternal punishment because he doesn't. The forces producing both are obviously in this world—good and evil. Meantime, the Catholic Church has plenty of evidence that there is a hell. Opponents have not a scrap of evidence that there is not. And no man can explain the terrible sufferings of Christ, granted his knowledge that there was no hell to save us from, and that we would all get to heaven in the end whether he suffered or not. He did not go through his Crucifixion for nothing.

552. Is any person so bad as to deserve eternal punishment?

Yes. The man who deliberately and finally despises and rejects the infinite love of God deserves to be deprived of it forever.

553. However bad people may be, I think it is against right ideas of God to speak of his punishing anyone forever.

Then what are you going to do with Satan? He is a creature of God even as we. Is he going to reform? Will he ever come out of the eternal fire prepared for the devil and his angels? No. And granting the fact that God is punishing one of his creatures like that, responsible human souls can certainly meet with the same fate. I do not like the thought of anyone suffering in hell any more than you do. But that will not make me deny the existence of hell. Hundreds of things we do not like are facts.

554. How can you reconcile hell with God's love, justice, and mercy?

If I could not that would but prove something wrong with my own ideas on the subject. For it is certain that God is loving, just, and merciful, and he has revealed that there is a hell. So the ideas cannot be repugnant. However, God's love, justice, and mercy demand that there is a hell. His love demands a hell, for the more he loves goodness, the more he must hate sin. To the man who says that God loves too much to send a man to hell, I simply reply that he sends no man there; men go there. And God has loved too much not to let them go there if they scorn, reject, and throw God's love back in his face. Again, his justice demands that if a man dies rejecting an infinite goodness he should endure a penalty of a never-ending nature. If there were no eternal punishment, a man could cry to God, "You say 'Thou shalt not not;' I say 'I shall.' Do your worst. You cannot punish me forever. What care I for your commandments or for yourself! You must either make me happy in the end or annihilate me when I shall have escaped your power." It is impossible for the drama of iniquity to end like that. That would not be justice. And as for God's mercy, already it is a mercy that man has the thought of hell as an emergency brake to stop his headlong rush into vice. The truth that there is a hell has mercifully saved many a soul from a life of blasphemy and sin, and still more often from death in a state of sin. And remember that God's mercy is offered to every man over and over again during life. Mercy is asked for, not forced upon people. Some men who are loudest in their protests against God's injustice would be the first to complain if God forced anything upon them, even his mercy. But men cannot have God's mercy and reject it at one and the same time.

555. The appeal to fear, to my mind, is not half so efficacious as the appeal to love.

I agree. Fear is a transitory emotion; love more lasting. But response to love supposes some generosity of character. Now, habitual sin dries up generosity. The sinner becomes more and more selfish. He is less sensitive to noble motives and is more affected by those that threaten his own comfort. This type will be more moved by fear than by love. But fear of God is but the beginning of wisdom. It is meant to make a man abandon his sins. But if he does so, and begins to lead a better life, selfishness wanes, nobility develops, and he begins to respond more to love than to his initial fears. And love will then show that it has the greater power to inspire positive virtue.

556. Are Judas and Adam in hell?

It has never been revealed that any particular soul is in hell. Christ said of Judas, "Better for him had he never been born." That does not look too hopeful in his case, for no matter what a man has to endure, if he attains eternal happiness in the end, much better to have been born. However, even of Judas, no man has absolute certainty. The question can be solved only by God. It is practically certain that Adam is in heaven and not in hell. Thus Scripture says, "Wisdom protected the first-formed father of the world ... she delivered him from his transgression" (Wis. 10:1). Adam was the type of the second Adam, Christ, and it is to be expected that Christ, the second Adam, would see to it that the first Adam was fully liberated from Satan. The Greek Church, from very ancient times, has celebrated the feast of Adam and Eve.

557. I am interested in your dogma concerning purgatory. Must I be a Catholic before I can understand that invention of your Church?

No. You must be a non-Catholic to suspect that the Church did invent it. The idea that there is no purgatory is the invention of

Protestants. The reformers corrupted the true doctrine, and many good Protestants, realizing this, are returning to the Catholic religion of their forefathers even as I myself have done. Meantime, if I could discover, or you could show me, when and where the Church invented this doctrine, I promise to spend the rest of my life exposing the Catholic Church as a merely human institution making outrageous claims upon men.

558. What is the nature of your doctrine on purgatory?

It can be summed up very briefly. At death the soul of man, if quite fit, goes at once to heaven; if not quite fit to purgatory; if quite unfit to hell. The soul that has repented of all its sins, and has fully expiated them in this life, is quite fit for heaven at once. The soul that departs this life in a state of unrepented mortal sin can never be fitted for heaven and goes to hell. But a soul that has sincerely repented of its sins, yet has not fully expiated them, secures immunity from hell by repentance and goes to purgatory until it has expiated all its deficiencies.

559. This dogma of purgatory was invented by Pope Gregory in the year 600 and was made an article of faith by the Council of Florence in 1439.

If not invented until A.D. 600, why did St. Monica, in the fourth century, implore her son St. Augustine, as she lay on her deathbed, to pray for her soul whenever he went to the altar to offer the Mass? And how would you account for the inscriptions in the catacombs recording prayers for the dead offered by the Christians of the first centuries? Or, if you would go back earlier, what will you do with the teaching of Scripture itself? The Council of Florence merely recalled previous definitions.

560. The Bible mentions only heaven and hell.

It does not. It certainly mentions an intermediate state to which the soul of Christ went after his death on the cross (1 Pet. 3:19). This state was neither heaven nor hell, but the limbo of the Fathers of the Old Law. In addition to this, Scripture mentions the purgatorial state. In any case, it would not matter if the Bible did mention but two places. My mentioning only London and New York could not prove the nonexistence of Paris. It would be a different matter if Christ had said, "There is no purgatory." But he did not.

It does not mention the precise word *purgatory*. But the intermediate state of purification described by that word is there. In Matthew 5:26, Christ in condemning sin speaks of liberation only after expiation. "You will never get out till you have paid the last penny." In Matthew 12:32, he speaks of sin that "will not be forgiven, either in this age or in the age to come." Any remission of the effects of sin in the next world can refer only to purgatory. Above all, St. Paul tells us that the day of judgment will try each man's work. That day is after death, when the soul goes to meet its God. What is the result of that judgment? If a man's work will not stand the test, St. Paul says that "he will suffer loss, though he himself will be saved, but only as through fire" (1 Cor. 3:15). This cannot refer to eternal loss in hell, for no one is saved there. Nor can it refer to heaven, for there is no suffering in heaven. Purgatory alone can explain this text. As a matter of fact, all Christians believed in purgatory until the Reformation, when the reformers began their rejection of Christian doctrines at will. Prayer for the dead was ever the prevailing custom, in accordance with the recommendation of the Bible itself. "If he was looking to the splendid reward that is laid up for those who fall asleep in godliness, it was a holy and pious thought. Therefore he made atonement for the dead, that they might be delivered from their sin" (2 Macc. 12:45). Prayer for the dead supposes a soul not in heaven where it does not need the help of prayer, nor in hell where prayer cannot assist it. Some intermediate state of purification and need, where prayer can help, is necessary. And the doctrine is most reasonable. "Nothing unclean shall enter [heaven]" (Rev. 21:27). Yet not all defilement should cost man the loss of his soul. Even in this life human justice does not inflict capital punishment for every crime. Small offenses are punished by fines or by temporary imprisonment, after which the delinquent is liberated. Those who deny purgatory teach the harder and more unreasonable doctrine.

561. Christ never told anyone to pray for the dead.

Not all that Christ said or did is recorded in the Gospels. They are fragmentary accounts only. Meantime, those who believe in Christ accept both Old and New Testaments as the word of God. Now, in the Old Testament we read, "It was a holy and pious thought ... he made atonement for the dead, that they might be delivered from their sin" (2 Macc. 12:45). In the New Testament St. Paul tells us that Christians are members of Christ and members, therefore, of one another, so that if one member suffers anything, all the members suffer with it. And St. James tells us to pray for one another, advice certainly not limited to this life only. So we find St. Paul praying for the departed soul of his fellow laborer, Onesiphorus.

562. God would not demand expiation after having forgiven the sin.

What you think God would or would not do cannot avail against that that he does do. When David repented of his great sin, God sent the prophet Nathan with the message to him, "The Lord has put away your sin; you shall not die. Nevertheless, because by this deed you have utterly scorned the Lord, the child that is born to you shall die" (2 Sam. 12:13-14). To forgive the guilt of sin, and purify the spiritual scar and stain, which that disease of the soul leaves, by expiatory suffering, is better than to leave the soul still unpurified and indebted to God's justice. I too could fully forgive a friend his offense should he have robbed me yet still insist that he make good the damage he has wrought me.

563. Where is purgatory?

God has not deigned to satisfy our curiosity on that point, and the knowledge is not of practical importance to us. The fact that there is a purgatory has been revealed by God. And when he reveals a fact we cannot say to him, "Well, I for one refuse to believe it until you tell me more about it." God proves a thing by saying it, for he is truth itself. We have but to prove that he said it.

564. How do you know that you can help the souls in purgatory by your prayers?

God would not have inspired the Jews to pray for the departed if such prayers were of no avail. Christians have always prayed for the dead, a practice fully warranted by the doctrine of the communion of saints. And if we can pray for our dear ones who are in trouble in this life, our prayers can certainly follow them in their future difficulties. All prayer is addressed to the same God who is as present to the souls of our dear departed as he is to us.

565. How do priests know when a soul escapes from purgatory?

Souls do not escape from purgatory as criminals from jail. When they are sufficiently purified for the vision of God they are admitted to heaven. And no one knows when this occurs, unless God gives a special revelation, a favor we have no right to ask.

566. Then you might be praying for a soul not in purgatory at all!

That is quite possible. Granted that we believe in purgatory, that our prayers can help the dead, and that we do not know for certain whether our dear ones are emancipated from their purifications or not, we continue praying for them. We give them, rather than ourselves, the benefit of any doubt. We argue that our prayers may possibly benefit them, not that they may possibly be wasted. And we would certainly risk saying too many for them rather than allow them to run the risk of being deprived of help.

567. I have heard Catholics speak of indulgences for the souls in purgatory? What are indulgences?

Do not mix up the ecclesiastical term *indulgence* with the modern idea of self-indulgence. An indulgence is not a permission to indulge in sin but is a remission of punishment due to sin. Now, in the early Christian Church certain sins were punished by long public penance, sometimes for days, at other times for years. But the Church was often indulgent, and loosed or freed Christians from all or part of their public penance, if they showed other good dispositions or performed certain works of charity. The Church had that power in the name of God as surely as the state has the power in its own name to commute a sentence or even release a criminal altogether under certain circumstances. Christ said to the Church, "Whatever you loose on earth shall be loosed in heaven" (Matt. 18:18). That the merits of Christ and of the martyrs and saints of the ages are at the disposal of the Church is also a consequence of the doctrine of the communion of saints. And that power of commuting or even of remitting penances and expiations exists in the Church today, being exercised by the granting of indulgences.

568. Pope Leo X sold indulgences in Germany to get money for St. Peter's. Do you think it right to sell pardons for sins?

An indulgence is not a pardon for sin. It can be gained only by one who is not in a state of sin and who has previously secured forgiveness of his sins by repentance and confession. Then, and then only, an indulgence is a remission of further penalties due to sin. It is absolutely wrong, of course, to sell indulgences. Pope Leo X did not do so. There were abuses by some individuals in this matter, but they were never with the sanction of the Church. The pope granted the favor of certain indulgences to those who would give alms toward the building of St. Peter's in Rome. But there is a difference between giving alms to a good work and giving money to purchase something of equivalent value. Remember that Christ had a special blessing for the widow who gave her mite as an alms to the temple in Jerusalem. Would you accuse him of selling that blessing for a mite?

569. Do departed souls retain memories of us and know what is still going on in this world?

There is every probability that they retain memories of those whom they loved or met during their life on Earth. But there is no real probability that they are aware of things that have occurred since their death, except insofar as God may choose to manifest such knowledge to them. The human soul secures its information concerning this world through the bodily senses—seeing, hearing, and touching things. Those senses are its normal means of contact with this earthly life. But when the soul leaves the body, it is separated from these sense-faculties and therefore loses the normal means of contact with the life we still experience.

570. Does your Church allow belief in reincarnation?

Catholic dogmatic teaching absolutely excludes belief in the doctrine of reincarnation, or the transmigration of souls, with their consequent reappearance in this world in other bodies.

571. After due purification in purgatory, you maintain that souls will be admitted to heaven. What is this heaven?

Heaven is the destiny in which a human soul will, if saved, be happy in the clear and immediate sight of God for all eternity. Before the resurrection of the body the soul alone enjoys this vision of God; after the resurrection, the body will be reunited with the soul and will share in its glory and joy.

572. How do you know that there is a heaven?

God has revealed the fact: "Rejoice and be glad," said Christ "for your reward is great in heaven" (Matt. 5:12). That heaven is not in this life, nor is it to be on this Earth: "I go and prepare a place for you, I will come again and will take you to myself, that where I am you may be also" (John 14:3). The conditions of heaven will differ from any we know in this life: "For when they rise from the dead, they neither marry nor are given in marriage, but are like angels in heaven" (Mark 12:25); "These all died … having acknowledged that they were strangers and exiles on the earth. For people who speak thus make it clear that they are seeking a homeland … they desire a better country, that is, a heavenly one" (Heb. 11:13-16). And St. John tells us that God "will wipe away every tear from their eyes, and death shall be no more, neither shall there be mourning nor crying nor pain any more, for the former things have passed away" (Rev. 21:4).

573. Where is heaven?

I cannot tell you in terms of longitude and latitude, as we mark out places on this Earth. Such terms suggest a place in space, and space is measured by distance, and distance in turn is calculated from the material conditions of bodies that have nothing in common with spiritualized beings. It is quite useless, then, to ask for an explanation of heaven in terms of geography and geometry. Such a request would be like asking for the geographical location of God. Spirit beings have no "where-ness" as we understand that notion. When Christ said, "I go and prepare a place for you, that where I am you may be also," he was speaking to human beings and used a language they could understand, although it was necessarily an inadequate explanation. Heaven and our ideas in our present state have no really common ground to work upon.

574. Is heaven a place where there are land, rivers, mountains, and the utilities of life, such as there are in this world?

No. St. Paul tells us that eye has not seen, nor ear heard, nor has it entered into the heart of man, what things God has prepared for those who love him. Therefore, so surely as you have seen, or heard, or touched things in this visible universe that are the objects of your senses, those things will not be constitutive elements of heaven. What heaven will be like I cannot, therefore, describe in human language, for our concepts are all derived from the visible universe and cannot convey adequate views of the next life. But at least I can say that there is a heaven and that it will mean everlasting happiness. God must intend life to lead to happiness rather than to misery, and he, therefore, intends virtue as leading to that happiness. The purpose of a Christian life, said Christ himself, is "that my joy may be in you, and that your joy may be full" (John 15:11). The chief happiness of heaven will be eternal union with God and the immediate vision of God. As surely as the eye can now see some transcendently beautiful natural scene, so will the mind be immediately conscious of God's infinite perfection and beauty in himself.

575. I cannot conceive a future state altogether satisfying. Will not heaven be monotonous—always existing with no hope of change?

There is a big difference between imagining a future life and conceiving it. I cannot imagine or picture the future life any more than you can. The only images we could form would be derived from this life, and they would fit this life, not the next. Not without reason does God say, "What no eye has seen, nor ear heard, nor the heart of man conceived, what God has prepared for those who love him" (1 Cor. 2:9). Yet although we cannot imagine what the next life will be like, we can conceive the fact that it will be, and also the intelligible principles by which it will be governed.

In heaven we shall be with Christ and as Christ. This supposes conditions of which we have no experience on Earth. It is little use guessing. We have but to accept the fact that there is a heaven, avoiding sin and serving God in order that we may attain to it. Speculate about heaven as we will, we must not miss our eternal happiness, for we cannot afford to be without it.

576. The brain power of babies is not developed, and that of the aged failing, when they die. Will they remain like that, or will all get the same level of intelligence in heaven?

Before answering this question, we must carefully distinguish between the brain and the intellect of man. The brain is a material bodily organ that the soul of man uses, just as any other organ, for the purpose of his composite life in this world. Now, the soul is a spiritual being endowed with a spiritual intellectual faculty, just as God, or the angels, have the spiritual power of intelligence. And just as the soul can exist without the body, so its intelligence can be operative without the brain, once it is released from the restrictions of union with the body. The material brain, therefore, belongs to the body; intelligence belongs to the soul. Now we may proceed further. When the soul is released from the body by death, it no longer derives its knowledge from sense-data, nor does it require the brain as a material organ of thought. It receives its knowledge either by God infusing necessary ideas or by the immediate intuition of God's own essential and infinite perfection and truth. In purgatory, it will receive infused ideas according to its relative necessities. But in heaven, all the souls of the blessed will have the same intuitive vision of the full truth in God. Yet whilst the same range of truth will be known to every intelligent soul, capacity to appreciate that truth and to rejoice in it will vary according to merit and virtue during one's life of probation on Earth. All this applies to separated souls of whatever age, prior to the resurrection of the body, to which the brain as a material organ belongs. At the resurrection, it is the common opinion of Catholic theologians that the bodies of all, whether of children or of the aged, will rise in a state of perfect development, yet wholly changed and spiritualized in character, even though essentially the same bodies as those in which we served God during life. If we can speak of brain power in such risen bodies, all will attain the same level of development.

577. Is heaven God alone, or will we be happy in the society of friends and relatives also?

Essentially, heaven is God alone, for he is the bond of union with all other beings. But contact with God does not exclude contact with our fellow creatures. Such relations with others will be richer and closer in God. We shall possess our loved ones as never on Earth. Earthly companions will be recognized, loved, and enjoyed. Grace does not destroy nature. It perfects nature. And since we are social beings by nature, there will be a social happiness in the communion of saints in heaven. But God gives us all this in giving us himself. Seek God, and attain your eternal union with him, and all the rest will be added. Of course, in all the mutual relationships of created beings in heaven, material interests will be entirely spiritualized.

578. If a mother and daughter die and go to heaven, will they know one another there, or will they be unable to see one another?

They will undoubtedly know one another and be happy in each other's company forever, even as both are happy in God's eternal company. We believe in the communion of saints, and that means in the common union of saints. All who die in God's love and friendship will be united in heaven and will appreciate that union. And the noble love of a mother and child, which is but a reflection of God's love, will have its own special joy in eternity.

579. Will men and women still fall in love with each other in heaven, or will there be no sex attraction there?

There will be no sex attraction in heaven, and men and women will certainly not fall in love with each other in any earthly sense of the word. All in heaven will love each other for purely spiritual reasons according to their union with and in God. Sex attraction will therefore cease with this earthly life. Our Lord himself simply said, "In the resurrection they neither marry nor are given in marriage, but are like angels in heaven" (Matt. 22:30). We know that God has implanted in bodily human nature two strong attractions or appetites, the appetite for food and the sex attraction. But it is obvious that both are chiefly concerned with life in this world. The hunger appetite is to induce people to eat, or in other words, it is to keep the individual alive. Sex attraction is intended for the purpose of keeping the human race alive. Now, just as the necessity of taking food is confined to this earthly existence, so that the individual who attains heaven and lives by the principles of a purely spiritual life will no longer experience hunger for material food, so also the sex attraction, which is ordained to the propagation of the human race on Earth, will cease with the conditions of earthly life. After all, sex attraction is but a means to an end and is based upon a difference not of soul but of material formation. When the end in view is abrogated, so also will be abrogated the means to that end. And above all we must note that the body itself will not remain subject to the conditions of its present material nature. St. Paul tells us that we bury a natural body, but that it will rise a spiritual body; that such as are heavenly things, so will be those who are heavenly; that we shall not be wholly changed but that we shall certainly be changed, the mortal putting on immortality.

580. If God wanted man to attain heaven, could he not have placed man there in the first place?

That would not have been in keeping with God's plan that man's destiny should be in his own hands. By his nature, man is made for Earth rather than for heaven and could have no natural right to be in heaven. God gave him all that his nature could rightly demand. In addition, God offered freely to man the prospect of an eternal supernatural happiness in heaven, provided man made a correct use of his mind and will by obedience to God's law. And he offered the help of divine grace for this purpose. Far from complaining that God did not do more for them, men should be grateful that he should have done so much in their favor.

581. If we are judged individually at death, why are we all to be judged again at the last day? God must already know.

God does not judge in order to discern guilt. At the particular judgment that takes place as individuals die, God apportions to each soul relative remuneration or retribution. But at the end of the world, all souls will be reunited to their bodies, the souls of the just not losing their happiness, the souls of the lost not escaping their misery. The general judgment will then take place for the general manifestation of God's justice. All men will then acknowledge his attributes, even those who have denied them during this earthly life. But those who availed themselves of God's mercy will have nothing to fear on that day.

582. When will the end of the world come?

No human being can say. Christ himself refused to give any definite information on the subject: "Of that day or that hour no one knows, not even the angels in heaven, nor the Son, but only the Father" (Mark 13:32). The uncertainty is deliberate, so that men will be encouraged to live good lives in constant expectation of the possible end. So, too, the moment of our death is uncertain, and for all practical purposes death is the final coming of Christ for us. For the soul is at once judged and declared definitely to be a subject of heaven or of hell.

583. Did not Christ himself believe that the end of the world was at hand? I refer you to Luke 9:27.

In that text Christ says, "I tell you truly, there are some standing here who will not taste death before they see the kingdom of God." But those words have no reference to the end of the world.

Christ often called his Church his kingdom. When he said to St. Peter, "I will build my Church ... I will give you the keys of the kingdom of heaven," he identified the two notions. Again, when he said that his kingdom was to be as a net holding good and bad fish, he obviously referred to his Church in this world. And within thirty years of his death, that kingdom of Christ had spread throughout the known world, many who had heard Christ living to see its establishment. Meantime, Christ's prediction that his Church would go to all nations, even to the uttermost parts of the Earth, and his promise to be with it all days even to the end of the world, show that he did not expect the end of that world to be at hand. Also, he proved abundantly his divinity and knowledge of the future. It is absurd to say that he was not aware of the subsequent history of the world as it has actually unfolded.

584. What is meant by a new heavens and a new Earth?

Even were the present universe left as it is, every soul that goes out of this life must see a new heavens and a new Earth, if only because it will see things from a completely different aspect. Science tells us that the atoms and molecules of even the most rigid objects are in motion and at an incalculable speed. If the soul could get a truly scientific vision of the dance of atoms and molecules, and of the very stars, it would certainly see the universe under a very new aspect. But the change to come should not be attributed only to the changed condition of the soul. There will be a change in the actual scheme of Earth and the heavens. There will be a new order and a perfect adaptation of all things to a new end. Christ will be the organizer, as he has organized the Church and humanity. It is quite possible that all may be spiritualized and submitted to the elect, the elect to Christ, and Christ to God. Thus, St. Paul himself says that all creation waits for the manifestation of the children of God. Exactly what will occur, of course, is a mystery that God has not deigned to reveal. But he has revealed the fact that Christ will come again in some glorious way to judge mankind. And we Catholics accept that fact on the authority of God's word.

585. St. Paul thought the end was imminent and told the Thessalonians that they would go to heaven with him.

St. Paul did not believe that the end was near. In 1 Thessalonians 4:16, he says that the Lord will certainly come again, adding, "Then we who are alive, who are left, shall be caught up together with them in the clouds to meet the Lord." But he does not say that he himself and his listeners would still be living when Christ comes. He could not intend such a thing, knowing that it is not given to any man to know the day or the hour of Christ's coming. He knew simply that there will still be some Christians living on Earth in that day and intended "such of us Christians as may still be living." When Christ comes, St. Paul's words will be fulfilled. Evidently some of the Thessalonians misunderstood his words, for in his second epistle to them he writes, "We beg you, brethren, not to be quickly shaken in mind or excited, either by spirit or by word, or by letter purporting to be from us, to the effect that the day of the Lord has come" (2 Thess. 2:1-2).

586. World events and the signs of the times prove that the end of the ages is at hand now in our own days.

I do not think there is a single age in the history of the Church when men have not said that. And history has proved them wrong. You may think present signs proof, but Christ said that it is not given to man to know. At best we can but conjecture, and your opinion is nothing more than a conjecture. Christ gave general signs, it is true, but he purposely left them obscure, telling us that the end would certainly come but not telling us when.

587. Never in history were there such plagues and rumors of war as today.

That is simply unhistorical. Hundreds of years ago the black death swept through Europe, and history is one long account of wars. I do not think that even the general signs given by Christ are approaching the completion of their fulfillment yet, and I do not think that the end is likely to occur in our own days. I do not claim to know, of course. You differ, thinking that the end is near at hand. But whether I am right or you are right, let us remember that as far as we are concerned individually, our own deaths will carry us to our personal judgments; and when our own deaths are to occur is God's secret. God can take me now as I am speaking to you, or you as you are listening to me. Let us both be ready to meet God with true sorrow for our sins and great love for him when he does take us from this world.

Chapter 10

Catholic Morality

588. Does Christianity expect me to love my neighbor when I don't even like him?

Yes. And it can be done. You must not mix up "loving" with "liking." Likes and dislikes concern your feelings. But love is a matter of the will to benefit another. It is bent on securing the good of another. "Liking" is a pleasure to self. "Loving" thinks not of self but of another's welfare. Thus you can like a person whom you do not love. If, to satisfy the pleasant feelings another awakens within you, you cooperate with him in evil conduct, you do not love him, for you assist in what is to his harm. But if, on the other hand, you do not like a man, yet overlook his faults, will his good, and do all you can for his true welfare, then you love that man. In practice you are his friend, even though you experience no friendly "feelings" toward him.

Another thing to remember is this. When Christianity bids you love your neighbor whether you like him or not, it really means that you must let your love of God overflow to your neighbor. You really see not your neighbor but God; and without diverting your attention from God, you let your love of him extend to all whom he thought worth making and loving. Your neighbor may have such faults that you can never get to like him. But you must abstract from those faults, never let your repugnance influence your conduct, and will only his good for the love of God.

589. My everyday religion is an earnest endeavor to be honest and to help others less fortunate, often at personal loss; still it suits my way of thought.

You therefore reject the Christian religion. Even as a Protestant, you have drifted pretty far. I do not mean to speak unkindly. But you must admit that what you call your everyday religion could be that of a good pagan. A man who professed complete unbelief in Christ could earnestly endeavor to be honest, and to help others even at personal inconvenience. He would be completely irreligious, for his one effort would be to retain his self-respect and be kind to his fellow man. But God would not enter into his scheme of things, nor would the man enter into any relations at all with God. And since religion inspires and regulates our relations with God your "everyday religion," as described, is not religion at all. Again, you justify your attitude by saying that it "suits your way of thought." Surely you can see that a Christian is one who adjusts his life to the teaching of Christ. His way of thought is the law for a Christian.

590. I am still convinced in my mind that if only one goes about trying to be good and to do good, God will notice the fact and judge accordingly.

It is certain that God notices all things, and that he will judge accordingly. But what will be his judgment? On the standard you give, Christ need not so much as set foot in this world. You reduce yourself to the level of those who have never heard of Christ. God notices that fact and will judge accordingly. You have been baptized as a Christian. Having received that sacrament, how will you justify before God your neglect of the other ordinances of Christ? Christ said, "If he refuses to listen even to the Church, let him be to you as a Gentile and a tax collector." But you obey no Church. As the very central act of worship to be offered in his name and on behalf of his people to God, he instituted the Sacrifice of the Mass. You repudiate the necessity of attending and assisting at that sacrifice. I cannot go through all the other obligations of Christians. But I have said enough to show that, if you still believe in Christianity, you do not fulfill Christian obligations. If, on the other hand, you no longer believe in Christianity, you owe it to yourself to know just on what grounds you have rejected it.

591. The moral theology of your Church is so dreadfully intolerant. If I follow apathetically the laws of that Church I might as well never have been endowed with free will.

Catholics follow the laws of their Church not apathetically but willingly. They know that her legislation rejoices in the authority of Christ. You might just as well say, "If I have to follow the Ten Commandments apathetically, I might as well have been born without free will." You are mixing up physical freedom with moral freedom. Man is physically free to do good or evil, but he is not morally free to do evil. And as morally we are not free to disobey God's commandments, so we are not morally free to disobey the Church Christ commissioned to teach in his name.

592. But Pope Pius IX condemned liberty of conscience straight out.

He did not. He condemned the proposition that any man is free to embrace any religion he pleases. But this has nothing to do with liberty of conscience. It simply asserts the principle that if God has given a definite revelation, it is man's duty to accept that revelation just as it is. Man cannot be morally free to reject a religion that he knows to have been revealed by God and choose some other religion at his own pleasure. If a man does not know the true religion, and is erroneously convinced that it is right to be a Wesleyan or a member of any other non-Catholic Church, then Catholic moral theology so respects his conscience that it will not allow him to be received into the Church as long as he has this conviction.

593. I know I can always say, "Follow your conscience. Conscience is the last court of appeal."

You cannot say that. Conscience is not the last court of appeal as the guide of conduct, whatever may be its value in relation to one's judgment by God. The last court of appeal, where right or wrong conduct is concerned, is the revealed law of God. The individual conscience can be objectively erroneous through lack of knowledge or through malice. For example, God says, "You shall not commit adultery." Yet there are people who say that they cannot conscientiously see any wrong in adultery. If they are telling the truth, then their conscience is wrong. They have distorted their conscience. God's law is the standard of right and wrong just as the sun is the standard of time. And conscience is right if it is conformed to God's law, just as a watch is right if it is in harmony with the sun.

594. I should be grateful if you would define conscience for me.

Conscience is simply a judgment of the intelligence applied to moral matters. In mathematics the mind concludes that two and two make four. In music it will judge as to whether the notes harmonize with one another or not. In moral conduct, it judges that good must be done and evil avoided. And when some particular course of action presents itself, it will decide as to whether that course of action is in harmony with good principles or not. Whence come the principles with which conduct is to be compared? They are part of our very nature, impressed upon us by the Creator himself. And in this sense conscience is the voice of God within us. Every human being is born with an urge to tend to a perfect development. But this will be possible only if life is well ordered. Hence, the innate conviction that the order of nature itself must be respected. As a creature, man has an innate tendency to respect the rights of the Creator; as social, he has an innate tendency to respect the rights of his fellow men; as intelligent and self-regulating, he tends to respect his own dignity. And conscience manifests itself by interior approval or reproach according to his observance or violation of these natural obligations imposed by the God who made man as he is.

595. Would the Catholic Church abolish religious liberty in America if it had the power?

I am quite sure that we differ in our ideas of what religious liberty means. The Catholic Church would give everybody the liberty to be religious. But liberty to propagate any religion at all is another matter. The abuse and misuse of liberty and freedom are dangerous things. A man can be subject to erroneous religions and free from the true religion. Or he can be subject to the true religion and free from erroneous religions. However, you evidently mean freedom to maintain and propagate any religion or all religions. To that thought I would say this. If all in America were Catholics, the Church would rightly forbid the danger to their faith by the introduction of error. But if erroneous religions were already established and their adherents were in good faith, the Church would permit their continued existence and liberty. And such is the case at present. The non-Catholics in America have never been her subjects, and she is not called upon to adopt such general protective measures as would be the case in a completely Catholic nation.

596. Is the temporal punishment of torture in accordance with the teachings of Christ?

It is quite lawful to inflict pain as a punishment, or no schoolmaster could punish a rebellious child. I am grateful now for many a punishment inflicted upon me by my parents in my childhood. In principle, the infliction of pain is lawful. The question rather concerns the degree of pain to be inflicted. Excessive pain is undoubtedly wrong, unjust, inhuman, and un-Christian.

597. But the history of your Church is one of excessive torture, unparalleled cruelty, and injustice.

You have read garbled accounts. No one denies the existence of cruelty and persecution in the history of the ages. But they have been exaggerated. Nor were they due to the Catholic point of view. They were in spite of the Catholic viewpoint, and due to the imperfect notions of the times, times in which Protestants were not less cruel than Catholics. My own course of reading as a Protestant bred in me the same repugnance for the Catholic Church as you now experience. I dreaded and hated the Church as a monstrous thing. Yet today I accept her as my mother, realizing that she has been caricatured by misunderstanding and misinformed writers. And over twenty years of association with the Catholic Church have only served to deepen my appreciation of her rational foundations, principles, and spirit.

598. Do you deny that your Church has been responsible for monstrous cruelties?

I do. I say that such a doctrine is a monstrous fable. History shows that human beings, whether Catholics, Protestants, Muslims, or pagans, have been guilty of great cruelties to one another. Even members of the clergy, if you wish, through their own fault and not through any teaching of their Church, have been guilty of excessive cruelty. Such excesses cannot be justified, but it was their own personal conduct. It was not inspired by their Catholicity, but by their own mistaken, or even evil, dispositions.

599. St. Thomas taught that heretics should be put to death.

He had in mind such men as had been Catholics and who labored to destroy the faith of other Catholics after their own lapse from the Church. And even then he puts the question speculatively. And he was quite logical. He argued that one who unjustly takes his neighbor's life by murder deserves death at the hands of the state. But he who destroys the faith of another robs him not of his temporal life but of his eternal life, which is far worse. The state, therefore, which is bound to safeguard the complete well-being of its citizens, would be justified in putting such a man to death, removing him permanently from among men to whom he can do so much damage. Speculatively, then, St. Thomas says that such a penalty would not be excessive. In practice he does not say that it should be done. And even if it were done, he writes that the Church whose mission is one of mercy must do all she can to win such a man from his sinful dispositions and destructive campaign, in order to save both his temporal and spiritual life if possible.

600. Do you personally believe that all non-Catholics deserve burning at the stake?

No. Present-day Protestants are not ex-Catholics in bad faith, and even if they were I would not wish to burn them. Some of them might deserve it. Some Catholics certainly do deserve it, for if a traitor to his country deserves death, so too does a traitor to God, who has a far greater claim to our loyalty than any country could possibly possess. However, thank God that neither non-Catholic people who might deserve it, nor bad Catholics who do deserve it, are likely to be burned today by their fellow men in this country. Your feelings are nearly as sensitive as my own on this point.

601. Could you please give me a brief summary of what the Inquisition was for?

The Inquisition was established to meet a very real need. The Church had the obligation to preserve the teachings of Christ free from corruption. When individual men took it upon themselves, not only to hold erroneous opinions, but to seek to propagate their errors, and destroy the faith of others, the Church had to undertake the defense of her children. She instituted the "Inquisition," or "Board of Inquiry" to trace errors to their source and prevent further dissemination of them. Just as the government has a "Pure Foods Act" to prevent contamination of the food we eat, and has inspectors to enforce the act, so the Church wisely had a "Pure Faith Act," and inspectors to prevent the adulteration of the life-giving doctrine of Christ. And this was most necessary. In Spain, for example, both Jews and Moors had pretended to be Christians, had received baptism, and had even worked their way into bishoprics, their one intention being to undermine both the nation and its religion. The Inquisition detected these false pretenses, and the Church expelled them from her communion, whilst the state dealt with them as traitors. It was a wise censorship based on principles acknowledged as necessary by all reasonable people. We admit even now that some censorship of films is required to preserve moral standards from corruption. People may disagree with the way that censorship is handled, but not many deny its necessity. And the same thing applies to the Inquisition. Many of its ways were in keeping with the spirit of the times when it flourished and would not be sanctioned by anybody today. And there were, of course, abuses of it by unscrupulous individuals. But in principle the idea was quite sound.

602. Still it is a fact that 300 years ago the Roman Church tortured heretics to make them renounce their heresy and believe in the Church.

That is not correct history. In the state of society that prevailed then, totally different from conditions prevailing today, the propagation of heresy was an offense also against the civil welfare.

It was for the Church to decide as to whether a man's teachings were indeed heretical; whilst the punishment of those guilty of disruptive agitation was left to the state. However, we can let that go. The thing to notice is that the authorities were well aware that they could not make any man interiorly renounce heretical opinions against his will, or interiorly accept the teachings of the Church if he did not want to do so. But they could compel individuals to keep their private opinions to themselves and cease public propagation of their errors. If men personally renounced the Faith, and engaged in seditious efforts to undermine the prevailing and legitimate civic order, both Church and state could cooperate to prevent such men from corrupting the faith of others and from subversive activities against the legitimately established order.

603. Do you consider that such methods of propagating the dogmas of the Church received divine approval?

You are laboring under a misapprehension. The Spanish Inquisition did not exist for the propagation of the dogmas of the Church. It existed to prevent the propagation of heretical doctrines in Spain, and also to suppress sedition against the state. It was, therefore, a mixed tribunal, ecclesiastical officials dealing with religious matters, and civil officials dealing with crimes against the state. As constituted, and from both points of view, the Spanish Inquisition would certainly meet with the divine approval. But unconstitutional abuses of their powers by the officials themselves would not meet with the divine approval. That such abuses occurred I do not deny, nor am I called upon to defend them. I condemn them as heartily as you would do, had you also the knowledge of them that I possess.

604. Do you feel proud of yourself when you read of Torquemada?

I do not feel very proud of myself. I am very proud of the Catholic Faith that, owing to God's sheer goodness, I now possess. But you have a wrong idea of Torquemada. He was head of the Inquisition in Spain, a great theologian and a good man. All the opprobrium associated with the Inquisition has been heaped upon his head, but unjustly. The cruelty and extravagance of other officials were despite him and despite the protests and instructions of the Church. Popes Sixtus IV and Innocent VIII protested strongly against the excesses of disobedient officials, their protests proving that such excesses were not committed in the name of the Church. Yet even whilst we admit excesses, we must remember that they have been greatly exaggerated by partisan writers.

605. You still justify an ecclesiastical Inquisition?

Of course. It is as lawful and wise a tribunal as that for the censorship of films. And although the Holy See condemned brutal excesses, the Spanish Inquisition was as necessary for both Church and state in Spain as the criminal investigation branch of the police department for the preservation of law and order in Chicago. There was no more need to suppress the institution altogether because of abuses than there is to enforce Prohibition because of individual abuses of drink, or to smash a pair of spectacles because dirt has spoiled their transparency.

606. How can you reconcile the Inquisition with the fact that God is love?

The fact that God is love does not forbid the imprisonment of a criminal nor the hanging of a murderer. If love for the murderer does not prompt it, at least love for law and order, and love for other citizens, suggests it. I am obliged to love my enemies, but not their crimes. Christ loved his enemies and prayed for them. Yet he told them that if they died in their sins they would be cast into hell for all eternity. Love does not forbid the punishment of crime. It insists that there should be some punishment so that men will not easily commit it.

607. Has not the Church always hindered the progress of science by her moral prohibitions?

No. The Catholic Church has ever conserved knowledge and encouraged true science. Her doctrine is that Catholic truth is of God, and that scientific truth is also of God. There cannot be a conflict therefore between Catholic truth rightly understood and demonstrated scientific truths. But the scientific truth must be demonstrated. A mere hypothesis may or may not be true, and as long as a doctrine is in the hypothetical stage, the Church is prudent in her judgment. If the doctrine has no religious consequences, the Church is all encouragement in the pursuit of inquiry. If religious consequences are involved, she encourages inquiry but forbids positive utterances until the hypothesis is proved definitely to be a fact. This has never hindered scientists but has spurred them on to securing, if possible, demonstrative proof of their theories.

608. *What does the Church teach concerning belief in astrology?*

That it is superstitious nonsense, and that it is sinful to place any serious reliance upon it.

609. How much is harmless, and how much dangerous?

None of it is really harmless, for even if one were to indulge in astrology on a lark, it would always be a danger of beginning to take oneself seriously. Real danger commences the moment one begins to entertain the thought that "there might be something in it." And there are many gullible and easily impressed people who do this. The end of the road is complete abandonment of both reason and religion. I have recently read a book by a prominent English "astrologer" in which he says that the sun itself is really God and that the planets are angels. He declares that the sun and the moon and the planets deserve our reverence and our worship, though people are not educated up to the stage of realizing that yet! However, according to him, as astrology becomes more popular, more and more people will come to discern its spiritual and religious significance. Catholics are bound in conscience to have nothing to do with astrology.

610. What reason would you give for not believing in the assertion that we are influenced by the stars?

I would give three reasons: the first based on an analysis of the stars; the second on an analysis of man; and the third on a study of history. Astronomy, by spectroscopic analysis, reveals the purely material constitution of the stars, and reason insists that there is no more reason why they, rather than any other material elements in the universe, should have any control over man's conduct. Reasonable people no more believe that they are influenced by stars than by starfish.

Secondly, an analysis of man reveals that he lives not only by bodily senses, which can be affected by material influences, but also by intelligence and will. And only the infinite intelligence of God can know what the free will of man will choose in the future. That cannot be known by us from a study of the stars.

Thirdly, a study of history shows a complete lack of consistency in the life and conduct of people born in the same astrological circumstances, and no trace of uniformity which should be present were the stars a reliable influence upon them.

611. Can fortune-tellers really tell the future of the persons consulting them?

No. Whether they give mere conjectures or have actually got in touch with occult sources of information, there is no certainty that what they predict will eventuate. Fortune telling is not a reliable source of knowledge but must be ranked as superstition.

612. Does the Church forbid Catholics to consult fortune-tellers?

Yes. By doing so, people seek a knowledge of the future that has not been revealed by God and that cannot be known in a natural way. Apart from revelation by God, we can know events in this world either by their actual occurrence or in their natural causes—as a meteorologist predicts future rain from present atmospheric conditions. But future events dependent upon the providence of God, and the free will of men is not contained in the lines on one's hand or in the throwing of dice, or in crystals and tea cups.

Any serious intention of discovering the hidden future by such means is forbidden by the Catholic Church as superstition and a sin against religion. And the Church is here repeating God's own law. In Deuteronomy 18:10-11, we read, "There shall not be found among you any one ... who practices divination, a soothsayer, or an augur, or a sorcerer, or a charmer, or a medium, or a wizard, or a necromancer." Such is the clear law given by Almighty God.

613. Would it be a serious sin to consult fortune-tellers?

I have said that it would be a sin. If you ask concerning the gravity of the sin, I would say that it is gravely sinful to do so with a serious intention of thus discovering the future.

614. What is the power or probable effect of a curse?

None whatever, if it proceeds from human ill will or malice. God certainly will not answer prayers inviting him to fulfill the sinful aims of men.

On the other hand, a curse might proceed not from ill will but from good will and for the good of some malefactor. Not malice but a love of justice, and a desire to prevent further iniquity, might impel an indignant man to say to one who has willfully shot another, "May God wither your arm that you may never shoot again." God could certainly make that curse realize its purpose, even though normally he would not do so. Under the inspiration of God the prophets of old have cursed sinners, but in those cases they have merely pronounced the sentence of God in the name of God.

615. May an ordinary individual call down the curse of God upon another?

To wish any evil to another with malice and the evil desire of seeing him suffer would be sinful. The gravity of the sin would depend upon the intensity of one's evil dispositions and the character of the affliction invoked. Normally speaking, it is mortal sin to curse a fellow human being. It could be a venial or lighter sin if no really serious evil were intended or the curse were uttered only impulsively and in a sudden rush of temper.

It could be lawful for an ordinary individual to wish evil to another provided he intended only the good of that other, and the good intended outweighed the evil invoked upon him. But it is better to abstain altogether from expressing such wishes. Human wisdom does not always rightly judge as to what is best. There is always danger of self-deception as to the motives prompting our actions, and it is easy to interpret our own ill will in terms of lofty, disinterested ideals. Also the invocation of God's name involves a great risk of irreverence and blasphemy.

616. Does the Catholic Church condemn secret societies?

The Catholic Church clearly distinguishes between lawful secrets and unlawful secrets. And she applies this distinction to societies as well as to individuals. A society may have its lawful secrets. Any family is a secret society in this sense—for many things are lawfully kept secret by its members. They are not obliged to tell their private affairs to everybody. But a society that obliges its members to keep secrets unlawfully in defiance of lawful authority is condemned.

617. Is Freemasonry condemned as a secret society?

Masonry is condemned as an unlawful secret society, upon the continent of Europe above all. Masons solemnly undertake to keep secret matters that are most dangerous to the public good. And the Church, of course, had Continental Masonry chiefly in mind when she condemned it. In fact, Masonry was secretly plotting many schemes aimed at the very destruction of the Catholic Church, and the Catholic Church could not but forbid Catholics to join such a society. Masonry in English-speaking countries is milder in its attitude toward the Church, but even so, the Masonic oath of secrecy is still unlawful, because the man who takes that oath has no guarantee that he is not binding himself to secrecy in unlawful matters. He may be told that, in taking the oaths, he will be asked to do nothing against his conscience. But any man of normal mentality would ask, "Whose conscience?" He has no guarantee that he is not handing his conscience over, to be adjusted to what others think right. No man may do that. Masonry, is, therefore, condemned as an unlawful secret society. I have its ritual, with its asterisks and blanks, and a good deal of literature of Masonic origin, and no man, in my opinion, can take upon himself such obligations. Other good men may persuade themselves otherwise, but Catholics, who act on the principle that the Catholic Church is the true guide as to what is morally right, cannot do so.

618. What would be the position of a Catholic who joined the Masonic Order?

Such a Catholic rebels against the divine authority of his Church, rejects the Catholic Church as the guide of his moral conduct, commits a grave sin of disobedience, and is excommunicated and deprived of all right to the reception of the sacraments and to Catholic burial. If he does not want any of his Catholic privileges and is indifferent to his eternal destiny, he won't worry about these penalties. But if he has any faith left at all, he will worry. And he will be able to escape the penalties and be restored to the communion of the faithful only provided he repents of his violation of the laws of the Church, resigns altogether from the Masonic Order, and promises to fulfill his ordinary Catholic obligations in the future.

619. Why does the Catholic Church forbid cremation?[3]

It was a pagan practice that Christians avoided from the very beginning. In the third century we find Christian writers, such as Minucius Felix, warning Christians against imitating the practice and bidding them retain the custom of earth burial. In comparatively recent times atheists and irreligious materialists have reintroduced it in order to destroy Christian belief and to impress in an imaginative way the doctrine that all is over at death. This, in itself, would be enough to justify the Church in her refusal to accept a practice credited with such closely associated ideas opposed to the doctrine of immortality. But there are many other reasons. It is opposed to human instinct and the better sentiments of the human heart. Filial piety protests against such treatment of, say, a deceased mother. Christian reverence for the dead also protests. The body that has

3 The Church no longer forbids cremation, provided, as the *Catechism* puts it, "that it does not demonstrate a denial of faith in the resurrection of the body" (2301). Fr. Rumble's replies, nonetheless, make a good case in favor of choosing traditional burial.

been anointed in baptism and that has been the temple of the Holy Spirit during life should not be treated as so much offal or refuse but should be allowed to disintegrate according to the ordinary laws of nature in God's earth. Again, the whole liturgy of the Catholic Church for Christian burial, from time immemorial, is adapted to earth burial, and she cannot be expected to change her sacred liturgy with fads of the times. If a Catholic is cremated, he forfeits the privileges of such Catholic burial, a liturgy of great benefit to the soul that inhabited that body. The man who does not bother about such things, and holds that once one is dead that is the end of it and that nothing else matters, is saying just what the advocates of cremation hoped that he would say. It is good to be buried in the Catholic way, in consecrated ground. That is the proper place for a Christian. We can add to these reasons the medicolegal aspect of the case. Cremation destroys all signs of violence or of poison and thus prevents exhumation and medical examination for the detection of crime. Many murders have been discovered by such examination after burial, and if cremation became a general practice, it would be an easy way out for the poisoner and murderer.

620. Is it a sin against the law of God to support cremation?

The natural law of morality does not forbid it, nor has God directly given a positive law in the matter. It is a disciplinary law of the Catholic Church, and a very grave one. The Church could suspend the law and permit cremation in certain circumstances, as in the case of an epidemic or in war time. But normally she insists upon retaining the law, and all Catholics are obliged to observe it. The Church speaks with the authority of God, and it is God who forbids cremation through his Church. Any Catholic who would violate the will of the Church in this matter would, by the very fact, be violating the will of God.

621. Does not the Church oppose cremation because she knows that it renders any idea of a resurrection impossible?

No. Cremation does not affect the question of the resurrection. Cremation means but a more rapid separation of the elements of the body, and even if the ashes be scattered to the winds, God can quite easily reassemble those elements. What is impossible to us is not impossible to God. Remember that there is no such thing as the absolute destruction of matter. There can be merely a transformation of matter. However many changes matter may go through, it is always there, still in existence. And the God who created matter can easily transform it back again into the bodies that he formed previously. No matter how men treat human bodies, or where they put them, some day they will all rise again.

622. Why does not your Church condemn gambling and lotteries as sinful and immoral?

Because they are not sinful and immoral in themselves. They can be made the occasion of sin, as when a passion for gambling leads a man to spend money that is not his own, or that is necessary for the upkeep of wife or children or to pay his lawful debts. But if one can honestly afford it, he is free to invest in lotteries, or to indulge in the amusement of a wager, unless he is violating a law of the state.

623. Does not God forbid gambling of any kind?

Nowhere does the law of God forbid gambling, provided no fraud, deceit, or injustice enters into it. If all is conducted fairly, and an investor keeps within his means, a man is free to purchase a proportionate chance of winning a bet or a lottery without offending God's laws in any way. But if a law of the state forbids gambling, such a law must be obeyed.

624. Christ drove the gamblers from the Temple.

When Christ expelled the money changers and the buyers and sellers from the Temple, their crime was not gambling. Their crime was the conducting of secular business in such a place and their own dishonesty in charging exorbitant prices for goods and exchange. But gambling as such was not involved in this matter.

625. What does the Catholic Church do to wipe out the evil drink that causes so much misery in so many homes? We Protestants fight for Prohibition.

The Catholic Church drills into every one of her children that drunkenness is an unjustifiable sin. But we refuse to admit that Prohibition should be enforced upon all. The particular abuses do not justify so sweeping a thing as abolition of drink altogether. You don't throttle a man because one tooth is aching. The Church does her duty in this matter in a sane way. Meantime, drunkenness is not the only evil. Drink itself is not forbidden by the law of God. Divorce and birth control are forbidden. What is Protestantism doing to wipe out these evils? It scarcely alludes to them; or if it does, it does so in order to sanction them.

626. Why does your Church oppose Prohibition?

Nowhere does God forbid wine or alcoholic drink. And the Catholic Church insists upon justice. It is unjust to forbid all men to drink even in moderation because a few take it to excess. This is an unjust interference with individual liberty. And in any case you cannot force people to be virtuous. The failure of the American experiment has shown that if a man cannot take drink moderately, the Church advises him to take the pledge and practice total abstinence. But Prohibition is like abolishing table knives because some men have used those implements for purposes of murder and suicide.

627. As there are no half-measures in this matter, your refusal of Prohibition favors the continuance of a sin repugnant to Christ.

What do you mean by no half-measures? For the man who cannot resist getting drunk, I admit that there are no half-measures. He must inflict rigorous prohibition on himself, and if necessary the law must forbid him to be served with drink. If you mean that Prohibition must be inflicted on everybody, I deny your assertion. Such Prohibition is as extravagant, and therefore as unreasonable, as the doctrine of a man who would insist that you must always employ a steamroller to crack walnuts. Would you agree with his argument that because you are opposed to the use of a steamroller to crack walnuts you are opposed to the cracking of walnuts at all?

We all agree about the sin of drunkenness. We disagree about the means to be employed in its prevention. Drunkenness is repugnant to our Lord. But his first miracle was to change water into wine for the simple joys of a wedding feast. He had no objection to the use of wine. He objects to the abuse of it. If some men abuse their liberty by thieving, we do not think to stop thieving by abolishing the use of liberty and locking everybody up in jail. And we are not the less Christian for sane conduct.

628. "Wine is a mocker, strong drink a brawler; and whoever is led astray by it is not wise" (Prov. 20:1).

The moral is that no man should be deceived into drinking to excess. Thus St. Paul wrote to the Ephesians, "Do not get drunk with wine" (Eph. 5:18). Yet in his first Epistle to Timothy, 5:23, he writes, "No longer drink only water, but use a little wine for the sake of your stomach and your frequent ailments." Our Lord himself blamed the Pharisees that they accused John the Baptist of having a devil because he abstained from drink, but when they saw Christ himself drinking wine in moderation, they said, "Behold, a glutton and a drunkard, a friend of tax collectors and sinners!" (Matt. 11:19). Let us have temperance by all means. But there is no warrant in Scripture or in reason for Prohibition.

629. Does drink enter Catholic presbyteries?

All of them have to keep special supplies of altar wine. Over and above this altar wine, reserved for sacramental use, drink enters some presbyteries but not others. It depends upon the needs of the individual priest. If a priest took drink to excess, he would be guilty of sin, and a worse sin than a layman would commit, owing to the scandal given by violating the dignity and requirements of his sacred office. Otherwise there would be no harm whatever in a priest taking drink in moderation.

630. Even Catholic bishops drink!

Some take it moderately; some do not take it at all. I have known one bishop who would eat none but brown bread, and another who would never touch it as not agreeing with his health. The advice given by one Catholic bishop to another I have recorded above in giving you St. Paul's words to Timothy.

631. Is there any virtue in taking strong drink?

That all depends upon the intention with which one takes it. If taken in moderation for the sake of health so that one may the better fulfill his duties for the love of God, it is virtue to take it. If taken merely for the sake of taking it, such use of drink would not be virtuous.

632. The Catholic attitude to drink shakes my faith in Christianity.

You have not understood the Catholic attitude. But, in any case, if you see a drunken man, it should affect your faith in that man, not your faith in Christianity. If the man professes to be a Christian, you must blame him for not living up to his belief. But Christianity is all right. If it told him to get drunk, it might be different. But it forbids him to do so. Don't lose your faith in Christianity, but persuade drunkards to live up to its obligations.

633. Does the Catholic Church make light of drunkenness? Isn't it sinful to cause blind misery and poverty in the home?

The Catholic Church does not make light of so grave a sin. It is an evil that leaves every one of us very miserable indeed. Man has obligations to God, to himself, and to his neighbor. Such drunkenness violates all three obligations. Few things so destroy God's image and likeness in man as excessive drink. Other vices leave him with reason at least. But, as Father Burke so well said, "Reeling from the hotel, the drunkard has laid the image of God upon the altar of the meanest and most despicable of all devils—gluttony." As regards himself, the drunkard loses health, respect, friends, happiness, and much else. For if a man dies in almost any other crime, he has his wits about him and can call upon God for mercy and forgiveness. But if he dies in drunkenness, he is incapable even of an act of repentance. And as regards his neighbor, surely first and foremost come his wife, and his children, his parents and other members of his family, not to speak of his duty to his employer and professional clients. Yet what greater misery can a man bring upon the woman who confided her youth and heart to him forever than that which his drunkenness inflicts upon her? And his own children are filled with shame, disgust, and scandal. No Prohibitionist can speak more strongly against drunkenness than the Catholic Church; for she has a heart full of compassion for the homes wrecked by this vice and of indignation that God should be so offended.

634. How do Catholics observe the Lord's Day?

They should sanctify Sunday by assisting at Mass, by prayer, and by abstaining from unnecessary servile works.

635. I think Catholic ideas most peculiar in this matter.

That is merely because Catholic ideas do not happen to fit in with your own religious upbringing. Things we don't agree with usually seem peculiar to us. But the whole point is, are your ideas right or are our ideas right? You have no proof whatever that your notions are right or that Catholic ideas are wrong.

636. Did not God command us to observe Saturday and not Sunday at all?

No. The command as given by Moses in the name of God to the Jews was that the Sabbath, and not Saturday, should be kept holy. The word *sabbath* means rest. The law includes two elements: one essential, that one day in seven should be dedicated to God; the other ceremonial, that the particular day should be chosen. The Jews selected Saturday.

637. God is eternally the same. Having once demanded the seventh day of the week, even he could not change it to the first day of the week.

On that argument he could not have changed from the Old Law to the New Law, nor from the Jews to the Christians. You should give up your Christian beliefs, and join the Jewish religion! Yet did not Christ say, "You have heard that it was said … but I say to you." And he deliberately abrogated certain Jewish legislation concerning marriage. He certainly admitted the possibility of some changes.

638. What are the reasons for the selection of Sunday rather than Saturday?

After Christ's Resurrection and the establishment of the Church of the New Law, Christians kept the substance of the Old Law in this matter by still retaining one day out of seven. But the apostles, as I have said, changed the specification of the day to Sunday. This they did for several reasons. Firstly, in order to honor the Resurrection of Christ from the dead on Sunday morning. St. Paul shows that this is the bedrock foundation of our faith when he says, "If Christ has not been raised, your faith is futile." Secondly, the advent of the Holy Spirit gave life to the Church on Pentecost Sunday. Thirdly, the change was calculated to impress upon our minds the transition from the Old Law to the New Law. Finally, Saturday had special significance as being dedicated to the completion of God's creative work. But God's redemptive work is greater than his creative work, and as a mark of honor the first day of the week was dedicated to the superior redemptive work of God.

639. Does Scripture in any way justify such a change as a fact?

Yes. Christ, of course, accepting the Old Law prior to fulfilling and perfecting it by his new revelation, observed Saturday. But he himself prepared the way for the change of day. He defended his disciples when the Jews accused them of not observing the Sabbath strictly in the traditional sense (Matt 12:1–8). He rebukes too severe an interpretation of the Sabbath law (Luke 13:10–16; 14:1–5; John 5:9–18; 7:23). He shows his authority to do as he may please with the Sabbath (Mark 2:27–28). Nowhere does he reassert the obligation of observing the Jewish Sabbath. Never does he quote this Jewish law. In marked contrast, the New Testament pays special honor to Sunday. Christ rose on Sunday and appeared to his apostles on Sunday. He chose the following Sunday to appear to them when St. Thomas was present. Fifty days later he chose Sunday for the bestowal of the Holy Spirit upon his Church. The first Christians themselves observed Sunday from the very beginning: "On the first day of the week, when we were gathered together to break bread" (Acts 20:7). St. Paul rebuked the Galatians because of their tendency to revert to Jewish customs, and above all in their observance of Jewish days as if they were still binding (Gal. 4:9-10). To the Corinthians he wrote, "As I directed the churches of Galatia, so you also are to do. On the first day of every week, each of you is to put something aside and store it up, as he may prosper, so that contributions need not be made when I come" (1 Cor. 16:1-2). In Revelation 1:10, St. John tells us that he was in the spirit "on the Lord's day," i.e., on the day on which Christ rose from the dead, and which was already dedicated to him as sacred in a special way.

640. Why are Catholics compelled to go to Mass on Sundays and holy days of obligation?

Because they owe to God the definite, regular, and public acknowledgment of their indebtedness to him by the practice of their religion, and because the Sacrifice of the Mass is the highest act of worship in their religion.

You must remember that religion is a form of justice by which we render to God what we owe to him. Catholics are compelled to fulfill the duties of their religion, just as honest people feel compelled to pay their just debts to their fellow men. Honest people want to discharge their obligations. And the fact that they have real obligations does not affect the fact that their fulfillment of them is voluntary. God exacts religious acknowledgment. He tells us to remember to keep holy the Sabbath day, and that is not permission to forget. Now, Catholics don't want to be unjust to God, and their Church tells them that they will be unjust to God unless they attend Mass on the days appointed. They are glad to know their obligations and attend Mass on those days rather than be guilty of serious injustice toward the one to whom they owe so much. As a matter of fact, God is good in himself; he has been good to us; we have not been very good to him; and we need his constant help. So we owe God adoration, thanksgiving, expiation of our sins, and the acknowledgment of our dependence on him by offering prayers of petition. And all four obligations are fulfilled by fervent assistance at Mass. The wisdom of the Catholic Church in appointing definite times for the fulfillment of these obligations should be evident. A general obligation never to be fulfilled at any particular time is often not fulfilled at all. So we see many non-Catholics omitting duties of religion altogether, or fulfilling them when they happen to feel like it, or turning to God only when things go wrong. But Catholics say, "It's not a matter of what is pleasant, nor merely of what is useful; it's a matter of what is right." Religion is a debt to be paid regularly. We want to pay that debt regularly. The Church is there to tell us how regularly we should do so, and we are grateful to her for giving us the information. And, in a spirit of justice to God and obedience to our Church, we feel compelled to fulfill the obligations of our religion. I hope that clears the matter up for you.

641. Why should Catholics be thus burdened?

Religion is a debt to God. We Catholics pay this debt regardless of our own comfort and pleasure. We do not pay earthly debts when it gives us pleasure and refuse to pay them when it displeases us. It is a matter of honesty and justice.

642. To keep a day holy means to keep it pious, godly, and sacred.

Catholics do keep the day holy. The day is consecrated to God by definite duties of religion. Innocent recreation does not desecrate it. Eating one's meals on Sunday is not in itself a pious act, yet it does not desecrate the day. To keep a day pious does not mean that every single act must be one of piety. Any act that is not sinful can be offered to God's greater honor and glory, even as David offered his dancing before the Ark of the Covenant. When the Pharisees complained to Christ that the disciples were doing what their traditions held to be unlawful, Christ replied that the Sabbath was made for man, not man for the Sabbath.

643. Is playing tennis keeping a day holy and as a day of rest?

Playing tennis is not sinful. It is neither holy nor wicked of itself. It is mental and bodily refreshment of one's forces. But how far will you go? If I may not play tennis, may I exercise my limbs by walking? If I may not use my legs, may I use my eyes in reading? If not that, may I use my lungs by breathing? Where are you going to stop in the use of one's faculties? Religion was not meant by God to be a straitjacket of gloom.

644. Our Protestant ministers forbid sport on Sunday.

If so, they do so on their own authority, not on the authority of Scripture.

645. God says, "You shall do no work," yet you permit housework on Sundays.

God forbade the ordinary work of the Jews by which they earned their living, and the work they allotted to their slaves and servants. Christ himself rebuked the Pharisees for their letter-of-the-law interpretation of this commandment. God's chief purpose was that all might be free for religious duties. We have to note what God intended, and fulfill the intentions of the legislator, in addition to making allowances for the vast difference between the spirit of the Old Law and that of the New. The Catholic Church forbids all unnecessary servile work on Sundays. If such work can be done during the week, it is not necessary on Sundays. Our Lord himself said that one would be justified in laboring to release an ox from a pit on the Sabbath. A man cannot find time always on weekdays for all things necessary to be done, and certainly some housework is reasonably necessary on Sundays.

646. You claim to legislate in purely spiritual things yet order fast and abstinence on certain days. There is nothing spiritual in forbidding people to eat meat.

I have never said that the Church legislates only in spiritual matters. Men are not purely spiritual beings, and in our composite nature, spiritual legislation must in some way affect our material being. The laws of the Church cover material things insofar as they affect our spiritual welfare. There is nothing spiritual about meat in itself. But spiritual virtue is exercised when we abstain from meat from a motive of self-denial, gratitude, and obedience to God.

647. Is there any Scripture warrant for fasting?

Yes. When the Pharisees complained to Christ that his disciples did not fast, he replied that they did not whilst he was with them, but that they would when he had gone from them (Mark 2:18-20). Now, the Catholic Church, ordered by Christ to teach all nations whatsoever Christ had said to her, tells us that at certain times we must fast in expiation of our sins. St. Paul wrote to the Corinthians, "As servants of God we commend ourselves in every way: through great endurance, in ... hunger" (2 Cor. 6:4-5). A Christian spirit of reparation says, "I indulged my senses at the expense of God's law; I will therefore now mortify them at the expense of my own comfort." However, it is part of Christian law, and those who say that the Catholic Church obliges fasting whilst other churches do not complain as usual that the Catholic Church is fulfilling the Christian law whilst others are not. And the Catholic Church appoints special days, for if it were left to individuals they would fast very irregularly, or not at all. It is much better to make it definite.

648. Why forbid meat on Fridays? Christ said that nothing from without defiles a man but that it is disposition of soul that counts (Mark 7:15).

It follows that meat is not evil in itself and that the Church does not forbid meat on Fridays because she thinks that meat will defile men. That should be evident from the fact that the Church permits meat on other days, as she could not do if she believed meat to be evil. Therefore it must be a question of the day and not of the meat. Why then does the Church forbid meat on Fridays?[4] Because on that day Christ gave his life for us in misery and suffering. If a Catholic eats meat on that day, the meat does not defile him, but his interior disposition of ingratitude and disobedience

4 The current Code of Canon Law (1251 & 1253) allows local bishops' conferences to substitute some other food in place of meat, or some other form of penance in place of abstinence. But abstinence from meat on Fridays remains normative, and Fr. Rumble's reply remains instructive.

certainly does. If a man is not prepared to give up a little meat on the day Christ gave up his life, he is not worthy to be ranked as a Christian. The Friday abstinence has kept our Lord's sacrifice and death before the minds of millions of Catholics for centuries. To the vast majority of the Protestant churches that abolished this beautiful practice merely because the Catholic Church had the grace to fulfill it, Friday is just like Tuesday, or Wednesday, or Thursday, and their members do not think week by week of the greatest event that ever occurred in history for love of us. I have never yet received a convert into the Church who has not seen the beauty of this devotedness to Christ, and of the loyalty with which the Church recalls Friday as the day of the greatest event in our redemption. That non-Catholics should be silent about this Catholic custom I could understand. But that they should still profess to be Christians and then blame the Catholic Church for such a generous and loving act in honor of Christ merely because they do not do it themselves is astonishing.

649. The Bible says that the Antichrist will bid men abstain from meats (1 Tim. 4:3).

The reference is to men who teach that meat is evil in itself and who declare that it is wicked to eat it under any circumstances. But Catholics do not believe or teach this. Almost any butcher will tell you that he supplies many Catholic customers regularly with meat.

650. When did the practice of Friday abstinence from meat begin?

In the very earliest ages of the Church. The practice is mentioned in the *Didache* or *Doctrine of the Twelve Apostles*, a booklet written by one of the immediate followers of the apostles in the year 90.

651. Who said that every man will go to hell if he eats meat on Friday?

No one. The Catholic Church says that it is a mortal sin for a *Catholic* to eat meat on Friday knowingly and willfully, without a sufficiently grave and excusing reason. Then that Church says that if a man dies in unrepented mortal sin, he will go to hell.

652. I don't blame Catholics for voluntarily abstaining from meat on Fridays, but to do so because ordered to do so is making a virtue of necessity.

That is not true. No Catholic is physically compelled to abstain from meat on Fridays. It is a moral obligation, adding the virtue of obedience to that of Christian mortification. On your method of reasoning you should say that a man should voluntarily abstain from stealing, and that it is wrong to do so because God has said, "You shall not steal." And do the laws of the land destroy the virtue of citizens because there is a moral obligation to observe them?

653. Who made the law of celibacy?

The Catholic Church, with God's approval and authority, following the example of Christ and the apostles.

654. Did not Pope Gregory VII originate it in the eleventh century?

No. He merely enforced the already existing law more rigidly in his efforts to correct abuses. Over 300 years before Gregory VII was pope, the Greeks met the Latin bishops at the Council of Trullo and admitted, "We know that the law of the Roman Church is to demand that married men, from the moment of their ordination, must separate from their wives forever." St. Jerome, over 300 years before that, wrote, "The Apostolic See accepts married men to be priests provided they live no longer as husbands to their wives." Marriage was never allowed after ordination. If a single man were ordained, he had to practice celibacy. If an aspirant were already married, he had to practice celibacy from the day he became a priest. Pope Siricius, in A.D. 385, said, "All we priests are obliged by an inviolable law dating from our ordination to be continent and chaste, and thus offer the sacrifice of our bodies to God." This same pope wrote also, "I have heard that a priest of Christ has married, defending his action by saying that the priests of the Old Law married. But the Church, the Spouse of Christ, has always loved chastity. Wherefore any priest who claims a privilege from the Old Law which is unlawful in the New must know that he is deprived by the authority of the Apostolic See of the ecclesiastical honor he has so misused, nor can he celebrate the divine mysteries." Pope Siricius was not beginning a new law in the Church but blaming an individual for not observing a law that had long been in existence. In 314 the Council of Neo-Caesaria had also said, "If a priest marries, let him be degraded." The Apostolic Constitutions gave the law, in the second century, "If a priest or deacon is not already married, he can never contract marriage." Thus right back to the second century you have explicit testimony that in the Catholic Church once a man became a priest he had to renounce marriage and practice celibacy.

655. God commanded all men to marry when he said, "Be fruitful and multiply."

That is a general precept for the whole human race and a general blessing upon marriage. But it does not bind each and every individual. If it did, every single marriageable man in the world is breaking God's commandment and is in a state of sin. Or when would a man begin to sin by not being married? At 18? 19? 20? Or only when he could afford to support a wife? And would you accuse Christ of violating God's will? Or if you exempt him because of his divinity, would you blame the apostles? Was St. John the Baptist so very evil? Or St. Paul, who wrote, "I wish that all were as I myself am . . . unmarried" (1 Cor. 7:7–8)? You quote the Bible and then give a teaching radically opposed to the doctrine of that Bible.

656. The Bible says that a man must leave father and mother and take a wife (Matt. 19:5).

The sense is simply that one who does take a wife has a duty to her and to his children that is so binding that he must leave even his parents in order to fulfill it in his newly adopted state. But Christ gave a special blessing to those who would renounce father and mother, and the prospects of a wife and children also, for his sake. Matthew 19:29 says, "And everyone who has left houses or brothers or sisters or father or mother or children or lands, for my name's sake, will receive a hundredfold, and inherit eternal life."

657. St. Paul says that a bishop must be the husband of one wife (1 Tim. 3:2).

St. Paul does not say that a bishop must be the husband of a wife but insists upon the expression "one wife." Had he meant that it was necessary to have a wife, he would have been violating the law himself. In the early Church, owing to the scarcity of single men eligible for the priesthood, married men who wished to be ordained could be accepted provided they had not been married twice. Those presenting themselves must have been the husband of but one wife. That is all that the text means. Catholic bishops and priests do not violate that law. A law forbidding a man to have had more than one wife does not order him to have one; nor is it violated by a man who has never had a wife at all. However, as Christianity grew and vocations became more plentiful, single men only were accepted and had to remain celibates, according to the advice of St. Paul that I have quoted.

658. St. Paul says that if a man cannot rule his own house, how shall he take care of the church (1 Tim. 3:4-5)?

That does not suggest that a bishop must be married but belongs to the same context as that which you have just quoted. If a man who has been married, but not to more than one wife, be chosen, he must be one who has been faithful and who has ruled well his own house. That discipline was most wise at a time when such a man could be chosen. But such discipline no longer holds.

659. Those who "forbid marriage" is given as one of the signs of false churches.

The Catholic Church does not forbid people to marry. The vast majority of Catholics marry with the blessing of the Church. The text refers to people who declare all marriage evil, as did many early heretics. Marriage is not evil, nor is any Catholic forbidden to marry, as you would suggest. It is true that priests may not marry. But no one can be obliged to become a priest; in fact every one who is a priest could have married instead of devoting his life to an ecclesiastical vocation, had he wished.

660. Priests are only natural human beings. Why are they forbidden to marry?

Because they do not wish to be only natural. They wish to be supernatural. St. Paul was human, but he did not marry. And like St. Paul, Catholic priests wish to center their interests in Christ and share their hearts with no one else. Meantime, they are not forbidden to marry as human beings. They are forbidden as priests. Prior to their choice of the priesthood, every priest could have chosen marriage instead had he wished.

661. Are priests different from other men?

As human beings—no; as called not to the state of marriage but to the priesthood—yes. For this reason, whilst like all others who for one reason or another do not marry, they are obliged to avoid all sins against chastity; they also take upon themselves an additional obligation to do so under pain of sacrilege by vows of chastity offered to God.

662. Priests ought to marry to set a higher example.

No one could give a higher moral example than Christ; and a priest does set a higher moral example by not marrying. When he encourages young people to live pure and chaste lives in a single state, he is not telling them to do what he is not obliged to do himself. He is unhampered by domestic cares so that he can go to the poorest mission for the love of God and can attend those dying of contagious diseases without thought of carrying infection to wife and children. And it is certain that our people have more confidence in their priests precisely because they are single men, above all in the confessional. Even in the Greek Orthodox Church, it is a known fact that the people go to confession by preference to single priests rather than to married priests.

663. Why more confidence in a single man as a confessor than in a married man?

Because single men can give undivided attention to their duties and have more time to study and know the law of God upon which they must base their advice. Then, too, people feel that one who has renounced earthly affections for the love of God has more opportunities of living a disinterested spiritual life, and that his words will be correspondingly more helpful. And last, but not least, a single man is not so likely to share his thoughts and worries with a better half, or betray a confidence through indiscretion or inadvertence.

664. How can priests advise as to the duties of the married state when they have no practical experience of it?

"The lips of a priest should guard knowledge, and men should seek instruction from his mouth" (Mal. 2:7). The married state is not exempt from God's laws, and the priests must know those laws. Every priest studies all the possible duties of marriage from a moral point of view during a long course of theology before he enters a confessional at all. If you say that a priest cannot explain those laws to people because he himself is not married, will you say that a trained lawyer has no right to explain the law of the land to a plumber concerning that individual's trade because he himself has never so much as fixed a leaking pipe?

665. Priests condemn prevention of life by birth control yet prevent life by their celibacy!

Those who undertake the duties of married life are forbidden deliberate and artificial birth prevention. Priests called not to married life but to a different state altogether have neither the rights nor duties of the married state. There is a vast difference between preventing children by setting God's natural laws in operation yet frustrating their effects, and simply omitting to have children. No one is obliged to set the natural productive laws in operation. So, too, the obligation to pay bills is not violated by the man who has no bills. I may omit having creditors, but if I have them, I must not prevent them from receiving what is due to them. That should make it clear. Human beings may omit those actions that God intends to result in life, but if they exercise them and then prevent human life, they violate God's law.

666. Where did Christ tell us to put ourselves away in monasteries or convents?

Nowhere. But he invited some people to renounce all things and to follow him by close imitation. "If you wish to be really perfect, sell all you have, give to the poor, and come, follow me." If a man marries, he cannot do that. He has a duty to his wife and children and cannot sell the house and furniture over their heads, leaving them stranded. From the very beginning many Christian young men and women renounced the prospects of marriage and property for the love of Christ. The Church arranged community houses wherein the members were to own nothing, merely receiving shelter from the weather and necessary food and clothing. For the rest they were to give themselves to prayer and to works of piety and charity, instructing children, preaching the gospel, nursing the sick, or feeding the hungry and destitute. Later these houses were called monasteries, after the Greek word *monos*, meaning *alone* or *single*. The fact that those who have renounced all in accordance with the invitation of Christ live in monasteries or convents makes no more difference than if they lived in tents.

667. Monks and nuns run away from temptation for selfish moral reasons, trying to be good in an easier life.

I am grateful for that admission that they try to be good. Meantime, if to take definite means to live a better life is to be guilty of a selfish moral end, then I wish that more men would labor for that selfish moral end. Those who enter monasteries or convents may escape certain classes of temptations, but they always have self with them, and at times the temptation to go back to the easier life they left. Nor must you think that monastic or convent life is one of idleness. Every monastery and convent is a hive of industry, each member being engaged at set hours in very definite and continuous duties of various kinds.

668. Please explain the attitude of the Church toward mixed marriages.

The law of the Catholic Church prohibits[5] the marriage of a Catholic with a non-Catholic. Bishops and priests therefore have the duty to advise Catholics strongly not to contract mixed marriages.

Her reasons are many and serious:

1. There is the danger to the faith of the Catholic.
2. There is the probability of domestic discord.
3. There is danger to the faith of the children.
4. The Catholic education of the children often involves great difficulty, even granted that they are baptized Catholics.
5. Even in the ceremony itself, the Catholic Church is naturally reluctant to admit to her rites those who are not members of the Church.

If, however, despite these obstacles, a Catholic in the judgment of the Church has good reasons for marrying a non-Catholic, above all in countries where a non-Catholic population predominates, the Catholic Church will grant a dispensation from the prohibiting law. But she grants this dispensation only on the following conditions:

1. The non-Catholic must be willing to receive instruction in Catholic teaching, whether he intends to become a Catholic or not. It is not fair to let a Catholic marry a non-Catholic when that non-Catholic knows nothing of the other's religious obligations.
2. The marriage must take place according to Catholic rites and in no other way.
3. The non-Catholic must give a promise in writing that he will in no way attempt to persuade the Catholic to give up her religion, but that he will give her full liberty to practice it.
4. Both parties must promise in writing that all children without exception will be baptized and brought up in the Catholic Faith.

In brief, because of the great dangers attaching to mixed marriages from a Catholic point of view, the Church forbids

5 Church discipline regarding mixed marriages has loosened somewhat since Fr. Rumble's time, but we include his reply for its still-sound reasons.

them. Granted sufficiently grave reasons, she will dispense from her prohibition, but only on condition that the marriage is safeguarded as far as possible from the dangers she foresees by the promises I have mentioned.

669. In a mixed marriage, why must the Protestant promise that all children will be Catholics?

You must try to see this through Catholic eyes. A non-Catholic does not, as a rule, believe that his is the only true religion, and on the principle that one religion is as good as another, his conscience does not forbid that his children should be brought up in the Catholic religion.

But a Catholic is in a very different position. He believes that his is the only true religion and does not believe that one religion is as good as another. Now, how can a Catholic in conscience hand over his children to what he knows to be a wrong religion? How say, "I shall have all the benefits of the true religion, but my children won't!" Or, "God will be worshipped by me in the way he commands but not by my children!" Even God could not authorize a Catholic to cling to the true Faith himself yet deny that Faith to his children. Without securing the promises, no Catholic could conscientiously enter upon such a marriage.

670. That all must be Catholics is very one-sided in favor of the Catholic Church!

It must seem like that to you, but in reality it is not. Parents cooperate with God in giving existence to children. But why is any man at all created? That he may save his soul and attain heaven. Marriage therefore has as its chief purpose the creating and training of children for their eternal destiny. And religion is therefore all important. Now, the Catholic believes that there is but one true religion. It does not matter whether others agree or not. And he believes that all other religions are wrong. Again it does not matter whether others agree or not. That is the Catholic conscience. It follows that no Catholic can in conscience consent to hand over his children to what he believes to be a false religion. Nor can a

Catholic say, "Give me the girls and you take the boys." The soul of a boy is just as dear to God as the soul of a girl. There can be no compromise. As for the one-sidedness, look at things this way. The Protestant who believes that one religion is as good as another need not mind if the children are brought up as Catholics. He does not violate his conscience and does not ask the Catholic to violate hers. They are square. The fact that the Catholic Church feels bound in conscience to demand all the children shows that she is conscious of having the truth and being the true Church. The fact that Protestants do not demand the children shows that they are not really conscious of possessing the truth.

671. If a Catholic cannot sign away the children, how can a Protestant do so?

If a Protestant wants to marry a Catholic, and his conscience does not protest against it, he may sign the promise in regard to the children. But if the Protestant really believed the Catholic faith to be evil, and that his personal religion was the only true religion, then he has no right to promise that any of his children will be Catholics. He should abandon the marriage rather than thus violate his conscience. He should demand that the children be brought up in his faith. But then of course a deadlock would result. He would have to refuse compromise, and as the Catholic is also obliged to refuse marriage unless the written promise is given, the marriage would be canceled. It is better to part with a human being than to part with loyalty to conscience in so grave a matter.

672. I do not understand all this talk about chastity. Personally, I can see no harm in people seeking outside marriage the pleasures you call sensual and immoral. I am an honest searcher after truth.

In other words, immorality for you is not a vice, and chastity is not a virtue. You see no harm in unbridled lust and think pleasure the only standard of conduct. No wonder you cannot appreciate the Catholic religion! But tell me, honest searcher after truth as you are, if later you do marry and have children, would you advise one of your own daughters to become a prostitute? Would you assure her that she would thus be entering a quite honorable profession, nobly contributing to the legitimate pleasure and happiness of mankind, and at the same time embracing a profitable career?

673. I can understand that stealing, murder, and such crimes must be avoided because they harm our neighbors, but sexual pleasures harm no one.

You are talking arrant nonsense. You give as a reason for avoiding stealing and murder the fact that they harm our neighbors. Do you deny that they are wrong in themselves? If you steal $100, is the only thing wrong the fact that your victim has lost the $100? Was there no dishonesty and moral depravity in your action considered in itself? And if you say your action was not wrong in itself, will you tell me why it is wrong in itself to harm your neighbor? What precisely is your standard of morality—if you have one? Your assertion that promiscuous sexual pleasures harm no one is, of course, merely stupid. Individually and socially they have caused untold harm. The man who has not learned to control his passions in accordance with the purpose intended by God will end by descending to a level lower than that of the brute beast. And in no passion is this more quickly verified than in the case of sensuality and lust. The man who thinks sensual pleasures an end in themselves to be sought quite lawfully whenever desired will himself end in a corrupt heart, an enfeebled intelligence, and a paralyzed will, his whole character ruined.

674. No one seems to be able to tell me why it is wrong to have sex relations with a woman before marriage.

You almost make me despair of humanity when you say that. The very first man you met should have been able to tell you. We are indeed reaping the fruits of secularism and driftage from Christianity! The Victorian rationalists attacked the Christian religion, and Protestantism was not able to resist that attack. Protestant writers compromised and watered down the Christian creed. Then the rationalists turned their guns on the Christian code. There exists today a vast conspiracy of modern intellectuals to destroy the very principles of sexual morality. And your letter is evidence of the extent to which their doctrines have percolated to the masses. You are one of those who have discovered that, having lost the Christian creed, you cannot keep the Christian moral code. As belief in a future life becomes dim; and God, and sin, and punishment for sin, pass into the region of fairy tales; pleasure becomes the rule of conduct. At the foot of the cross of Christ men found strength to deny themselves and take up their own cross. But, having lost faith in Christ, well, they are off to amuse themselves. But the state of affairs today is particularly depressing. History records that great wars were followed by loose morals for a period, after which there was a reaction to decent standards. But there are grave reasons to fear that there will be no reaction this time. In former ages the moral law was broken; but its truth was not questioned. But now thousands like yourself have lost the moral sense. You rank the old standards as outworn conventions. And denying virtue to be virtue, you will never want to recover it.

675. What other reason could there be for restricting sex-relations to the married state?

In other words, why is deliberate indulgence in sexual pleasure immoral, apart from marriage? Because chastity happens to be a virtue; and the opposite of virtue is vice. God forbids vicious conduct. Christ forbids it, and says, "Blessed are the pure in heart, for they shall see God" (Matt. 5:8). If you advocate impurity as being quite all right in itself, you fall lower than the ancient pagans. They at least were not blind to the beauty of chastity. Chastity is a virtue that controls in the married, and altogether excludes in the unmarried, all voluntary indulgence in the sensual and passionate pleasures associated with functions ordained by God for the reproduction of the human race. God implanted in us two great bodily appetites: the one for food to preserve the individual life, the other for sex relations to preserve the life of the race. The pleasure attached to these appetites is to induce people to do what is necessary for God's purpose. To enjoy the pleasure whilst fulfilling the duty is lawful. But the purpose, and not the pleasure, is the main thing. Take food. The virtuous man eats in order to live. The man given to the vice of gluttony lives in order to eat. He is ruled by his senses instead of controlling them; and that is immoral. Against his health the drunkard makes use of a function that should serve for health. The sex appetite is for social health. To seek indulgence in it without regard to its end or purpose is a crime against nature and a degradation. And the end or purpose is lawfully sought only in the state appointed by God for that purpose, the state of marriage.

676. Surely our natural inclinations give natural rights to enjoy sexual love.

That is natural to man which is in accordance with his complete nature. Now, man consists of both body and soul. He is both animal and spiritual. He has senses, but he has reason also. And his soul, the spiritual in man, should control by reason the lower animal passions and not be controlled by them. The soul must rule the body. The body must not rule the soul. That which accords only with the blind passions of man's lower animal self, but which is opposed to the dictates of reason and conscience, is not natural but unnatural to man. A mere animal gratification of the appetites is not the purpose of life. It is puerile because unreasoning; and it is degrading, for, as Cicero says, "Human nobility lies in that quality by which he differs from animals—his mind." The Christian, at least, is bound to fight for virtue; he must struggle to control blind passions. Unregulated self-indulgence is to grow flabby in one's character and impair one's will. The pleasure lover who talks of "self-expression," and laughs at the idea of "self-repression," ends in utter depravity. Chastity is the only law that has ever lifted life above the tyranny and bondage of the lusts of the flesh. It may be difficult, but to say that it is right to violate chastity because it is difficult is a complete renunciation of human dignity and nobility.

677. Do you mean that the only lovemaking that is morally justified is that of lawful courtship with possible marriage in view?

Correct. The instinct of love between male and female is implanted by God primarily for the production of children. The mutual attraction of the sexes toward one another, and its expression by lovemaking, kissing, and embracing gravitate of their very nature toward that complete bodily union that terminates in the child. There is no love between persons of opposite sex that does not spontaneously and consistently aim at this design of nature, however ignorant of the fact young people may be. Any couple indulging in flirting, lovemaking, kissing, petting, and cuddling is already inviting the prospective child, however remotely. And since parenthood is unlawful outside marriage, indulgence in free love for its own sake outside marriage and apart from all intentions of marriage is unlawful and sinful. Whoever is not in a position to meet nature's purposes in lawful wedlock is not morally free to indulge in exchanges of love primarily intended for the procreation of children and the conservation of the human race.

678. Why is the Catholic Church opposed to birth control?

She is not opposed to the controlling of the number of children by lawful means, such as by self-control and by mutual consent to abstain from the use of marital privileges. But she is opposed to birth control as commonly understood to mean the prevention of conception after indulgence in actions calculated to result in the generation of children. The use of such privileges and the deliberate frustration of their normal effects is a very grave sin against the law of God. And for this reason the Catholic Church cannot but forbid it.

679. Why is birth control wrong?

It is opposed to the natural dictates of morality. It is obvious, for example, that the accompanying pleasure in eating and drinking is secondary and in view of the primary end, that the individual life may be preserved by due nourishment. We have supreme contempt for the glutton who does not eat to live but rather lives to eat. No decent man eats merely for the sake of eating, even prepared to vomit in order to be able to eat again! And as appetite for food is an instinct ordained to the preservation of the individual life, so sex appetite is ordained to the preservation of the life of the race. The pleasure attached to the indulgence of sensual passion is but secondary, and in view of the primary purpose, the production of children. The birth controller satisfies passion for the sake of passion and violates the moral order established by God. The use of marital privileges together with the deliberate frustration of the justifying purpose is but reciprocal vice. It leads, too, to many sins of injustice, being often practiced without the consent of one party. It is destructive of marriage, for it often leads to the divorce court when those who have based their marriage on sensuality have tired of each other. And violated nature exacts a penalty sooner or later. When birth control is practiced in early married life, it leads to sterility and the impossibility of having children when they are wanted later on. The health of women is often gravely affected, neurosis, fibroid tumors, and other evils resulting. The health of women is undoubtedly better where there is a higher birth rate than where there is an artificially low one. Finally, it logically leads to the destruction of the human race by implying that one may indulge in the act of procreation for pleasure and yet frustrate the purpose of God in permitting that act.

680. It is not only recently that the Catholic Church forbade it?

No. But the recent publicity and advocacy given to this wretched vice have led to new statements of the permanent Catholic doctrine. This vice ruined pagan Rome, and Origen wrote against the pagan Celsus in the third century, "At least the more our people obey Christian doctrine, the more they love purity, abstaining from even lawful sex-pleasure that they may the more purely worship God. Christians marry as do others, and they have children; but they do not stifle their offspring. They are in bodies of flesh, but they do not live according to the flesh." In the fourth century St. Augustine wrote, "Relations with one's wife when conception is deliberately prevented are as unlawful and impure as the conduct of Onan who was slain." St. Thomas Aquinas, in the thirteenth century, taught clearly the constant doctrine of the Christian religion that birth control is a grave sin. He writes, "Next to murder, by which an actually existent human being is destroyed, we rank this sin by which the generation of a human being is prevented" (*Contra Gent.*, Bk. 3, c. 122). It is not a new law by any means.

681. Where does God forbid it?

God is the author of the natural moral law, and I have already shown that birth control is opposed to that law. However, in Genesis 38:10, we read that Onan was slain by God for this sin. "And what he did was displeasing in the sight of the Lord, and he slew him." The gravity of the punishment shows the gravity of the crime, and Cornelius a Lapide remarks, "If God so punished Onan, what must he think of Christians?" In the book of Tobit we find the angel Raphael instructing the youthful Tobias. "Hear me, and I will show thee who they are over whom the devil can prevail. For they who in such manner receive matrimony as to shut God out from themselves, and from their mind, and to give themselves to their lust as the horse and mule which have not understanding, over them the devil hath power" (Tob. 6:16-17, Douay-Rheims). And the prayer of Tobias is full of significance, "O Lord, I am not taking this sister of mine because of lust, but with sincerity" (Tob. 8:7). In the New Testament St. Paul repeatedly says that the lustful and sensuous will not inherit the kingdom of heaven and that even marital relations must be honorable. Such relations are justified only provided the conception of children be not deliberately and artificially prevented. The honorable nature of marriage is destroyed if it be turned into a merely sensual satisfaction. Christian marriage is a great symbol of the union between Christ and his Church. Can you imagine the Church deliberately preventing the spiritual life of grace in the souls of those whom her union with Christ should bring to God? Not only the natural law, but the positive revelation of God excludes birth control.

682. God dispensed from other laws given to the Jews.

He has never dispensed from such laws as involve the principles of natural morality. The violation of some laws is wrong because

God has forbidden a thing, or commanded some disciplinary measures. But contraception is not wrong because God forbids it. Rather, God has forbidden it because it is wrong in itself; and God could not dispense from it even as he could never sanction an essentially wrong thing.

683. Does contraception prevent souls from existing that God intended to be born?

People who practice contraception certainly prevent souls from coming into existence. Did God ordain them to be born? Certainly not by his absolute will, or he would not permit people to succeed in their crime. But he does ordain them to be born conditionally, that is, provided the parents do the right thing he intended them to do. If they fulfill the conditions required for the generation of children, he intends children to result. At the same time, whilst commanding parents to observe the law of nature, he leaves them physically free to serve him or to rebel, as in the case of any other commandments. Those who practice contraception violate God's law and deprive Christ of children to redeem. And if they die in such sin they will most certainly be lost. If they say that conscience does not reproach them, then they have warped their conscience and will have to answer for it.

684. Do you deny that one can follow his conscience?

One should follow a right conscience. But conscience can be warped just as any other judgment. Therefore a man needs some test by which he can know his conscience is true. What is that test? He must see whether his conscience squares with the known law of God. The Church tells us clearly that law in this matter, and once we know the law from the mouth of the Church, conscience bids us follow it.

685. Your teachings on birth control come with no weight from bachelor priests.

You seem to think that it is a law made by unmarried men. Get that idea out of your head. God made the law. The celibacy of priests has nothing to do with the question. God's law has the same force whether a bachelor priest declares the law, or a married layman. Would you say that the teachings of Christ are to be accepted in every case except when he refers to marriage, your exception being based on the fact that he was never married?

686. Is Catholic opposition to birth control an article of faith, or a temporary form of penance that a less prudish age will forsake?

This is not an ecclesiastical law but a divine law. No one on Earth can ever dispense man from it. The Catholic Church is not here to allow God's laws to be broken but to see that they are kept, so far as possible. Of course, she cannot force all her subjects to observe the law, even as God does not force all people to keep other commandments of moral obligation. Catholics must accept the condemnation of contraceptive birth control without reservation. If they fail in this matter, they cannot say that it is not a sin. They can but confess that they have sinned. The pope has definitely and irrevocably declared contraceptive birth control to be intrinsically wrong and declares that to be the authoritative teaching of the Catholic Church. Catholics, therefore, are not free in conscience to declare contraception to be moral and permissible. Nor will the Catholic Church yield in any way on this point whatever the character of future ages outside her fold, whether you choose to envisage those ages as "less prudish" or "more pagan." Protestants once claimed to be the champions of morality against the lax doctrines of Rome. That was ever an idle pretension. But today we are beginning to see things in their right colors; the Catholic Church standing rigidly for morality; non-Catholic churches significantly silent, or openly yielding to the demands of popular vice.

687. Is it not reasonable to think that contraception will be tolerated later, as Galileo's theories today?

No. Nor are the cases in any way parallel.

688. Many Catholics practice birth control, as is evident from their small families.

That is not evidence. Only on a man's own admission could we know that he is not limiting his children by practicing continence, he and his wife agreeing to abstain from marriage rights by mutual consent. But even if it be true that many Catholics sin in this manner, the fact that they sin could not justify the same sin in others. All cannot break a law because some do. Nor do such Catholics think themselves justified. They know they are sinning just as men sin by breaking any other law of God. Protestants have admitted to me over and over again that their consciences have protested against such conduct and that the Catholic law is undoubtedly right.

689. The motive of your Church is to increase her numbers.

Her motive is to obey God. Temporal advantages certainly do follow from the observance of God's law, but those advantages are not the primary motive of the prohibition of birth control. The Church cannot water down God's law to suit the passions of men; she must lift men to the observance of God's law. Whatever timeserving concessions other churches may make, the Catholic Church stands for the law of God because it is the law of God.

690. The world cannot look after its present inhabitants. What is to happen when the Earth is overpopulated?

Such considerations cannot affect the question. They are based upon the evil principle that the end can justify the means. You think you have a good purpose—let there be less of us to enjoy more. With this good end in view, you think to justify birth control even though by immoral means! It cannot be done. The Church can never teach that it is lawful. Even did she teach that it was lawful, that would not make it lawful. God made the law. Meantime, if the world lived moderately and justly, it could easily provide for those already in the world and for millions more. The fault is not with the children to be born but with the selfish men and women already in this world. The Earth is producing more than is sufficient for the people in it. Men are even complaining of over-production. And God is not to blame for men's failure to secure even distribution. Let men rectify their own fault. Finally, the Catholic Church is not opposed to the limitation of individual families where necessity and poverty justify it. If some families cannot afford to have further children, they are free not to have them. But the only way is by abstaining from the use of marital privileges, a continence possible by prudent separation, prayer, and the grace of God.

691. What if a doctor, a reliable doctor, says that death will result absolutely from any further conception?

In such a case the moral theology of the Catholic Church says that a wife is justified in refusing marital privileges to her husband and that he has an obligation to practice self-restraint and continence, thinking more of his wife than of himself. He must content himself with the other benefits of married life, mutual love, companionship, etc. But never can the Church permit contraceptive methods. The choice lies between offending God seriously with consequent risk to salvation, and continence.

It may seem hard, but there is no other possible choice. And such continence is possible if a man is prepared to live a truly spiritual life and to avoid proximate occasions of temptation in the matter. If such difficulties drive a man to God, to more fervent prayer and a consequent deepening of faith and merit, he will bless God for the necessity of such Christian mortification.

692. Would it not be better for thousands of children of physically, mentally, morally, or financially unfit parents never to have been born?

If there were no God; if there were no hope of any future life; and if I were not a Christian, I might be tempted to say yes. But there is a God who forbids contraception, and it is far better to accept what God's providence permits than to break any of his commandments. There is also a future life. A child does not consist of a body only. It has also a soul. If the child is baptized and attains salvation, far better be born no matter how physically deformed the body may be in this life. This life of so few years scarcely matters compared with eternity, where there will be no suffering and no deformity in heaven. Physical deformity often means pain, but pain is not an evil that really matters in the end. There was no real evil in Christ, yet he had much pain. Mental deficiency does not prevent the reception of baptism, and diminishes responsibility. God knows how to make all allowances for factors diminishing such responsibility for one's conduct. Financial deficiency means poverty, but Christ too had much of that. The opportunity of attaining eternal salvation and happiness is worth any privation in this life. Many a cripple has been full of gratitude to God and to his parents for existence and the chance to love God and to suffer with Christ. God's ways are not our ways. With twisted and deformed bodies, it is better to be born if we do no wrong culpably. With a strong and healthy body, it is better not to be born if we sin like Judas and die without having repented.

693. A higher standard of life and education is demanded today than in medieval times, and one can't do it with a large family.

That could not justify birth control by contraceptive methods. The choice today is between Christ and the modern pagan philosophy. If modern godless civilization is right and this life is all, then let us measure everything by utility and pleasure. If Christ is right and the beatitudes, directed against worldly wisdom, are the road to eternal happiness, then a small family cannot be had if it means sin and the recrucifixion of Christ in the name of sensuality. And is not the higher standard of living based on discontent with the necessities of life, and upon the desire to possess as many superfluous and pleasurable goods as possible? A man who is not content with Christian simplicity of life will lack what he considers fitting means to support children. His preference is for temporal comfort. The idea of providing Christ with little children to redeem, who may share a happiness he himself hopes to enjoy for all eternity, has little appeal for him. "The unspiritual man," says St. Paul, "does not receive the gifts of the Spirit of God." And remember that many of the greatest geniuses in the world have come from large but poor families, whilst men whose parents spent vast sums on their education have been failures. A child brought up without luxury is more energetic, more resourceful, and, if encouraged, can quite well make good in the world. Normally, it is good to give children a higher and a secondary, or even a university education, although they are not always the better for it. Character is the true education, and that is much better attained in a large family than in any other circumstances. The father and mother of a large family have more lovable qualities than those who restrict their families, and communicate their characteristics to a larger number of children who will glorify God and edify their fellow men.

694. You seem blind to the practical reasons against the Catholic doctrine.

I am not. But you are blind to the innate immorality of contraceptive practices, and your reasons are based upon expediency only. And if what is expedient is going to be lawful, then goodbye to morality. Slanderers of the Catholic Church have accused her of teaching the frightful doctrine that the end justifies the means. The Church has always indignantly denied such a doctrine. She has ever taught that men are not free to do what is morally wrong because they think they have some good end in view. But where the world used to say, "Those evil Catholics teach that one may do any harm that good may come," it now cries, "Look at that tyrannical Church! She dares to tell us that the end does not justify the means, and that we are not free to do anything we like if we have a good end in view." Once again I must say that you cannot have it both ways!

695. What is the Church's attitude toward sterilization of the unfit? Is it usurping the power of God over life and death, like birth control and the killing of incurables, or is it a lawful endeavor to safeguard national health, like the prevention and cure of disease?

The practice of sterilization of the unfit is absolutely forbidden by the Catholic Church as unlawful and gravely sinful. The commandment "You shall not kill" withdraws from man all jurisdiction over innocent life and forbids all notable mutilation of a morally innocent human being. Sterilization is a grave injury to a human person, depriving him of a power as integral to human nature as the power of sight or speech. The State did not give these powers and can no more remove them than it can amputate the hand of a pickpocket thief. The State can segregate a thief for a long or short period, but it has not the right to mutilate him. And the unfit are not even guilty of a crime by being unfit. Sterilization also renders marriage quite unproductive and therefore deprives such men of their natural rights to the offspring of marriage.

The State exists to protect its innocent citizens, not to injure and mutilate them. Anyway, sterilization is wrong in itself, and it is not lawful to do evil that good may come. No idea of safeguarding national health can justify evil means. As a preventive measure the State has other and lawful means, such as segregation and education. But sterilization is really an impossible measure in practice. It would not attain desired results.

It is not a cure, for the trouble is more psychical than physical; and if anything, it stimulates crime, merely removing fear of consequences. Despite sterilization we shall always have the degenerate with us, even as we shall always have the poor despite all our philanthropic legislation. Other difficulties abound.

The degree of mental or physical degeneracy cannot be determined. In less serious cases there will always be a doubt. In more serious cases, we have the disconcerting fact that heredity does not obey invariable laws. Nor can we deprive a man of a right now because of a possible future abuse of that right. And the Catholic Church rightly says that sterilization is an unlawful measure forbidden by the law of God.

696. Does not the Catholic Church condemn euthanasia?

Yes. Deliberately to terminate life either because of sickness or of old age is murder, and a violation of the commandment "You shall not kill," by whatever high-sounding names the process may be called.

697. Why did St. Thomas More advocate euthanasia in his book Utopia?

He did not do so. Sir Thomas More did not believe in Utopia, nor for a moment did he intend it as an expression of his own ideals. To think that is to misjudge him and to misapprehend the purpose of his work. The book was a rebuke to his own age. In it he describes an imaginary country that had no knowledge of the Christian religion. He sets down just what he thinks non-Christians would do at their very best. And he agrees that, if his Utopians could achieve such a peaceful and progressive society without the help of the Christian religion, what might not be achieved if people with the Catholic Faith would but seek first the kingdom of God and his justice! Naturally, in describing how a people not yet Christian would behave in this direction or that, Sir Thomas More introduced many manners and customs, including the idea of euthanasia, that were calculated to give a sense of reality to his non-Christian Utopia. It is altogether unjust to quote Sir Thomas More himself as favoring a custom he attributes to a society precisely because it is un-Christian. In fact, his words are a condemnation of the un-Christian ideals of those modern people who seek to introduce euthanasia. For they are doing the very thing Sir Thomas More predicted that an un-Christian people would do.

698. Why cannot a fellow human being, or the state, put a man out of his agony if he meets with a most painful accident and has no chance of living more than a few hours?

Because God the creator, author of life and death, has refused permission to human beings in this matter. God has said, "You shall not kill." He did not add, "Except when people are suffering and have no hope of recovery." Men may do their best to relieve human suffering and to deaden pain, but they may not take life where God has given them no authority to do so. Apart from this, we must remember that human judgment is often astray in its predictions of death, and the most unlikely recoveries are commonplace. Many a man is alive today, and glad to be alive, who would have been put to death by mistake, if the law allowed men to destroy those they thought unable to recover. Also, despite all sufferings, the last few hours of which you would deprive an afflicted man could easily be the most precious in his life. Medical men exist to save life, not to destroy it, and they must do their utmost in all lawful ways to save life as long as it exists in the patient.

699. I cannot understand why raving lunatics and sufferers from painful and incurable diseases are kept alive deliberately.

If you understood why you regard life as sacred, you would understand why we may not deprive innocent people of life. When you speak of their being "kept alive deliberately," you go further than merely saying that it is lawful to kill them. You suggest that it is sinful and criminal not to kill them. In that case you would be guilty of sin before God every time you meet an incurable sufferer and neglect to strangle him!

700. When we think of what a tremendous cost to the State these people are, we cannot but advocate that they be humanely relieved of further suffering.

In other words, they should be gently but firmly murdered, though guilty of no crime. The reference to the "tremendous cost to the State" is a pity. It spoils the thought that the sufferings of the poor lunatics are to be our only consideration. We are not asking the lunatics whether they want to die. We are asking other citizens whether they ought to be killed. And our lofty unselfishness seems to be called into question when, with the one breath, we suggest that the mentally afflicted be relieved of their sufferings, and that we be relieved of the taxation necessary to keep them. But enough. Suicide, and the killing off of those whose only fault is that they are afflicted, are both directly opposed to the law of God. And the Catholic Church will never hesitate to say so.

701. What is the law or teaching of the Catholic Church on the right or otherwise of a doctor to perform an abortion?

The Catholic Church teaches, and ever will teach, that no doctor has any right before God and in conscience to perform such an operation. The deliberate and direct destruction of innocent human life is forbidden by the commandment, "You shall not kill." Another principle insisted upon by the Catholic Church is that the end does not justify any morally evil means. And the commandment "You shall not kill" forbids the direct killing of an innocent human being before birth as well as after birth.

702. Does the law or teaching differ from accepted medical ethics?

No. But if it did, accepted medical ethics would be wrong. However, no medical man who observes the ethical principles generally acknowledged by the profession would perform such an operation. Doctors exist to save life, not to destroy it. And there are thousands of doctors, men of honor and integrity, who will have nothing to do with an operation to secure the deliberate abortion of a living child at any stage prior to viability. Even if the choice seems to be between the life of the mother or of the child, they will not deliberately destroy the life of the one in order to save the other. Admitting the equal rights of both to existence, they do their utmost to save both, leaving the issue to God's providence. And very often they do save both, finding their earlier opinion most happily mistaken.

703. At what stage of its development does a child receive its individual soul?

The soul is present the moment the active and passive principles of germination coalesce to form a definite entity. We therefore say that from the moment of conception, the soul is present. Our very doctrine of the Immaculate Conception of the Blessed Virgin Mary implies that doctrine. For we say that, from the moment of her conception, her soul was preserved immaculate, or free from any taint of original or inherited sin. Her soul, therefore, was created by God at the moment of her conception and long before human activity in the sense of discernible physical movement. In St. Luke we read that, when our Blessed Lady visited Elizabeth, the latter cried, "For behold, when the voice of your greeting came to my ears, the child in my womb leaped for joy" (Luke 1:44). Even before his birth, St. John the Baptist was able to know by revelation of the presence of the also yet-unborn Christ. And the souls of others are also created at the moment of their conception. The unborn child possesses an "earthly existence" every bit as much as the child lying in a cradle or romping in the streets. It is a living human being from the moment of conception.

704. You condemn abortion even when strongly recommended by a doctor?

Correct. No doctor has a moral right to recommend unjustifiable homicide. And the killing of a living unborn child is that.

705. Let us now consider that form of "self-defense" where one man kills another to save his own life. The taking of this other life is a violation of the commandment "You shall not kill."

That is not so, if there be no other way out. If an unjust aggressor seriously threatens to wound or even kill another man, that other has the right of self-defense. If less than death, such as wounding or disabling, is sufficient, to do more is sinful and against justice. But the right to defend one's own life is valid always against an unjust aggressor; and by his criminal conduct he encompasses his own death if he goes so far as to render so violent a defense necessary.

706. Now I submit that if the extreme form of self-defense is justified, then abortion is justified.

That does not follow, for the child is not an unjust aggressor, is guilty of no crime in being in its natural place, and is actuated by no malevolence toward the mother. The cases are not parallel, and the transition from one to the other is illogical.

707. Both involve the taking of life to preserve life and are opposed to the fifth commandment.

That is not true. In abortion the doctor directly intends the killing of an innocent child as a means to the end he desires to attain. He does not merely permit the child to die. He definitely kills it. The child is not responsible for its own death, unjustifiably exposing its life to danger. But in self-defense against an unjust aggressor, the attacked person intends directly his own protection, opposing violence to violence. The aggressor unjustifiably exposes his own life to danger if he walks into the zone of protection his sinister intentions have forced the attacked person to set up. The attacked person does not intend his aggressor to be an aggressor, nor to be killed. He intends his own safety and permits the aggressor to kill himself should he be so evil as to render his death necessary and put himself in the way of it. If the aggressor chooses to throw his own life away, it is he who breaks the fifth commandment. But the unborn child is not an unjust aggressor; is not choosing to throw its own life away; and, in abortion, is killed deliberately as a means to an end.

708. As a woman listener, I object to your assertion that abortion is murder.

The deliberate destruction of a living child prior to its birth is as much murder in the sight of God as its deliberate destruction after its birth.

709. So if a woman will lose her life if she has to bear a child, you say it is a sin to relieve her?

I never said that it would be a sin to relieve her. We are discussing the means to be taken in order to give her relief. I simply say that it would be sinful to destroy deliberately the life of her child as a means to the end desired. What you must face is the question as to whether it is a sin or not to kill an innocent living child. Will you answer that with a yes or no? Or will you say, "Of course that would be murder unless we had good reasons for it." Would you then say that murder ceases to be murder as soon as it happens to be expedient?

710. Truly you are a ruthless Church.

You do not know what you are saying. The Catholic Church forbids the direct killing of either mother or child. You advocate the deliberate murder of the child. Who is ruthless?

711. Good, loving, tolerant, God-fearing women who have to suffer the pangs of childbirth should make these laws, not men who have shirked the responsibilities of fatherhood and know nothing of what they are talking about, save in theory.

Neither women nor men may make any laws concerning this

matter. It is for God to make the laws. You speak of "good, tolerant, God-fearing women." If they are God-fearing, they will respect his laws and certainly will not tolerate the abortion you advocate, involving the murder of an innocent child as a means to some other end. As for priests not knowing what they are talking about, one does not have to be married in order to know the implications of the law "You shall not kill." If you think that priests do not understand the difficulties that the observance of God's law will cost in certain individual cases, you are very much mistaken. And if you think the priest devoid of sympathy, you are still more mistaken. But the priest knows that, even as he did not make the law, so he cannot abrogate it. He knows that it is useless for him to give a permission he has no authority to give and that God will not ratify. God has given the law. The priest must declare that law. Men may not do evil that good may come. It is morally evil in itself to destroy an innocent child's life. One may not do it, therefore, even to save the life of another. Abortion is murder, forbidden by the commandment "You shall not kill."

712. Perhaps in the future you may be man enough to have the courage of your real convictions and say, "Save the mother."

I go further. I say, "Save both." You say, "Murder the child." Think the whole matter over again. And don't imagine for a moment that I am simply refusing to understand your position. You mean well, but you have let your heart run away with your head. Concentrating on one aspect of the case you have lost sight of other aspects, and sentiment has obscured your vision of all the principles at stake. Owing to the limitations of the human mind, absorption by one idea can blot out all advertence to others, as in the case of the man who laughed uproariously whilst being flogged and gave as the reason for it, "You're flogging the wrong man." Concentration on the ludicrous aspect made him oblivious of physical pain. In your case thoughts only of pity for the mother (quite noble in themselves) have excluded from your mind all thoughts of the life of the child and its inalienable right to existence. And it is to that right I call your attention—a right vindicated by God's commandment "You shall not kill."

713. Is suicide a mortal sin?

In itself, the action of taking one's own life is mortally sinful. God is the author of life and of death, and he has never delegated to each individual the right to take his own life. The commandment "You shall not kill" extends to one's own life as well as that of others; and to take one's own life is to usurp an authority that belongs to God alone. But whilst I say that suicide is a mortally sinful action in itself, it does not follow that every man who commits suicide is guilty of mortal sin. To be guilty of mortal sin a man must not only do what is seriously forbidden by God; he must also know clearly that it is so forbidden, and be so in possession of his reason that the choice of his will is made with full freedom and deliberation. If we consider not the action but the man, charity demands that we give him the benefit of any doubts and believe that he was not quite himself at the time.

714. Does the Catholic Church grant burial to one who takes his own life?

The normal law of the Church forbids the Christian burial of a suicide when there is no reason at all to think that he was not in his proper senses at the time. She refuses her rites in such cases to impress upon people the gravity of such a crime against oneself, society, and almighty God. But when there are good reasons to believe that a suicide was not in his normal senses, and it is fairly common knowledge that the person was in ill health or oppressed by worries, the Church permits Catholic burial.

715. I can't understand why Catholics don't help more to prevent cruelty to animals.

That has no bearing on the question as to whether the Catholic Church is the true Church of Jesus Christ or not. The Catholic Church, of course, condemns as sinful all wanton cruelty to animals. If any Catholics are guilty of such wanton cruelty, then they sin in that matter, just as people sin in other matters. But that would be no reason for not joining the Catholic Church, which condemns such conduct. At the same time, whilst the Church condemns wanton cruelty to animals, she places no obligation on Catholics to take a special interest in societies for the prevention of cruelty to animals rather than in other good causes. And your own particular interest in this matter should not make you ready to condemn others who do not share your views of its importance but who devote their attention to other aspects of welfare work in this world.

716. There is a growing love for animals, and also a hatred of hurting anything or anybody, so that people don't like the thought of hell even for their enemies.

No Christian is allowed to like the thought of hell even for his enemies. But that does not justify us in denying the existence of hell and rejecting belief in the veracity of Christ. The growing love for animals of which you speak, and the hatred of hurting anything or anybody, are quite all right within due limits. But they can easily become excessive and distorted tendencies due to a loss of respect for the dignity of man and to the growth of effeminacy and degeneration, which are destructive of the fortitude and courage required for true manhood.

717. God is love, and our Savior said that God noted the fall of a sparrow. St. Francis of Assisi loved animals, I believe.

St. Francis of Assisi loved every creature of God, as all who love God should do. Meantime, you are wise in leaving the problem of the ultimate welfare of animals to God. But when you speak of our Savior's teaching that God notes even the fall of a sparrow, do not read into that more than he meant. Jesus is our Savior, not the Savior of animals; and in the passage you quote he was merely bringing out the providence of God. As a matter of fact, the strong contrast he makes is that if God has such care for creatures who do not matter so very much, far greater is his interest in those who do indeed matter: human beings whose souls are made in the very image and likeness of God.

718. May it not be that animals do not need saving? It is only man with his passions and dangerous temptations who needs saving.

It is quite certain that animals do not need saving from any eternal damnation. Animals lack moral responsibility, lacking reason and free will. And moral responsibility alone could warrant any such penalty as hell and eternal loss.

Man needs saving, not precisely because of his passions and dangerous temptations but because the whole human race fell from God's grace and friendship by the sin of our first parents, and because men have sinned personally and actually by yielding to their passions and temptations. The Son of God, therefore, died for us men and for our salvation. Whatever God's provision for animals, they do not enter into the redemptive plan save indirectly, insofar as men sin by their misuse of lower creatures and deprive themselves of grace and virtue.

719. I always include among my prayers one for the animals.

It would be better to pray for those human beings who ill-treat animals, that they may desist from doing so. You would thus be praying for those who are morally responsible for their cruelty and for the welfare of animals at the same time. The prayer, "Thy will be done on Earth as it is in heaven," is a prayer not only for men that they do God's will but that they may do so in all the relations with other things that life involves, even in their relations toward dumb creatures. Your attitude toward animals seems to me to savor of a sentimental exaggeration. Far more important is the saving of human souls, and there are thousands of them in real danger of eternal suffering, a fate impossible to conceive for animals. If you have any time to spare for prayer, devote it to the needs of those human souls for whom Christ died, rather than to animals for which Christ did not die and which belong to a sphere of existence quite other than that proper to mankind.

Chapter 11

Catholic Worship

720. What is holy water, and how does it differ from ordinary water?

Holy water is ordinary water sanctified by the blessing of the Church. It differs from ordinary water insofar as some salt has been added to it to signify preservation from corruption, and insofar as it conveys the blessing of the Church and of God where ordinary water does not do so. Holy water is placed at the doors of Catholic churches to remind us of the waters of baptism that once flowed over our foreheads, to signify that we are not worthy to enter into the presence of Christ without purification, and to forgive us those venial sins for which we are sorry, as well as remitting the temporal punishment due to our sins according to the measure of our regret and contrition. I do not know how you feel, but I know that I am not worthy to enter into the presence of God in a Catholic church. When Moses approached the burning bush, God said to him, "Do not come near; put off your shoes from your feet, for the place on which you are standing is holy ground." To Catholics it is a joy to be able to make straight for the holy water font on entering into the presence of God in the Blessed Sacrament and to make use of those waters of purification, asking God to make them a little more fit to appear before him.

721. Why do Catholics genuflect before entering the seats?

They do so to Christ personally present in the Holy Eucharist. When Christ allowed St. Thomas the apostle to touch the wounds in his hands and feet, St. Thomas said, "My Lord and my God." The same Christ left himself present in the Eucharist when he said, "This is my body," and when Catholics come into his presence they offer him the tribute of their deep reverence and worship by genuflection. You, too, would kneel before Christ if you believed as Catholics do.

722. I was rather amused by noticing how Catholics superstitiously cross themselves before beginning their prayers.

A professing Christian laughing at fellow Christians for making the sign of the cross is an anomaly! It shows how far Protestantism has drifted from the spirit of true Christianity. Catholics at least say with St. Paul, "Far be it from me to glory except in the cross of our Lord Jesus Christ" (Gal. 6:14). The early Christians made very much of the sign of the cross, even as Catholics do today. Tertullian, who died about A.D. 240, wrote, "In all our travels, in our coming in and going out, in putting on our clothes and our shoes, at table, in going to rest, whatever employment occupies us, we mark our forehead with the sign of the cross." St. Ephrem, who died in 373, wrote, "My son, mark all your actions with the sign of the life-giving cross. Do not go out from the door of your house till you have signed yourself with the cross. Do not neglect that sign whether in eating or drinking or going to sleep, or in the home or going on a journey. There is no habit to be compared with it. Let it be a protecting wall round all your conduct, and teach it to your children that they may earnestly learn the custom." An early Christian would certainly be at home amongst Catholics, but like a fish out of water amongst Protestants.

723. Why are Catholic churches decorated with images and statues, in direct violation of the second commandment?

The second commandment is, "You shall not take the name of the Lord your God in vain." Protestants, of course, call that the third commandment. But they are wrong in doing so, having taken that part of the first commandment that refers to images as the second of God's commandments. But do those words forbid the making of images? They do not. God was forbidding idolatry, not the making of images. He said, "You shall not make for yourself a graven image, or any likeness of anything that is in heaven above, or that is in the earth beneath … you shall not bow down to them or serve them." God deliberately adds those last words, yet you ignore them. He forbids men to make images in order to adore them. But he does not forbid the making of images. You will find the commandments given in Exodus 20. But in that same book, 25:18, you will find God ordering the Jews to make images of angels! Would you accuse God of not knowing the sense of his own law? He says, "You shall make two cherubim of gold; of hammered work shall you make them, on the two ends of the mercy seat." In other words, the Jews were to make images of things in the heaven above. And if your interpretation be true, why do you violate God's law by making images of things in the Earth beneath? Why images of kings and politicians in our parks? Why photographs of friends and relatives? On your theory you could not even take a snapshot of a gum tree. You would be making an image of a thing in the Earth beneath. You strain at a gnat and swallow a camel! This is the fruit of your private interpretation of Scripture. No. God does not forbid the making of images; he forbids the making of images in order to adore them.

724. I have seen Catholics on their knees adoring and praying to statues in their churches.

You have not. You have seen Catholics kneeling at prayer, and perhaps kneeling before an image of Christ, or of our Lady. But if you concluded that they were praying to the statues, that was not the fault of the Catholics. It was your own fault insofar as you judged them according to your own preconceived ideas. Without bothering to ask for information, you guessed, and guessed wrongly. Before an image of Mary, Catholics may go on their knees and pray to God through the intercession of that Mother of Christ whom the statue represents. But you have no right to accuse them of praying to the statue. Were you to kneel down by your bedside at night for a last prayer, could you be regarded as adoring or praying to your mattress?

725. But I have seen a Catholic kiss the feet of a statue of Christ.

If I kiss the photograph of my mother, am I honoring a piece of cardboard? Or is it a tribute of love and respect offered to my mother? A Catholic reverences images and statues only insofar as they remind him of God, of Christ, or of our Lady and the saints. Where a pagan adores and worships a thing of wood in itself, I kiss the cross not because it is a piece of wood but because it stands for Christ and for his sufferings on my behalf. And I am sure that our Lord looks down from heaven and says, "Bless the child; he at least appreciates my love for him." Your mistake is that you try to judge interior dispositions from exterior conduct—a dangerous policy always.

726. The Catholic Church omits the second commandment and then breaks up the tenth into two in order to avoid having only nine.

The reverse is the case. Protestants make the first commandment into two, and then, to escape having eleven, turn the ninth and tenth into one! The first commandment as given in the Bible, is as follows: "I am the Lord your God, who brought you out of the land of Egypt, out of the house of bondage. You shall have no other gods before me. You shall not make for yourself a graven image, or any likeness of anything that is in heaven above, or that is in the earth beneath, or that is in the water under the earth; you shall not bow down to them or serve them; for I the Lord your God am a jealous God, etc." (Ex. 20:2-5).

727. And you deny that you have changed the commandment?

I do. You notice words only, paying little or no attention to the legal substance of those words. To simplify the wording whilst retaining the full sense is certainly not to change the commandment. If you say, "He is under an obligation not to give expression to his thoughts at the present moment," I do not change the substance of what you say if I repeat to some small child, "He must not speak now." The first commandment contains within its involved Hebrew amplification two essential points: that we must acknowledge the true God, and that we must avoid false gods. Those two essential points are put briefly and simply in the catechism for children who are more at home with short and easy sentences.

728. All the liturgy of the Catholic Church seems very different from the simple teaching of Jesus, doesn't it?

The teachings of Jesus were not so simple as many people suppose. Only an inadequate knowledge of those teachings can speak like that. His doctrines are most profound, and many people profess that they cannot solve what seems to them so involved and at times paradoxical.

But the teachings of Jesus are not really involved in your question. The liturgy of the Church concerns her forms of worship. Now, I admit that the forms of worship in the Catholic Church today are much more elaborate than in the time of Christ. But they are in full keeping with the principles he laid down. An oak tree is a much more elaborate thing than an acorn; but its development is in full accordance with the potentialities of the acorn. The growth and development of the Catholic Church through two thousand years must affect her in all aspects of her being. But essentially and fundamentally she remains the same. Outwardly, to take one example of her liturgy, the Mass seems very different from the simple Last Supper. But precisely what was done at the Last Supper is done during the Mass.

729. Christ was poor and humble. Yet Catholic ceremonial is full of pomp and display. Does your religion teach humility?

Yes. We are taught to be humble. And Christian humility orders a man to be unassuming and gentle. But it does not forbid a man to worship God as befits God. In fact, the more humble a man is, the more he magnifies and glorifies God and depreciates self. The Catholic Church says, "God certainly deserves the best we can give him. Whatever else we may do, let us not be mean in anything where God is concerned. We personally deserve very little, and if by our gifts God's worship is magnificent and we the poorer, that is how it should be." Christ himself commended the poor widow for giving all she had to the Temple. Yet he was the one who taught humility.

730. Is it not opposed to the simplicity of his principles?

No. Christ was God, and in the Old Testament God dictated a ceremonial every bit as lavish as Catholic ceremonial. So that it cannot be against his principles. And Christ never condemned ceremonial. He instituted the ceremonial of baptism with water. With ceremony he breathed upon the apostles when giving them the power to forgive sins. He came to fulfill the law, not to destroy it. But above all, he founded his Church, giving into her care the guardianship of his religion, and conferring upon her the power to regulate its worship. Whatever the Church has sanctioned in this matter she has done in virtue of the commission given her by her Founder.

731. The ceremonial of the Church shows a great change since the time of Christ.

You won't find the leaves of an oak tree wrapped up inside an acorn. Christ sowed the seed and said that the small seed he planted would grow into a vast tree. Such growth supposes external changes without loss of identity. Because an acorn has no branches or foliage, will you deny its identity with the tree into which it grows?

732. The Last Supper had no elaborate ceremonial rites, yet look at the Mass today.

The essential rites of the Mass are exactly the same as those of the Last Supper. Remember that before the simple Last Supper Christ had fulfilled the full ceremonial of the Jewish Feast. He ceremoniously washed the disciples' feet. And the growth of the surrounding rites in the Mass has been in accordance with principles dictated by God to the Jews, and by the actions of Christ throughout his public ministry when he used so many ceremonies in the miracles he worked.

733. Why do priests vest so elaborately when going to say Mass?

In Exodus 28:2-3, we read of God's prescriptions of the vestments befitting the dignity of his religion. "You shall make holy garments for Aaron your brother, for glory and for beauty. And you shall speak to all who have ability, whom I have endowed with an able mind, that they make Aaron's garments to consecrate him for my priesthood." Throughout the rest of the chapter God deigns to give the most minute directions as to the various vestments Aaron was to use. Not for a moment would Christ have condemned the principle of vestments after such a sanction by the infinitely wise God. He would be contradicting himself. There can be nothing wrong with vestments in principle.

734. Christ dressed with the utmost simplicity and talked to God in the most humble places.

Priests also dress with simplicity. They are not always in vestments. As for Christ, he too went to the Temple and took part in its worship, never condemning its ritual. With the establishment of his own Church in fulfillment of the Old Law, he ordained his own priests after the order of Melchizedek in place of the Levitical priesthood and left it to the Church to regulate the ceremonial surrounding the substantial form of worship he had prescribed. As I have said, he would have been the last to condemn a dignified ceremonial, and Anglican Protestants of the High Church group are rapidly trying to resume the vestments prescribed by the Catholic Church, vestments their forefathers so eagerly got rid of; mistakenly, now say the High Church Anglicans.

735. Christ was not concerned with ceremonies and doctrines but with men's souls.

Precisely because he was concerned with men's souls he was very much concerned with ceremonies and doctrines. By ceremonies religion is adapted to the needs of men who are so conditioned by their senses and so dependent upon visible and tangible manifestations of realities. Therefore Christ constantly made use of ceremonies and prescribed ceremonies.

Again, he came to teach truth; and it is impossible to teach a truth without giving a doctrine. A doctrine is merely a teaching. Why did Christ tell the apostles to teach all nations all things whatsoever he had made known to them, saying that he who believes not shall be condemned? The very welfare of men's souls depends upon their acceptance of the doctrines taught them by the Son of God.

736. Why the proud display of processions such as those of eucharistic congresses?

There is nothing wrong with processions. Christ entered Jerusalem with a procession of the populace crying hosanna, waving palms and strewing their garments on the roadway, making it as elaborate as they could. And he rebuked those who would have prevented it. Remember that eucharistic congresses are not in honor of ourselves but of Christ, and love of him suggests that nothing can be too good for him.

737. When I think of the expense, I think too of the poor, and ask why so much money should be wasted.

Such an objection recalls the words of Judas, "Why was this ointment not sold for three hundred denarii and given to the poor?" (John 12:5). In any case, the lavish generosity of the Catholic Church in the worship of God does not interfere with her work for the poor. She is the most active of all churches in that work. No other church has so many institutions, hospitals, homes, and orphanages; and in many parishes there is a weekly distribution of money and food to the poor through the St. Vincent de Paul or some other society.

738. Cathedrals costing thousands are nothing to God. He is a Spirit and would love just as much without the earthly show.

But man would not love so much! You fail to grasp a fundamental point. It takes two to make a religion, God and man. God is a pure spirit but man is not. Man is a composite of the spiritual and the material. And he must worship God according to his twofold nature. Man not only possesses spiritual thoughts; he gives them expression in speech, writing, music, art, and architecture. And, where God is concerned, he dedicates all these things to God's service in religion. God himself ordered the Jews to do so, commanding the erection of the glorious Temple at Jerusalem. God wants the service not of half our being but of our complete being.

739. In Europe I found glorious cathedrals and pitiable poverty side by side.

The present-day poverty is not due to the cathedrals, which were built long ago by others who gave their time and services as a voluntary offering to God. The poverty due to modern industrial conditions should not be attributed to buildings erected in other and happier ages. Meantime, those beautiful cathedrals do no harm to men. If the poor pulled them down stone by stone, they could not eat the stones. And even if they could sell them for thirty pieces of silver, the relief would be of a very temporary nature. Believe me, future generations would be just as poor temporally, and much poorer spiritually, with no inspiring cathedrals.

740. Should not the government at least confiscate all gifts and ornaments, and distribute their value to the poor?

No. They are gifts of the people, and if people wish to dedicate tokens of gratitude to the house of God, no one has any right to their possession. People are not free to distribute what is not their own to the poor. There were many poor in Israel when God demanded the dedication of a richly ornamented Temple to his worship.

741. Why does the Church cling to Latin, a dead language?

For one reason, precisely because it is dead! In modern and living languages, words are constantly changing their meaning, whilst in a dead language, such as Latin, they do not. The essential doctrine and significance of Christianity must not change, and the safest way to preserve it intact is to keep it in an unchangeable language. Again, a universal Church must have at least her chief form of worship in a universal language. Christ came to save all men, and wherever a member of the true Church may be in this world he should be able to find himself at home at the central act of Christian worship. The Mass, being said in Latin, is the same in all lands. If a Frenchman, who could not understand a word of English, were to enter a Catholic church in London, he would be at home the moment the Mass began. An English service would be a mystery to him. I myself have said Mass with as many as fifteen different nationalities present, and not all could follow my discourse when I spoke to those present though I spoke for a few minutes in English, in French, and in Italian. There were still many who could not understand any of these languages, but being all Catholics, they were quite at home the moment I turned to the altar and went on with the Mass in Latin. It brings out the wisdom and the universality of the Catholic Church. The priest ascends the altar to intercede with God on behalf of the people. Those present kneel, and in their hearts pour out their prayers for their own necessities. They feel no more need to know just what the priest is saying than the Jews who knelt at the foot of the mountain felt the need of knowing just what Moses was saying to God on their behalf at the top. And here once again let me say that if anyone should complain of the use of Latin, it should be those who have to endure it. And I have never yet heard a Catholic soul complain that it caused difficulty, or that he or she would like it changed.

742. At evening devotions in a Catholic church I heard many prayers to Mary. I cannot find in Scripture where Mary is to be worshipped in the same way as Christ.

I am not surprised, for such a doctrine is nowhere taught in Scripture. Moreover, if any Catholic dared to worship Mary in the same way as he worships Christ he would be guilty of a most serious sin, and no Catholic priest could give him absolution unless he promised never to do so again. But that does not mean that one must deprive Mary of all honor.

743. St. Bonaventure said, "Into thy hands, O Lady, I commend my spirit." Thus he served the creature more than the Creator, to whom alone such words should be addressed.

St. Bonaventure did not serve the creature more than the Creator. In commending his soul to Mary he was not commending it to anyone opposed to God. He did it because of God, who chose Mary as the second Eve. Eve brought us forth to misery and to death; Mary brought us forth to happiness and to life when she brought forth our Savior. Like the kings from the East, St. Bonaventure knew that after the long journey through this life, he would also find the child Jesus with Mary his mother, and that if he commended his soul to the mother he would necessarily find himself in the presence of the child, even in eternity. Gladly on my own deathbed would I utter the words used by St. Bonaventure. As Jesus came to us through Mary, so we shall go to him through her, whether we think of it or not.

744. When someone praised Mary, Christ paid no attention, but said that only those are blessed who keep the word of God (Luke 11:28).

The Gospels are fragmentary accounts, and we do not know all that transpired on that occasion. But even so, the actual text is not opposed in any way to the honor we give to Mary. Someone praised Mary. Christ replied, "Blessed rather are those who hear the word of God and keep it!" Not for a moment did he intend to deny that Mary had done this. He practically says, "Yes. She is blest in being my mother. But it is a greater blessing to serve God." And, from one point of view, the fidelity with which Mary undoubtedly served God was a greater blessing to her than merely being the mother of Christ. Any idea that Christ, the best of sons, was trying to belittle his mother is absurd. And if you have such faith in Scripture, what do you do as regards the prophecy of Mary in Luke 1:48? "Henceforth." she predicted, "all generations will call me blessed." Yet blessed are they who hear the word of God and keep it! We Catholics call Mary blessed indeed, whilst many Protestants search Scripture in the fond hope of proving something to her discredit!

745. Christ called her "woman" when he said, "Woman, behold your son."

In the language Christ spoke, that word was a term of great respect, however harshly it may sound in our modern English language. Our Lord would have been the last to slight his mother, a thing we despise in every man; and above all in his last and most tender words to her. Nor are we likely to please him by seeking to dishonor her.

746. Did he not say to her at the marriage feast of Cana, "O woman, what have you to do with me?"

He did. But most certainly he intended no reproach to Mary. Her action was one of pure charity to others. Foreseeing the possible distress of others, she asked him to relieve them; and he would not rebuke so unselfish a thought. Nor would he speak to her with any trace of disrespect. Then, too, had Mary asked a wrong thing, Christ would not have done it, nor would he have sanctioned a request he had to rebuke. And Mary knew that she had not been reprehended, or she would not have told the waiters to do what her Son would tell them. She would have dropped the matter. Why, then, did Christ speak thus? It was his first miracle, the first public sign of his divinity wrought by himself. And he wanted to bring out publicly the fact that he was doing it not as the son of an earthly mother and according to his human nature, but calling upon his divine nature as the eternal Son of God. He did it because his mother requested it but he did not do it by any power derived from his mother. He thus brought out both for the listeners and for us that this beginning of miracles was proof of his divinity, although in appearance he seemed but man.

747. Why do you call Mary Queen of Heaven?

Because Mary is undoubtedly in heaven, and Jesus is King of heaven. Since Jesus is "King of kings and Lord of lords," it is certain that Mary his mother rejoices in queenly dignity.

748. Catholics worship Mary and her Child; Hindus worship Lankhria, Queen of Heaven, and her Son, Devi, King of Heaven.

A little knowledge is a dangerous thing. You understand neither the Catholic religion nor the Hindu religion. And you are not, therefore, in a position to compare them. It is true that we Catholics worship Jesus as God. We do not worship Mary as a goddess.

Your statement of the Hindu teaching is equally astray. The ancient Hindu or Vedic religion taught straight-out pantheism. In reality one alone exists—Brahman. The thought that anything else exists is illusion.

Five centuries after the birth of Christ a new Hindu sect arose called the Tautrikas or Saktas. They taught a subordinate god named Siva, gave him a wife named Durga, and declared that she was identical with him and in no way different from him. She was worshipped as a goddess, though identical with Siva the god! The Hindu sect made her supreme, because they said she was the "power" of Siva, the active side of his nature. This Durga was called Devi, which means "the" goddess. How can you make Devi the King of Heaven, when the very word means "the" goddess? Any ordinary encyclopedia would tell you that, in Hindu mythology, Devi was regarded as a goddess and not King of Heaven or of anywhere else. Nor have these Indian mythological characters any historical reality such as all the world acknowledges in the case of Christ and his mother, Mary.

749. Why pray to Mary at all?

Because God wills that we should do so, and because such prayers to her are of the utmost value. God often wills to give certain favors only on condition that we go to some secondary agent. Sodom was to be spared through the intercession of Abraham; Naaman, the leper, was to be cured only through the waters of the Jordan. Now Mary is, and must ever remain, the mother of Christ. She still has a mother's rights and privileges and is able to obtain for us many graces. But let us view things reasonably. If I desire to pray, I can certainly pray to God directly. Yet would you blame me if, at times, I were to ask my own earthly mother to pray for me also? Such a request is really a prayer to her that she may intercede for me with God. Certainly, if I met the mother of Christ on Earth, I would ask her to pray for me, and she would do so. And in her more perfect state with Christ in heaven she is not less able to help me.

750. But a prayer to God directly must be more efficacious than a prayer to Mary.

Not necessarily. It might well be that God intends to honor our Lady by granting the favor I seek through her intercession in a particular way. In that case the grace is to be given through her provided I honor her by addressing myself to her. Again, every prayer to Mary is in reality the asking of a favor from God, even as the mother of Christ is requested to ask the same favor also. It is often better to ask God for a favor and to have someone else praying to God with one for the same favor. Two prayers are better than one. And above all when the other one praying is Christ's own mother.

751. There is but one mediator; there is no place for Mary.

Christ is the principal mediator in his own right. Mary is a secondary mediatrix, through, with, and in Christ. Without him she would have no power, and therefore he is the source of all mediation with God on behalf of men.

752. How can you blend the mediation of others with that of Christ?

It follows from the doctrine of the communion of saints. Remember that by baptism every Christian is incorporated with Christ. St. Paul says, The head of every man is Christ." So close is this union that Christ says, "Whoever gives you a cup of water to drink because you bear the name of Christ, will by no means lose his reward" (Mark 9:41). Every Christian is Christ in a most intimate way. St. Paul tells us that if a baptized person sins, he takes the members of Christ and makes them the members of iniquity! When that same St. Paul was persecuting the Christians before his conversion, Christ appeared to him and said, "Saul, Saul, why do you persecute me?" He did not say, "Why do you persecute my disciples?" He could equally say, when we pray to Mary or to the saints, "What asketh thou of me?" When we honor our Lady or the saints, we honor not their own merely human and created nature but we honor Christ in them according to the doctrine of Scripture. The Catholic Church is the only completely scriptural Church.

753. Attending a Catholic church one evening I was disgusted by the rigmarole called the rosary. What is that rosary?

The rosary is a special form of devotion to Mary. One takes a set of beads, divided into five sections, each section consisting of one large bead and ten small ones. Holding the large bead, one says the Our Father, and on each of the small ones, the Hail Mary. Between each section, or decade, the Gloria is said. Whilst saying the prayers, one meditates or thinks of the joys, or sorrows, or glories of Christ's life and of that of his Mother. It is a very beautiful form of prayer with which you were disgusted merely because you did not understand it.

754. The rosary is a relic of the superstitious Middle Ages, when it was meant for ignorant people.

The use of beads dates from the earliest centuries. The prayers embodied in the rosary were composed by Christ himself in the case of the Our Father, and by the Angel Gabriel, St. Elizabeth, and the Council of Ephesus in the fifth century, in the case of the Hail Mary. We are in very good company with those prayers. As a devotion, with its loving contemplation of the mysteries of the life, death, and resurrection of our Lord, it appeals to rich and poor, to learned and ignorant alike, as Christianity itself was meant to do.

755. When were beads invented, and what do they symbolize?

It is impossible to say when beads were first used. As an aid to memory, the early Christians used to put a number of pebbles in one pocket transferring them to another as they said each prayer, so that they could be sure of completing such prayers each day as their devotion inspired. Later, berries or pebbles were strung together for the purpose. In the Middle Ages sections of these beads were adapted to the different meditations that compose the rosary, the sections being a numerical help to meditate for a given period of time upon each allotted subject. The symbolism is expressed in the word rosary. A rosary is a garland of flowers. One rose does not make a rosary. Prayers are the flowers of the spiritual life, and in offering that group of prayers known as the rosary, we lay a garland of spiritual flowers at the feet of God.

756. Between each Our Father to God, it throws in ten prayers to Mary!

You've got it the wrong way around. Between each ten Hail Marys an Our Father is said. The rosary is essentially a devotion to Mary, honoring her whom God himself so honored. And it honors her particularly in her relation to Christ, whose life is the subject of the meditations. The Our Father abstracts from the Incarnation of Christ; the Hail Mary is full of reverence to our Lord's birth into this world for us.

757. Christ said, "In praying do not heap up empty phrases as the Gentiles do; for they think that they will be heard for their many words."

Vain repetition in the manner of heathens is forbidden, but not useful repetition that is not in the manner of heathens. Vain repetition relies mechanically upon the mere number of prayers or formulas uttered. But Catholics do not rely on the mere repetition of prayers, nor upon their multiplication, but on the intrinsic worth of each prayer and upon the fervor and earnestness with which it is said. Two prayers said well, one immediately after the other, are as good as the same two prayers said well with twenty-four hours between them. Time is nothing to God, in whose sight a thousand years are but as a day. He does not mind whether there be two seconds between our prayers or two years; the prayers themselves are just as pleasing to him. If you take the principle behind your objection and push it to its full conclusion, you could say the Our Father but once in your life. If you said it once each year, it would be repetition. How often may you say it? Once a month? Once a week? Once a day? If daily, what would be wrong with saying it hourly? If you have just concluded one Our Father, why may you not begin it again at once? Does it suddenly become an evil prayer?

758. If repetition adds to effectiveness, why stop at ten Hail Marys? Why not more?

It is the nature of this devotion that the rosary should be composed of decades, or groups of ten. It would not be the rosary otherwise. Repetition certainly adds to effectiveness, if the prayers are said well. Just before his Passion, Christ prayed "the third time, saying the same words" (Matt. 26:44). He thought it good to say the same prayer three times in succession. Why did he limit it to three times? If good to say it three times, why not twenty times? He thought three sufficient for his purpose. So, too, we consider the period taken by the recital of ten Hail Marys sufficient time for the amount of reflection we desire to give to each mystery of the rosary.

759. Why do not the Protestant churches teach us anything about Mary's power of intercession for us?

Because they have wrested Scripture to the destruction of all true understanding of Christian revelation and have been led into many grave errors by an exaggerated literalism. Concentrating on the fact that Christ is the one principal Mediator, they have made no allowance for the equally clear doctrine of secondary mediation of one human being for another with, in, and through Christ. Though they repeat the words of the Creed, "I believe in the communion of saints," they have no idea of the practical significance of those words. They do not understand that they mean the common union in Christ of all who love him, so that he lives in them as in his very members, and in them as his own mystical body. But we Catholics understand this doctrine and know that member can help member. We accept the teaching of St. James that the prayer of a just soul availeth much. And first and foremost among the just is the Mother of Christ. She is with God; she shared in the redemptive work of Christ; she is interested in all whom Jesus died to redeem; and as he makes constant intercession in heaven for us now, she associates her intercession with his, and we rightly ask for a share in her intercession as well as in his.

760. Why do you omit from the Our Father the words "For thine is the kingdom, the power, and the glory forever and ever"?

Because our Lord did not add those words to the prayer as he taught it. There is nothing wrong with the words in themselves. In fact, they are very beautiful. But they are not Sacred Scripture. Some early Catholic copyists wrote those words in a margin; later copyists mistakenly transcribed them into the text; and the Protestant translators made use of a copy of the New

Testament with the words thus included. All scholars today admit the words to be an interpolation. We Catholics do not use them.

761. Why pray to saints? Is it not better to pray to God direct?

Not always. The same answer applies here as in the case of prayers to the Virgin Mary, who after all is the greatest of the saints. God may wish to give certain favors through the intercession of some given saint. In such a case, it is better to seek the intercession of that saint as God wishes. I can decide to give you a gift myself, or to do so through a friend. In the latter case you do me greater honor by accepting it from my friend than by refusing my way of giving it to you, and insolently demanding it directly from myself in person.

762. I pray that you may see the futility of praying to saints who can do nothing for you. Christ is the only mediator.

By your very prayer you are attempting to mediate between God and myself on my behalf. I do not criticize the principle of praying for others. I believe in that. But I do criticize your praying for me in violation of your own principles. If the saints cannot be mediators by praying for me, nor can you. Your prayers would be futile; they could do nothing for me; and you would be wasting your time.

763. The Lord's Prayer shows that God himself hears our prayers.

Correct. And he hears the prayers we address to the saints, and their prayers also on our behalf. And those prayers, added to our own, give us additional claims to be heard by God in a favorable way.

764. When did God tell anyone to pray to human beings?

When the Catholic Church teaches us that prayer to the saints is right and useful, it is God teaching us that truth through his Church. But the doctrine is clearly enough indicated in Scripture also. I have mentioned Abraham's prayer for Sodom. The Jews asked Moses to go to speak to God on their behalf. God himself said to Eliphaz the Temanite, "My wrath is kindled against you ... my servant Job shall pray for you, for I will accept his prayer not to deal with you according to your folly" (Job 42:7–8). Earlier in that same book we read, "Call now; is there any one who will answer you? To which of the holy ones will you turn?" (5:1). His enemies meant that Job was too wicked to be heard, but they knew that it was lawful to invoke the saints. Long after the death of Jeremiah, Onias said of that prophet, "This is a man who loves the brethren and prays much for the people and the holy city, Jeremiah, the prophet of God" (2 Macc. 15:14). St. James says that "the prayer of a righteous man has great power in its effects." If his prayer is valuable, it is worthwhile to ask his prayers. If you say, "Yes. That is all right whilst a man is still in this life and on Earth," I ask whether you think he has less power when in heaven with God? In Revelation 8:4, St. John says that "the smoke of the incense rose with the prayers of the saints from the hand of the angel before God." If I can ask my own mother to pray for me whilst she is still in this life, surely I can do so when she is with God! She does not know less when she rejoices in the vision of God; she has not less interest in me; and she is not less charitably disposed toward me then. We Catholics believe in the communion of saints and are in communion with them. But for you the doctrine of the Apostle's Creed, "I believe in the communion of saints," must be a meaningless formula. Christ is not particularly honored by our ignoring those who loved and served him best and whom he loves so much.

765. By what authority does the Catholic Church make saints?

The decree of canonization does not make a saint. It simply declares infallibly that a given person has lived such a holy life with the help of God's grace that he is a saint. When someone like a Francis of Assisi lives such a holy life that all people are compelled to admire it, the Church is often asked to say whether such a person is worthy to be honored publicly as a saint. The Church then carefully collects all possible information, and, after due consideration, says yes or no. If the Church says yes, the name of the person to be venerated is put into the canon or catalogue of those who have become saints by their heroic lives of virtue. The Church has the authority of Christ for these decisions, for he sent her with his authority to teach all nations in matters of faith and morals, and she could not tell us officially that a given person was a perfect model of Christian virtue if such a person were not.

766. Why do Catholics worship relics of saints?

They do not worship relics as they worship God, by adoration. If you mean worship in the sense of honor or veneration, then Catholics certainly venerate the relics of saints. The law "Honor your father and mother" extends to their persons, body and soul; to their reputations and to all connected with them. We reverence their remains even after death. And if we are not to venerate the remains and relics of the saints who have been so entirely consecrated to God, are we to desecrate them? Or are we to be blandly indifferent to them as to the bleached bones of some dead animal lying in the fields? The Catholic doctrine, forbidding adoration yet commanding respect and veneration, is the only possible Christian conduct.

767. I don't object to that kind of veneration. I object to the expecting of favors through relics.

No real difficulty arises in this matter. No one holds that material relics of themselves possess any innate talismanic value. But God himself can certainly grant favors even of a temporal nature through the relics of saints, thus honoring his saints and rewarding the faith and piety of some given Catholic. St. Matthew tells us that the diseased came to Christ. They "begged him that they might only touch the fringe of his garment; and as many as touched it were made well" (Matt. 14:36). Again, we read of a woman who touched the hem of Christ's garment and who was cured. "And Jesus, perceiving in himself that power had gone forth from him, immediately turned about in the crowd, and said, 'Who touched my garments?'" (Mark 5:30). You may reply that these incidents concerned Christ, and that whilst he was still living in this world. But that does not affect the principle that God can grant temporal favors through inanimate things. And if you look up 2 Kings 13:21 in your own Protestant version of the Bible, you will find that a dead man, who was being buried in the sepulcher of Elisha, was restored to life the moment his body came into contact with the bones of that great prophet of God. In the Acts of the Apostles, too, we read of a most Catholic and most un-Protestant procedure. "God did extraordinary miracles by the hands of Paul, so that handkerchiefs or aprons were carried away from his body to the sick, and diseases left them and the evil spirits came out of them" (Acts 19:11-12). But you will notice that it was God who wrought these miracles. And we Catholics say that God can quite easily do similar things even in our own days. As a matter of historical fact, he has wrought such things throughout the course of the ages within the Catholic Church.

768. Are not relics received and venerated without a particle of proof that they are genuine?

No. The Catholic Church is very prudent in this matter, and her law declares that those relics alone may be publicly venerated that have authentic documents accompanying them and proving them to be genuine. These documents can be given only by one authorized by the Holy See to grant them. If the documents are lost, no relic may be offered for public veneration by the faithful without a special decree from a bishop who can guarantee the relic as genuine. But even should a Catholic venerate as a relic some object that is not authentic, such veneration is at least well meant and directed toward the one whom the object is believed to represent.

769. Christmas Day is always on December 25th. Why are not our Lord's death and resurrection celebrated on the same day each year?

For the sake of convenience, the world has forsaken the Jewish calendar, which is based on the movement of the moon round the Earth, in favor of the Roman calendar, based on the movement of the Earth round the sun. Now, the normal procedure of the Church is to arrange her festival days according to the accepted

Roman calendar. By way of exception, however, the Church retains the Jewish calendar for the celebration of Christ's death and resurrection. Since the movement of the moon around the Earth does not keep proportionate time with that of the Earth around the sun, Easter necessarily becomes variable in relation to the Roman calendar. Easter Sunday is always the Sunday after the first full moon to occur after March 21st. It can fall on any day between March 22nd and April 25th. The reason why the Church has retained the Jewish method in the case of the death and resurrection of Christ is chiefly based upon the religious significance of these events. The paschal lamb of the Old Law, celebrating the liberation of the Jews from captivity in Egypt by the slaying of a lamb to preserve them from the slaughter of the children of the Egyptians, was but a type or figure of Christ, the true Lamb of God. By his death and resurrection we are liberated from the captivity of Satan. In order to bring out the identity between the figurative paschal lamb of the Old Law and the true Lamb of God in the New, the Church insists that Easter be celebrated at that very time when the Jews used to celebrate the Passover. In other festivals the Church follows the Roman, or rather, the Gregorian calendar, which is a modification of the Roman calendar.

770. What is Ash Wednesday?

Ash Wednesday is the first day of Lent, ushering in the forty days of fasting and penance prior to the celebration of Easter and the Resurrection of Christ. On that day the Catholic priest blesses some powdered ashes and signs the foreheads of the people with them as they come to the altar rails. As he marks them with the ashes, he says over each, "Remember, man, that thou art dust, and into dust thou shalt return" (Gen. 3:19). The ashes remind us of the shortness of life, enkindle serious thoughts of eternity, and are a symbol of repentance.

771. The assembly of the Free Presbyterian Church strongly protests against the recognition of Good Friday as a holy day, there being no scriptural authority for so regarding it.

A strong protest against things offensive to Christ would be a little more intelligible. But a protest against an effort to honor Christ from a body of professing Christians is an enigma. The authority of Scripture for the fact that our Lord died for us on Good Friday is more than enough warrant for our regarding the day as one demanding special reverence. Would the Free Presbyterians quarrel with the recognition of their own birthdays as having an importance not belonging to other days? And do they, or do they not, believe that the death of their Savior has meant more to them than their birth into a state from which they needed redemption?

Or again, is Christmas Day, the very birthday of Christ, sacred to the Free Presbyterians? Yet they have no more, and no less, scriptural warrant for its observance. And do they think they will block the desecration of the Sabbath day by asking people not even to recall all that Christ did for them on Good Friday? It is a weird idea to propose that since Christ is not honored as he should be on Sundays, we must see to it that he is not honored as he should be on Good Friday.

The Catholic Church at least remains loyal to all that our Lord's death has meant to those who love him. Every Friday throughout the year she calls upon Catholics to give up the pleasure of taking meat on the day Christ gave up his very life for them. She prepares for the annual commemoration of the death of Jesus on Good Friday by the forty days of Lenten observance, and devotes the whole of Holy Week to recollection, prayer, and fitting religious services. If people want fidelity to the memory of Christ they will find it nowhere as they will find it in the Catholic Church.

772. *Concerning the origin of "Easter Day," ancient secular history records the origin of the vernal or spring equinox feast as being in existence for centuries before the Christian era.*

The existence of a spring equinox feast centuries before the Christian era has nothing whatever to do with the origin of "Easter Day." The argument from superficial similarities to causal connection teems with fallacies. One might as well say, "As regards the origin of swimming in the Domain baths, history shows that people used to swim in the river Ganges centuries before Australia was discovered." Did we therefore build the Domain baths because people used to swim in the Ganges some centuries ago? The celebration of festivals is as natural to man as to wash. Again, where religion is concerned, it is not the act that counts but the motive and intention. A feast in honor of springtime is not the same thing as a feast that is in honor of something else and that merely happens to occur during the spring season. Ancient celebrations of spring equinox feasts contained no trace of the significance of the Christian Easter.

773. In the Babylonian mythology we read that a large egg fell from heaven into the river Euphrates and out came the goddess "Ishtar" or "Easter," and hence the egg became the symbol of Astarte, or Ishtar.

In the first place, the word *Easter* has no connection with the name of Ishtar, the goddess of the Babylonians. The word *Easter* is an Anglo-Saxon word from the Teutonic "Eostre," an ancient German goddess of light. To think that Easter and Ishtar are synonyms because they have a remote resemblance in sound is simply a barbarism. From an etymological point of view one would have a better case in trying to trace the origin of the Christian Easter to ancient German mythology than to that of the ancient Babylonians. But even that would not work. Not only because the significance of the Christian Easter is not to be found in German mythology but because the feast designated by the word *Easter* existed long before that term was applied to it. Easter is but an Anglo-Saxon designation of a feast observed by Christians from the very beginning, and by Christians who had never heard the word and who would not have recognized the Anglo-Saxon method of alluding to it. The early Christians knew Easter as "Paschal" time. And the Greek word *pascha* was derived from the Hebrew *pesach,* meaning "passover." The Christian liturgy adopted the feast from the Jewish religion, because the paschal feast in that religion was prophetic of Christianity. The paschal lamb slain by the Jews was typical of Christ, and as Christ died on the Jewish paschal day, or as we say in English "Easter" day, that day has been retained. And it happens to fall in the spring season. Babylonian mythology had nothing to do with this, and Christians had no idea of honoring spring any more than they thought of dishonoring summer, autumn, or winter.

774. So from Babylon of old the egg has always been associated with the festival of Easter. Buns also figured in the Babylonian rites, as they do now.

Eggs and buns were certainly usual symbols in use at springtime long before Christianity came on the scene. The egg was a symbol of germinating life, and buns symbolized the fruits of the Earth. Since Easter happened to occur in the springtime, those symbols were in use amongst the pagans of early ages precisely when Christians were celebrating Easter. And as those symbols were as harmless as the lifting of one's hat to symbolize reverence toward a lady friend, the Church allowed converted pagans to retain the custom of eggs and buns. But the essential significance of Easter as representing the fulfillment of Jewish paschal predictions in Christ was absolutely foreign to their paganism. And an entirely new symbolism was given to their simple habits of feasting on eggs and buns. No longer did these things symbolize any religious devotion to Ishtar the goddess of spring, but they now symbolized the new life won for humanity by the Resurrection of Christ, and the fact that he is the bread of our true, supernatural, and eternal life.

775. The observance of the Easter festival was introduced into the Catholic Church in order to conciliate the pagans to nominal Christianity.

That is sheer nonsense. The Easter festival originated with the Church herself and was a legitimate continuation of the Jewish paschal season. It would be interesting were people, fond of glib assertions, to give the date when their supposed additions to Christianity were made. Eusebius quotes a controversy in the time of Pope St. Victor in the year 190 as to the right day for the celebration of Easter. St. Irenaeus shows a diversity of practice in the time of Pope Sixtus, about the year 120. The feast was in existence then or there could not have grown up diversity of usages in different places. St. Irenaeus also mentions that St. Polycarp kept Easter on the 14th of Nisan, clinging rigidly to the Jewish date and claiming that he was following the custom of St. John the apostle, whose disciple he had been.

The idea that the feast was introduced in order to conciliate pagans to nominal Christianity is just wild extravagance. The feast was not introduced to conciliate pagans; its Christian significance and utter repudiation of all pagan Ishtar-worship could not have conciliated them in any case; and such pagans as were converted were not invited to become nominal Christians. The early ages of the Church were not the times for nominal Christians. The invitation to become a Christian was practically an invitation to martyrdom.

776. The Church, pursuing its usual methods, took measures to get the Christian and pagan festivals amalgamated.

No Christian and pagan festivals were amalgamated. The Church followed her usual methods in tolerating harmless practices to which pagans were attached provided they renounced and repudiated all pagan significance. If I converted a pagan today who attached a religious significance to the growing of a beard, I would demand that he renounce his religious idea, but I would not order him to shave. Things pagan of their very nature the Church forbade absolutely.

777. Is the Catholic burial service in any way designed to benefit the soul of the departed?

Most decidedly. In fact, abstracting from the fact that it is essentially a part of our liturgical worship offered to God and a bond of union between living members of the visible Church on Earth, the whole of the service is one of prayer for the soul of the departed person, imploring God's mercy for that soul, forgiveness of his sins, an early deliverance from expiations due to past infidelities, and a more generous share in the happiness of heaven insofar as our intercession can secure these things for him according to our fellowship in the communion of saints.

778. What is the meaning of absolution given to the dead?

Strictly speaking, there is no such thing as absolution given to the dead. If we take absolution in the sacramental sense, as part of the sacrament of penance, it is evident that the person to be absolved must still be a living subject of the Church in this world. At times, however, you may hear of the "last absolution" being given at a requiem Mass, that absolution being pronounced over the dead person lying before the altar. But that absolution is not to be taken in the strict sense of the word, as if it had sacramental efficacy. Rather it is a liturgical prayer for the repose of the soul of the departed person—a prayer that would be of no avail to that person did he die in a state of mortal sin.

779. I thought absolution could be given only to the living insofar as they are disposed to receive it.

That is correct. Sacramental absolution cannot be given to dead people. If people are unconscious, or have even apparently died but a short time before the arrival of a priest, the priest can give but conditional absolution, which would avail only insofar as the subject is capable of responding to it in the sight of God. God alone can know whether such a conditional absolution has its effect or not. But in any doubt, the priest gives the benefit of the doubt to the unconscious person and absolves conditionally in the hope that the sacrament may be of actual benefit.

780. Where in the Bible did Jesus tell his disciples to teach us to burn candles for our dead?

Nowhere. Yet the Bible recommends prayer for the dead, and nowhere forbids the burning of a candle from religious motives as an expression of prayer and a symbol of our belief in Christ as the light of the world.

781. I have read in a Catholic paper of the votive lamp system and would like to know something about it.

You are welcome to ask any questions you wish about Catholic teachings or practices. But there is no such thing in the Catholic religion as "votive lamp system." In itself, the lighting of a lamp before an altar or a shrine as an expression of piety is quite a legitimate practice. A person, unable to give himself continuously to prayer, may leave a lamp burning as a tangible expression of his faith, love, and devotedness to God. And he may even regard it as a silent prayer to God, asking God's blessing and protection. A modern writer has recently said, "I am always strangely moved when I see the white beams of the votive candles in a church, modestly crowded together in some corner by the altar—as if they were living souls shining there, and consuming away in their own fire; the faithful candles which we put there. We have to go; but they remain in our place in the sacred building, until their service has wasted them to the last drop." As a simple religious practice, therefore, votive candles are quite justifiable. But, as with all religious practices, excess is possible, and excesses are always to be condemned. Moderation is necessary in all things.

782. I read in a Catholic paper that those who wear the brown scapular of our Lady will not go to hell and will be released from purgatory the first Saturday after their death. All a Catholic needs to do is to wear the scapular!

No Catholic believes that that is all that is needed. Now, let me explain briefly. The scapular is a small piece of cloth that is part of the religious habit of the Carmelite order. Those who join the Confraternity of the Scapular are in a certain degree affiliated with that order and share in all their prayers and good works. And as the Carmelite order is established in honor of the Mother of Christ, those who wear the scapular in a spirit of true devotion and love have a special claim to her intercession and protection. Historical documents tell us that our Lady appeared to St. Simon Stock, an English monk, and promised a special protection of all who would wear the badge known as the scapular. But the promise that one's soul would be preserved from hell supposes sincere dispositions and excludes absolutely the sin of presumption. If anyone were to wear the scapular and presumptuously think that enough, and that despite any and every sin salvation would be secure, such a one would certainly not be preserved from hell. And every Catholic knows this. But granted sincere devotion to our Lady and sincere efforts to live a life worthy of Christ her Son, the scapular does give the well-founded hope that Mary will obtain for one the privilege of death in God's grace and friendship and consequently preservation from hell, even though the soul must yet endure purification in purgatory. The additional promise of release from purgatory on the Saturday following one's death—it is called the Sabbatine privilege—supposes additional conditions of prayer and Christian mortification throughout life, conditions not easily fulfilled.

However, it is enough to say that all presumption is excluded; that no magic power attaches to the scapular or the wearing of it; and that the spiritual privileges are strictly dependent upon the dispositions of soul with which one adopts the scapular and tries to live a good Christian life.

783. I would be surprised if you could show me where this is mentioned in Scripture.

You would have more cause for wonder if I could, since the scapular devotion arose in the Church some thousand years after Scripture was written. But there is nothing in the idea of scapulars that in any way contradicts any principle in Scripture. It is in perfect harmony with Gospel principles. A piece of cloth worn with piety and devotion is just as able to convey a blessing to the wearer as clay made from earth and spittle was able to be an agent of blessings to the blind man cured by Christ, or as the handkerchiefs and aprons that had touched the body of St. Paul were able to heal the sick and convey spiritual benefits (Acts 19:12).

Chapter 12

Catholic Social Teaching

784. The Catholic Church is a blight on social welfare, asking the public to support too many religious institutions.

The irreligious man perhaps thinks that there are too many. But the religious man will say that there are not really enough. God is not likely to complain that works of mercy are being multiplied in his name. And what public is called upon to support these Catholic institutions? Let those complain who do so. Catholic institutions are supported in the main by Catholics and by such generous non-Catholics who admire their charitable work. And the man who does not support them is not the one who should complain. If those who do support them had no wish to do so for the love of God and their fellow men, they would cease to give. But they must be allowed to do with their own property what they wish. If they wish to devote some of their earnings to charitable and religious works, those who selfishly reserve all for their own comfort or amusement should at least have the grace to keep silent.

785. If Catholicism is true, why are the most backward countries Catholic and the most enlightened and progressive countries Protestant?

Let me lay this ghost to rest once and for all. The assertion implicit in such a question ignores the facts of history. A few centuries ago Spain was the dominant nation, and it rose to power as a Catholic nation. On your principles, pagan Romans could have argued that their paganism was true, pointing with scorn to Druid-ridden England and its lack of culture. Italy, under Mussolini, is today leaping to the front and disturbing politicians of other countries; and its rapid advance has not demanded the relinquishing of Catholicity. As for enlightenment, Protestant artists and architects go to study the great masters and the architectural gems in Catholic countries and are inspired by Catholic culture! Temporal progress is a fluctuating thing, dependent on political, geographical, racial, economic, and personal factors, and that quite independently of religion. I have mentioned that the assertion violates logic from the Christian point of view, since Christ did not promise temporal welfare. And it is absurd, on the face of it. For it is like arguing, "Jones is a millionaire; his religion must be true. Jones has become a bankrupt; the same religion must be false!" Finally, if Protestantism is justified by the present temporal prosperity of Protestant nations, it will be falsified by the future collapse of those nations. You can be quite sure that the present relative position of the nations of this world is not going to remain unchanged until the end of the world. That would be against all the laws of history and of the mutability of men. Alexander the Great longed for more worlds to conquer—his empire has crumbled and gone. The Roman Empire has crumbled and gone. The British Empire will crumble and go—yielding to further political changes and regimes, ever fluctuating and variable. Protestantism is changing daily and will go even as the religions of the Greek and Roman Empires. The Catholic Church alone is changeless and will last through all political and national upheavals, as she has done through all the changes of the last two thousand years. Talk about the relative temporal enlightenment and progress of various countries impresses no thinking man in the matter of religion. It is a phase that neither proves nor disproves the truth of a religion but is simply irrelevant.

786. Catholic countries, burdened by Church institutions, cannot progress.

They have done so, and they do. And what do you mean by Catholic countries being thus burdened? The women of Jerusalem wept in their health and strength as they saw Jesus carrying his cross. But instead of accepting their compassion, he said, "Do not weep for me, but weep for yourselves and for your children." Catholics, too, say to you, "Weep not over us. Have your progress in worldly advantages, comforts, and pleasures.

Christ promised happiness in self-renunciation and generosity. The comfort-lover does not know what these things mean." The Catholic Church is mainly interested in progress in holiness and virtue; and that is the only progress worthwhile in the end. The nations that have progressed in worldly goods have religiously progressed into indifference. As with individuals, the more these nations have, the less they want God. But this is not the fault of progress as such. It is the unhappy result of a Protestantism that came into being just as the swing toward scientific progress came upon the world. That swing would have come in any case. It did not come because of Protestantism; but Protestantism was unable to hold the religious allegiance of men in the midst of temporal prosperity. And in their luxuries, men are forgetting God.

787. What is your attitude toward State schools? Do you think them satanic and their founders devils?

I accuse the founders of no conscious error. But I say that the system, whilst not positively teaching satanic doctrine, is truly an agent of the devil rather than of Christ insofar as it omits religious formation as an integral part of its program. The child may be taught to be outwardly respectable, but he finds no adequate interior motive for his private conduct. He is animal rather than spiritual. He is not conscious of being a child very dear to God. What religion he may have secured in other ways is not consolidated and it soon disappears. A very small proportion of children thus trained bother about religion after they have set out on the path of life. And all this is certainly not a matter of grief to Satan. An Anglican clergyman once said sadly to me, "We Anglicans played the part of Judas when we handed our children over to the tender mercies of the state by approving the state school system."

You can't have a Catholic atmosphere in a school where 75 percent of the children are non-Catholics. Children's convictions are formed or deformed in the playground every bit as much as in the classroom. For children are impressionable and greatly influenced by the opinions and assertions of their companions. And a Catholic child who constantly hears non-Catholic children giving utterance to their parents' peculiar religious or irreligious opinions is certainly not being well grounded in the Catholic Faith. If Catholic parents want to bring up their children as good Catholics, they must send them to a school where they will come into contact with a consistent Catholic teaching, both in classroom and playground.

788. The State offers the best schools in the world, irrespective of religion.

That is self-contradictory. Education that abstracts from religion, the very soul of true education, cannot be the best. That is not true education that fills the mind with facts and figures but that does not form the whole man, intellectually, morally, and religiously. Every bit as much, if not more time, should be given to the child's moral and religious formation.

789. State education is just as good as yours.

A system that does not teach the truths necessary for right living cannot be as good as one that does. All my own primary education was done in state schools. I did not become a Catholic until after I had left school and started out in business. I do not remember having had a teacher who was not a naturally good man, bent on teaching us to be naturally good and honest. But all the knowledge of religion I and my companions picked up in virtue of our state education would not fill a thimble. Religious motives were not taught. Religious duties were ignored, and man's greatest duty to God simply omitted. The result of such education is that the child is impressed with the idea that this life is all, and that an earthly career and one's relations with one's fellow men are the supreme duty. Motto cards on the walls advising boys to be brave and girls to be good are no sufficient substitute. The Catholic Church could not in conscience accept such a system. And Catholics made the very great sacrifice of building their own schools at the cost of double taxation. They are compelled to subscribe just as non-Catholics toward the support of state schools that they cannot in conscience use, and in addition they have to subscribe for the support of their own schools. But at least their children are taught that their first and greatest duty is to know, love, and serve God in this life, and that their true destiny is to be happy with him in the next.

790. Do you know that American factories, kept going at full efficiency, could supply this world, and four others, with all necessary material requirements?

I have no hesitation in describing that as a hopeless exaggeration. But that is a minor point. Let us go on.

791. If so, why the poor?

Because whatever the efficacy of production, the limitations of human wisdom and the moral deficiencies in human character will always result in an uneven distribution. The poor will not always be a reality amongst men because good men want them to be poor. They will be a reality because even the best of men will fail to devise a really perfect system of administration; and because there will always be ambitious, covetous, evil, yet clever men who will want to be rich at the expense of others. And Christ predicted the sad fact of continued poverty precisely because he knew both the limitations of human wisdom and the moral depravity ever likely to assert itself in human nature. We must do our best to improve human knowledge and correct the moral depravity. But so long as the human race exists we shall never entirely succeed in our task. Our Lord foresaw this and foretold it. But you ignore the realities of life, take it for granted that human nature is what it is not, and live in a world of dreams.

792. Is not poverty the enemy of God?

Not necessarily. When the eternal Son of God came into this world, he embraced poverty and promised special blessings to the poor. If anything, he condemned the other extreme of wealth, and declared that riches are much more likely to take men from God than poverty.

At the same time, a great deal of the poverty in this world is due to the injustice of the rich. And that injustice is undoubtedly the enemy of God. Again, abject poverty can be, and often is, the occasion of temptations to crime. And in this sense, poverty could be regarded as the enemy of God.

793. If poverty be in any way the enemy of God, why do we Christians hesitate in abolishing it?

Men will never succeed in abolishing poverty entirely. Our Lord has said, "The poor you always have with you." But that does not alter the fact that there are far too many poor and that the cause of their poverty is not according to God's will. Why, then, do we Christians hesitate in abolishing this excessive poverty of so many people? For the simple reason that the vast majority of those who are really Christians are amongst the very poor whose lot is to be remedied. In other words, we Christians have not within our hands the means whereby we can abolish such injustice. Our Lord warned us that the more money a man gets, the less likely he is to be a good Christian. And the wealth of the world is concentrated in the hands of rich men who have no Christian inspiration to use their power for the alleviation of poverty and the bettering of the lot of the poor at what they regard as their own expense. It is because they won't obey Christian principles that the poor also abandon Christian principles, turn Communist, and proceed to take by force what the rich unjustly reserve for themselves. It takes a lot of Christian principle on the part of the poor to refrain from Communism and appeal to social justice by constitutional means, whilst those who control the goods of this world are quite deaf to the claims of social justice.

794. Jesus satisfied the hunger of the people after three days.

You must not make the mistake of thinking that Jesus came to fill the stomachs of hungry people. He multiplied bread for the particular group that was with him. But there were other hungry people elsewhere, and, as God, he knew of their existence. Yet he did not multiply bread for them. And why did he multiply bread for those to whom he had been speaking? Was it merely to satisfy their hunger? No. He did so as a miraculous guarantee of the truth of his teaching. But, like many other people, they were not interested in spiritual truth; they were interested only in their full stomachs. And if you look up John 6:26-27, you will see Christ's reaction to that. For he said, "Truly, truly, I say to you, you seek me, not because you saw signs, but because you ate your fill of the loaves. Do not labor for the food which perishes, but for the food which endures to eternal life, which the Son of Man will give to you." In other words, Christ wrought the miracle to lead them to faith in him and to the eternal life above and beyond this life. But they ignored that primary purpose and took only a materialistic view based on present earthly benefits. He blamed them, as he would blame you for quoting his action in favor of a purely economic relief. Are you interested in soup—or in salvation?

795. On what grounds do you condemn Communism?

I could reply in a few words by saying, "On the ground of insanity." But you will want the insanity proved. Does Communism violate reason to such an extent that it can be called madness? I maintain that it does. It is bad for the individual, for the family, and for society itself. The individual right of ownership is destroyed. Communism restricts or even abolishes the right to private property sanctioned by the natural law and positive legislation of God. No true incentive to self-development and progress is left. Liberty, so prized by every reasonable human being, is abolished. Men are but cogs in a machine, and the so-called will of the people ends in the will of a tyrannical group of leaders. In addition, the family is broken, and children are deprived of true parental care and education. Russia, in great part, is a huge foundling home; if it can be called a home at all. The State itself cannot provide for its own citizens. It cannot regulate supplies in accordance with demands, and people starve in outlying quarters if only because overlooked by authorities. Few people realize the immense flood of misery and suffering Communism has meant in Russia. But, in addition to the dictates of reason prompted by the thought of the individual, the family, and the State itself, Communism is the declared enemy of religion. And religion is absolutely essential to the welfare of man, quite independently of the fact that God has the foremost right to man's acknowledgment and service. Also, because Communism seeks to place all man's happiness in material things only, it is a denial of the true spiritual nobility of man. A Catholic who supports Communism is supporting a force that aims at the destruction of religion and above all of the Catholic Church. Your question is really like asking, "Why cannot a child assist the murderer of its mother?"

796. Why does the Catholic Church defend the capitalist and attack the worker?

She does not do these things. The Catholic Church defends law and order and human rights. She is ever ready to denounce injustice, whether of the government or of any private individual. If a wealthy Catholic did not pay just wages and were seriously defrauding his employees, the Catholic Church would be the first to condemn such conduct and warn him that if he continued in such conduct he would risk eternal damnation. On the other hand, if an employee accepted good wages, and did not render equivalent service, he too, would be condemned by the Church. The Catholic Church neither denies nor approves present-day miseries. And since the world will not listen to her principles, she turns around and tries to relieve all the misery she can by every possible kind of charitable organization.

797. Why don't you condemn all rich men as criminals?

Some may be, and then they sin, and are condemned by the Church. But not all rich men are criminals. A man can lawfully acquire property and wealth and build up a legitimate state in life by his diligence and ability.

798. When did the Catholic Church first endorse the holding of private property?

The right of private property is a natural right and has always been held by the Church. When God gave the commandment,

"You shall not steal," he acknowledged that men could acquire property to which others had no right.

799. St. Augustine says that the superfluities of the rich are the necessities of the poor. Therefore those who possess superfluities possess the goods of the poor and are robbers.

The Catholic Church agrees with St. Augustine in this matter and declares that all who possess superfluities, that is, goods which are over and above that which is necessary for the upkeep of their state in life, are obliged under pain of sin to share their superfluities with their less fortunate fellow men. The hundreds of orphanages, hospitals, and other works of charity established by the Catholic Church are supported by contributions from such superfluities, as well as by contributions from Catholics who are sacrificing much that they could legitimately retain.

800. Considering that Christ preferred to die amongst thieves, what would he say of the rich today?

Although Christ was crucified between two thieves, he had friends amongst the rich and often dined in the houses of the wealthy. If the rich today are unjust and violate God's laws, Christ would condemn them according to the measure of their iniquity. He would not condemn them otherwise. He never condemned riches as such. When Job was a rich man, he was commended by God and loved by him. God does condemn the bad use of riches and orders all men to be poor in spirit. Every man must be prepared to sacrifice all his earthly goods rather than commit sin to retain or increase them.

801. Why not take literally Christ's words that it is easier for a camel to go through the eye of a needle than for a rich man to enter heaven? And that means impossibility.

Normally the rich man experiences greater difficulty than the poor man, for the rich man has much upon which to set his heart, even to the forgetting of God.

That Christ did not intend to say that it is impossible for a rich man to enter heaven is evident from the preceding verse where he says, "It will be hard for a rich man to enter the kingdom of heaven." To express this difficulty more strongly he merely fell back on a proverbial expression, and once we know that he is using a proverb we know that we must not take the literal but the proverbial sense of the words. Now, the camel and the needle formed a common proverb among the Jews at the time to express any improbability. If a Jew said, "Caesar himself is coming to Jerusalem," another would express his doubts by replying, "Yes—and a camel will walk through the eye of a needle." The Jews had many similar proverbs to express unlikelihood—such as "You'll tell me next that a tortoise can race a hare," or "Why don't you tell me you have an elephant in your purse"—or again, "I'd rather believe that a woman was at a loss for words." But the proverb chosen by Christ was particularly suitable. It symbolized a rich man, his back burdened with goods as the back of a camel with a hump, trying to pass through the narrow gate in the walls of Jerusalem known as the Needle, or to limit his desires to the narrow restrictions of virtue imposed by the law of God. Our Lord's words, therefore, are to be taken proverbially, not literally; and his expression in the previous verse shows without doubt that he meant to say riches are an obstacle in the way of salvation, not that riches render such salvation absolutely impossible.

802. Can you give me one case where the Church has actively assisted the lower orders against the oppression of higher powers?

Certainly. In Catholic times, when the Church had power, the people of England owed Magna Carta, or the great Charter of their liberties against the royal tyranny, to Stephen Langton, the Catholic Archbishop of Canterbury and Primate of England. In 1929 Lord Strickland tried to trample upon the rights of the people in Malta. He was endowed with the "Divine right of Kings" theory. The Church fought him. The newspapers distorted the facts in favor of Strickland and against the Church. But England appointed a commission that found against Strickland on almost every count. This was not given the same publicity as the earlier anti-Catholic cables.

Still later the pope, notwithstanding all the concessions of Mussolini for the sake of the Concordat, fought him for the rights and liberties of the people, prepared to sacrifice the Concordat itself. Once more the newspapers tried to give the impression that the pope was trying to interfere unjustly in political matters. But he was vindicating the elementary rights and privileges of the people.

803. These things were in Catholic times and Catholic countries; but what is the Church doing for the downtrodden workers throughout the world?

The Church has always consistently used what power she has in the cause of the worker. With the very rise of the present industrialism Pope Leo XIII insisted on the rights of labor in a series of almost revolutionary encyclicals. He insisted that in justice the workers must receive wages that not only provide moderate comforts of life for themselves and their families, but enough to leave a surplus so that the thrifty may be able to save enough to provide for their future, and even to establish themselves in business and become employers also. Each pope since Leo has reiterated his protest against injustice, whilst defending, of course, fundamental rights to property. Pope Pius XI, the present ruling pontiff, says clearly, however, "If anything, the workers need the assistance of the Church in the obtaining of their rights, not the wealthy in the conservation of their rights." And he gives as his reason the fact that the workers have less means of securing their rights because the wealthy have the control of the political machinery and of the press.

804. Why does the Church denounce the abuses of capitalism instead of denouncing the whole existing system as evil and as existing only for profit and not for use? The Church ought to say, "Away with capitalized industry."

You take too much for granted. It is easy to say that modern industry under capitalism exists for profit and not for use. But it is not true. Industry produces things for the use of those who need them. The public pays for the value of the thing and something additional for the trouble of making it. A portion of this something extra is distributed in wages, and a portion is returned to those who have invested their savings in the enterprise. If you think that the portion returned to investors is always excessive, just note the dividends paid by the average business today. It is too sweeping to say that capitalized industry exists for profit and not for use. This is but a catchword that can impress only the unthinking or those who want to believe it. I am not denying that abuses exist. Some wealthy owners are unwilling to let their dividends decrease and would rather permit wages to decrease. They are wrong and eaten up with self-interest. But wholesale condemnation is nearly always exaggerated. The present system as a system is a mixture of advantages and disadvantages. It has its uses and abuses. And the Catholic Church does not support it with unqualified approval. Yet whilst condemning the abuses, she does ask us to beware, lest in washing the dish we break it.

805. You excuse the Church's lack of interest in these matters by saying that she exists to save souls.

The Church does exist to save souls, even as Christ died for that purpose. But she does not lack interest in the social well-being of mankind. Moral law rules even man's social conduct, and since moral injustice can and does occur in the behavior of men toward each other in their social relations, it is the duty of the Church to give us correct moral principles covering such conduct. In addition to this, the Church makes very much of the corporal works of mercy, and the duty of Christians to benefit their neighbors even in the purely temporal order.

806. Christ came to give life more abundantly. How does the Church give life to the workers more abundantly?

The text you have in mind does not refer to earthly life with its temporal comforts, but to eternal life—a far richer, fuller, and more satisfactory life than this world can possibly offer. He defined the life he offered when he said, "This is eternal life, that they know you the only true God, and Jesus Christ whom you have sent." He who secures the life of God's grace has life more abundantly than this world can give it. And to thousands of souls daily the Catholic Church gives this life. The workers who throng the confessionals and the altar rails in the Catholic Church know that every absolution and every Holy Communion is giving them life more abundantly than this world ever could do.

807. Would you tell us the view your Church takes of socialism?

Socialism is a very broad term that men interpret in many different ways. Communistic socialism is, of course, condemned by the Catholic Church. Mitigated forms of socialism that aim at social reform but ignore religion and rely upon purely materialistic methods, are also condemned. In these and similar senses of the word no Catholic can be a socialist. The Catholic program is social reform that demands true consideration of the workers by employers according to the demands of both justice and Christian charity, at the same time demanding of the workers a just quantity of work together with respect for other peoples' lawful possessions according to God's commandment "You shall not steal."

The Catholic program of reform is badly needed and is the only way out. Economic reconstruction will not succeed unless it takes Catholic social principles into account. On the whole the sympathy of the Church is with the worker, who has less means of defense; and the capitalist is the one who should voluntarily begin to rectify the many abuses that undoubtedly exist. But no policy of socialism that aims at the destruction of all social inequalities can be tolerated. Social inequalities are essential to the general good of mankind; some men being employed on necessary manual works; others in intellectual pursuits; whilst various grades of ability or genius required in the work done demand various grades of remuneration. And this of course means social inequality. God himself never condemned the employment of man-servants and maid-servants but vindicated both their rights and the rights of their employers.

808. Was Christ a socialist when he said, "Our Father, give us our bread" instead of saying, "My Father, give me my bread"?

No. Those words have no reference to any particular civil or economic structure of society.

809. When he multiplied bread he did not sell the loaves and reap profit. He gave them away.

His distribution of the bread has no reference to the matter under discussion. Firstly, it cost him no effort so to multiply bread miraculously. If men could produce things miraculously, they would not mind giving them away. But ordinary human production costs the producer the employment of his own means of support, and he has a right to an equivalent return. Secondly, Christ's purpose in performing that miracle was to prove his claims to the religious convictions and adherence of the people. He blamed them for concentrating solely upon the provision of their temporal needs. "You seek me," he said, "not because you saw signs, but because you ate your fill of the loaves. Do not labor for the food which perishes, but for the food which endures to eternal life." Remember, too, that Christ paid for his necessities, Judas carrying the purse to buy those things that Christ and the apostles needed.

810. God gave manna to the Jews in the desert. Those who gathered little had sufficient; those who gathered much had but enough. Was not that socialism?

No. It was the provision by God of a miraculous food for the Jews in crossing the desert, where their own efforts could not secure it. When they were able to provide for themselves, the manna ceased. Socialism, in its wildest dreams, does not think of leading us all out into the desert and relying upon God to rain down food miraculously.

811. The sufferings of the workers have made me a communist. I believe that we should destroy the Church and work for universal freedom, brotherhood, and peace.

I am afraid you are a communist only whilst other people have what you do not possess. Would you remain a communist if you had the goods and others had not? It is easy to remain a communist when you want others to give you their property; but I know few who would remain communists when it is their turn to give away. And you seem to forget the communist objection to the shame of almsgiving when you demand that those who have more should give to those who have less. Or, instead of allowing them to practice charity, would you practice injustice by confiscating the possessions of others? And if you are out for universal freedom, why do you deny the freedom to men to better their positions by ability and diligence? If you want universal brotherhood and peace, why do you distort and ridicule the religion of Christians?

812. Does not this scheme conform with the principles given in the pope's encyclicals?

The pope does not mention explicitly the particular system of social credit. But in theory the system does not seem to conflict with any of the pope's principles. He has insisted that the goods of the earth must be made to minister to the needs of all; that the present financial system is preventing this, with consequent injustice to the worker, and that therefore the worker's lot must be improved by further means of income. But the pope insists rather upon the just wage than upon the social credit "just price" plus a national dividend. However, the national dividend idea does not seem to be opposed to ethical principles in itself.

813. You sanction the great shame of almsgiving.

It is inconsistent to demand that the rich share their superfluities with their less fortunate fellow men and then to say that almsgiving is shameful. The Catholic Church teaches those who are endowed with this world's goods that they must redeem their sins by almsgiving, as God himself commands. And there is certainly no shame in the giving of alms. You think that there is shame in the acceptance of alms. There is shame in merely human philanthropy, in which only too often money is thrown to the poor as a bone to a dog, the giver glorying in his superiority. But Christianity robs almsgiving of any element of shame. He who accepts alms given in a Christian spirit accepts what is really given to Christ and given by him to his poor. Catholics are taught to see Christ in the poor and to give to him in the persons of the poor. Such gifts are not thrown to the poor in any spirit of contempt but are offered to Christ for the love of Christ, and are shared by Christ with his loved though poverty-stricken friends.

814. Are the Catholics of Germany bound to refuse to support this order of government that alone offers hope to them?

I deny that the present form of government in Germany alone offers hope even from the national point of view. From the viewpoint of their religion, it offers Catholics but death and destruction. Yet it means persecution, misery, and death if they do not submit in general to the prevailing tyranny. And I can but say of Catholics in Germany what the pope himself said of Catholics in Italy as regards the Fascist regime. Here are his words: "We must say that one is not a Catholic—except in baptism and by name as opposed to his obligations—who adopts and develops a program so opposed to the rights of the Church of Jesus Christ, and of souls." But he adds that he realizes how, for countless persons, daily bread and life itself are at stake. So he says that, if they are compelled externally to support the "Totalitarian State," they must in their own consciences make the reservation "insofar as the laws of God and the Church permit," or "in accordance with the duties of a good Christian." And they must be prepared, if need be, to declare their reservation externally should they be asked to choose between the State and their religion. That judgment concerning the position of Catholics in Fascist Italy could apply to Catholics in Fascist Germany. The only difference is that Catholics in Germany are much more likely to meet with the necessity of rejecting State demands in the name of God, and of suffering the consequences of their fidelity to conscience.

815. Is it not well known that the Church of Rome accepts Fascism, which is akin to Communism?

Fascism is not essentially akin to Communism, although it can be perverted in the communistic direction, as in Germany. The Catholic Church prescribes no political policy and sanctions any form of government within the bounds of social justice. She does not accept Fascism any more than she accepts the present British constitution. She tolerates both, and would be quite prepared to condemn any abuses that might arise in these different forms of government.

816. Yet Fascism is as great a curse as Communism, aiming to destroy the worker where the latter wants to destroy capitalists.

Fascism does not aim at the destruction of the worker. Mussolini's Fascism sanctions and supports religion and aims at the well-being of every individual in the State; and for that purpose demands that every individual must contribute toward the service, discipline, and progressive construction of the national well-being. Remonstrance by the Church against a few initial abuses secured their rectification. Hitler's imitation of Fascism in Germany is no true indication of what real Fascism is. He has not understood at all the aims and principles of Fascism. Meantime, whilst Communism's objective has been to dethrone both religion and capitalism, it has succeeded in destroying the worker and has merely imposed a new and worse tyranny. Nor only that. The Soviet is rapidly turning back toward capitalism and is working on capitalistic principles in its own name.

817. Why did Christians fight, killing men they never knew and who never did them any harm?

Every war is a misery and is due to injustice of some kind, or to misunderstanding. And whoever is really responsible for war is very guilty before God. But God alone can judge as to the guilt of the respective parties. As for the killing of men we never knew, remember that men can be considered as individuals or as units of another nation. If one nation is defending itself against the injustice of another nation, then the soldiers are considered not as individuals but as national units. War is unchristian, but it is not unchristian for individuals to fight for their country.

818. I submit that no war is justified and that it is wrong for individuals to kill each other in wartime.

You are confusing various aspects of the question. It is wrong for any nation or any group of politicians to give cause for war by unjust treatment of others, or by deliberate aggression. But if another nation wants to slaughter us unjustly, then, although the war as a war is unjustifiable, we are certainly justified in defending ourselves; and our soldiers are justified in killing the soldiers of the unjustly aggressive army.

819. God says, "You shall not kill." How can my country send me forth to kill?

"You shall not kill" means without just cause. For example, if a thief is on the point of shooting me, I may kill him first if possible, provided I know that my merely wounding him is not likely to save my life. Therefore I am allowed to kill an unjust aggressor. And if my country is defending itself against an unjust attack, or defending its rights by just attack, it is not a crime to fight on her behalf. Loyalty to one's country is a virtue. As a rule, individual soldiers cannot decide whether the powers that be in a given country are right or wrong in their decision upon so extreme a measure as war. And with the good motive of defending what he conceives to be the rights of his country, the ordinary soldier is justified in his participation.

820. Christ said, "Love your enemies."

He did. But he did not say, "Love their enmity." They do wrong in being my enemies, and the sooner I stop them from being my enemies the better for them.

821. Roman theology dispenses a man from the commandment, "You shall not kill" in wartime; it dispenses a man from the commandment "You shall not steal" in times of grave necessity; why not from "You shall not commit adultery" whilst the Church is at it?

There is no parity between this last commandment and the two former ones under the circumstances of their application. We must be careful about the right interpretation of these laws. "You shall not kill" does not prevent just and lawful killing. Legitimate public authority may condemn a man to death because the common good is more important than the individual good. Nor only is it lawful for the State to remove murderers completely from society by death. An individual may kill an unjust aggressor if it is necessary for the preservation of his own life.

And in Scripture we notice how God himself sanctioned war over and over again when other means did not avail to secure justice.

"You shall not steal" means that you can never take unjustly the goods of another against his reasonable will. But every word of this explanation must be noted. If a man is actually dying of starvation, he may take food from those who have more than they need. But that is not stealing, for it is not unjust in extreme necessity to take food that is the product of the earth for the nutrition of the human race, nor is it against the reasonable will of the owner. It would be unreasonable to hold more food than you need and watch a fellow human being die of starvation.

But there can never be any exception from the commandment, "You shall not commit adultery." That commandment is absolute, because it can never be necessary to dispense from it in the interests of justice or for the necessities of human life. Adultery is always a serious evil, and therefore always seriously forbidden.

822. Is every individual soldier bound to satisfy himself as to the justice of his side before participating in war?

Catholic theologians say that volunteers must satisfy themselves that the cause is not unjust. Conscript soldiers are not obliged to solve the problem, but may obey orders, unless the war be clearly and obviously unjust. In this latter case they would be obliged in conscience to refuse service.

823. Was Christ incapable of taking life in the same sense?

Had he been an ordinary human being and not the Son of God come into this world for the salvation of souls, and had he been a soldier in the employ of his country, he would not have been incapable of fulfilling the duties of a soldier, even if it meant killing enemy soldiers in actual warfare. But you must notice the two suppositions. In reality Christ, who was the Son of God, and the eternal King with a kingdom not of this world, cannot be made the standard of such a comparison with an ordinary soldier, who is obviously the subject of a kingdom that is of this world and to which he has duties in the natural order, besides his duties to Christ in the spiritual order. You will notice in the Gospels that Christ met several military men, yet never once did he condemn their occupation; nor did he ever condemn war. He abstracted from the temporal concerns of this world and preached the kingdom of God, bidding men to attend to the spiritual welfare of their souls and to make sure of securing their eternal welfare, whatever might be their success or disasters in this life. So, for example, in a somewhat similar way, he refused to interfere in the litigation of two brothers over a legacy from their parents. One of them said to him, "Teacher, bid my brother divide the inheritance with me." But our Lord replied, "Who made me a judge or divider over you?" And he simply took the occasion to say, "Take heed, and beware of all covetousness; for a man's life does not consist in the abundance of his possessions" (Luke 12:14-15). In other words, Christ refused to decide who was right and who was wrong in this dispute over interests concerned with this world. He left that to be solved by the ordinary human administration of justice. From the contentions of nations he also abstracted, and condemned neither the military profession nor its employment, when deemed necessary by the countries concerned in actual warfare.

824. If so, could you imagine Jesus with a bayonet dripping with blood, which he had just withdrawn from the entrails of another individual?

I cannot. But why? Is it because all war is necessarily wrong? No. If you had no weapon but a bayonet, and you could not stop an unjust aggressor from killing you save by running the bayonet through him, you would not be guilty of any crime before God by doing so. You are not obliged to sacrifice your innocent life for the sake of sparing his guilty life. And the same principle can be extended to nations. Nor did Jesus ever condemn war in a just cause. His condemnation of all injustice would, of course, include an unjust war.

But even though it could be lawful to engage in war, why cannot I imagine Jesus engaged in such strife? For the simple reason that, whilst fighting for one's temporal well-being can be lawful, Jesus came for our eternal rather than our temporal welfare. He came to teach us detachment from earthly concerns and to set an example of that detachment. He never condemned a moderate and necessary interest in earthly concerns, but he himself was not interested in them and bade us to seek first the kingdom of God. He abstracted from the material, bodily pursuits of men and concentrated on spiritual welfare of their souls. I can no more imagine him wielding a bayonet than I can imagine him frequenting the stock exchange in order to try to amass an earthly fortune. His kingdom might be in this world, but it was not to be of this world. And it is impossible to imagine him absorbed by any of the affairs of this world.

825. Is it not a fact that Jesus was immovably a pacifist?

It is not a fact. Though temporal, political, and national matters were outside the scope of his mission, he did not condemn them. His mission was to teach men spiritual truths for the good of their souls and to redeem them from sin. Without any condemnation of earthly warfare, he even chose analogies from it in order to illustrate his higher teachings. And he treated war as quite a normal event, incidental to the imperfections of this worldly existence given over to the administration of men. Thus in Luke 14:31, he says, "What king, going to encounter another king in war, will not sit down first and take counsel whether he is able with the ten thousand to meet him who comes against him with twenty thousand?" Accepting this as human prudence, he warns us to use similar prudence with God.

826. If Jesus was not a pacifist, can you picture him with a gas mask, decked out in all the equipment of civilized warfare?

There is no need to do so.

827. Would you pray to such a conception of Christ?

Since Christ is God, I would pray to him no matter what he might choose to do or not to do. But as my conception of Christ does not happen to include your fanciful hypothesis, I am not called upon to pray to him under such conditions.

828. Yet you can picture followers, or alleged followers of Jesus, with bayonets, killing their fellow Christians.

I can picture a citizen of one country, who happens to be a follower of Jesus, fulfilling military duties in his country's cause against the soldiers of another opposing country, even though those soldiers also happen to profess the Christian religion. A man engages in war not precisely as a follower of Jesus but as a citizen of his own country; and his intention is in no way to kill fellow Christians. His intention is to put the soldiers of enemy forces out of action. If he wanted to kill fellow Christians, he would have to interrogate every enemy he met regarding his religion on the score that he was looking for fellow Christians in order to exterminate them. Your introduction of the Christian religion in such a way is quite irrelevant and a violation of reason.

829. At Gethsemane, Jesus bade Peter sheathe the sword by means of which he might have defended the "Son of God."

That incident occurred. Christ forbade Peter to defend him by means of the sword.

830. If Peter was not justified in fighting on such an occasion, how can any group of people be justified in killing, even to defend human life?

That question is inconsequent. The fact that Christ forbade Peter to use his sword in the particular circumstances mentioned affords no basis for any conclusion concerning the morality of war. For Christ did not forbid Peter to use his sword on the score that violent defense against unjust aggressors was wrong in itself. He forbade Peter to use the sword on this particular occasion for several reasons. Firstly, Christ knew that the time had come according to God's will when he should enter upon his Passion, and it was not right to seek to escape it. Secondly, and in any case, Peter and the apostles were utterly unequal to the armed throng that had come to secure him, and thought for them urged Christ to advise the prudent course. Thirdly, their defense of Christ was really unnecessary, for he told them that if he really wanted to escape he could easily do so, if only by commanding "twelve legions of angels" to defend him. It should be obvious to you that Christ was not attacking the right of armed self-defense in general.

831. If war is, under certain circumstances, a justifiable business, why does not the Church allow priests to fight as ordinary soldiers?

War is not a justifiable business. Whenever it occurs, it supposes injustice on somebody's part, and even as that injustice is evil, so war is evil. Don't imagine that, because I protest against your violations of logic and reason, I do not protest against violations of peace and harmony between nations. I protest against war, and vehemently. But if warfare is unjustly forced upon a peaceful people, then that people is justified in defending itself by force of arms if necessary.

At the same time, whilst ordinary citizens are justified in the violent repulsion of violent aggressors, the Church forbids priests to engage in an occupation involving unavoidable bloodshed.

Even apart from war there are many occupations quite lawful in themselves, and to other people, that would be most incongruous for priests. For example, it is not sinful to be a bartender, but it would be most unbecoming for a priest to engage in such a duty. The Church forbids priests to engage in many forms of ordinary commercial and industrial activity normal to others. And above all, when war breaks out, and citizens enlist for the armed support of their country's cause, priests should abstain from active violence. By his very vocation the priest stands for unworldly ideals. Heart and soul he must labor for the eternal and spiritual rather than the temporal and material welfare of men. He is concerned with a heavenly rather than with an earthly kingdom. He represents Christ and the claims of Christ rather than the demands of an earthly allegiance. And as when men's worldly careers come to an end they must turn their thoughts to another and higher realm altogether, so the priest must be one whom they have regarded as apart from worldly interests and dissociated from their own earthly concerns. As they are ceasing to belong to the world about them, they find help in one who has already ceased to belong to this world in spirit and profession. Again, the priest represents the love of God, the peace of Christ, and the mercy of a Master who would far rather be crucified than crucify. And he should abstain from that active fighting in which ferocity and hatred are so easily enkindled as opposed to love; in which peace is destroyed by a storm of conflicting emotions; and in which man is the agent of death rather than of life. For even when a nation is justly at war, these sad consequences cannot but arise. Let the priest shed his blood, if necessary, for Christ and for souls; but let him not shed blood. The Church even goes so far as to forbid priests to engage in surgery. He must abstain from all unbecoming duties; be in the world, but not of it; fulfill his personal spiritual duties, destroying his enemy, sin, inculcating virtue, devoting himself to prayer and the worship of God; and be ready to assist any men, friends or enemies, who need his ministrations.

832. You insist that the State has the right to inflict capital punishment.

The State possesses the right on the same principle as an individual who may kill an unjust aggressor, if there is no other efficacious way in which to preserve his own life. Those whose crimes gravely threaten the well-being of society may be put to death by social authority when lesser penalties prove inefficacious as a control upon them. God himself sanctioned this law in Hebrew society, and it is entirely reasonable. If the extreme penalty could not be lawfully inflicted by the State upon enemies of the common good, much greater and more widespread evils would ensue.

833. Is not the executioner guilty of murder? He kills an individual person whom he knows by name, and intends to do so.

He knows he is hanging an individual person, and the name of the person. But he is not guilty of murder. Firstly, he acts not as a private person but as the agent of the State exercising lawful authority.

Secondly, his intention is not one of personal revenge but of doing a lawful act for the common good. His fulfillment of duty, far from being evil, could be quite meritorious. Motive makes morality.

834. I cannot admit your version of the commandment "You shall not kill," except by lawful authority.

The very Bible that gives you the commandment also records God's authorization of death as a penalty when inflicted by lawful authority.

835. Is it a crime to sympathize with the criminal going to his doom?

Not at all. Nor is anyone expected to be inhuman. But in this, as in many other cases, there are two sides to the question. It is quite possible to have great sympathy for an individual who encounters disaster, yet to experience a reasonable relief that other good ends have been attained; and that a sufficient sanction and deterrent has been upheld for the good of the community.

836. You oppose sterilization of the mentally deficient for the common good, yet you justify the taking of the criminal's very life!

There is all the difference in the world between these two things. Where sterilization of the unfit is in question, many other factors come into the case besides the common good. The State has no direct right over the life and members of its subjects. It has an indirect right to sentence to death as a punishment for grave crimes. But sterilization of the mentally deficient is a measure directed against those lacking moral responsibility and who are guilty of no crime in being mentally deficient through no fault of their own. Nor could we support sterilization of those who have been guilty of sex crimes and who are not mentally deficient, for sterilization is not proportionate as a punishment; and far from being a deterrent for the future, it leaves a man with all his passions and no fear of the consequences. Sterilization is useless both as a punitive measure and as a reformative measure; and it is not justifiable even where the death penalty is.

Index

Subject

H

J

Biblical

www.ingramcontent.com/pod-product-compliance
Lightning Source LLC
Jackson TN
JSHW082127281225
95929JS00001B/1

* 9 7 8 1 9 3 8 9 8 3 7 4 0 *